Biographies for Birdwatchers

Photographs were supplied by, or are reproduced by, kind permission of the following:

United Kingdom — *H. S. Gladstone collection*: Alexander, Allen, Aristotle, Baillon, Baird, Barrow, Bartram, Bewick, Blyth, Bonaparte, Brünnich (*Copenhagen University Library, Denmark*), Bulwer, Canute, Cory, Eversmann, Finsch, J.E. Gray, G.R. Gray, Hornemann (*Det Nationalhistoriske Museum på Frederiksborg, Denmark*), Hume, Nordmann, Pallas, Radde, Sabine, Savi, Swinhoe, Temminck, Tengmalm (*Svenska Porträttarkivet, Stockholm, Sweden*), Tristram, Verreaux, Wilson. *Trustees of the National Library of Scotland, Edinburgh*: Denham, Hodgson, Lichtenstein, Tickell, Whitehead. *National Portrait Gallery, London*: Franklin, Arctic Council (Ross), Swainson. *National Army Museum, London*: Dunn. *Royal Entomological Society, London*: Ménétries. *Linnean Society of London*: Montagu. *The British Library, London*: White. *C. F. Butler*: Butler. *M. Cordeaux*: Upcher. *B. and R. Mearns*: Eleonora.
France — *Bibliothèque Centrale du Muséum National d'Histoire Naturelle, Paris*: Audouin, Clot, Leschenault. *Bibliothèque de Société de Géographie, Paris*: Berthelot. *Bibliothèque Municipale, Sézanne*: Levaillant. *Archives de l'Académie des Sciences, Paris*: Moquin-Tandon. *F. Roux*: Jouanin.
Belgium — *J.-P. Ledant*: Ledant.
The Netherlands — *Academisch Historisch Museum, Riksuniversiteit te Leiden*: Schlegel.
Italy — *Università di Sassari, Sardinia*: Cetti. *Dipartimento di Biologia Animale, Università di Torino*: Bonelli. *Professor P. Passerin d'Entrèves*: Gené, Marmora.
Austria — *Bild-Archiv der Österreichischen Nationalbibliothek, Vienna*: Forster.
F.R.G. — *Forschungsinstitut Senckenberg, Frankfurt am Main*: Cretzschmar, Hey, Rüppell. *Stadtarchiv, Mainz, BPS*: Kittlitz. *Stadtsbibliothek, Berlin*: Bolle, Krüper.
D.D.R. — *L. Baege*: Brehm, J.A. Naumann, J.F. Naumann, Sturm.
Poland — *Library of the Institute of Zoology of the Polish Academy of Sciences, Warsaw*: Godlewski, Młokosiewicz.
U.S.S.R. — *Library of the Academy of Sciences of the U.S.S.R., Leningrad*: Fischer, Schrenck. *Scientific Library of the Tartu State University, Estonia*: Schwarz.
U.S.A. — *Mead Art Museum, Amherst College, Massachusetts*: Amherst. *Moulton Library, Bangor Theological Seminary, Maine*: Bruce.

The publishers and authors have made every attempt to contact the copyright holders of the portraits. In the few instances where they have been unsuccessful, they invite the copyright holders to contact them direct.

Biographies for Birdwatchers
The Lives of Those Commemorated in Western Palearctic Bird Names

Barbara and Richard Mearns

Illustrated by Darren Rees

1988

ACADEMIC PRESS
Harcourt Brace Jovanovich, Publishers
London · San Diego · New York · Berkeley · Boston · Sydney · Tokyo · Toronto

ACADEMIC PRESS LIMITED
24–28 Oval Road
London NW1

United States Edition published by
ACADEMIC PRESS INC.
San Diego, CA 92101

British Library Cataloguing in Publication Data
Mearns, B.
    Biographies for birdwatchers: the lives
    of those commemorated in western palearctic
    bird names.——(Books about birds).
    1. Ornithology. Biographies. Collections
    I. Title II. Mearns, R. III. Series
    598'.092'2

    ISBN 0–12–487422–3

Typeset by Photo·graphics, Honiton, Devon, England
Printed by The Alden Press,
Oxford, London and Northampton,
England

Contents

Maps

"Surely, the gentlemen whose names are applied to these birds have not so slight a hold on fame as to require such aids as these to attain it, if indeed aids they be, which I question; for such nomenclature *cannot* stand the test of time."

Letter to *The Auk*, 1885

Foreword

Every winter, hundreds of Bewick's Swans which have bred on the Soviet arctic tundras come south-westwards to the Wildfowl Trust Centre at Slimbridge, where they feed and roost on 'Swan Lake'. For me, they are an endless source of interest, beauty and enjoyment. Some years ago I was able to acquire Thomas Bewick's telescope, which now lives on the shelf below my studio window. I have always admired Bewick's exquisite woodcuts, and enjoyed his early observations, described in his famous book *The History of British Birds*.

Like many other birdwatchers I know all too little about most of the other naturalists who have had birds named after them, so I am delighted that Barbara and Richard Mearns have brought together this delightfully miscellaneous collection of men and women from many different centuries, cultures and countries so that we can all learn about their lives, and their contributions to the development of ornithology.

There are few birdbooks which appeal equally to complete beginners and to ornithologists of long experience, but this must be one of them. Whatever your degree of knowledge, I am sure that you will be fascinated by the stories of endurance and adventure, success and tragedy, hard work and dedication which lie behind the names so often used by birdwatchers.

Sir Peter Scott

Preface

Richard's curiosity about the identity of people with birds named after them was first aroused in 1959, at the time of his ninth birthday, when he was presented with a copy of E. Thomas Gilliard's *Living Birds of the World*. Among the birds listed for Mexico and the southern United States he found Mearns's Quail and wondered if Mearns was related to his family.

The interest lay more or less dormant until the spring of 1983 when we travelled together in Alaska. There, in the course of just a few weeks, we watched Wilson's Warblers flitting through willow scrub, Sabine's Gulls flying over tundra pools, Bonaparte's Gulls roosting on sandy beaches, Steller's Eiders diving offshore, Barrow's Goldeneyes swimming on fast-flowing rivers and Baird's Sandpipers leading their chicks across stony coastal hills. We realised that although we had both been watching birds since early childhood, neither of us knew much about these people. The fact that we were near Point Barrow and the Baird Mountains heightened our resolve to investigate further.

On our return to Scotland we looked for a book which would explain all these avian eponyms, but found that no such book existed. We therefore took on the task ourselves, trusting that other birdwatchers would also enjoy the combination of ornithological history, travel and adventure that such a book could reveal.

During the early stages of our research we had an unexpected boost. In our local public library, in the *Transactions and Journal of Proceedings of the Dumfriesshire and Galloway Natural History and Antiquarian Society* for 1940–44, we found an article entitled 'British Birds Named After Persons', which described the lives of Cetti, Bulwer and Temminck. It had been written by the late Sir Hugh Gladstone, who had lived just ten miles from our home, and so we visited his grandson to ask if there was more information on the subject. We were invited to hunt for anything of interest amidst a pile of files and boxes stacked beneath a large table in a large and imposing hall. Without any great expectations we spent a morning sorting through files of congratulatory letters received on the occasion of Sir Hugh's knighthood in 1941, files of correspondence for the Wild Bird Advisory Committee, the minutes of The Thornhill Young Gentlewomens' Friendly Society, ledgers of accounts and newspaper clippings, a small box of sawdust (carefully labelled 'sawdust'), and a large box containing Sir Hugh's khaki uniform from the Boer War.

Amongst this dusty miscellany we at last uncovered a big dress box, faintly marked in pencil, 'Birds named after Persons'! Inside lay unpublished manuscripts, correspondence and photographs concerning Bewick, Bonaparte, Montagu, Pallas, Savi and many others, extending even to Macqueen, Sykes, Feldegg and Holböll,

Nisus and Athene, Tammy Norie, Jackdaw and Robin. All had lain untouched and forgotten since Gladstone's death in 1949.

Sir Hugh Gladstone had confined his interest to the birds of the British Isles, but had included races as well as names from Greek and Roman mythology. Despite the difference in our scope there was much of value to us. Our first acknowledgement and greatest debt is, therefore, to Sir Hugh Gladstone of Capenoch and to Mr and Mrs Robert Gladstone who generously allowed us to use the manuscripts and the collection of photographs and who made us welcome on numerous visits. Our biographies of Bulwer, Cetti, Eversmann, Hornemann, Montagu and Nordmann, in particular, owe much to Gladstone's investigations.

On our many trips to Edinburgh, Mick, Anne, Ruth and Duncan Marquiss unfailingly provided us with a home away from home, and so we thank them for their friendship and hospitality. We are also grateful to Mike and Jo Moser, and Steve Tilley, for their kindness on other library visits.

Special thanks are due to those who undertook translation work for us, as without their help, many of the chapters could not have been written. They are: Christopher and Rosamund Mearns (French); Benjamin Engel and Eileen Tilley (German); Ann-Marie Knox, Clare Pearson and Vicky Robinson (Italian); and Donald MacKerron (Russian). For their help with the photographs we wish to thank Edmund Fellowes, Brian Turner and Jim Young.

We must also acknowledge the assistance of a host of library, museum and university staff, especially, Ludwig Baege (Naumann Museum, Köthen, East Germany), Linda Birch (Alexander Library, Edward Grey Institute, Oxford), June Chatfied (Gilbert White Museum, Selborne), Eileen Holt (University College of Swansea), Brenda Leonard (Royal Entomological Society, London), Pietro Passerin d'Entrèves (University of Turin), and Anne Vale (British Museum (Natural History), Tring). Staff from the following institutions provided us with much valuable information, but are too numerous to thank individually: Edinburgh University Library, National Library of Scotland, Scottish Ornithologists' Club Library, Edinburgh; Glasgow University Library, Mitchell Library, Glasgow; Balfour Library, Cambridge; Liverpool Museum, Liverpool; Linnean Society, Kew Gardens, National Army Museum, British Library (Manuscripts Department), London; the Public Libraries of Bath, Bromley, Bury St Edmunds, Cheltenham, Dumfries, Durham, Folkestone, Great Yarmouth, Norwich, Paisley, Plymouth, Sevenoaks, Shrewsbury and Weymouth; Bibiothèque Municipale de Sézanne; Bibliothèque Municipale de Vienne; Bibliothèque Nationale, Paris; Forschungsinstitut Senckenberg, Frankfurt am Main; Bibliotheek der Rijksuniversiteit te Leiden, Rijksmuseum van Natuurlijke Historie, Leiden; Kungliga Biblioteket, Stockholm; Library of the Academy of Sciences, Leningrad; State Public Library, Tbilisi; American Philosophical Society, Philadelphia; New York Botanical Garden Library, New York; Meade Art Museum, Amherst (Mass.); Bangor Theological Seminary, (Maine).

Lord Amherst, Clarence and Joyce Butler, Mildred Cordeaux, Angus Dunn and Sir Douglas Elphinstone, who are all related to subjects of the book, were most helpful regarding our enquiries and their assistance was much appreciated. Christian Jouanin kindly provided us with all the information about himself and the identification of Moussier is entirely due to his efforts. We are also very grateful to Jean-Paul Ledant for his own biographical details.

Our thanks must also be extended to those who gave us early help and encouragement or who read through some of the chapters and made valuable suggestions: Joan Curzio, Colin Kinloch, Jean Kinloch, Mick and Anne Marquiss, Kathleen Mearns, Bill Neill, Ian Newton and Tom Pow. We are indebted to Tim Birkhead who kindly commented on the entire manuscript.

The authors would welcome information concerning the location of any of Lady Amherst's diaries (other than 1823); the existence of pictures of any of our main subjects whose portrait has not been included here; and any further information about Moussier, Neumayer and Richard, as well as any details that would confirm the identity of Dupont.

Introduction

The History of Nomenclature

For centuries the traditional bird names were perfectly adequate for the use of country people, the majority of whom were both sedentary and illiterate. Inevitably, a multitude of names arose in different localities for a relatively small number of easily distinguishable birds and, conversely, groups of similar species were often referred to together under single names. In the eighteenth century, as the study of birds gathered momentum, the need arose for the creation of new names for the many newly discovered species and for the standardization of the existing folk names.

Just as the standardization of vernacular names became essential for people within a country to understand each other quickly and easily, so it became necessary for naturalists from different countries to understand each other, hence the importance of the Latinized names for every species. Many naturalists were not classicists and so names were formed from a type of technical Latin, Latinized Greek or even just bad Latin; it is, therefore, preferable to call them scientific names even though there has been nothing scientific about their formulation. The relatively stable nomenclature of the present day was preceded by years of ambiguity and inconsistency. In 1753 Carl Linné, or Linnaeus of Sweden introduced a binomial system of classification which was later adopted throughout the scientific community. All botanical names in use before 1753 and all zoological names in use before 1758 are now judged to be Pre-Linnaean and have been discarded. This even applies to many names which Linnaeus himself formulated before these dates—they too are Pre-Linnaean!

The Linnaean system was not accepted at once. Well into the nineteenth century several authors on natural history used their own system of classification and nomenclature or another of their choice. Some bird species thereby acquired long lists of different names and it was not unusual for particularly 'difficult' species, such as redpolls and crossbills, to have ten or more scientific names on the authority of as many naturalists. One of the most extreme examples occurs in Henry Dresser's *A History of the Birds of Europe* (1871–81), where the Crested Lark sports no less than sixty-four synonyms which take up two full pages before the bird itself can be discussed.

These synonyms arose partly because of the desire of some authors to have their own system universally accepted but also because of the limited contact between naturalists. Many of them worked in isolation without access to either foreign literature or large skin collections so that a single species was often described as new over and over again. Sometimes this could have been avoided by a little more research, but on other occasions, repetition was inevitable. Who, for instance, would have suspected that a pipit found breeding in the Arctic, in north-west Russia in 1875, would already have been shot and described in south-east China a few years earlier? Or that another pipit, named from a specimen collected in France, had already been discovered in New Zealand?

It soon became obvious that a set of rules was necessary to control the number of synonyms and other problems that existed. Unfortunately, such a variety of systems were proposed that in time:

> "English systematists were following the Stricklandian Code; French systematists were following the International Code; German systematists were following the German Code; American systematists were divided between Stricklandian, the A.O.U., the Dall and the International Code; systematists in special groups were in some cases following special or even personal codes; and systematists of Italy, Russia and some other countries were following either the International or some other code."[1]

All of these have now, thankfully, been superseded by the single International Code of Zoological Nomenclature.

The Rule of Priority

In addition to the general decision to adopt the Linnaean system of nomenclature, one of the earliest and most fundamental rules was the Rule of Priority: the oldest published specific name had priority over any other. Even this is not as simple as it sounds, as some early descriptions are barely recognizable, being so vague that it could not be agreed whether they constituted valid descriptions or not. Moreover, descriptions were sometimes discovered in the very old literature pre-dating those which had been accepted for decades. To obviate change under these circumstances, a fifty-year rule was proposed, whereby any name which had been out of use for fifty years or more should not be allowed. Somewhat predictably, even this rule is sometimes debated.

The Naming of New Species

The scientific name of each species now consists of two words, as introduced by Linnaeus. The first, generic name tells us to which genus the species belongs, and it always has an initial capital letter. The second word is the specific name and does not, now, begin with a capital letter, even if it refers to a place or person, e.g. Arctic Redpoll, *Acanthis hornemanni*. If the species can be separated into races, then this binomial sytem can be extended to a trinomial one, e.g. *Acanthis hornemanni exilipes*. The first race to be described is known as the nominate race, i.e. *A. h. hornemanni*, regardless of whether it is the most widespread or the most typical of the species.

When a new species is named a single specimen, thereafter known as the type specimen, must have a name and description published in sufficient detail for it to be distinguished from any other closely allied species. The type locality is the term given to the location where the specimen was obtained.

When the full scientific name of a bird is formally given, it is followed by the name of the person who gave the original description of it and the date of the publication, e.g. Kestrel *Falco tinnunculus* Linnaeus, 1758. Occasional revisions in classification mean that sometimes the generic name has been changed, in which case the describer's name is placed in brackets, e.g. Sparrowhawk *Accipiter nisus* (Linnaeus), 1758; Linnaeus originally named it *Falco Nisus*. Occasionally, as in the chapter headings of this book, the full reference for the publication and the type locality is given.

The Origins of Bird Names

Most birds are named after some obvious distinguishing feature. This may may be their colour (e.g. Blue Tit, Isabelline Wheatear, *Sturnus roseus*); their basic structure (e.g. Tufted Duck, Broad-billed Sandpiper, *Mergus serrator*); their size (e.g. Little Tern, Goliath Heron, *Parus major*); their call (e.g. Cuckoo, Kittiwake, *Crex crex*); or some aspect of their behaviour (e.g. Turnstone, Dipper, *Vanellus gregarius*). Alternatively a bird may be named after a location where it was discovered or where it often occurs, either in a geographical sense (e.g. Dartford Warbler, Terek Sandpiper, *Serinus syriacus*) or with reference to its supposed or actual preferred habitat (e.g. Meadow Pipit, Wood Sandpiper, *Ammomanes deserti*).

However, when one considers that the warblers of the world include the Green, Greenish, Olive, Olivaceous, Olive-backed, Yellow, Yellow-green, Yellow-headed, Yellow-browed, Yellow-throated, Icterine, Citrine, Golden-cheeked, Golden-winged and Golden-bellied, one can appreciate that simple descriptive titles can become totally inadequate.

Birds Named After People—Avian Eponyms

The early botanists started to name species after people and the idea was adopted by Linnaeus and extended to the naming of birds. By the beginning of the nineteenth century the practice had become widespread in both the scientific and common names of birds. It was not just the original discoverers, describers and eminent naturalists who were honoured in this way, but also their wives, daughters, patrons and friends. It is this varied group of people; naturalists, explorers, sailors, soldiers, farmers, pharmacists, artists, consuls, doctors and priests who form the subject of this book.

All the individuals, living or dead, who now have one or more Western Palearctic birds named after them in either the scientific or vernacular English name have been included. Those whose names are only attached to a race have been excluded, as have mythological characters. The length of each biography is in no way a measure of the subject's contribution to ornithology, nor does it reflect the status of the bird species within the Western Palearctic—the Western

Palearctic being a zoogeographical region which includes Europe, North Africa, the Middle East and the U.S.S.R. west of the Ural Mountains.

Ninety-one biographical sketches are presented, (in eighty-nine chapters), of which three concern women. If the subjects are divided by nationality—a difficult exercise due to the many territorial changes during the eighteenth and nineteenth centuries—twenty-nine are British; twenty-five German, Prussian or Polish; fourteen French; seven Italian; five American; three Danish and two Dutch. There are also single representatives from a number of other countries. The majority of them deserve to be classed as either professional or serious amateur naturalists. More than forty of them were full-time naturalists, either earning their living through the study of natural history as museum directors or assistants, university professors, explorers, collectors or artists, or as men of independent means who had devoted their lives to the subject. It is notable that most were naturalists in the true sense of the word; only in this century has it become common to specialize in ornithology.

Although it is sometimes suggested that clergymen were the most influential group of early naturalists, only six are represented in this miscellany. The medical profession occur more frequently than any other, although many, in time, found *Homo sapiens* the least interesting species and turned their attention to other animals.

Many of the early naturalists were great travellers and between them, our subjects explored almost every corner of the world. If some sketches are read in groups, the reader will get an idea of the development of ornithology in various countries, e.g. North America–Wilson, Swainson, Baird; Soviet Union–Steller, Pallas, Radde; South Africa—Lichtenstein, Verreaux; Middle East—Hemprich, Rüppell, Tristram; India—Blyth, Hodgson, Hume; China and East Indies—Swinhoe, Whitehead; Australia and New Zealand—Forster, Leschenault, Finsch. The famous search for the North-west Passage is well represented in the accounts concerning Adams, Barrow, Franklin, Ross and Sabine.

The survival of eponyms has been largely a matter of chance. The old literature is full of bird names such as Richardson's Skua, Jerdon's Warbler, Strickland's Bunting, Ehrenberg's Chat and many others which mean nothing to young ornithologists. As each succeeding generation becomes more distanced from these early naturalists less and less is remembered about most of them. But whether one approves of such eponyms or not it cannot be denied that many have now stood the test of time and their names remain in constant use by birdwatchers. Unless a revolutionary new system of scientific nomenclature is forthcoming, or there is a complete revision of popular names which seems even less likely, most of the current eponyms will continue in use.

It is our sincere hope that the names which still honour the work of outstanding naturalists will remain. The contributions made to the development of ornithology by such men as Charles Bonaparte, George Montagu, Henry Baker Tristram, Georg Steller and Alexander Wilson deserve to be commemorated by every generation.

Edward Adams†
(1824-1856)

WHITE-BILLED DIVER *Gavia adamsii* (G. R. Gray)

Colymbus adamsii G. R. Gray, 1859. *Proceedings of the Zoological Society of London*, p. 167: Alaska

"This fine species is named after the late Mr. Adams Surgeon of H.M.S. *Enterprise*, commanded by Captain Collinson, in the voyage made by him through Behring's Straits. Mr. Adams employed his pencil in producing beautiful drawings of the remarkable birds obtained during the voyage."[1]

These words by George Gray relate to his friend Edward Adams,[2] an unfortunate naturalist who survived two rigorous and exciting expeditions to the Arctic only to die soon afterwards. Because of his early death, an ornithological paper written by Adams in western Alaska between October 1850 and July 1851 was overlooked for many years. It was eventually found by his brother William among other manuscripts and drawings and was belatedly published, under the title 'Notes on the Birds of Michalaski, Norton Sound', in *The Ibis* of 1878. But by then Robert Kennicott, William Dall and others had visited the same area and Adams's labours were of less consequence. Nevertheless Edward Adams remains a pioneer Alaskan ornithologist.

He was born at Great Barton, near Bury St Edmunds in Suffolk, on 24 February 1824 and spent a great part of his youth pursuing his interest in natural history. He entered the medical profession and qualified as a surgeon in April 1847, at the age of twenty-three. In August of the same year he obtained a commission in the Royal Navy as assistant surgeon and was appointed to Haslar Hospital, Chatham, but after three months he was transferred to the Naval Hospital at Devonport. His service here was also brief because after four months he volunteered to join James Ross's expedition to the Arctic to search for Sir John Franklin. Adams's interest in natural history no doubt aided his selection and he was appointed as assistant surgeon and naturalist to the *Investigator* under Captain Bird; James Ross commanding the *Enterprise*.

The two ships left England on 8 May 1848 and sailed northwards to Baffin Bay and Lancaster Sound to winter near Somerset Island. The search was fruitless in that they found no trace of Franklin, but Adams collected birds and geological specimens and sketched a number of Arctic scenes. Ironically, Adams and Ross

†No portrait traced.

were close to the Boothia Peninsula where, in the 1830s, Ross had spent three winters trapped in the ice and had returned with three skins of the White-billed Diver! Edward Sabine, however, had persuaded Ross "against his own better judgement" that these examples were only very old males of the similar Great Northern Diver.[3]

After eighteen months the two ships arrived back in England and were immediately prepared for a second search expedition that was to approach the islands of the Canadian Arctic from the west, by way of the Bering Straits. This time Edward Adams was appointed assistant surgeon to the *Enterprise* under Captain Richard Collinson, while the *Investigator* was commanded by Robert McClure. They left Plymouth on 20 January 1850, after less than three months in England; and the *Enterprise* did not return for another five years. (For a map of Adams's travels with Collinson, see Franklin, p. 162).

The *Investigator* was the slower of the two ships but, in true tortoise-and-hare fashion, she arrived in the Arctic first, and choosing a route north of Victoria Island tried to force her way eastward. The *Enterprise*, with the young Adams on board, had been becalmed north of Hawaii and did not arrive in the Bering Straits until August. They were astonished to hear that McClure had gone on ahead but by then it was too late for them to follow because winter was already closing in. Putting into Port Clarence, north of Nome, Collinson heard several stories from the captain of the *Plover* concerning possible survivors from Franklin's expedition, some of which came from the Eskimos while others had been passed on to him by the Russians who were then colonizing the region. The most promising account told of two officers and eight men in a "distressed state" who had bartered guns for food at a place 550 miles upriver from the mouth of the Yukon. Collinson determined to investigate this report and Lieutenant Barnard, Adams and Thomas Cousins (a seaman who had been with Franklin and Richardson when they explored the Mackenzie River) were all put ashore at St Michael, just north of the flat and marshy expanses of the Yukon Delta. Barnard waited until winter before setting off so that he could travel with the Russian Governor and his interpreter, believing that this would speed up his enquiries. Adams remained behind, but on the 25 February he received a note saying that the Russian trading post of Nulato had been attacked by Indians and that Barnard was "dangerously wounded". The doctor left at once but by the time he arrived Barnard was dead.

White-billed Diver

The Russians enjoyed good relations with the Athabascan Indians and had therefore not been on their guard against them. Some Indians from further north had surprised the Russians as they slept, killed the Governor, fled after a struggle with Barnard and then killed a number of local Indians on their return northward. The interpreter had also been wounded but was saved by Adams's surgical skills. There was no sign of the white men whom Barnard had been looking for; they were probably only fur-trappers who had arrived on the Yukon overland from the Mackenzie.

On his return to St Michael, Adams continued his observations on the bird life around the fort, enjoying especially the brief period between the arrival of spring in mid-May and the arrival of the *Plover*, which took Adams and Cousins back to Port Clarence to rejoin their ship on 4 July. By then Adams had made notes on many of the typical birds of the area including Red-necked Phalaropes, Golden Plovers, Sandhill Cranes, Sabine's Gulls, King Eiders, Spectacled Eiders and Lapland Buntings. He was the first to record the Bluethroat in America and also saw the Yellow Wagtail, another North American 'rarity' whose breeding range only just extends from Siberia across the Bering Sea into Alaska. On the 9 and 10 May Adams witnessed the curious phenomenon of thousands of Snow Geese flying overhead *southwards* and the Russians and Eskimos confirmed that these birds flew *north* as winter approached. Adams deduced that the apparent anomaly was due to the birds' habit, on migration, of closely following the coastline which is sharply convoluted in the region of St Michael.

Concerning the White-billed Diver, the naturalist noted that the "Natives kill numbers of these birds at sea during the autumn. They have plenty of skins, both old and young, which they convert into bags for their tools. I saw none of the birds myself." Although Adams saw plenty of these divers later on, he was not likely to have seen them on this part of the expedition because they are at sea from October to May and then move far to the north of Norton Sound to nest. They are almost circumpolar in range, breeding in the high Arctic of eastern Canada westwards to the Russian–Norwegian border.

After leaving St Michael the previous autumn Collinson had taken the *Enterprise* southwards to the Russian capital of Sitka, then crossed the Pacific to Hong Kong where he spent the winter and replenished the ship's supplies before returning to Alaska in July. With Adams and Cousins on board once again, they entered the Arctic and taking a more southerly route than the *Investigator* had done, below Banks and Victoria Islands, they succeeded in penetrating further east than any other ship had done before. In the spring of 1853 some of Collinson's crew reached as far as Gateshead Island by sledge and although they found not the slightest trace of the missing men and only one piece of wreckage (of doubtful origin) they were only a few miles from the position where Franklin had perished—as long ago as 1847.

The senior surgeon and Adams made worthwhile collections of insects, flowers and birds, although more often than not any shooting was for the pot. Eighty-eight birds of various kinds were later presented to the British Museum but no account of the expedition's natural history discoveries was ever prepared.

The *Enterprise* did not meet up with McClure again (who was trapped in the ice, well to the north) and in all they spent three years in complete isolation within the Arctic before returning homewards. Their brief call at Hong Kong, where they took on board twenty men from a hospital ship, caused Collinson to remark that "the relaxation and run ashore did our men more damage than all the exposure to the northward". Some men died and Adams himself contracted a lung disorder that made him ill for the remainder of the voyage.

Their welcome by the Admiralty was less than enthusiastic. McClure had already claimed the credit and been given the prize money for completing the North-west Passage, even though he had not actually sailed his ship through; the *Investigator* had been crushed and lost in the ice and the crew had been transferred to another ship which had approached from the opposite direction. Four other ships had also been lost in the Arctic causing the Admiralty to lose interest in the search for Franklin and they made little of Collinson's achievements.

In the course of a two-month rest Adams appeared to recover and after passing his full naval surgeon's exams he was appointed to the steam sloop *Hecla*, joining her at Devonport in November 1855. When the ship was ordered to the coast of West Africa in the following May, Adams suspected that he would never return because of the humid climate there. After only a month in the region he was set ashore as an invalid while the *Hecla* carried out her duties elsewhere for three weeks. When she returned Adams was taken on board in the hope of taking him back to England but an attack of typhus was too much for him and he died on 12 November. His burial at a small cemetery in Sierra Leone was attended by most of the ship's company, the Governor and the whole garrison. He was but thirty-two years old. A brother officer wrote:

"To you who knew him, I need hardly say how deeply his loss is felt, not only by us, his messmates, but by all who were fortunate enough to be able to appreciate his sterling good qualities; but as an accomplished natural historian, and a most efficient member of a learned profession, his death will affect a larger circle than that of his immediate friends."

Boyd Alexander (1873-1910)

CAPE VERDE SWIFT *Apus alexandri* Hartert

Apus unicolor alexandri Hartert, 1901. *Novitates Zoologicae* 8, p. 328: São Nicolau, Cape Verde Islands

At the beginning of this century, the name of Boyd Alexander was known around the world due to the success of the Alexander–Gosling Expedition, which crossed Africa from the Niger to the Nile and explored the Lake Chad area. As well as being a great explorer, Alexander was also an outstanding ornithologist whose writings displayed his enthusiasm for the birds of his native Kent as much as for the exotic species that he discovered in Africa.

Boyd and his twin brother, Robert, were born on 16 January 1873, the first sons of Lt Col. B. F. Alexander of Swift's Place, Cranbrook. Like many other small boys they revelled in birds' nesting, and being fortunate enough to live on a large estate, their opportunities were ample. As soon as he was allowed to handle a gun, Boyd learnt to shoot and skin birds which he mounted and displayed along with his egg collections in a large room which became known to the family as Boyd's Museum.

His courage and his determination to pursue birds were indicated in a characteristic adventure at the age of eleven, when he and two of his brothers were scouring the countryside for eggs on the first day of their summer holidays. A pair of Swallows had built their nest in the rafters of a disused barn, but the door was locked. Robert and Herbert were still trying to find a way in when they heard an exultant shout from Boyd, who had somehow got up into the roof. He stretched his hand up to count the eggs, and the next thing which the boys outside heard was a crashing in the rafters and a sickening thud. Peering through a crack in the door, they could see their brother lying with his head in a pool of blood, but despite kicking at the door and tearing at the boards, they were unable to reach him. Fortunately, they spotted a labourer in a nearby field, who broke down the door and carried the unconscious body out into the sunshine. They succeeded in reviving him with some water, but three of his teeth were broken. Due back for lunch and fearing that a dramatic and messy arrival home would prevent such forays in the future, Boyd cleaned himself up, struggled home on foot and tried to eat lunch as though nothing had happened.

W..t & Son, Phot. B.B., Vol. iv., Pl. i.

Boyd Alexander

ALEXANDER. *BRITISH ARMY OFFICER AND AFRICAN EXPLORER. A SUPERB FIELD-ORNITHOLOGIST, HE AMASSED IMPORTANT COLLECTIONS FROM THE CAPE VERDE ISLANDS, FERNANDO PO AND WEST-CENTRAL AFRICA.*

Inevitably, his dazed condition and battered face were soon noticed, but his parents never heard the full details of the incident and his freedom continued.

At the age of twenty the twins separated when they joined different regiments of the Rifle Brigade. Boyd's first published notes appeared three years later in three issues of the *Zoologist* of 1896. In the first he discussed the increased disturbance of breeding birds along the Kentish coast, particularly at Lydd Beach which had been affected by the opening of the Dungeness railway and by nearby artillery practice. Once an extensive wilderness, with breeding Stone Curlews and Kentish Plovers, the stony expanse with its large ponds was seriously threatened. Redshanks, too, were decreasing, partly because of the drainage of their nesting habitat and also through the taking of their eggs by country people for food. From mid-May onwards young Grey Herons invaded the ditches and shallow pools in search of eels, but many were shot by the farmers, as they too made good eating.

Boyd's next contribution described the birds of Kent in the late summer, as Swifts and Swallows gathered for their departure and Linnets resorted in large flocks to the fallow fields. That year he had found a great many Red-backed Shrike nests, often in close proximity to each other, and had enjoyed watching the fledglings hunting from wooden fences, or perched on outgrowing branches of the stout hedgerows.

The 'Ornithological Notes from Rye' was his third paper and took the form of a beautifully written, evocative diary of the autumn migration, a harmonious combination of careful records and delightful, appreciative descriptions of birds and their surroundings, such as is rarely found in more recent journals and magazines. On warm, fine days Boyd watched the parties of Herring and Black-headed Gulls clustering along the water's edge, while inland, beyond the sea-wall, Curlews cried noisily in large flocks. By late August masses of Starlings were appearing offshore like driven smoke, buffeted by the strong south-westerlies. On 27 August there was an unusual influx of Yellow Wagtails, so that the bean and stubble fields seemed to be alive with them, while others perched on the telegraph wires, like Swallows. In the second week of October late broods of House Martins arrived on the coast, weary and exhausted, huddling together on the eaves of the cottages; but most other migrants, by then, were scarce.

In 1897 Boyd made two visits to the Cape Verde Islands, accompanied by a friend and two professional taxidermists. On 10 February they landed at São Vicente and spent the next four months observing and collecting the ornithological specialities of the group. On 15 March they set out to explore three small, uninhabited islands, devoid of both fresh water and vegetation. On Cima, Boyd found a mixed colony of petrels breeding on low, flat, gravelly land, completely honeycombed by their many burrows. During the day, the birds remained underground with their eggs or chicks, but as it grew dark, their mates returned with food, and Boyd later described the scene as the island came to life:

"When the night shadows began to brood vaguely over this lone waste of an island, the petrels came abroad and filled the still air with their weird cries. They mustered strongly, flitting to and fro over the low-lying ground in hundreds. Among the number the most noticeable was *Puffinus assimilis* [the Little Shearwater], as it

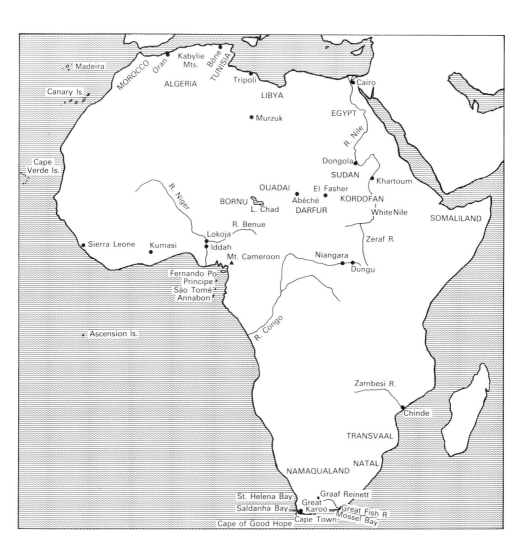

PLACES IN AFRICA VISITED BY ALEXANDER, ALLEN, BUTLER, DENHAM, DUNN, LEDANT,
LEVAILLANT AND LICHTENSTEIN

glided like some large soft-winged bat over the small sand hills, and even sometimes brushing past our camp fire, for ever uttering its weird cry '*karki-karrou, karki karrow, karki-karrou*' while amid these a similar but softer one would often strike fitfully upon the ear, coming from *Oceanodroma* [*castro*] [the Madeiran Storm-petrel] as it flitted over the island . . . As the night wore on, the cries of these petrels died away, only to recommence, however, with redoubled energy just as dawn arrived, and then, as soon as the dusky light waxed clear, these voices ceased as suddenly as they had commenced, indicating that their owners had crept noiselessly into their dark retreats, there to remain till the heat had once more abated."[1]

Boyd collected a good series of Little Shearwater skins on Cape Verde. They were later described as a separate race, named *Puffinus assimilis boydi* in his honour.

The Cape Verde Swift is endemic to the Cape Verde Islands and is very similar in appearance to the Plain Swift *Apus unicolor* which breeds only in the Canaries and Madeira. When Hartert first described the Cape Verde Swift in 1901, from a specimen which Boyd shot on São Nicolau, he named it *Apus unicolor alexandri*, believing it to be just a race of the Plain Swift. Some still share this opinion, but in *The Birds of the Western Palearctic*, Vol. IV (1985) it is given specific status, pending further study of its biology. Boyd found the swifts breeding in the crevices of cliffs, but they also use caves and sometimes the roofs of houses, where they lay freckled red-brown eggs, quite unlike the white eggs of the Plain Swift.

When Alexander returned to England, he brought with him a Portuguese boy called José Lopes, who showed promise as a collector and who remained his faithful assistant throughout his African travels. Boyd's lifelong interest in the birds of that continent prompted his friendship with Captain G. E. Shelley, who had written extensively on that subject, and on one occasion he invited Shelley to his home. Boyd's mother had not yet realized that ornithology could become a serious life-study, and by way of making conversation at dinner on the first evening, she asked the elderly gentleman, "And are birds as much a hobby with you as they are with my boy?" She was rather startled, as well as amused, when he replied, "Lord, yes! I'd 'a shot my mother if she'd had wings."

In the summer of 1898 Boyd travelled across mainland Africa for the first time. He set out from Chinde, on the coast of Mozambique, as one of nine members of the 'Cape to Cairo Expedition'. Boyd was responsible for the exploration of the lower part of the Zambesi River and one of its tributaries,

Cape Verde Swift

and collected nearly 1000 skins of 212 bird species, several of which were new to science.

Afterwards he spent only a short time in England before returning to Africa to serve with the Gold Coast Constabulary, and took part in the relief of Kumasi in 1900, accompanied by Lopes who followed behind the relief column collecting birds. Shortly after the beleaguered fort had been occupied, Captain Alexander was found to be missing. General Sir James Willcocks instituted a search, and Boyd and Lopes were discovered in their tent in the surrounding forest, in serious danger of being attacked by hostile Ashanti tribesmen. When told to account for his behaviour, Boyd explained that if he had stayed inside the fort he would have been called upon for duty, whereas in the forest he had undisturbed opportunities to collect birds! Despite this splendid assessment of priorities, Boyd won a medal and clasp for his part in the attack on the fort and must have remained on good terms with his superior, as he later named a new species of honey-guide *Indicator willcocksi*.

When Boyd returned to England he was offered a commission in his old regiment of the Rifle Brigade and he accepted. At the same time, he began to plan an expedition to the island of Fernando Po, which lies off the coast of Cameroon, and he made the trip during a three-month period of leave at the end of 1902. Other naturalists, including Louis Fraser of the 1841 Niger River Expedition, had previously collected on the island, but none had traversed the mountains, which are clothed almost to their summits with thick bush and damp virgin forest. It was Boyd's ambition to ascend the highest range, topped by Clarence Peak at 10,800 ft.

At the end of October Boyd and Lopes sailed into the beautiful little bay of Santa Isobel at the north end of the island, accompanied by 25 carriers whom they had brought from Calabar. They spent the day assembling their baggage and organizing the required stores: bags of rice and trade goods such as beads, tobacco, rum, gunpowder and clothes. To the amazement of the natives, they were ready to set off early the following morning and travelled in heavy rain along slippery tracks past cocoa plantations and through thick vegetation. For days they followed the low ground of the eastern coast as far as Bakaki and as they passed through the villages they tried to hire guides, but without any success. Boyd decided to strike inland without local help, and carrying all their provisions and water they climbed the steep slopes of the mountain, cutting their way through the jungle until they reached nearly 8000 ft, where they began to find many new and rare forest birds. Unfortunately, the hard physical labour and the continual wearing of wet clothes took its toll and Lopes came down with fever, so that the party had to hurry back to Bakaki, where they stayed until he had recovered.

At the end of November they set out again for the peak which was shrouded by heavy mist which drenched and darkened the tracks. Often they had to crawl on hands and knees through the dense undergrowth and all loads over 20 lb, including the tents, had to be abandoned. It was a continual struggle to keep the guns and powder dry, but they managed to obtain a number of interesting species, and often stopped to appreciate the beauty of the many lovely orchids and mountain ferns which grew abundantly on the sheltered slopes. On the fourth day they at last reached the summit where they were suddenly exposed to cold winds which bent and blasted the few stunted and scattered trees which survived there. Bird life was scarce but they had achieved their objective and after acquiring what specimens they could they turned back towards the east coast and returned to Santa Isobel in a couple of large surf boats, lent to them by some English cocoa farmers.

Boyd then sailed homewards, leaving Lopes to work the southern portion of the island. The whole expedition resulted in a series of nearly 500 specimens representing three new genera and 103 species, of which no less than 35 were found to be entirely new.

For the next three years Boyd was again in Africa on his famous Niger to the Nile Expedition, accompanied by his brother Claud, Captain G. B. Gosling and Lopes. They sailed from Liverpool at the end of February 1904, and a few weeks later they reached the mouth of the Niger River where they boarded a sternwheeler which took them 250 miles upriver to Lokoja. Their plan was to survey parts of eastern Nigeria, Lake Chad and rivers to the east of it, travelling as far as they could in two steel boats which they had brought from Essex, and, if possible, to reach the Nile and return home via Egypt. Boyd's chief interest, as ever, was in the ornithology of the region, and he hoped to establish the extent to which the avifauna of the west coast and the Nile were related, and to investigate the little known birds of Lake Chad.

Much was achieved during the first six months, with the expedition members splitting up to explore separate areas. Claud made a thorough survey of the Murchison Range, but in October fell ill with enteric fever and died at the British fort of Maifoni in November, aged only 26. Boyd and Gosling carried on to Lake Chad, where they spent many months exploring its shores and islands. The flat, sandy pastures around the lake were inhabited by Chestnut-bellied Sandgrouse which flew high over the camp in batches every morning and evening to drink from the lake. In the distance the country was wooded with gum and mimosa trees, but the bird life seemed to be identical with that of the Sudan, and the only species which Boyd discovered was a new reed warbler. Denham and Clapperton had made a small collection in the same area some 80 years before and when Boyd and his companions landed on some of the islands they often disturbed Denham's Bustards which had hitherto been concealed by the long grass. Gosling studied the fishes and found that with one or two exceptions the species were common to both the Niger and the Nile.

By May 1906 Gosling was seriously ill with blackwater fever and in June he died at Niangara. Boyd continued with a heavy heart, determined to reach the Nile by the least-known route. From Dungu he followed the River Kibali which had not previously been navigated and the remnant of the expedition was almost lost in its rapids. Despite frequent attacks of fever, Boyd reached the Nile late in the year and arrived back in England in February to a hero's welcome.

Some of the tributes bestowed on Boyd afforded him less pleasure than was intended, for the ordeal of public speaking at dinners and lectures struck him with greater terror than any of the dangers which he had encountered in Africa.

Troubled by shyness since his childhood he found himself ill at ease in social situations, especially when he returned from an expedition after being cut off from all society for a long time. The Royal Geographical Societies of London and Antwerp awarded him their gold medals and he was elected an Honorary Member of the R.G.S. of Scotland. Boyd's family expressed their mixed pride and grief in a rather unusual way; his twin brother Robert constructed a lake at Swift's Place, making it a small scale replica of Lake Chad, with boat house and duck huts representing the reed-built huts of the Buduma tribe.

After less than two years in England Boyd sailed back to Africa, accompanied only by Lopes. His plan consisted of four phases: to make ornithological collections on the islands of São Tomé, Principe and Annabon in the Gulf of Guinea, and then to do the same on Mt Cameroon. Afterwards he intended to travel northwards through Cameroon, visit Claud's grave in Bornu and then undertake the most hazardous, but principal object of the expedition, which he had discussed only with his brother Herbert, for fear of official interference.

After satisfactory visits to the the three islands, Boyd and Lopes sailed to Cameroon and ascended the volcanic peak discovering at an altitude of 7000 ft a new and remarkable francolin: the Cameroon Mountain Francolin. From Victoria Boyd wrote to Ogilvie-Grant on 30 April 1909, reporting that:

> "I have worked pretty hard on the peak of Cameroon and I do not think I have ever had more difficult collecting. The forest is so thick that I lose nearly half of what I kill. I had an appalling time of it on the mountain during the first night of the earthquake. My camp was at an altitude of 8000 feet. At each boom from the mountain above us the ground danced like a live thing and torrents of stone poured down the hill not half a mile from where we were camped, forest-trees came crashing down and snapped in two like match-sticks, and the cries of terrified monkeys flying before the torrent added, if that was possible, to the dreadful scene. I abandoned my camp at three in the morning and only just in time, for an hour later the place was destroyed."

After this lucky escape Boyd and Lopes travelled to Bornu, by Lake Chad, and made their way eastwards to Ouadai, hoping to reach El Fasher, the capital of Darfur. Darfur was ruled by the great Sultan Ali Dinar and it was Boyd's secret ambition to win his confidence and persuade him that a full acknowledgement of Britain's suzerainty, with his active cooperation in the abolition of the slave trade, was by far the best policy for the welfare of Darfur, as Boyd himself believed it to be. Without this urgent humanitarian mission, Boyd would not have considered repeating his stupendous journey.

At Abéché in the French territory of Ouadai they were held up for a month because of fierce fighting in the surrounding areas. They travelled on at the end of March and on 2 April set up camp at a little village called Illarne, near Nyeri. During the evening they were visited by an unruly group of villagers and soldiers who tried to persuade Boyd to go with them to the local sultan. Having already sent a note to say that he would call next morning, Boyd refused, but they then tried to take him by force. The explorers' weapons were in the baggage and Lopes ran for them, but they were unloaded and he could not find the ammunition. He pointed his rifle at the mob and by pretending that he was about to fire, gained sufficient time to escape, but by then Boyd had been felled by a single shot and clubbed to death.

The body was recovered later that same week by French officers and taken to Abéché, then borne to Maifoni under José Lopes's charge. There, Boyd Alexander was laid to rest beside Claud under a tall, white-flowered acacia tree, at the place which he had chosen for his brother five years earlier.

ALLEN. *ENGLISH NAVAL OFFICER WHO ROSE TO THE RANK OF REAR ADMIRAL. HE TOOK PART IN TWO DISASTROUS EXPEDITIONS TO WEST AFRICA AND LATER DEVISED AN EXTRAORDINARY ENGINEERING PROJECT FOR PALESTINE.*

William Allen
(1793-1864)

ALLEN'S GALLINULE *Porphyrula alleni* (Thomson)

Porphyrio alleni Thomson, 1842. *Annals and Magazine of Natural History* 10, p. 204: Idda, Niger River

During the course of his long naval career which spanned almost sixty years, William Allen took part in, and was lucky to survive, two ill-fated expeditions up the Niger River. His degree of interest in ornithology is hard to determine, since the account of the second expedition, his most important work which contains references to birds, was co-authored by the naval surgeon and zoologist Dr T. R. H. Thomson.

Born at Weymouth in November 1793, Allen entered the Royal Navy as a first class volunteer at the age of twelve and served in the Mediterranean and Baltic until 1805. Two years later he was in the Dardanelles and in 1808 assisted in the capture of an Italian brig-of-war in the Adriatic. His next appointment took him to the East Indies where he was involved in attacks on pirate settlements on the coast of Borneo, and he did not return to England until September 1815, by which time he had attained the rank of Lieutenant.

In 1832 Allen volunteered to join, at his own expense, Richard Lander's Niger River Expedition which was mainly a commercial enterprise, backed by some prosperous Liverpool merchants. Unfortunately, the reports concerning the amount of ivory available close to the river had been exaggerated and they arrived so late in the season that they had to navigate a falling river. One of the steamers was grounded about 300 miles upriver and it remained fast until the next rainy season. The expedition eventually retired to the island of Fernando Po, but later when re-ascending the Niger in a canoe Lander was hit in the thigh by a musket-ball fired from the river bank. He was taken back to Fernando Po where he died in early February 1834. All these events, coupled with the ravages of blackwater fever, turned the venture into a complete disaster. Of the forty-seven officers and men only nine survived.

On his safe return to England Allen was appointed to the *William and Mary* yacht, then surveying the Thames and Medway. He contributed two papers to the 1834 *Proceedings of the Zoological Society:* 'On a Collection of Objects of Zoology, made in the interior of Africa' and 'On some drawings of Fishes of the river Quorra [the Niger]'. He had also sketched and charted the course of the river as far as Rabba on the Niger and eighty miles upriver on the Benue, and these observations proved most useful when he returned to the region in 1841.

The main objective of this second Niger expedition was to establish treaties with some of the African chiefs whereby commerce would replace the trade in slaves. They were also to set up a model farm, explore the rivers, collect natural history specimens and make magnetic observations. Three vessels took part, all steamers: the *Albert* under Captain Henry Dundas Trotter, the *Wilberforce* under Commander William Allen, and, rather confusingly, the smaller *Soudan* was captained by Commander Bird Allen. Civilians on board the *Albert* included the botanist Dr Vogel and Louis Fraser, a well-known ornithologist of the period.

The project was supported by Prince Albert who was then President of the Society for the Extinction of the Slave Trade and the Civilisation of Africa. He presented each of the three captains with a fine gold chronometer just before their grand send-off from Woolwich on 22 April 1841. At Sierra Leone they took on a hundred Africans who were accustomed to serving on ships in the tropics and it was hoped that they would spare the British sailors from working in the hot and humid conditions on the Niger. They could not, of course, protect them from fever and the first British death occurred as soon as they entered the Niger Delta.

This time the river was swollen with rain which helped their passage by reducing the risk of grounding. They saw several species of terns skimming over the mud-brown water and caught glimpses of weaver birds, sunbirds and hornbills in the dense vegetation that lined the river banks. On 8 September, about a month after entering the river, they had reached Idda, and that night anchored between the village and a long low island. The narrative describes how, "Among the reeds, which yet appeared on parts of English Island, a very beautiful and new species of Sultana or water-hen was procured . . . The prevailing colours of this bird were rich dark green above, softening off into violet; the upper part of head, deep violet, breast blue and vent white . . . Dr Thomson called it Alleni in honour of his distinguished commander Captain William Allen R.N."[1]

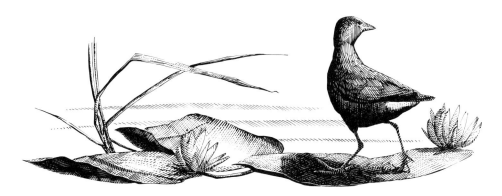

Allen's Gallinule

On the same day as the gallinule was shot Allen was reported as "unwell due to fatigue and exposure" and within a month nearly everybody's health had deteriorated. Captain Trotter and most of the crews were incapacitated and it was decided to go downriver and retreat to Fernando Po. But the situation did not improve and Dr Vogel and Commander Bird Allen were among those who died there. The sight of the two disintegrating steamers from the previous expedition only added to the general feeling of despondency. Trotter returned to England and Allen withdrew into the Atlantic to Ascension. The final death toll among the 145 officers and crew was forty and almost everyone had had very severe attacks of fever.

After a spell of recuperation Allen prepared to re-enter the Niger but the Government ordered the expedition home because of the appalling loss of life and mediocre achievements. By 1848 Allen and Thomson had completed *A Narrative of the Expedition sent by H. M. Government to the River Niger in 1841*, which dealt mainly with the exploits of the *Wilberforce*. The text contains many references to wildlife and plants and is followed by a natural history appendix compiled chiefly by Thomson. A description of Allen's Gallinule and some of the more important discoveries had already appeared in the *Annals and Magazine of Natural History in 1842*. Louis Fraser of the *Albert* published some of his ornithological material in his own *Zoologia typica* (1849); a good proportion of his new birds being from the forests of Fernando Po.

The overall results of the expedition were not good. The few treaties made with the African chiefs along the river did not last and slavery continued in the area; the model farm was not established and the insect specimens were all lost. On top of this, the overworked Edward Sabine, to whom all the magnetic observations had been given, had not analysed them in time for their inclusion in the narrative. Disaster had been inevitable because so little was known then about tropical diseases; not for nothing was that region of Africa known as the white man's graveyard. Blackwater fever is one of the severest forms of malaria causing anaemia and sometimes renal failure; it is still imperfectly understood and is still a killer disease. It can now usually be kept at bay by regular doses of quinine but Allen and Thomson actually commented: "As regards the influence of diet in the prevention of fever, we had the clearest proofs that tolerable good living, with a moderate proportion of wine and Bass's ale, was the most proper course to be adopted."

Their narrative further contains a long discourse on the evils of the slave trade which Allen later expanded upon in his *Plan for the immediate Extinction of the Slave Trade, for the relief of the West India Colonies and for the Diffusion of Civilisation and Christianity in Africa by the co-operation of Mammon and Philanthropy*, published in 1849. In that same year, Allen, who had often travelled on the Continent when not on active service, extended his horizons eastwards by visiting Syria and Palestine accompanied by his nephew. He later wrote *The Dead Sea, a New Route to India* (1855), which contained some seemingly bizarre proposals. Had they been adopted one can only wonder to what extent Allen would have altered the course of world history.

The Suez Canal did not then exist. The Dead Sea, the Sea of Galilee and much of the Jordan Valley are below sea-level and Allen suggested that a canal should be dug between the Jordan and Haifa so that the Mediterranean could pour into the valley. Another canal constructed between Aqaba and this new large sea would create a shipping route between the Red Sea and the Mediterranean, with a sheltered deep-water port at both ends. The total length of the proposed canal was less than a hundred miles because so much of the Jordan Valley would be deeply flooded. Elsewhere in the book (which contains scant reference to natural history) Allen discusses the biblical prophecies concerning the return of the Jews to the Holy Land.

After five months in the Middle East, Allen and his nephew returned to England. Twelve years later, in 1862, he retired from the Royal Navy as a Rear Admiral and died, a seventy-one year old bachelor, on 23 January 1864, at his home town of Weymouth.

A report in *The Gentleman's Magazine* described Allen in his latter years and gives us a few details about his character:

> 'In person the Admiral was rather under than over the middle height, with very handsome features, remarkably frank and open in their expression, and beaming with benevolence and good humour. Perhaps the most striking evidence that can be aduced of the simplicity and geniality of his disposition is his excessive love of children, of whom he was the idol.'

There have been a number of diligent ornithologists with the name of Allen but William Allen R.N. does not appear to have been one of them. He was a fellow of the Royal Society, a member of the Royal Geographical Society and a corresponding member of the Zoological Society. He wrote seven papers of a geographical nature but contributed only two papers and a letter to the *Proceedings of the Zoological Society*. None of his contributions were specifically about birds, although he no doubt possessed more than a passing interest in the subject.

In addition to his varied scientific pursuits Allen was a capable musician and a talented artist. As well as providing the illustrations for his books, he produced two volumes of *Picturesque Views* (1838–40), carried out on Ascension and on the Niger, and five of his landscape paintings were exhibited at the Royal Academy between 1828 and 1847.

Lady Amherst
née The Hon. Sarah Archer
(1762-1838)

LADY AMHERST'S PHEASANT *Chrysolophus amherstiae* (Leadbeater)

Phasianus Amherstiae Leadbeater, 1829. *Transactions of the Linnean Society of London* 16, p. 129, Pl. 15: "Mountains of Cochin China", error for Yunnan

Sarah was born on 19 July 1762, the eldest daughter of Andrew, the 2nd Lord Archer, Baron of Umberslade. Her childhood was spent in Warwickshire at Umberslade Park, near Tanworth-in-Arden, where the estate with its lakes and woods extended for nearly 1800 acres. Followers of the old Earls of Warwick, the Archers had long been settled there and also owned land at Pirgo in Essex. However, Sarah probably owed her interest in botany and ornithology to the other side of the family, for her maternal grandfather, James West of Alscot, was for a time the President of the Royal Society.

At the age of twenty-five Sarah married Other Hickman, the 5th Earl of Plymouth, who owned estates at Hewell Grange, Worcestershire, and at Peel Hall in Cheshire. The Earl, then aged thirty-six, was Sarah's cousin, and the wedding took place in London on 20 May 1788. A year later their only son, Other Archer, was born, followed by a daughter, Maria, in 1790. Sarah and her husband visited Rome in 1794, and while they were there, they made the acquaintance of William Pitt Amherst, whose company they much enjoyed. Having only recently left Oxford, Amherst was on a 'Grand Tour' of the continent and taking every opportunity to study languages, the mastery of which was later a great advantage in his diplomatic career. In the summer of 1797 Sarah gave birth to another daughter, Harriet, but less than two years later became widowed.

Sarah was the Countess Dowager of Plymouth for less than a year. In July 1800 she married the young man whom she had met in Rome, now Lord Amherst. The wedding was at St Georges, Hanover Square, in London, and afterwards they resided, with her three children, at *Montreal*, Lord Amherst's comfortable mansion which lay on gentle slopes between Riverhead and Sevenoaks in Kent.

AMHERST. *ENGLISH AMATEUR NATURALIST. HER ACTIVITIES WERE CURTAILED BY FAMILY RESPONSIBILITIES BUT SHE BOTANIZED DURING FIVE YEARS IN INDIA.*

Sarah's second husband was ten years her junior. Orphaned at the age of eight, he and his sister had been adopted by their uncle Jeffery, Lord Amherst, and brought up at his home, *Montreal*. The house had been named after one of Lord Amherst's greatest victories when he was Commander-in-Chief of the British Armed Forces in North America from 1758 to 1764. During the course of just two years he had secured all of Canada for Britain. After his return to England he was created Baron, and on his death his nephew inherited his estate and title, as well as the large Georgian house.

In 1802 the new Lord Amherst became Lord of the Bedchamber to George III, and in August Lady Amherst gave birth to their first son, Jeffery, at *Montreal*. Three years later their son William was born in London, followed by Frederick in 1807. They also had one daughter whom they named Sarah.

When Lord Amherst was sent to Sicily as Ambassador Extraordinary in 1809, his wife remained in England. Although Lady Amherst's young family prevented her from travelling and from pursuing her interest in natural history as she would have liked, she had specimens sent to her by collectors; one of her correspondents being Rafinesque, who, in 1810, was sending her plants from Sicily.

In 1815 Lord Amherst was made a Privy Councillor, and the next year the Prince Regent sent him as Ambassador to China. Again, Lady Amherst stayed at home, but the fourteen year old Jeffery accompanied his father on the long voyage, via Rio de Janeiro. Although the mission was an exciting adventure for Jeffery, it was not a diplomatic success, for Amherst refused to kow-tow to the Celestial Occupant of the Dragon Throne. The return journey almost ended in tragedy when they were shipwrecked off Java, but they eventually returned safely to England in 1817, after calling at St Helena where Amherst had a memorable interview with Napoleon. In their discussion of world politics, the exiled emperor asserted his conviction that one day India and all the British colonies would achieve independence, that the Italians and Germans would eventually enjoy national unity and that the rights of man would prevail. But: "If Russia organises Poland", he told Lord Amherst, "she will be irresistable".

After years of periodic insanity George III died and the Prince Regent ascended the throne, in 1820, as George IV. Three years later he appointed Lord Amherst the Governor-General of India. For the first time, Lady Amherst was able to go with her husband on an official posting abroad. She was now aged sixty and her three children by her first marriage were all settled: her son Other, the 6th Earl of Plymouth, who had chosen a career in the army, had for many years been married to Mary, the eldest daughter of the Duke of Dorset, who lived within sight of *Montreal*, at Knole; Maria and Harriet were both also married. Lord and Lady Amherst decided that of their own children, only Jeffery and Sarah should travel with them. William would soon be going up to Oxford, and Frederick also remained behind to continue his education.

Lord Amherst was recovering from a serious illness when they sailed from Southampton, on 15 March 1823; they called at the Canaries and Rio de Janeiro, and on the 18 July they reached Madras where they landed in state. Lady Amherst was wreathed with flowers and anointed with attar of roses and there were great festivities in their honour. Soon, however, they embarked on the last leg of their voyage up the east coast, and on the 1 August they sailed up the Hooghley which was crowded with small vessels, while the forts on either side fired their salutes. As they landed at Calcutta they were escorted through a seething mass of spectators to Government House, where Lord Amherst took his oath in the Council Chamber, and then they were welcomed by a public breakfast in the great marble hall. During the next six years most of their time was spent at Fort William in Calcutta, or at their country residence about 16 miles north of the town at Barrackpur.

Lord Amherst was now the ruler of a motley assortment of conquered states which varied enormously in their customs, religions, dialects and attitudes to colonial rule. At that time the British government had not yet assumed direct responsibility for the government of India. Authority was exercised through the Governor-General who was paid by the East India Company, the vast trading organization which, in effect, controlled much of the country. It was a country burdened with profoundly complicated social, economic and military problems. Lord Amherst's position was made much more tolerable by the support and encouragement of his wife, who played a large and gracious part in life, both at court and during their various journeys. A fortnight after their arrival she held her first 'drawing-room', attended by a great number of officers in full uniform and their ladies in brilliantly coloured gowns. Throughout her years in India, Lady Amherst kept a detailed diary in which she chronicled such social events, along with dainty sketches, pressed flowers and leaves, newspaper cuttings and letters.

The Amhersts had barely settled in when Bishop Heber arrived with his family and on 11 October he was installed at the elegant Cathedral, dining afterwards at Government House with the Amhersts, who welcomed him warmly. The next month, Lady Amherst and Sarah with five attendants carrying gilt sticks and maces, swords and spears, took Bishop Heber on a tour of the Botanical Gardens, which the East India Company had established forty years before, to provide a nursery for the cultivation of rare and useful plants of economic importance. The Director of the Gardens was the outstanding Danish botanist, Nathaniel Wallich, through whose devotion the park had become a place which in the Bishop's view more perfectly resembled Milton's idea of Paradise than anywhere else he had ever seen. It was certainly a paradise for Lady Amherst and her daughter, who spent many happy days investigating and learning about its botanical delights, for the garden harboured over 3000 species of plants.

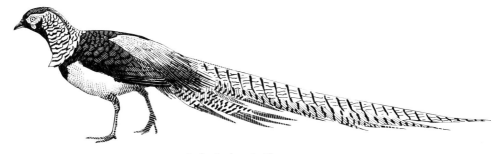

Lady Amherst's Pheasant

Bishop Heber invited Lady Amherst to be patroness of the Native Female Schools, run by the Church Missionary Society, a position which she gladly accepted. The primary object of the work was to teach the young Indian girls to read, so that they would be sufficiently well educated to be able to read Holy Scripture for themselves, and to choose which religion they wanted to follow. On 12 December Lady Amherst accompanied the Bishop and others to examine one of the schools, and watched as the girls, sitting on the ground, wrote their letters in the sand or on banana leaves and read the Bible stories.

The Amherst family spent their first Indian Christmas at Barrackpur on the banks of the Hooghley. From the house there was a fine view across the river to the neat, white buildings of the Dutch settlement of Serampoor. The park extended for several hundred acres, and contained many different trees and colourful flowering shrubs. There was also a huge menagerie of local birds and animals there, in which Lady Amherst took much interest.

The new year brought grave problems for Lord Amherst, who, though a diplomat at heart and pacific by nature, was compelled by the pretensions of the King of Burma to declare war. The early stages of the conflict were disastrous for the British and, at the end of that traumatic year, the Indian troops mutinied at Barrackpur, where the Amhersts were then residing, and for twenty-four hours their lives were in great danger until the rebels were suppressed. The war in Burma continued into 1825 and in June, finding the heat of Calcutta unbearable, the Amherst family made an excursion in the government yacht. Accompanied as usual by Dr Clarke Abel (a keen botanist who had been Lord Amherst's personal physician since his embassy to China) as well as other friends and servants, they sailed upriver to above Murshidabad. The banks were lined with palm trees, banana trees and indigo plantations and they passed many tumbledown villages haunted by crocodiles. Whenever they went ashore Lady Amherst and Sarah took the opportunity to collect many interesting insects and plants. Late in July they returned to Calcutta, feeling rejuvenated by their cruise, but in August Lady Amherst suffered from cholera, and wrote:

> "This dreadful scourge still rages at Calcutta, and its environs, and Barrackpur. Dead bodies lie in heaps by the river-side. At Achipur the same disease extends, notwithstanding a great sacrifice by the Hindus of a live buffalo, a goat and a dog."

Suttee was consequently very common, and, like all westerners, Lady Amherst was appalled by the custom, as she witnessed many of the widows being dragged by the Brahmans to their death.

At last, to the great relief of Lord Amherst and his family, the war turned in Britain's favour. After the defeat of Prome, the capital of lower Burma, by Sir Archibald Campbell, the King of Burma sued for peace. He was forced to relinquish Tenasserim with its superb hardwood forests, Assam with its valuable tea plantations and Arakan, one of the world's greatest rice growing areas. When Sir Archibald Campbell visited the Governor-General in Calcutta, he brought Lady Amherst two very beautiful pheasants which had been presented to him by the King of Burma, and the birds were added to her aviary at Barrackpur.

Although the war had ended in victory, Lord Amherst was severely criticized by the directors of the East India Company for his conduct of the war, especially during the early heavy losses. When the long campaign was finally over, the Amhersts at last felt free to plan a tour of the Upper Provinces. However, at the end of July 1826, a few weeks before they were due to set out, Lord Amherst and Jeffery both suffered an attack of 'epidemic fever', bouts of which usually lasted just three days. When Jeffery recovered he joined his parents at Barrackpur, but suddenly he relapsed, and after two days of violent fever during which he was tended by his mother, he passed away on the morning of 2 August, as she sat by his bedside. At the end of the year, Lady Amherst wrote in her diary:

> "This year, full of momentous events, has nearly drawn to a close. Upon the whole the most miserable of my life . . . I used to try to console Lord Amherst by saying so long as it pleases God to grant our children and ourselves tolerable health, we must be thankful. That great luminary, truth, must in time bring all things to light; but the heavy and awful visitation of the sudden and very unexpected removal of our beloved Jeff overset us. This death was the bitterest pang I ever felt and shall continue to feel as long as I live."

In the meantime the distraught family had to begin the long excursion up the Ganges and across the lowland plains to Simla, a thousand miles away in the foothills of the Himalayas. The day after Jeffery's interment, just three weeks before his twenty-fourth birthday, the Amhersts with Sarah and Dr Abel went aboard the government yacht, in which they travelled as far as Allahabad. During the following months they made frequent excursions ashore to meet the local dignitaries who entertained them with feasts and fireworks and numerous other forms of amusement. From Allahabad they travelled by land, often hunting and hawking with their hosts, but near the end of the year the party was deeply saddened when Dr Abel fell ill and died at Kanpur.

In January they reached Agra, where, as usual, Lord Amherst held a levee. After solemn promises were made that no men would be present, Lady Amherst was allowed to hold a reception for the wives of the local ruler, and through an interpreter she enjoyed much conversation with them. The ladies stayed for three hours and presented their hostess with many precious gifts, including twenty-four trays of jewels, twenty-seven trays of muslin and one female elephant. One of the Indian women later wrote an account of the meeting:

> "The great lady [Lady Amherst] was sitting on a golden Musnid of curious workmanship and resembling the mountain Kaila's in splendour; she did not sit cross-legs like your Highness, but with her feet hanging down to the ground in a strange manner which I cannot describe, but which I think must be very painful . . . She did not wear a Sary or Dossuttah or even Pyjamas: neither did she wear nose rings, which was very surprising; but what caused me most astonishment was that her throat and neck were quite uncovered. This shocked me very much. There were a great many more of the great lord's wives present; some were very handsome, but most of them so horridly white that they appeared like figures of marble."

Towards the end of March the heat of the northern plains became very trying and the cool heights of the Himalayas grew increasingly attractive. They reached Simla early in April after enduring the unaccustomed shock of being soaked to the skin by heavy showers of hail and snow. The party rested for ten weeks at

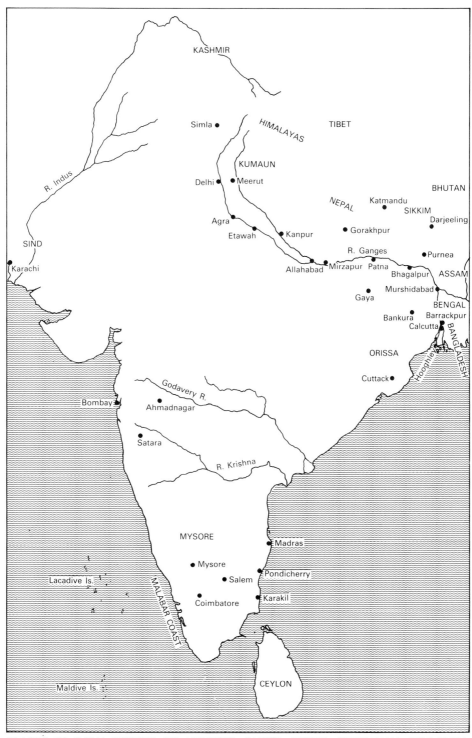

PLACES IN INDIA VISITED BY AMHERST, BLYTH, BRUCE, BUCHANAN, HODGSON,
HUME, TICKELL AND LESCHENAULT

the remote hill station, glorying in the cool fresh air and the majestic scenery. Sarah and Lady Amherst were in their element, and, although the latter was now aged sixty-four, they both rose early every morning and went out on excursions with the native botanist, delighting in the many new and lovely plants and shrubs which grew only in the mountains. They gathered and pressed the leaves and flowers, and also collected seeds, many of which they sent to England to be grown there for the first time. Among the flowers which they introduced to British gardens are *Anemone vitifolia* and *Clematis montana*, one of the most popular and easily cultivated of flowering climbers.

At the end of May good news reached Lord Amherst at Simla. The directors of the East India Company had withdrawn their earlier criticism, and in the light of more recent events, were fulsome in their praise of his decisions. Furthermore, King George IV had created him 'Earl Amherst of Arakan in the East Indies and Viscount Holmesdale in Kent'.

Lady Amherst was given an honour of a very different kind. While she was earning her reputation as a pioneer of Himalayan botany, the Director of the Calcutta Garden, Nathaniel Wallich, was exploring the forests of Burma with the task of assessing their economic potential. In the mountains north-east of Ava, Wallich found 300 new species of plants in just four days. He also searched for a very rare and spectacular tree which his colleague, John Crawfurd, had discovered on an earlier visit. One of the loveliest of all flowering trees, bearing long dangling racemes of pale-red blossoms, he hunted for it without success and eventually had to visit the neglected monastery garden on the bank of the Salween River where he found Crawfurd's original specimen. He was able to obtain some layers from the tree which he later established in the garden at Calcutta. Wallich named the tree *Amherstia nobilis* in honour of Lady Amherst and her daughter, with whom he had often delighted in sharing his enthusiasm for all things botanical.

Lord Amherst was the first Governor-General to make Simla a place of summer retreat, but thereafter it was the official summer residence of the Governor-General and his retinue and a popular resort among other Europeans in northern India. In the middle of June they reluctantly began the return journey across the plains to Calcutta. Cholera was again raging through many areas but they returned safely to Barrackpur. Lord Amherst's term of office was now nearing its end and Lady Amherst was fully occupied in making preparations for the voyage home. In addition to the usual household baggage and many mementoes of their stay, she had to pack her extensive botanical and zoological collections for safe transit. The two Burmese pheasants, which had survived in her aviary for two years, were assigned to their coops after she had cut off their tail feathers about two inches from the body. This enabled the birds to move about more freely and preserved the superb black and white tail-feathers which were more than three feet long.

Shortly before they sailed in March, Sarah became seriously ill and had to be carried on board, but she recovered during the voyage and they arrived safely at Spithead on 22 July 1828. As soon as they had anchored they were reunited with Lady Amherst's son by her first marriage, the Earl of Plymouth, as well as William and Frederick.

The pheasants had survived the long voyage, but, sadly, they died just a few weeks later. Lady Amherst showed them to Benjamin Leadbeater, a natural history dealer, who described them in the *Transactions of the Linnean Society* and named them *Phasianus Amherstiae* "as a tribute due to the distinguished lady to whom ornithologists are indebted". More of these spectacular pheasants were introduced to Britain over the years, but they were not bred successfully in captivity until 1871. There is a long-established feral population thriving in Bedfordshire and some other parts of southern England, but in the wild their range is limited to the mountains of south-west China, adjacent parts of Tibet and upper Burma.

After Lady Amherst returned to England her husband resumed his former duties as Lord of the Bedchamber to George IV, and their son William became the MP for East Grinstead. In October 1829 the family were again bereaved when Frederick died, unmarried, at the age of twenty-two. Four years later Lady Amherst lost her eldest son, the Earl of Plymouth, when he collapsed suddenly, aged forty-four, on board his yacht at Deptford.

Lady Amherst died on 27 May 1838, at the age of seventy-five, while staying at Grosvenor Street, London. She was laid to rest at Riverhead, survived by her husband, her three daughters Maria, Harriet and Sarah and one son, William.

Strangely, Lord Amherst married again a year later to Mary, who was, as his first wife had once been, the Countess Dowager of Plymouth. Mary was the widow of Lady Amherst's first son, the 6th Earl of Plymouth, and she had inherited her father's home at *Knole*, near Riverhead. Lord Amherst and his second wife lived there quietly until his death, in 1857, within sight of *Montreal*.

ARISTOTLE. *GREEK SCHOLAR, PHILOSOPHER AND NATURALIST.*

Aristotle
(384-322 BC)

SHAG *Phalacrocorax aristotelis* (Linnaeus)

Pelecanus aristotelis Linnaeus, 1761. *Fauna Suecica, Faunula*, revised edn, p. 5 and No. 146, *ex.* p. 51: Sweden

Linnaeus gave scientific names to about 4400 species of animals, and an even greater number of plants. It would have been surprising if he had not once chosen to commemorate the name of Aristotle, who, apart from providing a great wealth of ideas on philosophy and other subjects, left us with some of the oldest written ideas on natural history.

The facts concerning Aristotle's life are sparse and some of the following generally accepted events may only be conjecture. He was born at Stagyra in Macedon in 384 BC but lost his parents when he was about seventeen years old and moved to Athens where he became a pupil of Plato. When Plato died twenty years later Aristotle was not appointed as his successor and, perhaps for this reason, he moved to the court of his philosophical friend Hermias in Asia Minor. Here he married Pythias, the ruler's niece, but after the assassination of Hermias, Aristotle fled to Mitylene, the Island of Lesbos. In 342 BC he was invited by Philip of Macedon to educate his son, Alexander, who was his pupil for at least three years.

Aristotle then returned to Athens, spent most of the last thirteen years of his life there and founded a famous school called the Lyceum. On the death of

Shag

Alexander, in 323 BC, the anti-Macedonian faction in the city forced Aristotle to move to Chalcis in Euboea where he died the following year of chronic stomach disease.

After his death, his library and unfinished manuscripts had a complicated and curious history. They were left to his favourite pupil who on his death thirty-five years later bequeathed them to his own pupil, by whom they were taken from Athens to Scepsis in Asia Minor. His heirs buried them for fear that they would be seized by the King of Pergamus for his own libraries, and they remained undisturbed until 100 BC when a wealthy book collector unearthed them and took them back to Athens. The Aristotolean manuscripts had been lost to the world for 187 years.

Leaving aside his other works which include discussions on the art of rhetoric, politics, ethics and the soul, Aristotle wrote no less than fifty books on zoology, of which twenty-five have been preserved. Tradition maintains that his former pupil, Alexander the Great, sent back zoological specimens gathered during his conquests in the East, and this first-hand material, together with Aristotle's own library of works by preceding naturalists and his own observations, helped him in the formation of his treatise, 'Researches about Animals'. On the subject of ornithology he mentioned more than 140 birds but many of these cannot be identified because he did not supply enough information about them.

Some scholars have credited him with the first attempts at avian classification and he did indeed divide birds into eight groupings chiefly from an exterior descriptive viewpoint. He also broadly categorized birds according to whether or not they were birds of the land or water or water's edge. Aristotle was the first person to actively promote ornithology, but all branches of zoology, in his view, were worthy of investigation:

> "We therefore must not recoil with childish aversion from the examination of the humbler animals. Every realm of nature is marvellous . . . for each and all will reveal to us something natural and something beautiful."[1]

Jean Victor Audouin (1797-1841)

AUDOUIN'S GULL *Larus audouinii* Payraudeau

Larus Audouinii Payraudeau, 1826. *Annales des Sciences Naturelles* 8, p. 462: Sardinia and Corsica

Jean Victor Audouin was born in Paris on 27 April 1797 and he died in the same city on 9 November 1841, aged only forty-four. During his short academic career he became well known in scientific circles for his entomological studies but he also contributed to several other branches of natural history, including ornithology.

A lawyer's son of moderate means, Jean Victor studied firstly at the College of Reims and later at the Lycée Louis le Grand. He then spent some time in Italy, staying with a relative at Lucca, near Florence, only returning to Paris following the fall of Napoleon's Empire. His father obtained a post for him with a firm of lawyers but young Audouin did not enjoy his legal studies and eventually persuaded his father to let him study medicine, and so he was twenty-five years old by the time he gained his doctor's degree. His thesis concerned the Spanish Fly, or blister beetle, *Cantharis*, at that time used extensively for medicinal purposes.

One day, whilst out walking in the woods between Versailles and the centre of Paris, Audouin met Alexandre Brogniart who also happened to be searching for insects. Brogniart worked at the Paris Museum and had a similar keen interest in entomology; he was so impressed by Audouin that he employed him at the museum, became his advisor and helped him in his new profession. He also allowed Audouin to marry his daughter.

Circumstances at the museum further advanced Audouin's career. In 1825 Lamarck became blind and was replaced by Latreille, but he too became ill and Audouin was provisionally appointed to take over the study and teaching of entomology. When Latreille died in 1833 Audouin was created Professor of Entomology, and under his direction the museum's insect collection accumulated so rapidly that eight years later the insect specimens numbered more than half a million; 120,000 species of 10,000 different genera. His first publication on the subject had appeared in 1818 when he was only twenty-one years old, and two years afterwards a paper on the anatomy of insects had earned for him the praise of Baron Cuvier. Thereafter, Audouin published a number of works on the physiology, anatomy and classification of insects, his last major contribution

AUDOUIN. *FRENCH ZOOLOGIST WHOSE MAIN INTEREST WAS ENTOMOLOGY. HE COMPILED THE ORNITHOLOGICAL SEC-TION OF SAVIGNY'S* DESCRIPTION DE L'ÉGYPTE.

being a 'History of Insects which infest the Vine' (1840–43); he had already studied silkworms and the economic effects of their diseases. Such works as these, of commercial significance, helped to secure his election to the Academy of Sciences in 1838. Audouin was also a founder member and the driving force behind the French Entomological Society. William Swainson described him as "the most philosophic, profound and accurate entomologist in Europe".

Audouin's other zoological interests included the co-authorship of the *Dictionaire Classique d'Histoire Naturelle* (1822) and a collaboration with Henri Milne-Edwards in an exhaustive study of marine animals from French inshore waters. Large numbers of new species were described in this latter work for which Audouin had to visit many parts of the coast.

Audouin also began to contribute ornithological material to the *Description de l'Égypte*, a vast compendium intended as a summary of the scientific researches carried out during and after Napoleon's 1798 invasion of that country. When Savigny was forced to abandon work on the project because of failing eyesight, Audouin was entrusted by the French Government with the task of completing the zoological section. His edited version of the ornithology was finally completed in 1826 as the *Explication sommaire des Planches d'Oiseaux de l'Égypte et de la Syrie*. In the same year B. C. Payraudeau published in the *Annales des Sciences Naturelles* the first scientific description of Audouin's Gull. Payraudeau had recently returned from Sardinia and Corsica reporting 246 bird species during the course of his travels. He had found the gulls "tolerably abundant" around the two islands, especially in the southern part of Corsica and the Straits of Bonifacio, where there are numerous rocky reefs and islets. He correctly speculated that this rare gull (with a current world population of about 3500 pairs) might also be found along the coast of North Africa. Although he named the gull after his "excellent ami, M. Audouin", who was one of the editors of the journal, Payraudeau does not mention any direct link between this eminent naturalist and the gull. It was perhaps a return compliment for *Pyrrhula payraudoei*, a name (not now used) which Audouin had given to the Trumpeter Finch in his study of Egyptian birds.

Audouin's Gull

BAILLON. *FRENCH NATURAL HISTORY DEALER WHO LIVED IN NORTHERN FRANCE AND COLLECTED LOCALLY. NO POR- TRAIT EXISTS, ONLY THIS POSTHUMOUS BUST DONE FROM MEMORY BY PIERRE SAUVAGE. IN 1857 A REPLICA WAS PLACED IN THE MUSEUM AT ABBEVILLE.*

Louis Antoine François Baillon (1778-1855)

BAILLON'S CRAKE *Porzana pusilla* (Pallas)

Rallus pusillus Pallas, 1776. *Reise durch verschiedene Provinzen des Russischen Reichs*, Vol. 3, p. 700: Dauria

L. A. F. Baillon was born at Montreuil, to the south of Boulogne, in February 1778. His father, Jean François Emmanuel Baillon, was a lawyer who devoted all his spare time to the study of natural history and corresponded regularly with the leading French naturalists of his day, including Buffon and Cuvier. From an early age Louis came into contact with his father's scientific friends and by the age of eleven, when the rioting mobs stormed the Bastille in Paris, he was already a budding naturalist. Throughout the following years of violent revolution Louis continued to assist his father and around 1792 they moved about twenty-five miles south to Abbeville on the Somme. From there they collected, prepared and dispatched specimens in response to the uninterrupted demand for them.

At the age of twenty Louis went to Paris to take up the post of assistant naturalist at the Jardin d'Histoire Naturelle and as such was exempted from

Baillon's Crake

military conscription. He stayed for four years, during which time Napoleon executed his *coup d'état* and became First Consul. In 1802 the elder Baillon died and Louis returned to Abbeville. For the rest of his life he dedicated himself whole-heartedly to the study of the local fauna, corresponding and exchanging specimens with other European collectors. He took up the study of insects in response to the many requests for them and he made daily visits to the fish market, sometimes discovering rare or new species there. He developed an interest in capturing and keeping live birds and also amassed a considerable collection of bird skins which became well known far beyond the confines of Abbeville. Baillon sent a number of specimens to Louis Vieillot, including, in 1819, a small crake which Vieillot named *Rallus Bailloni*: "the name which I have given to this species is that of the naturalist to whom I owe all the information concerning it, and who first discovered it in Picardy where it arrives in the month of April."[1] The nominate race had already been described by Pallas from birds obtained on the borders of Manchuria, two years before Baillon was born. In 1804 Hermann had named the western European race *P.p. intermedia* but it is Vieillot's later name for the species that has been carried into the French and English vernacular.

Baillon's only publication was a catalogue of the mammals, birds, reptiles, fish and marine molluscs which occurred around Abbeville, but he also collaborated with Pauguy on the *Flore du département de la Somme*. Baillon died at Abbeville on 3 December 1855 and his collections were dispersed shortly afterwards.

Spencer Fullerton Baird (1823-1887)

BAIRD'S SANDPIPER *Calidris bairdii* (Coues)

Actodromas Bairdii Coues, 1861. *Proceedings of the Academy of Natural Sciences of Philadelphia* [13], p. 194: Fort Resolution, Great Slave Lake, Mackenzie

Among the most significant publications of the great Elliott Coues was his *Key to North American Birds* which went into no less than six editions. The revised second edition of 1884 had a precise twenty-page 'Historical Preface' in which Coues reviewed the history of North American ornithology. He divided it into six epochs together with those ornithologists whom he considered to have exerted the most influence:

The Archaic Epoch: to 1700—John Smith, Thomas Morton.
The Pre-Linnaean Epoch: 1700–1785—Mark Catesby, George Edwards.
The Post-Linnaean Epoch: 1785–1800—John Forster, Thomas Pennant, William Bartram.
The Wilsonian Epoch: 1800–1824—Louis J.P. Vieillot, Alexander Wilson.
The Audubonian Epoch: 1824–1853—Charles L. Bonaparte, William Swainson, John Richardson, Thomas Nuttall, John James Audubon.
The Bairdian Epoch: 1853–18[87]—John Cassin, George N. Lawrence, Thomas M. Brewer, Spencer Fullerton Baird.[1]

Not surprisingly for a continent in the process of being colonized, its noted ornithologists, up until the 1850s, included recent immigrants from Europe as well as visiting Europeans. Others such as Edwards, Pennant and Swainson never went to North America but nevertheless contributed to its ornithology through their publications. Only in Coues's last mentioned, Bairdian Epoch, did American ornithology become more or less independent of outside stimulation and assistance, and flourish through the efforts of its own new native Americans. During this period ornithologists became more specialized and professional. They also began to organize themselves on a more national basis: the Nuttall Ornithological Club was established in 1873 and was followed ten years later by the formation of the American Ornithologists' Union and the establishment of its journal, *The Auk*.

Spencer F. Baird, through his work at the now prestigious Smithsonian Institute, inspired succeeding generations by his books and gave encouragement

BAIRD. *AMERICAN ORNITHOLOGIST, BIRD-COLLECTOR AND AUTHOR. AS A YOUNG MAN HE WAS BEFRIENDED BY AUDUBON. HE LATER BECAME DIRECTOR OF THE SMITHSONIAN INSTITUTE AND USED HIS POSITION TO ORGANIZE NATURAL HISTORY COLLECTING IN MANY PARTS OF NORTH AMERICA ON A GRAND SCALE.*

and direction to the younger enthusiasts of that time. Among these was Elliott Coues who was just eighteen years old when he discovered a new species of sandpiper while working through a bird collection at the Institute, sent there from the Great Slave Lake by Robert Kennicott and Bernard Ross. Coues dedicated it "To Spencer F. Baird . . . as a slight testimonial of respect for scientific acquirements of the highest order, and in grateful remembrance of the unvarying kindness which has rendered my almost daily intercourse a source of so great pleasure, and of the friendly encouragement to which I shall ever feel indebted for whatever progress I may hereafter make in ornithology."[2]

Coues went on to discover many new species, but he was perhaps disappointed to learn that a warbler which he had found in Arizona, and which he believed to be yet-undescribed had already been named Lucy's Warbler by James G. Cooper, another Baird protegé. The bird was named after the Bairds' only child, Lucy Hunter Baird, to whom we owe many of the existing details about their family life.

Spencer's father, Samuel Baird, who was of Scottish descent, practised law at Reading, in Pennsylvania. The family was comfortably well off and Samuel decided that they should live on a reasonable minimum, without luxuries, and he gave away the surplus for the benefit of the poor. Unfortunately, when Spencer was only ten his father died during a cholera epidemic leaving his mother with four sons and three daughters to support. The family moved to nearby Carlisle to be closer to relatives and were soon joined by a recently widowed aunt and her two children. However, sufficient money remained to educate the boys at school and later at Dickinson College in Carlisle.

For a young naturalist, it was a superb area in which to grow up. To the north and south were the wooded slopes of the Appalachian Mountains with many limestone cliffs rich in fossil remains; on the lower ground were marshes, lakes and rivers and more deciduous woodland. Baird was very soon proficient with a gun and began to list the birds he shot on his rambles. One day when he was sixteen he walked twenty-five miles hunting for birds and game. The following day he was too tired to attend college and instead studied a borrowed copy of Wilson's *American Ornithology*. In the same year he found that he had a heart palpitation.

At seventeen, he obtained two flycatchers which he could not identify and speculated that they belonged to an undescribed species. Spencer sent a full description to the famous artist and naturalist J. J. Audubon and received confirmation of his discovery and an encouraging reply. Their correspondence continued over the years and they developed a lifelong attachment. While Audubon was at work on his *Viviparous Quadrupeds of North America* he took the opportunity to enlist the help of young Baird:

> "I have thought that you might have it in your power to procure several of the smaller species for me, and thereby assist me greatly.
> Please to collect all the Shrews, Mice, (field or wood), rats, bats, Squirrels, etc., and put them in a jar in common Rum, not whiskey, brandy or alcohol. All the latter spirits are sure to injure the subjects."

After graduating from Dickinson College Baird went to New York to study medicine. The day after his arrival he went to visit Audubon and his family for the first time. Whilst in the city he became well acquainted with the naturalists George Lawrence, Titian Peale and Major Le Conte, the latter being a cousin of his grandmother. With money sent to him by his brother William who had a long-standing similar interest, Baird continued to add to their skin collection by buying specimens in the markets and by receiving duplicate skins from Audubon and other collectors. The collection and his ornithological knowledge were now very impressive, but he suffered two early disappointments.

The first of these occurred when the Wilkes Exploring Expedition returned with a huge hoard of specimens from the Antarctic. Baird enlisted the support of Audubon in the hope of being allowed to catalogue the discoveries but he was unsuccessful, and the task went to others less interested and less competent than himself. Years later when the bulk of the collections went to the Smithsonian Institute he was able to help organize its proper investigation.

The second disappointment came when Baird reluctantly had to refuse an invitation to join Audubon on a trip westwards to the Yellowstone River. He declined at first because he did not have the necessary $500, but Audubon was so keen to have the knowledgeable and enthusiastic young naturalist with him that he undertook to bear the costs. Baird's relatives, however, reminded him of his heart trouble and were also worried about the danger from rattlesnakes and Indians. On his safe return Audubon admitted that not a single rattlesnake had been seen and that the trip had not been arduous. Baird had missed a great opportunity. Certainly it seems as though, at that age, he was fit enough to go; he was in the habit of walking tremendous distances. In his nineteenth year he calculated that he had walked over two thousand miles, and one day, returning from an extended trip along the Susquehanna River, he had covered sixty miles. In a letter to his brother William he wrote of this occasion:

"Walking time 15 hours. I was a good deal fatigued . . . having passed so many mountains and hills, but on reaching Carlisle I felt as if I could have gone ten miles further; got up next morning at 7 without the slightest stiffness or Pain. Walked in all 400 miles."

It was by now obvious that Baird had little intention of following on with his medical career. His brother offered to finance his winter lodgings in New York but he had already decided to quit, despite William's warning that "No means of livelihood... is to be obtained in America from ornithology..."

Baird's first publication in 1843 concerned his Yellow-bellied Flycatcher discovery and he now concentrated on his list of birds of Cumberland County which was succeeded by a similar work on the trees and shrubs. Still not yet twenty, he was a member of several natural history societies, and, in order to be able to read more ornithological literature, he began to study German and a number of other foreign languages. In 1846 John Cassin financed him for a short trip to Boston to check on the synonomy of various bird species, a subject which also greatly interested Baird. He crammed the work into a few days and found time to call upon the botanist Asa Gray and to view Thomas Brewer's vast collection of eggs. On his return through New York he visited Audubon and came away with more duplicate skins that the artist had pressed upon him. By now Baird was acquainted with most of the prominent ornithologists working on the east coast and his name became even more widely known when Audubon, in a new edition of his *Birds of America*, named a new bird Baird's Bunting (since renamed Baird's Sparrow).

Back at Carlisle Baird continued to collect avidly and having discovered a source of the diminutive Least Bittern he "went out there next morning and in an hour had four of them, 3 males. Not being satisfied with these I went again on Monday and got four more, all females. I probably could have got more, but I began to be ashamed of murdering them so." His brother, to whom these words were written, had by now given up collecting to concentrate on his law career, but he always maintained an interest in his younger brother's exploits.

When Baird was twenty-two he was created Honorary Professor of Natural History and Curator of the Cabinet at Dickinson College. At first there was little to do but in the following year when he was made a full Professor he received a small salary and began to teach. His students were often not much younger than himself. An innovation of his, which arose independently elsewhere and became a common practice, was to take his students on country rambles in order to instruct them in botany, zoology and geology. They had to be fit to keep up with him because he was over six feet tall and used to walking at his own pace. At the college he kept barrels of snakes and other animals, and he now began to collect and study fish, using tadpoles to strip carcasses down to bare skeletons.

At a quiet family wedding, on 8 August 1846, he married Mary Churchill. The bride's father, Colonel Churchill, was in Mexico on extended military duty but he had agreed to the wedding if the newlyweds moved in with Mrs Churchill to keep her company. They lived there for two years until Lucy was born. To test his theory that fear of snakes was not innate but acquired through life, he forbade anyone to prejudice his daughter against the reptiles and he gave her harmless species to play with: they never frightened her. Baird adored his little girl and often made up long fairy stories for her. He also had a good rapport with other children.

When James Smithson, the illegitimate son of the Duke of Northumberland, died, he left over half a million dollars for the setting up "at Washington under the name of the Smithsonian Institute, an Establishment for the increase and diffusion of knowledge among men". When Baird heard that a curator was

Baird's Sandpiper

required for the newly formed Institute he was determined to get the post and began a campaign of letters eliciting the support of Audubon, Cassin and other influential friends. He had to wait some time for his appointment to be confirmed because the building was not yet finished, but he started as Assistant Secretary in October 1850, taking with him his own huge collection to form the nucleus of the natural history department. One of his many correspondents warned him, somewhat prophetically: "Take care of yourself, my dear boy. You are destined to great things, if you do not exhaust yourself too early by over-work."

The Secretary at the Smithsonian was the physicist Professor Joseph Henry and he and Professor Baird got on well together, developing a father-and-son-like relationship. Baird did not disappoint Henry but plunged into the work at once and was soon working twelve to fifteen hours a day. Much of his time was taken up with arranging and cataloguing collections, bundling up exchanges of books and papers for foreign institutions and dealing with an ever increasing amount of world-wide correspondence. In one year alone he dealt with over three thousand letters but such was his remarkable memory that he was always able to handle them efficiently. On one occasion a friend sat in amazement as Baird, apparently without effort, dictated the replies to twenty-seven letters without hesitation or reference to the original letters received the day before.

In 1858 Baird produced his classic *Catalogue of North American Birds* but as he took upon himself an increasing number of administrative duties he was less able to produce original work. Nevertheless, working with Thomas Brewer and Robert Ridgway he later helped to complete the five volume *History of North American Birds* (1874–84). Baird also became involved in a monograph on fishes to be written mostly by Louis Agassiz, but because of the latter's other commitments the work was never finished. It did, however, deepen Baird's interest in that direction.

One of Professor Baird's major accomplishments, if not the greatest, was the way in which he inspired and trained young naturalists and then succeeded in placing them in the government-sponsored surveys exploring the West. Among the many expeditions of the period were the U.S. Northern Boundary Commission Survey and the U.S. Geological Survey expedition to Colorado, both with Elliott Coues as collector and naturalist.

The Western Union Telegraph Company's search for an overland telegraph line between America and Siberia was led by Robert Kennicott, who had also studied at the Smithsonian. He had already spent several years in the Arctic enlisting the help of the trappers and factors of the Hudson's Bay Company in collecting and preparing bird skins, and, directly or indirectly, was responsible for sending more specimens to Baird than any other man.

Baird himself continued to collect, but limited his travels to eastern North America, visiting the Adirondack Mountains, Lake Champlain and the regions around Montreal and Quebec. He also travelled extensively in western Wisconsin with Jared Kirtland, specializing more and more on fish. In 1863 because of this interest, and his own and his wife's increasingly poor health, he spent some time by the sea at Wood's Hole in Massachusetts. Nine years later this place was chosen as the site for the U.S. Fish Commission's first laboratory—now world famous.

The Fish Commission was set up in 1871, with Baird as its unsalaried first director, with the original purpose of investigating the decline of the inshore fish stocks. It was expected to last only one or two seasons but Baird became responsible for directing marine research on the east coast for the next sixteen years. With the acquisition of the steamer *Albatross* he also supervised research into the fauna of the Gulf Stream and the waters of the West Indies.

On the death of Joseph Henry in 1878 Baird became Secretary of the Smithsonian Institute but the additional duties, combined with those of the Fish Commission imposed a huge work load upon him and he was eventually advised by his doctors to take a complete year off work. He complied by spending some time in the Adirondacks, but after some slight improvement he returned to Wood's Hole where he died of heart problems in August 1887, at the age of sixty-four. He was buried at Washington's Oak Hill Cemetery. His wife, who died four years later and his daughter Lucy, who died unmarried in 1913 were interred beside him.

Baird's death was indeed the end of an era. He had set the pace and direction of North American ornithology for nearly forty years, but although the study of birds had progressed, some recent developments in the natural world were deeply disturbing. Leonard Stejneger, commissioned by Baird to visit Bering Island, had returned with the report that Steller's Sea Cow was long extinct and the Spectacled Cormorant more recently so. In Baird's lifetime the Great Auk and Labrador Duck had been exterminated and the large populations of Carolina Parakeets, Eskimo Curlews and Passenger Pigeons had already plummeted. Baird of course had noticed these changes and may well have wondered about the effects of large-scale collecting which he had so long encouraged. In a letter written a few months before he died, to a sister whose son wanted advice about collecting eggs, he certainly gave the boy no encouragement:

> "I am inclined to ascribe the reduction in the number of our home birds as much to the taking of eggs for various purposes, or driving away the parents, as to the actual extermination of the birds themselves. However, the most effective way of preventing the difficulty is by prohibiting the taking of eggs entirely which I would earnestly recommend."

Baird's involvement with the Fish Commission was therefore especially valuable to him because he was able to achieve positive results of economic importance. The reasons for the decline in fish stocks had been self-evident: every possible trap and device was being used to catch fish, so that fewer and fewer ever reached their spawning grounds. In the absence of strict legislature, which could have controlled the problem, Baird improved the situation by setting up hatching ponds to produce both marine and freshwater fish for distribution along the coast and elsewhere. The success of this enterprise and many others no doubt pleased him greatly.

BARROW. *INFLUENTIAL AND POWERFUL BRITISH ADMINISTRATOR WHO STRONGLY SUPPORTED THE EXPLORATION OF AFRICA AND THE SEARCH FOR THE NORTH-WEST PASSAGE.*

John Barrow
(1764-1848)

BARROW'S GOLDENEYE *Bucephela islandica*
(J. F. Gmelin)

Anas islandica J. F. Gmelin, 1789. *Systema Naturae*, Vol. 1, Pt 2, p. 541: Iceland

Point Barrow, Barrow Sound and Barrow Straits in the Arctic, and Cape Barrow in the Antarctic, are perhaps surprising memorials to a man who, for half his life, held what was essentially a desk job in London. Sir John Barrow was Second Secretary to the Admiralty for over forty years, and was responsible for the civil administration of the Royal Navy over a period that included the latter part of the Napoleonic Wars. When peace came in 1815, Barrow was able to suggest to Lord Melville, first Sea-Lord, a plan for resuming the search for a sea route north of mainland America to the Far East: the North-west Passage. This quest virtually dominated Barrow's thoughts for the rest of his life; apart from those who actively took part in the search, he contributed more to Arctic exploration than any other man.

In 1818 John Ross sailed to Baffin Bay to search for a route westwards but in Lancaster Sound, believing his way to be blocked by a range of mountains, he retreated and sailed back to England. This unfortunate decision resulted in a long-standing and bitter feud between Ross and Barrow, who was convinced that a more thorough investigation should have been carried out. Barrow was all the more vehement because he had already stated publicly that he believed in the existence of such a 'Passage'. His claims were supported in the following year when William Parry sailed right through Lancaster Sound into Melville Sound and called the narrow opening between, Barrow Straits. Nevertheless, almost thirty years later, sufficient ill-feeling remained for Barrow to devote two chapters in his *Voyages of Discovery and Research within the Arctic Regions* (1846) to a virulent attack upon Ross. Once aroused he had become inexplicably vindictive and Ross's misfortune served as a warning to all other explorers on the many succeeding Arctic expeditions.

Ross's nephew, James Clark Ross, continued to support Barrow, and so did all the other officers involved in Arctic exploration at that time. They had no alternative if they wanted to further their naval careers. Years later, when the younger Ross sighted the Antarctic continent he named some of the first land he saw after Edward Sabine and John Barrow; the latter Ross described, in his narrative of the voyage, as "the father of modern arctic discovery, by whose energy, zeal and talent our geographical knowledge of those regions has been so greatly increased; and we may hope, by God's guidance and blessing attending the exertions of the [Franklin] expedition that has so recently left our shores, he may live to see the great object of his heart, the discovery of a North West passage through Barrow Straits to the Pacific Ocean, accomplished."[1]

To John Barrow the existence and discovery of the 'Passage' was a matter of both personal conviction and national pride. In the *Journal of the Royal Geographical Society* he wrote: "If we should allow the completion to be snatched from us by any other power, we shall sustain a humiliating defeat." In fact, although technically completed by dying members of Franklin's last expedition just a few months before Barrow's death, it was a Norwegian, Raold Amundsen, who first sailed through, but not until 1903–06.

By exerting his influence as a powerful naval bureaucrat Barrow was largely responsible for a great many Arctic expeditions and the explorers whom he had a hand in sending northwards included James Clark Ross, Edward Sabine, John Franklin and Dr John Richardson. Barrow therefore indirectly instigated the study of North American Arctic biology of which Richardson's *Fauna Boreali-Americana* was the most important early work. In the second volume, on the birds, which was published in 1831 and co-written by William Swainson, a species of duck, which they understood to be new, was described under the name *Clangula Barrovi*. The "specific appelation [was] intended as a tribute to Mr. Barrow's varied talents, and his unwearied exertions for the promotion of science", though Swainson admitted that "the name of Barrow . . . will not be solely indebted to us for its imperishable record".[2] Their specimen was a male shot in the Rocky Mountains by Thomas Drummond; they gave the bird the vernacular name Rocky Mountain Garrot unaware that there were earlier names and descriptions by J. F. Gmelin and Latham. It has since become known as Barrow's Goldeneye in both Britain and North America.

There is therefore no direct connection between the bird and the man, but an examination of Barrow's earlier life reveals that he was not uninterested in natural history. Although his later years were mainly sedentary they contrasted sharply with the first half of his life in which he travelled extensively. He was born of humble parentage near the village of Dragley Beck, on the northern shores of Morecambe Bay, on 19 June 1764. His parents' small thatched cottage, with three or four fields attached, faced seawards. Educated mainly at Ulverston, Barrow excelled at mathematics and taught the subject to a one-armed midshipman in return for lessons in navigation. While still at school he spent two months carrying out a survey of nearby Conishead Priory, which proved to be the first of many detailed surveys that he later undertook. His parents wanted him to enter the Church in the mistaken belief that salvation for the family was best secured by having a son in the clergy. Instead, he became a time-keeper at a Liverpool iron-foundry for three years.

By chance he was introduced to a man who ran an academy at Greenwich, London, and Barrow was invited to teach mathematics there. In his spare time he taught the wife of Sir George Beaumont and the son of Sir George Staunton, and naturally became acquainted with the boy's father. Barrow confided later that he was indebted for all the good fortune of his life to Staunton, for it was he who introduced him to Lord McCartney: Barrow soon found himself employed by McCartney as 'Comptroller of the Household' amongst a party of seventeen on their way to visit the Emperor of China!

Sailing in HMS *Lion* they eventually arrived at Tientsin and then proceeded to Peking. McCartney travelled on to the Royal Palace at Gehol while Barrow stayed behind to supervise a display of gifts for the Emperor. When the Emperor came to Peking to view them Barrow described the visit in his *Travels in China* (1804) as a long and thorough examination. McCartney's party then travelled overland for a thousand miles to Canton, the young Barrow, not yet thirty years old, taking every opportunity to travel independently of the main group. Fifty years later Barrow affirmed that his two years in China had been the most interesting period in his life. Disappointingly, McCartney's mission was not a diplomatic success because he refused to prostrate himself, or *kow-tow*, nine times before the Emperor; he would only compromise by kneeling before him. The next ambassador to China, Lord Amherst, was equally ineffectual in gaining concessions for Britain.

Back in London Barrow stayed with Sir George Staunton and assisted him in his literary work. When time allowed he botanized at Kew but his studies were cut short when he went away again with Lord McCartney, this time to South Africa as his private secretary.

As soon as they arrived McCartney sent him on a mission to reconcile the Boers and Kaffirs, and to obtain more accurate topographical knowledge of the area; at that time there was no map that covered even a tenth of the Cape Colony. Among his equipment he took with him only two books: Aiton's *Hortus Kewensis* and Linnaeus's *Systema Naturae*. Barrow soon had his first encounters with south African wildlife. He was particularly impressed by a huge swarm of locusts, reckoning that about 18,000 square miles were covered, or had been covered by them. A strong north-west wind later blew the insects out to sea and many were washed ashore in banks three or four feet high along fifty miles of coastline. On one of his surveying expeditions he shot a hippopotamus

Barrow's Goldeneye

and had the skull sent to his friend, the young George Staunton. Many years later at a meeting of the Linnean Society of London, when a hippopotamus skull was being examined Barrow boasted that during his time in south Africa he had shot one, but that it had, of course, been far bigger. The skull in fact turned out to be the same one that Barrow had collected; a present to the Society by Staunton! It says much for Barrow's sense of humour that he told this story against himself.

After seven years it appears that Barrow was preparing to settle in the Colony for he married a Miss Trüter and bought a house looking toward Table Mountain. However, the Colony was ceded to the Dutch by the Treaty of Amiens of 1802, and so Barrow, his wife and young daughter moved to England. Barrow then wrote an *Account of Travels into the Interior of Southern Africa* which was published in two volumes in 1801 and 1804. It was the best written account of the Cape Colony, its topography, native inhabitants, mineralogy and natural history, containing frequent references to the birds he had encountered. His map was superior to any that had yet been compiled and the whole work, together with his political dealings with the Boers and Kaffirs, were sufficient recommendation for Lord Melville, who had known Barrow in Cape Town, to appoint him Second Secretary to the Admiralty.

When there was a change of Sea-Lords in 1806 Barrow was removed from office with a £1000 a year pension, but the following year he was reinstated. In the intervening period he wrote his 'Life of Lord McCartney', became a member of the London Literary Society and was elected a Fellow of the Royal Society through the influence of Sir Joseph Banks. Banks and Barrow often co-operated in the selection and placement of civilian naturalists on Royal Navy expeditions that went all over the world. In 1816 Barrow was instrumental in sending the Navy's first steam vessel, HMS *Congo*, to explore the River Congo in order to determine whether the Niger was indeed part of that great river as Mungo Park had suggested. It was the first of the many expeditions that Barrow helped to organize and it was a complete disaster. Two hundred miles upriver all the officers and all the scientists died of fever. In his autobiography Barrow failed to mention his interest in the exploration of central Africa, perhaps because of this infamous Congo expedition and because he had been a supporter of the erroneous theory that the Niger flowed into the Nile. Barrow thereafter turned most of his attentions northwards and began to promote the exploration of the Arctic. In time he became one of the main founders of the [Royal] Geographical Society and was Chairman at its first public meeting in 1830. His son John was also an active member of the society.

Barrow rarely wrote for the *Geographical Journal* but he contributed 159 articles to the *Quarterly Review* in which he examined accounts of various voyages, descriptions of foreign countries, recent discoveries in natural history and the arts, naval improvements and a host of other subjects, the majority of which were of a geographical nature. He also found time to compile a 'Life of Peter the Great' (1832), biographies of Lord Howe (1838) and Lord Anson (1839), and *The Eventful History of the Mutiny and Piratical Seizure of HMS Bounty* (1831). The latter remained in print far longer than any of his other works and is one of the better accounts of the mutiny, giving the first extracts from Captain Bligh's journal and the court martial proceedings to which Barrow was able to gain access.

During all this literary work and behind the scenes activity he continued to work at the Admiralty. From 1807 to 1845 he remained Second Secretary under thirteen naval administrations, often under far less competent First Secretaries, and in effect, Barrow was all powerful. He never became First Secretary because that position could only be filled by a member of the House of Commons. An incident in 1815 demonstrating his influence and high ranking contacts is contained in a letter from Lord Liverpool, the Prime Minister, to Lord Castlereagh, his Foreign Secretary, concerning the recently defeated Napoleon: "Since I wrote to you last, Lord Melville and I have conversed with Mr. Barrow on the subject, and he decidedly recommended St. Helena as the place in the world best calculated for the confinement of such a person . . . At such a distance and in such a place, all intrigue would be impossible . . ."[3] Barrow knew because he had been there!

When the Duke of Clarence, who had been First Sea-Lord for a short period, became King William IV he made Barrow a baronet. And when Barrow retired, at the age of eighty-one, he received the thanks of the Prime Minister, but the service of plate presented to him by the officers engaged in Arctic discovery is said to have given him the greater pleasure. The accompanying letter was signed by Franklin, James Ross, Parry and George Back, while others who had contributed included Francis Crozier, Sabine and Richardson. One of the favours that Barrow requested when he retired was a knighthood for Richardson; the other was promotion to Captain for James Fitzjames, then sailing with Franklin and soon to die with him.

In November 1848, at the age of eighty-four, Barrow died suddenly while writing at his home. He was buried at Pratt Street, Camden Town, where a marble obelisk was set up. In 1850 a large lighthouse-like monument was erected to his memory on the Hill of Hoad, above Ulverston, from which fine views of the sands of Morecambe Bay can be obtained.

Where did Barrow's long interest in the North-west Passage originate? Perhaps it arose from an episode in his early life that occurred just before he moved from Liverpool to London. A relative of the iron-foundry owner, a Captain Potts, had offered him a place on a whaler bound for Bear Island and Spitzbergen. Barrow accepted and began to learn the skills of a sailor, taking a hand at the oars of the small whale-boats when the hunt was on. He also discovered what it was like to be beset by ice, but he himself never went north again.

BARTRAM. *ENTHUSIASTIC AMERICAN BOTANIST WHO ASSISTED MANY YOUNG NATURALISTS, ESPECIALLY ALEXANDER WILSON.*

William Bartram (1739-1823)

UPLAND SANDPIPER *Bartramia longicauda* (Bechstein)

Bartramia Lesson, 1831. *Traité d'Ornithologie*, Pt 7, p. 553. Type by monotypy, *Bartramia laticauda* Lesson = *Tringa longicauda* Bechstein
Tringa longicauda Bechstein, 1812. In J. Latham, *Allgemeine Uebersicht der Vögel*, Vol. 4, Pt 2, p. 453: North America

> "This bird being as far as I can discover a new species, undescribed by any former author, I have honoured it with the name of my very worthy friend, near whose Botanic Gardens, on the banks of the river Schuylkill [near Philadelphia], I first found it."[1]

So wrote Alexander Wilson in his *American Ornithology* (1808–14) about the Upland Sandpiper, which he called *Tringa Bartramia*. He added that "they are remarkable plump birds weighing upwards of three quarters of a pound; their flesh is superior, in point of delicacy, tenderness and flavour, to any other of the tribe with which I am acquainted." Wilson first observed these curious waders one August, and never having seen them on the seashore, he rightly assumed that they bred in meadows and such-like places in the interior of North America.

Bartram's garden, which was nearby, had not been established by William but by his distinguished father, John Bartram, whom Linnaeus had called the greatest natural botanist in the world. The garden was an unrivalled collection of native trees and shrubs which John had procured on his many travels between Florida and Lake Ontario, and European and Oriental plants sent to him by his many correspondents. Wilson spent some of his happiest hours there. William Bartram was already in his sixties when Wilson met him but the friendship flourished through their shared passion for ornithology. William had developed a profound love and respect for all aspects of natural history in his childhood and by the age of sixteen he was already a well-trained observer, sending skins and his own drawings of birds to George Edwards, the British nature artist.

When his father was nearly seventy, William travelled to Florida with him, and they explored the 400 miles of the St John River until they reached its source. When the elder Bartram returned to Philadelphia, William stayed behind, determined to become a rice planter, but within the year he had to admit failure and returned home. He tried his hand at various occupations, but never settled into any career and remained unmarried. His only vocation was recognized by a Seminole chief who named him *Puc Puggy*, the Flower Hunter, when he returned to Florida.

He published a description of this excursion which lasted from March 1773 to January 1777, calling it *Travels Through North and South Carolina, Georgia, East and West Florida, the Cherokee Country, the Extensive Territories of the Muscogulges, or Creek Confederacy, and the Country of the Chactaws, Containing an Account of the Soil and Natural Productions of Those Regions, Together with Observations on the Manners of the Indians* (1791). It met with an unenthusiastic response in America. However, William Bartram's *Travels* went into nine foreign editions during the next decade and powerfully influenced the Romantic movement in England. It fired the imagination of Samuel Taylor Coleridge whose land of Xanadu was inspired by Bartram's vivid descriptions of the fountains and caverns of Florida. The water snakes, "Blue, glossy green, and velvet black" which swam around the cursed ship of the *Ancient Mariner* had already been painted by Bartram's pen.

William Wordsworth so treasured the journal that when he lost it while travelling through Germany, he immediately wrote home asking that a new copy of the 'Travels' be sent to him. His poem *Ruth* springs directly from an encounter which Bartram had with some young Cherokee girls. Coming over the summit of a ridge, he surprised them as they were gathering berries, while others whose baskets were already full reclined in the shade amongst the fragrant bowers of magnolia, azalea, philadelphus and calycanthus. Much of Wordsworth's writing reflects Bartram's experiences, language and philosophy.

While others marvelled at his adventures, William Bartram was thereafter content to remain by the Schuylkill River, tending his garden and enjoying the company of his many eminent visitors. He became a good friend of Thomas Jefferson, who vainly tried to persuade him to explore the vast unknown lands west of the Mississippi. Instead, he continued to botanize locally and spent much of his time studying and cataloguing the American birds. His list of 215 species was the most extensive in existence until Wilson's *Ornithology*. Wilson benefited enormously from Bartram's experience and encouragement. So also

Upland Sandpiper

did Thomas Say, Bartram's great-nephew, who often helped in the garden and went bird hunting with Wilson. Say later produced the *American Entomology* (1824–28) and had a phoebe (*Sayornis saya*), named after him by Charles Bonaparte.

Like many other American naturalists, Wilson and Say owed an enormous debt to *Puc Puggy*.

Carl Heinrich Bergius†
(c.1790-1818)

SWIFT TERN *Sterna bergii* Lichtenstein

Sterna Bergii Lichtenstein, 1823. *Verzeichniss der Doubletten des Zoologischen Museums der Koenigliche Universitaet zu Berlin . . .*, p. 80: Cape of Good Hope

Bergius was born in Germany around 1790 and was one of a large family. He went to school with the naturalist Leopold Mund, afterwards serving for a time in the Prussian Army, probably during Napoleon's Russian Campaign of 1812–14, and was awarded the Iron Cross.

He then studied pharmacy in Berlin, where his flair for botanizing brought him to the attention of Dr M. H. C. Lichtenstein, the Director of the Berlin Zoological Museum, who had spent three years at the Cape of Good Hope and had travelled and collected extensively throughout the Colony. Lichtenstein sent out a number of promising young naturalists to collect for his museum, and he arranged for Bergius to go to southern Africa as an assistant pharmacist to his friends Messrs Pallas and Polemann who owned the first chemist shop to be established in Cape Town.

Bergius arrived there early in 1815, and during the next three years wrote a number of letters to his patron, four of which have survived. They reveal his enthusiasm for the project, his great love for, and knowledge about plants and animals and his determination to work incessantly under even the most trying conditions. They also chronicle his isolated, poverty-stricken existence, the bitter disappointment of his most cherished hopes and the rapid deterioration of his health, leading up to his death from pulmonary tuberculosis in January 1818.

In the first letter to Lichtenstein, dated 24 August 1815, Bergius recorded his delight at the potential opportunities for making original observations and discoveries, but that he had so far had little chance to do so, because he was working in the pharmacy from sunrise until after 10 p.m. each night, with only one evening off each week for his own study.

Seven months later he wrote again, mentioning that after more than a year at the Cape, he was disappointed not to have received a single letter from Lichtenstein and only one from his own family. His domestic situation had become extremely unpleasant, for the Pallas family with whom he was staying insulted and humiliated him, complained about the standard of his work and expected him to take his meals alone in his room. His greatest grievance,

†No known portrait.

however, lay in the fact that he was allowed only one day's holiday every month, and so had far less to send to Berlin than he had hoped for. He usually occupied his free days in plant collecting, but had also bought a number of interesting birds, including a live gannet which he suspected of being hitherto undescribed. His assumption was correct, but Lichtenstein did not publish a description until 1823, five years after Bergius had died, when he named the Cape Gannet *Sula capensis*.

Bergius also procured for the museum a specimen of a large and graceful tern with a yellow bill, which breeds colonially along the coast of southern Africa and locally eastwards to as far as Polynesia. It was posthumously named in his memory by Lichtenstein, who called it *Sterna Bergii*.

In October of 1816 Bergius was cheered by the arrival of his old schoolfriend, Mund, bearing letters from his family and Lichtenstein. He also brought news of recent scientific advances in Europe for which Bergius had craved. They made a number of botanical excursions together, to Table Mountain and elsewhere in the vicinity.

In January Bergius wrote again to his patron, mentioning the continual problem of preserving his zoological collections, particularly those which needed to be stored in spirits, as he could acquire few suitable containers. Everything had to be kept in his own small room, so that he was constantly surrounded by plants, animal skins, snakes, lizards and scorpions from which the stench was at times almost overpowering. He had at last made up his mind to resign from the pharmacy, but had to wait until Polemann found a successor.

The last letter was written on 28 December 1817. It was a poignant, pathetic and rather rambling letter, affirming his hope of completing a book on the Cape orchids, which he was undertaking with Mund, the orchids having a special place in the affections of both naturalists. He was worried about an expensive shipment dispatched to Berlin some twenty months earlier, of which he had heard no word, nor had he received any correspondence or remuneration from Lichtenstein for well over a year. He was embarrassed and frustrated by the lack of basic necessities experienced by himself and his fellow Prussians, when the British, French and Dutch collectors were arriving with copies of the newest scientific works, instruments of all types and liberal supplies of every kind.

He described some of the difficulties surrounding the termination of his contract with Polemann; he had eventually acquired his independence at the end of May, but was now in debt to the pharmacy, and was living in extreme

Swift Tern

poverty, supported only by the sales of his small collections. During his first few months of freedom he had made several excursions with Mund and with Ludwig Krebs, his replacement, but poor health and his financial limitations had prevented him from travelling far afield. He had been coughing up blood and continually felt too weak and ill to do much work, and his savings had come to an end, though Mund had lent him a small amount of money.

The letter was sent with a small collection of unknown insects and ten days later, Bergius died.

BERTHELOT. *FRENCH NATURALIST KNOWN PRINCI-
PALLY FOR HIS STUDIES IN THE CANARY ISLANDS. THIS
PHOTOGRAPH WAS TAKEN THE YEAR BEFORE HE DIED.*

Sabin Berthelot
(1794-1880)

BERTHELOT'S PIPIT *Anthus berthelotii* Bolle

Anthus Berthelotii Bolle, 1862. *Journal für Ornithologie* 10, p. 357: Canaries

Kittlitz, when he visited Tenerife in 1826, was perhaps the first naturalist to remark upon this species of pipit:

> "They were the first birds we saw running along the road. I shot one, and found it to differ but little from the Water Pipit . . . having the legs lighter in colour, and the hind claws shorter, being, as it seemed to me, intermediate between that species and Anthus campestris [Tawny Pipit]."[1]

Other observers examined and described the differences but there was some debate over its status as a distinct species. No decision was reached until Carl Bolle redescribed and named the pipit in 1862, in the *Journal für Ornithologie*:

> "Berthelot's pipit inhabits the entire Canarian Archipelago where it is exceedingly common . . . Wherever in the volcanic region there is a less luxuriant vegetation and bare places, it is sure to be found . . . From its love of open spaces it frequents, like the Crested Lark, the roads, and it is familiar with the sight of man; hence its local names of *Correcamino* and *Caminero*; and according to Berthelot, it bears a third appellation, that of *Pajaró*."[2]

Bolle named the pipit after his friend Sabin Berthelot, who was at that time the French Consul at Santa Cruz on Tenerife. Berthelot, along with Gregorio Chil and René Vernau, was one of three great historical scholars at work in the Canaries during the nineteenth century. Altogether Berthelot lived and worked there for 44 years, studying whenever he could the early history of the islands and their people.

Born on the 4 April 1794, the son of a merchant of Marseilles, Berthelot joined the French Navy and served as a midshipman during the latter part of the Napoleonic Wars. When peace came he transferred to the merchant fleet and for a time plied between Marseilles and the West Indies. He did not go to the Canaries until 1820, by which time he was twenty-six years old. To earn a living he taught at a school on Tenerife and also managed the botanical gardens at Orotava for the Marquis of Villaneuva del Prato, a rich landowner on the island. Over the next eight years Berthelot studied throughout the islands and collected a small herbarium for himself. In 1828 he met up with the English botanist Philip Barker-Webb, who had just arrived, and their long association together led to the creation of the most important early work on the natural history of the Canaries.

Webb had been educated at Harrow and Oxford and had studied Italian and Spanish. On the death of his father he inherited a large fortune and spent much of the rest of his life travelling and botanizing; he had already visited many parts of the Mediterranean, northern Morocco and latterly, Portugal. In May 1828, he sailed from Lisbon to Madeira and in September pressed onwards to Tenerife. Webb was actually on his way to Brazil, but he never completed the voyage; instead he spent two years in the Canaries visiting all the islands with his new French friend, Berthelot.

They made a complete natural, physical and statistical history of the islands. They collected plants, mammals, birds, fishes, mollusc shells and insects; they examined rocks, analysed water, made weather observations and studied the peoples and their languages. Berthelot searched for traces of the original islanders, or *Guanches*, thought to have come from North Africa, and by using the criteria of speech, surnames, dances and traditional farming methods he discovered survival groups at Güimar and Santiago, on Tenerife. These and other observations were later expanded upon in *Les Guanches* (1841 and 1845), *La Conquête des Canaries* (1879) and *Antiquités Canariennes* (1879).

Firstly, however, Berthelot concentrated on working with Webb on their projected *L' Histoire Naturelle des Îles Canaries*. In 1830, having collected most of their material they left the islands, visited Algeria and some other Mediterranean countries and, prevented from entering France by revolution, they set themselves up at Geneva. In June 1833 they were able to move to Paris and the first volume of their work was brought out there in 1835. It was not finally completed until 1850 and, in all, contained more than 400 plates by the best artists available. Berthelot completed the ethnography, history of the conquest by Europeans from the fourteenth century onwards, and the general geography of the islands; Webb wrote on the botany, mammology and geology, while other specialists contributed sections on the insects and reptiles. The ornithological section, which was published in 1842, was mainly written by Alfred Moquin-Tandon, and contains descriptions of the preferred habitat of each species along with several observations relating to the birds themselves.

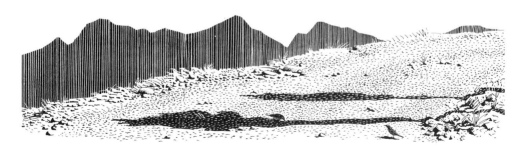

Berthelot's Pipit

During the fourteen years of preparation for this monumental publication, Webb confined his travelling to trips between Paris and his English home at Milford Haven. Although almost the same age as Berthelot he died in 1854; his huge collection of plants, one of the best in private hands, was bequeathed to the Grand Duke of Tuscany and was afterwards exhibited in a room of its own at Florence. Berthelot, in the meantime, had been nominated Secretary of the Geographical Society in Paris and spent four years editing their bulletins. The sedentary nature of this position did not suit him and he quickly accepted a proposal that he investigate the fishing grounds between Monaco and Gibraltar. He had already shown his interest in the subject by writing an account of the fish of the west coast of Africa; and his Mediterranean work led to similar publications.

In 1845 Berthelot founded the Société d'Ethnologique and in the following year he returned to the Canaries in order to survey and study the coastline of Tenerife. Two years later he was nominated the French consular agent for the island and was promoted to full Consul in 1867. He retired in August 1874, at the age of eighty, and was given the freedom of the city of Santa Cruz where he died on 10 November 1880.

Although Berthelot chose to specialize in the early history of the Canaries and was not a single-minded ornithologist, he was nevertheless deeply interested in all aspects relating to the islands and knew a great deal about their flora and fauna. His interest in birds should not be underestimated. The remarkable Blue Chaffinch, described by Bannerman as "the most beautiful of all the feathered inhabitants of the Canary Islands", was first discovered by Sabin Berthelot. In 1825 he saw eight of these birds at the base of the Pico de Teide but it was four years before he was able to secure two specimens, driven down from the pine forests of the mountains by severe weather. More importantly, Berthelot contributed much of the information to Moquin-Tandon's ornithological section of *L'Histoire Naturelle des Îles Canaries*, the publication of which gave most European ornithologists their first inkling of the extraordinary richness of the islands.

BEWICK. *ENGLISH ARTIST, BEST KNOWN FOR THE WOODCUT ILLUS-TRATIONS IN HIS* HISTORY OF BRITISH BIRDS. *HE HAD AN ENORMOUS INFLUENCE ON BIRD-ART, BUT HE WAS "IN THE STRICT SENSE OF THE WORD", ACCORDING TO H. K. SWANN, "HARDLY AN ORNITHOLOGIST AT ALL".*

Thomas Bewick
(1753-1828)

BEWICK'S SWAN *Cygnus columbianus* (Ord)

Anas Columbianus Ord, 1815. In W. Guthrie, *Geographical, Historical and Commercial Grammar*, 2nd Am. edn, p. 319: Columbia River

Bewick's Swan was almost the last large bird regularly occurring in Britain to be recognized and described by the scientific community. It has recently been categorized as a race of the North American Whistling Swan, but up until the early part of the nineteenth century the Bewick's Swan and Whooper Swan were classed together as 'Wild Swans'. Any attempt to assess their early individual status is complicated by the problem of correct field identification. This confusion is also reflected in the history of their eventual separation.

It had been known for some time that the sizes and weights of wild swans varied enormously. In 1824, John Latham described a 'Lesser Swan' from a specimen in the collection of the Reverend Kerr Vaughan (an old friend of George Montagu), who had bought the swan from a collection known as the 'Bath Museum'. Latham noted that it was "not so large as the Hooping Swan . . . in fact, it imitates the Wild Swan in miniature . . ."[1] Having only a single skin he was unwilling to say whether it was a hybrid, a freak of nature or a distinct species.

Five years later, in October 1829, Richard Wingate, a Newcastle taxidermist, read a paper to the Natural History Society of Northumberland which concerned his discovery of a new swan. He described it in detail but omitted to provide the bird with a name. This essential detail was required for scientific recognition and was soon supplied by his friend P. J. Selby in a paper published in the Society's Transactions in August 1830[2] in which the swan was referred to as the 'Cygnus Bewickii of Wingate'. The paper acknowledged the help of Sir William Jardine and William Yarrell, two distinguished naturalists who had been drawn into the discussion. Yarrell then wrote another account of the new species which appeared in the *Transactions of the Linnean Society*:

"In the winter of 1823–4, I prepared and preserved the trachea and part of the bones of a young Wild Swan, shot in this country, which possessing peculiarities I had never observed in the Hooper at any age, induced me to believe it would prove to belong to a distinct species."

He "proposed to call it Bewick's Swan, thus devoting it to the memory of one whose beautiful and animated delineations of subjects in natural history entitle him to this tribute."[3]

Yarrell has received the credit as the original describer of Bewick's Swan; not because he claimed to have been aware of it first but because his description was actually published before Selby's. It created some ill-feeling at the time as many felt that Wingate deserved the recognition. Fortunately, all parties were happy with the choice of name, although it is not now clear who suggested it initially. Wingate was an old friend of Bewick and Yarrell had often sent the artist bird skins and had met him in London in 1828.

Thomas Bewick, therefore, has no direct connection with Cygnus Bewickii; indeed it was not named until 1830, two years after his death. However, the woodcut of a swan's head which is appended to the text concerning the 'Wild Swan', in Bewick's *History of British Birds*, looks suspiciously like a Bewick's Swan!

Bewick's contribution to *ornithology* was slight. His real achievement was to popularize the subject through his skills as an artist and wood engraver. The content of his works in no way compares to Yarrell's own *History of British Birds* (1837–43).

Growing up in the Northumberland countryside on his father's small farm, Thomas Bewick was the eldest of eight children. He drew and sketched almost from the very start of life, first with pen and ink, or even blackberry juice, before moving on to brush and colour. He had a great feeling for his home area and after he left Cherryburn House in the parish of Ovingham, to travel the few miles to Newcastle to become apprenticed to the engraver Ralph Beilby, he wrote:

> "I liked my master, I liked the business, but to part from the country and to leave all its beauties behind me, with which I had all my life been charmed in an extreme degree, and in a way I cannot describe—I can only say my heart was like to break . . ."

The work with Beilby was varied; they engraved pipe moulds, bottle moulds, coffin plates, stamps and seals, billheads and many other items and so Bewick

Bewick's Swan

etched in metal long before he began to dominate the wood engraving side of the business. At that time the art of wood block cutting was at a low ebb, copper plates having superseded wood almost entirely, but Bewick brought fresh life to the art by reviving old techniques to produce the effects that he wanted. Five of his early wood blocks for Gay's *Fables* (1779) were thought to be so good that Beilby sent them to the Society for the Encouragement of Arts who awarded seven guineas to Bewick for his efforts.

After seven years Bewick's apprenticeship ended and he set out from Newcastle on a walking tour visiting Carlisle, Glasgow, the southern Highlands and Edinburgh. At Leith he took a boat back to Newcastle and soon after sailed on a collier for London. Although he easily found work he was, after a while, pleased to return to Newcastle where he entered into partnership with his old master, Beilby.

During this period of his life many of Bewick's works were miscellaneous engravings and if he was working in wood it often involved copying, but also improving, other artist's work. This helped his designing ability and at the same time allowed his skill as an engraver to develop, coming to fruition at last in his *General History of Quadrupeds*. He began work on it in 1785, when he was aged thirty-two, most of the cuts and vignettes being carried out after working hours. Beilby supplied much of the text. Published in 1790, it sold rapidly and went into several subsequent editions; those animals that Bewick was familiar with were successfully represented but others such as the bison and hippopotamus, of which he had only seen stuffed examples, were poor. This may have influenced his next choice of work, *The History of British Birds*, for which he knew a greater proportion of the species from first-hand knowledge and for which he was able to obtain fresh specimens. The first volume on *Land Birds* (1797) had the text written by Beilby, largely amended and edited by Bewick. The second volume on *Water Birds* (1804) was written by Bewick with 'literary corrections' by the Rev. Cotes of Bedlington, his partnership with Beilby having been dissolved by then. These two volumes also went into numerous subsequent editions, six in Bewick's lifetime, one of which was completely re-arranged by John Hancock to suit the nomenclature of Temminck. Bewick illustrated other books after *Quadrupeds* and *British Birds* including Burns's *Poetical Works* (1808) and *Fables of Aesop* (1818) but he did not live to see the completion of *The History of British Fishes*. None achieved the standard and popularity of the two earlier works.

In 1827 the American artist John James Audubon visited Bewick and "found him at all times a most agreeable, kind, and benevolent friend."[4] Audubon later named a North American species, Bewick's Wren, in honour of Bewick's achievements, among which the hard-up Audubon no doubt included Bewick's discovery of eight new subscribers for his monumental *Birds of America* (1827–39).

On 8 November 1828, two years after the death of his wife and only a year after Audubon's visit, Thomas Bewick died at Gateshead at the age of seventy-five. He had continued to work until his very last days and was buried at Ovingham beside his wife. His son Robert was also an engraver who had helped in the preparation of the *Fables of Aesop* and the *History of British Fishes*, but he never achieved the greatness of his father. Bewick's eldest daughter Jane is chiefly remembered for editing and issuing *A Memoir of Thomas Bewick, written by Himself* (1862), which remains the standard authority on his personal history. He was undoubtedly hard working, methodical and honest, as well as unassuming and devoted to his family and Tyneside. His woodcuts of birds (and a few watercolours) are excelled by his small vignettes of country scenes. The latter have stood the test of time far better; they are lively, full of interest and humour, and have no equal.

Edward Blyth (1810-1873)

BLYTH'S PIPIT *Anthus godlewskii* (Taczanowski)

Agrodroma Godlewskii Taczanowski, 1876. *Bulletin de la Société Zoologique de France* 1, p. 158: Argun River, south Dauria

BLYTH'S REED WARBLER *Acrocephalus dumetorum* Blyth

Acrocephalus dumetorum Blyth, 1849. *Journal of the Asiatic Society of Bengal* 18, p. 815: No locality = Calcutta

Edward Blyth was one of the most highly regarded ornithologists of his generation. He followed his early studies in England with twenty years service in the Museum of the Asiatic Society of Bengal, where, prevented from doing much field-work himself, he received, described and classified specimens from all over India. During the 1860s there was scarcely an issue of *The Ibis* that did not contain papers or letters by Blyth relating to his ornithological work in Asia. His death prompted his friend Allan Hume to eulogize:

> "It is impossible to over-rate the extent and importance of Blyth's many sided labours. Starting in life without one single advantage, by sheer strength of will, ability and industry he achieved a reputation rarely surpassed, and did an amount of sterling work such as no other single labourer in this field has ever compassed . . . Neither neglect, nor harshness could drive, nor wealth nor worldly advantages tempt him, from what he deemed the nobler path. Ill-paid, and subjected as he was to ceaseless humiliations, he felt that the position he held gave him opportunities for that work which was his mission, such as no other then could, and he clung to it with a single-hearted constancy nothing short of heroic."[1]

The eldest of four children, Edward Blyth was born in London on 23 December 1810. His father died when he was ten and his mother sent him to Wimbledon School where it seems he would have distinguished himself academically but for his inclination to be out exploring the fields and woods nearby. He left school at fifteen to study chemistry and it was hoped that he would later go to university and afterwards into the Church. Edward, however, was possessed by his interest in natural history and would often rise at 3 or 4 o'clock in the morning so that he could either read, make notes and sketch, or go out collecting birds, insects and other animals. When he came of age he used his small inheritance to buy

BLYTH. *ENGLISH ZOOLOGIST WHO SPENT MUCH OF HIS WORKING LIFE AT THE CALCUTTA NATURAL HISTORY MUSEUM. HE MADE A HUGE CONTRIBUTION TO EARLY INDIAN ORNITHOLOGY.*

a druggist's store on the outskirts of London. He often wrote about the birds he had studied locally and this is why the British race of the Yellow Wagtail has the unlikely-sounding type locality of Tooting.

Blyth gave scant attention to his business and even took a room in Pall Mall so that he could be closer to libraries and the British Museum. He managed to supplement his income with the proceeds from various publications and he also contributed papers to several scientific journals. Between 1833 and 1836 the subjects that interested him varied from 'Habits of the Bearded Tit' and 'The Predaceous Habits of the Shrike' to 'Observations on the Cuckoo' and 'The Occurrence of the Carrion Crow in Ireland'. In 1836 an edition of Gilbert White's *Selborne* was issued with zoological notations by Blyth; Seebohm went so far as to call Blyth's contribution "of equal merit to the text"! Blyth wrote regularly for Rennie's *Field Naturalist* but often changed the names of birds that he considered to be unsuitable, so much so that not even the Robin escaped his attentions. Hugh Strickland protested successfully and later Blyth carefully adhered to the Code of Nomenclature, realizing the need for uniformity amongst bird names.

Almost inevitably Blyth's business at Tooting failed. For a time he acted as Curator of the Ornithological Society of London, but his health was now poor and he was professionally advised to seek a warmer climate abroad. When he was offered the paid position of Curator of the Museum of the Asiatic Society of Bengal he readily accepted the post and arrived in Calcutta in September 1841. For the next twenty years he devoted his life to the study of the natural history of British India and at once set about improving the Museum collection and upgrading the catalogues. In 1849 he published a *Catalogue of the Birds of the Asiatic Society* and had begun to contribute regularly to the Society's journal. He also sent articles to the *Indian Field, Indian Sporting Review* and the *Calcutta Review*.

Blyth's field-work was limited by his poor health and difficult financial position; his salary never increased all the time he was in India. He had to content himself with visits to Khulna, less than a hundred miles to the east, the jungles of Midnapore, a similar distance to the west, and one visit to Burma. The receipt of the occasional consignment of bird skins must have been his chief consolation in an otherwise mundane existence. He received specimens from Hume, Tickell and numerous other collectors in India, and sometimes Swinhoe sent batches of skins from Formosa and China.

Blyth's Pipit

Many species have been named in honour of Edward Blyth. They include Blyth's Kingfisher, Blyth's Hawk Eagle, and Blyth's Tragopan as well as Blyth's Reed Warbler and Blyth's Pipit. The warbler was first described by Blyth as *Acrocephalus dumetorum* and Henry Dresser bestowed upon it its current vernacular name in 1876. Blyth was also the first to provide a description of Blyth's Pipit, but the scientific name which he proposed is not now accepted because of some complicated rules of nomenclature (see Godlewski).

When he was forty-four years old he married Mrs Sutton Hodges, a widow he had known in England, but his happiness was short-lived as she died only three years later; Blyth never really recovering from the loss. To add to his sorrows, his request for an increase in salary and a promise of a pension were repeatedly turned down and, in 1861, his health had declined to such an extent that he returned to England the following year. No sooner had he left India than he was granted a pension of £150 a year by his employers. In his absence the *Catalogue of the Mammalia* was seen through the presses by his friend Dr Jerdon, another of the great early Indian ornithologists.

On his return to England, Blyth persisted with his

Blyth's Reed Warbler

interests and in the eleven years of life that remained to him, paper after paper appeared in the *Annals and Magazine of Natural History*, *The Zoologist* and *The Ibis*. Under the *nom de plume* of *Zoophilus* he contributed regularly to *Land and Water* and *The Field*; the latter being a more substantial publication than it is at present and his 'Natural History of the Cranes' which appeared in it, in the year of his death, was later published as a separate work. In 1860 he had become one of the original Honorary Members of the B.O.U. and was afterwards an Extraordinary Member until his death.

During his time in India Blyth corresponded with Charles Darwin, and it appears that Darwin read all of Blyth's papers that discussed variation, the struggle for existence, and sexual and natural selection. Blyth believed that the best adapted individual would be most likely to survive and thereby "transmit its superior qualities to a greater number of offspring". Although he never received much acknowledgement for his influence, Blyth was probably responsible for implanting many ideas in Darwin's mind and it may well have been Blyth who first warned Darwin of Wallace's similar ideas on evolution.

A humble and self-effacing character, devoted to the study of ornithology and blessed with a remarkably retentive memory, Blyth died from heart disease on 27 December 1873, a few days after his sixty-third birthday. Gould provided a fitting epitaph when he wrote:

"One of the first *zoologists* of his time and the founder of that science in India."[2]

Carl Bolle
1839.

BOLLE. *WEALTHY GERMAN NATURALIST, RESPONSIBLE FOR SOME OF THE EARLIEST WORK ON THE BIRDS OF THE CANARY ISLANDS.*

Carl August Bolle
(1821-1909)

BOLLE'S LAUREL PIGEON *Columba bollii* Godman

Columba bollii Godman, 1872. *Ibis*, p. 217: Tenerife, Canaries

A manuscript dated to about 1400, but not rediscovered until 1889, gives the earliest indication that a distinctive species of pigeon was to be found in the Canary Islands:

> "The Land is very rich in birds: herons, bustards, river birds with a different plumage to ours, big pigeons with their tails marked with white, and ordinary pigeons, always taken by the hawks, and quails, larks and numberless others."[1]

Nineteenth century ornithologists knew of the existence of the Laurel Pigeon, as did the native inhabitants of the islands who called it *rabiblanco* (white-tail). Carl Bolle was the first to point out that there were *two* species of these laurel pigeons, but although he saw both species he was unable to secure specimens of each, and was therefore unable to make a clear distinction between them. This was achieved by Frederick du Cane Godman, an English ornithologist who visited the islands, obtained sufficient evidence to differentiate between them and named the second species *Columba bollii*. In *The Ibis* of 1872 Godman wrote concerning the new species:

> "The first I shot in a ravine above Orotava, where I had been told they came to feed in the early morning upon the fruit of the laurel . . . I afterwards found this bird more abundant in the forest of Taganana, at the east end of the island [of Tenerife], about 5000 ft above the sea where I procured the rest of my specimens. It is a very shy bird . . ."

With the destruction of the laurel forests which began after the rediscovery and conquest of the Canaries by Europeans in the fourteenth century, the suitable habitat for laurel pigeons has become increasingly restricted. The Laurel Pigeon is mainly confined to La Palma and Gomera. Bolle's Laurel Pigeon has long been extinct on Gran Canaria and is now found only on Gomera, La Palma and Tenerife (and recently on Hierro). Both species are considered to be endangered, Bolle's Laurel Pigeon especially so.

Like many a traveller, Carl Bolle visited the Atlantic Islands partly for the sake of his health; firstly in 1852 and again in 1856. He was a wealthy German naturalist who had been born in Berlin to an old and well-respected family that had made its fortune from the brewing industry. He studied medicine and natural science at Berlin and Bonn gaining his doctorate, at the age of twenty-five, with a dissertation on botany. Thereafter his inheritance enabled him to pursue his own private studies howsoever he wished.

For his visit to the Cape Verde Islands, his ornithological notes were brief and rather disappointing. His list of forty-eight species included birds he had not seen for himself and the 'sea eagles' he claimed for ten of the islands were undoubtedly Ospreys. Nevertheless it was a first attempt at a bird list for the islands and was later vastly improved upon by the Italian collector, Leonardo Fea, and the Kentish-born adventurer, Boyd Alexander. For the Canary Islands, Bolle wrote a series of much more useful accounts which appeared in the *Journal für Ornithologie* between 1854 and 1862. His fluent and elegant style was well suited to the period and through these papers his name soon became well known in many European countries. Travelling did not really appeal to him, and thereafter he preferred to remain quietly settled on the family estates at Schaffenberg, near Brandenburg, some 40 miles west of Berlin. Almost all of his future writing, whether ethnographical, botanical or ornithological, was centred on his home territories. Between 1855 and 1896 he produced more than thirty major ornithological papers, half of which were in the *Journal für Ornithologie*, many of the remainder in *Naumannia* and others in more local publications.

Dr Bolle was a founder member of the D.O-G. (German Ornithological Society) which was created in 1867; he regularly attended their meetings throughout the 1870s and 1880s, and became Chairman after the death of Alfred Brehm in November 1884. Bolle refused to accept Darwinism and declined to involve himself in controversies over nomenclature. Gradually he began to withdraw from his former associates and turned his attention to the study of plants and trees, expressing his inner feelings for nature through poetry. He eventually became more and more reclusive and died in his eighty-eighth year, on 17 February 1909, completely alienated from his old circle of scientific friends; an isolation entirely of his own making.

Bolle's Laurel Pigeon

Charles Lucien Jules Laurent Bonaparte (1803-1857)

BONAPARTE'S GULL *Larus philadelphia* (Ord)

Sterna Philadelphia Ord, 1815. In W. Guthrie, *Geographical, Historical and Commercial Grammar*, 2nd Am. edn, p. 319: No locality = near Philadelphia, Pennsylvania

The birth of Charles Bonaparte, in Paris, on 24 May 1803 was followed five months later by the secret marriage of his parents, at Plessé. Napoleon, the First Consul of France, was enraged when he heard about his brother's wedding, as he was already planning to bestow on himself the title of Emperor and wanted Lucien, Charles' father, to make a suitably grand royal alliance. Instead, Lucien had married the beautiful widow of a Paris banker, with whom he had been having an affair since the spring of 1802.

Napoleon tried to persuade his younger brother to seek a divorce, so that he could appoint him as one of his heirs, but after a bitter argument Lucien left Paris with his wife and the infant Charles, to seek papal protection in Italy. The Bonapartes enjoyed a life of luxury in Rome until Pius VII was imprisoned and deported by the Emperor. Fearing for the safety of himself and his increasing family, Lucien decided to escape to North America. By then (in 1810) there were two daughters by his first wife and one daughter of Madame Bonaparte and her former husband, as well as Charles, his brother and two sisters.

In August, at the height of the Napoleonic War, they embarked on an American ship at Civitavecchia, near Rome, but foul weather forced the captain to seek the shelter of Cagliari Bay, on the coast of Sardinia. As the island was then under the control of the Royal Navy, the British envoy there quickly learned the identity of the passengers and informed Lucien that he and all on board were prisoners. Hoping that the British would not risk attacking a neutral vessel the captain set sail, but once outside the harbour they were intercepted by two British frigates. The Bonapartes were taken to Malta and held there until the end of December when the seven year old Charles and his family, together with their retinue of twenty-three musicians and servants all sailed for England. They should have been there in a fortnight, but the captain had been instructed to give the French coast a very wide berth and Atlantic gales prolonged the miserable voyage by four weeks.

BONAPARTE. *NEPHEW OF THE EMPEROR NAPOLEON. HE DABBLED BRIEFLY IN POLITICS, BUT DEDICATED HIS LIFE TO THE AWESOME TASK OF PREPARING A SCIENTIFIC CLASSIFICATION OF THE BIRDS OF THE WORLD. HE SUCCESSIVELY SET UP HOME IN PHILADELPHIA, ROME, LONDON AND PARIS, AND EXAMINED ALL THE MAJOR BIRD COLLECTIONS OF EUROPE.*

The long-suffering party eventually arrived in Shropshire where they lived at Dinham House, close to Ludlow Castle, for the next six months, forbidden to travel more than two miles from their home. Naturally, there was strong anti-French feeling in the neighbourhood and sometimes Charles and the other children had stones thrown at them, but their father succeeded in establishing friendly relationships with some of the local gentry, including Thomas Knight, who was a member of the Royal and Linnean Societies and who had particularly studied the cultivation of fruit trees and vegetables. After the Bonapartes moved, in July, to Thorngrove Estate near Grimley, in Worcestershire, Knight sent them shrubs and potatoes for their garden. The friendship between the families flourished and Knight may well have influenced and encouraged Charles, who was already asking questions about the birds, insects and flowers which he watched and collected on the estate. He also began to learn about astronomy when his father bought a huge telescope for 50,000 francs and installed it in their observatory.

The Bonapartes had all their letters censored and were now confined to a ten-mile radius, but they were allowed to entertain visitors and entered into the social life of the area. Every Sunday evening the Bonapartes held a concert, in which their own children and the guests took part, and Charles also acted in two comedies written by his father, which the family performed in their private theatre before an audience of two hundred neighbours.

After the peace of 1814 the family returned to Italy, dividing their time between their country estates in the hills near Viterbo, some forty miles north of Rome and their palace in the city. Pope Pius VII created Lucien Prince of Canino and Charles as his eldest son became Prince of Musignano. For the next seven years the young prince delved into the scientific literature of Europe, reading English, French, Italian and Latin with equal facility. He built up extensive natural history collections, identifying the birds from the first two published volumes of Temminck's *Manuel d'ornithologie*. There was one streaky brown warbler, however, which he shot while still in his teens which he could not find in the book, so he prepared the specimen and sent it to the famous author in Leyden. Temminck agreed that it was a species new to science and included it in his next great work, *Planches coloriées*, as *[Acrocephalus] melanopogon*, the Moustached Warbler; a bird so similar to the Sedge Warbler that the separation of the two species was no small achievement for the youthful beginner.

Shortly after his nineteenth birthday, the ardent young naturalist travelled to Brussels to marry his cousin Zenaide. She was twenty-one years old, the eldest daughter of Joseph Bonaparte, who had been King of Naples and Spain and who now lived in extravagant luxury near Philadelphia. It was an arranged marriage and Joseph sent Lucien the generous dowry of 730,000 francs.

Charles had inherited the restless energy and striking physical features, though not the political ambitions of his uncle Napoleon who had, on this occasion at least, let it be known to the family that he approved of the union, although he died in exile on St Helena before the wedding actually took place.

Soon after the marriage, the young couple sailed for Philadelphia, Charles beginning his study of the American birds before he even arrived there by observing and capturing some of the petrels which followed the ship. They provided the basis of the material for his first ornithological paper, 'An Account of Four Species of Stormy Petrels' published by the *Journal of the Academy of Natural Sciences of Philadelphia*, in 1824. The vernacular name of Wilson's Storm-petrel stems from a proposal made in this article to honour Alexander Wilson (who had died in Philadelphia just ten years before Charles arrived there), "as a small testimony to the memory of the author of the *American Ornithology . . .*"

For the next three years Charles and Zenaide resided in a villa on Joseph's extensive estate of Point Breeze, on the banks of the Delaware River. It was an ideal location for Charles, who quickly became a leader among Philadelphia's ornithologists, and a close friend of the artist Titian Peale, the entomologist Thomas Say and the naturalist William Cooper. Through studying Wilson's *Ornithology* and the skin collections of his fellow enthusiasts, and by making excursions to the forests and meadows, creeks and salt marshes, Charles became familiar with the birds of the eastern United States in a remarkably short period of time.

He soon conceived the idea of producing a supplement to Wilson's work which would incorporate recently discovered species, the females and immatures of many common species which were still undescribed and his revisions of Wilson's nomenclature. *The American Ornithology; or, The Natural History of Birds Inhabiting the United States Not Given by Wilson* was published in four volumes. It included the Cooper's Hawk and Say's Phoebe which Charles named after his friends, and the first illustrations of the females of the American Goldfinch, the Golden-winged Warbler and the Cape May Warbler. The latter had been shot on migration by Charles himself, but he was primarily a closet naturalist, producing his best work in the environment of musty museums and quiet libraries. His great and incalculable influence on the development of ornithology was due to his remarkable talent for the systematic arrangement of genera and species, for which he was particularly well equipped by his first-hand knowledge of the birds of both the Old and New Worlds.

The first volume of the supplement appeared in 1825, and in the autumn of that year, Charles was described by a visitor to the Academy of Natural Sciences:

> "He is a little set, blackeyed fellow, quite talkative, and withal an interesting and companionable fellow. He devotes his attention to ornithology and has published

Bonaparte's Gull

a continuation of Wilson's work on the above subject . . . He read a memoir on the 'golden Plover'. To a novice it seems curious, that men of the first intelligence should pay so much attention to web-footed gentry with wings."[1]

It was this "companionable fellow" who had first introduced Audubon to the Academy of Sciences in 1824, when the artist had returned to Philadelphia in search of an engraver and publisher for his spectacular bird paintings. Charles greatly admired the originality and liveliness of Audubon's style, and would have liked him to do some of the drawings for his supplement, but Alexander Lawson, who had been Wilson's engraver and was now producing the sequel, was appalled by the suggestion. "You may buy them", he coldly told Bonaparte, "but I will not engrave them, because ornithology requires truth in the forms and correctness in the lines. Here are neither!" Lawson was not alone in his criticism and so Charles encouraged the artist to seek a publisher in Europe, with the result that Audubon's *Birds of America* was eventually produced in Britain. Despite Lawson's protestations, one of Bonaparte's plates (the Boat-tailed Grackle), was drawn by Audubon.

In 1824 Zenaide gave birth to a son who was the first of their twelve children, four of whom died in infancy. Despite the size of their brood, the direct male line of Charles Bonaparte's branch of the Imperial Family became extinct in the next generation: their eldest son died without heirs, the second became a cardinal and the third, Napoleon Charles, married the Princess Ruspoli of Etruria, by whom he had only two daughters. Charles declared his affection for his wife by naming a genus of doves, *Zenaida*, but after the first few years their marriage was not a very happy relationship, and their problems were compounded by their impecunious state for which Charles' father was at least partly responsible. Lucien had used a substantial part of Zenaide's handsome dowry to pay off some of his many debts.

At the end of 1826 Charles left America and sailed to Europe with his family, hoping to retrieve part of the dowry. Prohibited from travelling through France they continued their journey to Italy via Germany and Switzerland. Charles therefore took the opportunity to visit the newly established Senckenberg Museum in Frankfurt, where the director, Dr Cretzschmar, gave him two Black-winged Kites which Eduard Rüppell had recently sent from Egypt, and several other skins. The Bonapartes then visited Zenaide's mother in Florence, before going on to Rome where they stayed with Lucien, but discovered that he had already run through most of their fortune.

They returned to England where Charles continued his studies throughout the summer using various libraries and collections. He met J. E. Gray at the British Museum, delighted in the birds brought back from Sumatra by Raffles, was made a foreign member of the Linnean Society and enjoyed a reunion with Audubon who was surprised and dismayed to find that the prince allowed his servants to call him "your Royal Highness". "I thought this ridiculous in the extreme", remarked the American. Charles finished the second and third volumes of his *American Ornithology* in London and made a brief trip to Philadelphia in the autumn, to arrange for their publication.

In 1828 the Bonapartes moved to Rome and made their home there for the next twenty years.

It was while Charles was working in Italy that his name was first attached to the small gull which breeds beside ponds and lakes in the northern forests of Alaska and Canada. It had first been called *Sterna Philadelphia* by George Ord in 1815 and *Larus capistratus* by Bonaparte himself in 1826, but in 1831, Richardson and Swainson suggested the name of *Larus Bonapartii* in their *Fauna Boreali-Americana*.[2] Although the specific scientific title has reverted to the original, the prince's name remains in the French, English, Swedish, Spanish and German languages. Sir John Richardson later wrote about these interesting and unusual gulls, recording that:

> "One of the birds which we traced up to its breeding places on Bear Lake River, but not to the sea coast, is the pretty little Bonapartean Gull . . . This arrives very early in the season, before the ground is denuded of snow, and seeks its food in the first pools of water which form on the borders of Great Bear Lake, and wherein it finds multitudes of minute crustacean animals and larvae of insects. It flies in flocks and builds its nest in a colony resembling a rookery, seven or eight on a tree; the nests being framed of sticks laid flatly. Its voice and mode of flying are like those of a Tern, and, like that bird, it rushes fiercely at the head of anyone who intrudes on its haunts, screaming loudly. It has, moreover, the strange practice, considering the form of its feet, of perching on posts and trees; and it may often be seen standing gracefully on the summit of a small spruce fir."[3]

Meanwhile Bonaparte had turned his attention from the birds of America to the birds and animals of Italy. Between 1832 and 1841 he published his three-volume *Iconografia della Fauna Italica*. It contained 180 hand-coloured lithographic plates and at that time was the most complete and elaborate work on the vertebrate animals of any country in the world. In 1837 he introduced a new system of classification for the Vertebrates which received widespread acclamation and he also visited England. While in London he met up with Audubon again and began to attend the meetings of the British Association for the Advancement of Science. When he returned to Italy he founded a similar association which met in Pisa from 1839 onwards and of which he was president of the zoological section until the events of 1847. On the death of his father in 1840 Charles styled himself Charles Lucien Bonaparte, Prince of Canino and Musignano. He had hitherto kept himself apart from politics but the rise of the nationalist movement in northern Italy aroused his republican sympathies, which had been nurtured by his father and strengthened during his years in the United States. At a scientific congress in Venice, in 1847, he expressed his revolutionary sympathies and was promptly expelled from the Austrian territories.

For the next two years he threw himself into the cause of freedom and became a leader of the increasingly powerful radical party. In November 1848 the Pope fled from Rome and in February of the following year Bonaparte became vice-president of the legislative council of the Roman Constituent Assembly. Five weeks later he signed a proclamation calling the Romans to arms on behalf of a united Italy, but his great hopes were dashed by none other than his own cousin, Louis Napoleon, President of France. Rome was attacked by a French expeditionary force and it fell on 3 July.

Charles had to flee from the city and sailed to Marseilles but Louis Napoleon ordered him to leave the country. Charles ignored the command and continued his journey towards Paris, only to suffer the humiliation of being arrested in Orleans and conducted under arrest to Le Havre, where he was compelled to embark for England.

He had many friends in London who welcomed him warmly, but he left almost immediately to attend a meeting of the British Association in Birmingham, then travelled to southern Scotland to visit Sir William Jardine who lived ten miles from Dumfries and who had just received an interesting collection of rare Himalayan birds from Edward Blyth. For many years Charles had been planning to make a methodical classification of all the birds of the world. Now, as a refugee, without any of his own collections, reference books or preparatory notes which he had been gathering for twenty years, he hoped to complete the task by visiting private collectors and museums in many parts of Europe. To begin the work in earnest he went to Leyden, where the friendship and advice of Hermann Schlegel and the 12,000 birds in his museum offered some compensation for his losses. In May, Schlegel and Bonaparte travelled to Berlin to examine Lichtenstein's collections, then visited the aged J. F. Naumann and other German naturalists before returning to Leyden. In the summer Charles unexpectedly received a message from Louis Napoleon declaring that he would now be most welcome in France.

Bonaparte wasted no time in returning to the city of his birth and though he continued to travel relentlessly between the museums of Europe, he made Paris his home for the rest of his life. He frequently studied at the Museum d'Histoire Naturelle, working daily on his *Conspectus Generum Avium*, and in its pages expressed his contempt for Louis Napoleon in naming a new bird of paradise *[Diphyllodes] respublica*:

> "There are those who are much inclined to name their most beautiful species for princes; since I am not in the least enamored of the authority of any princes, I have adorned this extraordinarily beautiful bird of paradise with the name of Republic: of that Republic which would be a Paradise, if it had not been made into a Tartarus by the evil intrigues and the ambitions of Republicans who are unworthy of the name they have taken. But since there is not to be a paradisiacal Republic, there shall at least be a republican bird of paradise . . ."[4]

It was not surprising that this indulgence disgusted many of his fellow ornithologists, including the owner of the specimen!

On another occasion, in December 1851, Charles and his cousin Plon-Plon went around the suburbs of Paris trying to arouse the workers to resist Louis Napoleon's coup d'état. Even though the two princes were wearing workmens' clothing they were soon recognized and had to abandon the attempt.

In August 1854 Charles' wife, Zenaide, died in Naples after living apart from her husband for some time. His own health was deteriorating, so that he was forced to work day and night in a desperate attempt to complete his synopsis. When Gustav Hartlaub visited the Prince at his home in the Rue de Lille, in Paris, he found him working on the *Conspectus* in his bath! At that time Bonaparte was suffering from swollen and ulcerative legs, but even on his death-bed he continued to produce further sections of his book, finally losing the race against time on 29 July 1857. The second volume of his incomplete *Conspectus* was published later that same year, edited by Schlegel. It was unfortunate that

Bonaparte had not had time to work through the auks, divers, grebes, wildfowl, pheasants and some other groups, but while any taxonomic work is open to criticism, his enormous experience and his perceptive eye had combined to produce an arrangement of genera more like our present system than that of any of his contemporaries and it is still sometimes consulted, even today.

Charles Bonaparte's obituary in the *Proceedings of the Linnean Society* of 1859 contained the following tribute:

> "[His] extreme ardour in the pursuit of science, and the unremitting attention which he devoted to it, increasing even as his physical powers gave way, were his most striking characteristics. Confining himself to Vertebrated zoology, and especially conversant with the class of Birds, which few men have studied more successfully, his labours have contributed largely to our knowledge of the faunas of Europe and of North America in particular, to the improvement of their systematic arrangement, to the establishment of many well-marked genera, and to the distinction and description of a multitude of new or imperfectly-known species. Of his conduct in public life it is not my business to speak; but I only echo the general sentiment in saying that in private he was amiable and estimable, a warm friend, and an agreeable companion."

Franco Andrea Bonelli
(1784-1830)

BONELLI'S EAGLE *Hieraaetus fasciatus* (Vieillot)

Aquila fasciata Vieillot, 1822. *Mémoires de la Société Linnéene de Paris* 2, Pt 2, p. 152: Fontainebleau [France] and Sardinia

BONELLI'S WARBLER *Phylloscopus bonelli* (Vieillot)

Sylvia Bonelli Vieillot, 1819. *Nouveau Dictionnaire d'Histoire Naturelle, Nouvelle édition*, Vol. 28, p. 91: "Piémont"

Franco Andrea was the twelfth son of Tommaso and Veronica Bonelli, born on 10 November 1784[1] at Cuneo, in the Piedmont. The family later moved north to Turin and it was here, in the Po valley, that the young Bonelli learned to hunt wild birds and animals, to prepare the specimens and catalogue his collections. During his teenage years he kept detailed ornithological notebooks; those written in 1801 and 1802 describe 146 different methods of catching birds. For example, he explained how Magpies could be attracted to bowls of walnut oil and caught as they attacked their reflections, and he drew a sketch of a man, disguised as a cow, ringing a bell as he herded partridges into a funnel trap ahead of him.

He later became engrossed in the study of entomology and at the age of twenty-five published one of his first works, on subalpine fauna. His next publication on the *Carabidae*, or ground-beetles, brought him much acclaim

Bonelli's Eagle

BONELLI. *ITALIAN NATURALIST WHO BECAME PROFESSOR OF ZOOLOGY AT TURIN UNIVERSITY. HE IS DEPICTED HERE IN HIS STUDY SHORTLY BEFORE HIS DEATH, WITH A BONELLI'S EAGLE.*

and the French naturalist Baron Cuvier asked to meet him when he visited Turin in 1810. Cuvier invited the young man to come to Paris, where he benefited from Cuvier's teaching on comparative anatomy, but was also strongly influenced by Lamarck's evolutionary theories.

In the autumn of 1811 Bonelli returned to Italy and became Professor of Zoology at Turin University, with responsibility for the zoological museum. He was particularly interested in the fauna of his own corner of Italy, and that year he completed a *Catalogue des Oiseaux du Piémont*, which listed 264 species, giving their scientific, French and Piedmontese names. After this, with financial assistance from the Savoy family who ruled Sardinia and Piedmont, Bonelli expanded his horizons by gathering collections from the Alps, the hills of Liguria and Sardinia. One of his most zealous correspondents was Alberto della Marmora, an experienced soldier who served on Sardinia and who sent him butterflies and moths and many other natural history specimens.

In December 1815 Bonelli acquired a leaf warbler with a yellowish rump, from the Piedmont, and sent it to L. A. F. Baillon, in Abbeville. Vieillot examined the specimen while he was working on his *Nouveau Dictionaire d'Histoire Naturelle*, and described the warbler in volume 28, naming it *Sylvia Bonelli*. Bonelli's Eagle was also first described by Vieillot, from an individual shot in Fontainebleau woods near Paris, and another sent to him by Bonelli, which had been collected on Sardinia by Marmora. Vieillot named the new eagle *Aquila fasciata*—l'aigle à queue barée. It was Temminck who later proposed, in his *Planches coloriées*,[2] that the bird should be called after Bonelli, as it

Bonelli's Warbler

was Bonelli who had sent him the specimen to examine, and who, moreover, had by then earned widespread admiration among European naturalists. Temminck's name of *Falco Bonelli* is no longer valid, because of the law of priority, but his suggestion is still retained in the English, French and Italian names for this fine eagle. Bonelli so admired the species that he kept one in captivity for some time and gathered information on plumage changes which he hoped would clear up the confusion which then existed because young birds were sometimes misidentified as a separate species.

One of the most highly respected Italian naturalists of his day, Bonelli raised the status of the Turin University Museum to that of Pavia, the foremost in the country. His lecture courses, which reflected his ideas of evolution along Lamarckian lines were considered to be highly revolutionary. Despite his lifelong interest and influence on Italian ornithology much of his work on the subject was never published; most of his papers were entomological.

In 1815 Bonelli had married Ferdinanda Dancona, but at about that time his health started to deteriorate. After many years of illness, he died at the age of forty-six, on 18 November 1830.

THEKLA. *ONLY DAUGHTER OF THE CELEBRATED GERMAN ORNITHOLOGIST C. L. BREHM.*

Thekla Klothilde Bertha Brehm (1833-1857)

THEKLA LARK *Galerida theklae* (C. L. Brehm)

Galerita Theklae C. L. Brehm, 1858. *Naumannia*, p. 210: Jativa near Valencia and Sierra Nevada, Spain

   Thekla was the only daughter of the German ornithologist Christian Ludwig Brehm. She was born on 24 April 1833 in the village of Renthendorf, near Triptis, about fifty miles south of Leipzig. By the time of Thekla's birth, her father, a Lutheran minister, had lived in the manse for twenty years and had been collecting birds for nearly three decades; the house was filled with display cases of German birds and the attic was stacked with boxes of skins.

   When J. F. Naumann wrote his great work on the birds of Germany, *Naturgeschichte der Vögel Deutschlands* (1820–1844), he constantly drew on C. L. Brehm's *Beiträge zur Vögelkunde* [Contributions to Ornithology] which was published in three volumes between 1820 and 1822. The minister also published some two hundred papers, mostly about birds, and his collection (now in the museum at New York) eventually grew to about fifteen thousand skins. It is particularly valuable because he labelled every specimen with meticulous care. Unfortunately, Brehm consulted very few reference books and was frequently criticized for describing, as new species, birds which had been

Thekla Lark

discovered long before. He also caused much confusion by naming many subspecies in the same way as species, using just a binomial. It was Naumann who created a more lasting influence on German ornithology.

Thekla Brehm had no particular interest in birds, but as the only girl in the family she held a very special place in the affection of her parents and her six brothers. Sadly, she was of a delicate constitution and never married. She died of a heart disease, at Renthendorf, on 6 July 1857,[1] at the age of only twenty-four. In the following year, in the ornithological journal *Naumannia*, her grieving father published a description of a lark which had been collected in Spain by her elder brothers Alfred and Reinhold. Brehm named the bird Thekla's Haubenlerche [Thekla's Crested Lark], in memory of his much loved and "unforgettable" daughter.

Alfred Brehm later became well known as a zoologist, writer and explorer. He travelled in Spain, North Africa and Lapland and accompanied Otto Finsch on his expedition to western Siberia in 1876. When his own daughter was born, in 1864, he called her Thekla in remembrance of his little sister.

Henry James Bruce
(1835-1909)

STRIATED SCOPS OWL *Otus brucei* (Hume)

Ephialtes Brucei Hume, 1873. *Stray Feathers* 1, p. 8: Rahuri, Ahmadnagar, Bombay Presidency

The Reverend H. J. Bruce was an American, born at Hardwick, Massachusetts, on 5 February 1835. At the age of twenty-four he graduated from Amherst College and then studied for the ministry at Bangor Theological Seminary and Andover Seminary, being ordained at Springfield, Massachusetts, in September 1862. A month later he married Miss Hepzibeth P. Goodnow and at the end of October they sailed from Boston for India, where they served with the Marathi Mission for the next forty-six years.

The Mission was supported through the American Board of Commissioners for Foreign Missions (A.B.C.F.M.), and was based at Ahmadnagar, in the hills about 140 miles east of Bombay. The first outstation to which the Bruces were sent was at Khokar, some 35 miles north of Ahmadnagar, and south of the great Godavari River, which the Hindus revered as being sacred and a sister of the Ganges. With a native pastor and twelve helpers, Bruce ministered to his own villagers and travelled throughout the area, often preaching the gospel to men and women who had never before heard the name of Jesus Christ.

During those early years, as Bruce endeavoured to learn all that he could about the region where he was to spend the rest of his life, he became interested in its natural history, as well as in the languages, religions and customs of the local people. He began to study the many birds of the district and to correspond with Allan Hume in northern India, and to send him specimens. After a number of years Bruce moved about ten miles south-westwards to Rahurio, and from there he sent Hume a pale, greyish owl with bright yellow eyes, which he had obtained on 20 January 1870. Realizing that it was an unknown species, Hume described the bird in the first issue of his new quarterly journal, *Stray Feathers*, along with a number of other 'novelties' which included the black and white chat now known as Hume's Wheatear.

Rahurio was situated on the bank of the Mula River, in the broad, open valley of the Godavari. Around the village were a large number of highly cultivated gardens, irrigated by water drawn from the wells by bullocks. Beyond were fertile plains and Bruce found that the whole area abounded in bird life. From

BRUCE. AMERICAN MISSIONARY WHO DEDICATED HIS LIFE TO CHRISTIAN SERVICE IN WEST-CENTRAL INDIA. WHILE THERE HE DEVELOPED AN INTEREST IN THE LOCAL BIRDS AND SENT SPECIMENS TO ALLAN HUME. BRUCE (SEATED ON RIGHT, WITH PITH HELMET ON KNEE) IS WITH THE AMERICAN MARATHI MISSION AND DEPUTATION OF 1901.

his study window he could watch Red-vented Bulbuls, Blue Rock Thrushes, Indian Rollers, flocks of Little Swifts and the common Indian Mynas. On one occasion, when a pair of mynas built their nest near his window, Bruce was alerted by their alarm calls and rushed out with a stick; an unfortunate cobra was soon safely housed in a jar of alcohol. Amongst the raptors which hunted around the bungalow were Egyptian Vultures, Booted Eagles, White-eyed Buzzard Eagles and Black Kites. One of the missionary's small children was repeatedly terrorized by one particular kite which made a habit of swooping down and seizing whatever snack the child was carrying when he went out to play in the shade. Needless to say, the hapless bird was also added to Bruce's natural history collection. However, the greatest pests, according to Bruce, were the Indian House Sparrows, for he admitted that his patience had frequently been sorely tried by them when preaching in local churches, as it was impossible to keep the sparrows out of the buildings and their noisy chirping throughout the services almost drove him to distraction. He was appalled by the attempts then being made to introduce the House Sparrow to North America.

One day when Bruce was relaxing on his veranda during heavy rain which followed several weeks of drought, he noticed a number of Collared Doves which welcomed the shower by lying on the ground, on their sides, each with their upper wing spread and raised above the back, apparently attempting to cool off; this may well be the first account of this dove's occasional habit of rain-bathing. He described this interesting behaviour amongst other varied ornithological observations in an article on 'Some of the Familiar Birds of India', which appeared in the *American Naturalist* of 1872.

In addition to his ornithological and botanical publications Bruce wrote regularly for the *Missionary Herald* of the A.B.C.F.M. One such article, entitled 'Missionary Touring in India', was issued in March 1875 by which time he had more than ten years of experience to draw upon. He wrote that touring was only attempted during 'the cold season', and even then, every effort was made to find a large shady tree under which to pitch the tents, to protect them from the heat of the sun. Bruce was usually accompanied by his growing family and his assistant, the Rev. Kassimbhai. They would select a central village, camping near it for a week or more and from that base go out in a small covered wagon, drawn by ponies or bullocks, to preach in all the villages within a radius of four

Striated Scops Owl

or five miles. At each place they would give a simple explanation of the way of salvation, often using music to gather and hold their audience, and on other occasions, in the cool, dark evenings, Bruce would use his magic lantern to entertain and instruct the marvelling congregation who had generally seen nothing of the kind before. At the end of one such performance, the missionary heard a man say, with great satisfaction, "Now I have seen it all. What is there left for me to see?" "Poor man!" commented Bruce, "If he will but receive the truth as it is in Jesus, he will behold greater things than these."

It was typical of Bruce that even in this short religious article he mentioned the Demoiselle Cranes which sometimes appeared in great numbers during the cooler months, flying like geese in straight parallel lines or in V formation, often at a very great height.

Bruce and his family later moved to Satara, less than 60 miles from the coast and about 120 miles south of Bombay. At the end of January 1877 he set off on a fifteen-day tour of the Koyna valley, accompanied by two native helpers, and porters who carried their tents and baggage on the rough footpaths through the jungle. Bruce had never before met with so much eagerness for the good news of the gospel, and as word of his journey spread through the community, messengers sought him out, asking him to come and speak at their villages. There was one day when Bruce was constrained to preach to six different audiences, and it was with great heaviness of heart that he left the people to return to Satara, with the resolve that if at all possible he would send them a teacher. Bruce and his wife worked in the area for the next thirty years, helped in time by their daughter Clara, who also became a missionary. There was such a dire lack of Christian literature for the use of the local people that Bruce bought and operated a printing press, and although the work was laborious and expensive, in less than ten years he published over three million copies of tracts.

The family made several brief furloughs back to the United States, but Bruce had no desire to retire there, and he continued his labours in India until the age of seventy-three, when he became too ill to carry on. He moved to Panchgani and rested there until his death the following year on 4 May 1909. Bruce was buried at Satara, the place which he had loved so much, after a service of praise and thanksgiving. He was survived by his wife, his daughter Clara, his eldest son who was then working in Europe and two sons and two daughters in America.

Morten Thrane Brünnich (1737-1827)

BRÜNNICH'S GUILLEMOT *Uria lomvia* (Linnaeus)

Alca Lomvia Linnaeus, 1758. *Systema Naturae*, 10th edn, p. 130: "Europa boreali", restricted to Greenland by Hartert

Brünnich was born in Copenhagen on 30 September 1737, the son of a portrait painter who prospered sufficiently to give the boy an excellent education. At the age of twenty Brünnich took his B.A. and went on to study oriental languages and theology, but under the influence of Linnaeus's writings and lectures by Danish naturalists, he turned to the study of the natural sciences.

Within just a couple of years he was making original observations about the insects of his native country and he contributed to the entomological section of Pontopiddon's *Danske Atlas* (1763–81). In 1762 Brünnich was given the superintendence of the large natural history collections of Counsellor Thott and Judge Christian Fleischer, and, as a result, he became increasingly absorbed in the study of ornithology. Fleischer had obtained many northern birds from the countries then allied with Denmark (the Faeroe Isles, Norway, Greenland and Iceland) and these specimens formed the basis of Brünnich's *Ornithologia Borealis*, published when he was only twenty-six. It was the first Danish work of any importance on the subject, and included the first descriptions of the Great Northern Diver and the Manx Shearwater from specimens killed in the Faeroes and of the Jack Snipe from the tiny island of Christiansø, east of Bornholm, Denmark. The book also included both Brünnich's Guillemot and the Common Guillemot, and though the former had previously been described by Linnaeus in 1758 and the latter by Pontopiddon in 1763, Brünnich was the first to describe both these species, realizing that they were different, as they had frequently been confused in previous years. Indeed, Brünnich unfortunately added to the confusion by giving his bird the scientific name *Uria Troile*, then used in Britain for the Common Guillemot. In 1818 Edward Sabine proposed the name *Uria Brünnichii* to clarify the matter, when he listed the bird amongst those which he had encountered off the coast of Greenland, while seeking the North-west Passage.[1] By the law of priority Linnaeus's name for this northern guillemot now stands, but Sabine's suggestion remains in the English vernacular.

Brünnich also wrote 'A History of the Eider Duck' which was published in Copenhagen in 1763, and he corresponded with many foreign naturalists including Linnaeus, Pallas and Thomas Pennant. The latter had studied Fleischer's

BRÜNNICH. *DANISH NATURALIST WHO WROTE THE* ORNI-
THOLOGIA BOREALIS. *THIS PORTRAIT WAS PAINTED WHEN
HE WAS SIXTY-TWO YEARS OLD.*

same bird collection while preparing his *British Zoology* (1766), and on Brünnich's authority, when writing about the Storm Petrel, he commented that "the inhabitants of the Faeroe Isles make them serve the purposes of a candle, by drawing a wick through the mouth and rump, which being lighted, is fed by the fat and oil of the body."[2]

In the same year that his *Ornithologia Borealis* was published, his *Entomologia* also appeared, thus demonstrating Brünnich's enormous capacity for work. Through the influence of Pontopiddon and other eminent naturalists who recognized his outstanding energy and abilities, Brünnich was appointed Lecturer in Natural History and Economy at Copenhagen University. He took up the post after a long tour of Europe, during which he visited the tin mines of Cornwall and many other mines and quarries in Hungary and Transylvania. He also spent time studying Mediterranean fish while staying in Marseilles and on the Dalmatian coast, and in 1768 issued his *Icthyologia Massiliensis* on that subject. At that time Copenhagen University did not have a natural history museum, so Brünnich therefore endeavoured to establish one, building up a considerable collection within just a few years. Finding that suitable textbooks for his students were lacking, Brünnich wrote his own: the *Zoologiae fundamenta* (1771).

For the rest of his life, however, he almost abandoned the study of zoology, in favour of mineralogy, although he did work for a time on the collections in his museum. In 1782 he brought out the first volume of 'A History of Animals and the Zoological Collection in the Natural History Museum of the University'. Unfortunately the successive volumes were never produced, because both the manuscripts and twenty-four copper plates were destroyed by fire in 1795. Nevertheless, the single work does give a unique picture of the early history of Danish natural science. The vast majority of Brünnich's publications were concerned with mineralogy and copies of all his books, which include an autobiography, are now in the Copenhagen University Library.

Brünnich had married Vibecke Schou, from Salling in Jutland, when he was thirty-eight; he outlived his wife, who was nine years younger, by seven years, and he died in Copenhagen on 19 September 1827 at almost ninety years of age. He was regarded as the founder of Danish zoology and in the style of that period, Linnaeus once wrote: "would that we had more Brünnichs; natural history would then soon be perfect."!

Brünnich's Guillemot

Francis Buchanan-Hamilton[†] (1762-1829)

GREY-NECKED BUNTING *Emberiza buchanani* Blyth

E. [mberiza] Buchanani Blyth, 1845 (1844). *Journal of the Asiatic Society of Bengal* 13, p. 957: "Indian peninsula"

The Grey-necked Bunting breeds high in the mountains of Iran, Afghanistan and central Asia, migrating southwards in the autumn to flock on the stony hillsides and dry stubble fields of west and central India. It was one of the many birds which Francis Buchanan painted during the twenty years he spent in India surveying vast areas in Nepal, Malabar and Bengal. In 1844 Edward Blyth described and named the bunting in the *Journal of the Asiatic Society of Bengal* from one of Buchanan's illustrations.

Buchanan was a Scot, born in the parish of Callander, in Perthshire, on 15 February 1762, the third son of Thomas Buchanan of Spittal and Elizabeth Hamilton, heiress of Bardowie in Stirling. He obtained his M.A. from Glasgow University at the early age of seventeen, and then, as his father had done, he studied medicine in Edinburgh, graduating in 1783.

One of Buchanan's fellow students was James Edward Smith, an ardent young naturalist who, at the age of twenty-four, bought the entire natural history collections, correspondence and libraries of Linnaeus from his widow, for a thousand guineas, and had them transferred from Sweden to England. In 1788 he founded the Linnean Society of London which Buchanan joined that same year.

During his twenties and early thirties Buchanan made four voyages to India and China as Surgeon to an Indiaman, and in 1794 he became an assistant surgeon with the Bengal Establishment of the Honourable East India Company. The following February he sailed for Burma with an embassy to the Court of Ava, and took every opportunity offered throughout the next ten months to expand his botanical collections. During the next two years while stationed in south-east Bengal he wrote about the botany, zoology, geography and religions of Burma, while trying unsuccessfully to return there. At the end of 1798 he was sent to Barrackpur, just north of Calcutta and there he began his monumental work on the fishes of the Ganges, making several journeys down to the mouths of that great river. He employed an elderly Hindu to draw the outlines of the fishes which he later filled in himself, in colour, but after two years the work had to be temporarily abandoned when he was sent to Nepal.

†No known portrait.

The Governor-General of India was at that time the Marquis of Wellesley, a man gifted with the ability to recognize and make the best possible use of the talents of his subordinates. Buchanan was a more than competent surgeon, but when some of his reports on the natural history of the country were brought to Wellesley's attention, his exceptional skills of investigation and observation immediately impressed the Governor-General who recalled him from the frontier and sent him to survey Malabar. Buchanan was instructed "to travel through and report upon the countries of Mysore, Canara, and Malabar, investigating the state of agriculture, arts and commerce; the religion, manners and customs; the history, natural and civil and antiquities in the dominions of the Raja of Mysore and the countries acquired by the Hon. East India Co. in the late and former wars from Tipoo Sultan."

Buchanan sailed to Madras and at the end of April began the long journey inland and through the mountains to the coast of Malabar. He sent back seeds to the Botanical Gardens at Calcutta and returned at the end of the following summer, later producing an exceedingly lengthy report on all the required topics. He was again posted to Katmandu for a year and produced a *History of Nepal*, but was delighted when he was transferred to Barrackpur once more and attached to Lord Wellesley's staff as his surgeon. He was also given the responsibility of looking after the extensive menagerie there, a task continued by the Amhersts and their staff some twenty years later. When Wellesley returned to England in 1805, Buchanan accompanied him, and he gave all his Nepalese specimens (some 1500 of them), along with all his drawings and manuscripts into the safe keeping of his old friend Dr J. E. Smith.

However, the thoroughness of Buchanan's survey of Malabar ensured that he was not allowed to remain long in Britain. At the age of forty-five he was given the daunting task of preparing a full topographical account of all the territories which formed the Presidency of Bengal, an area of approximately half a million square miles. It extended from the southern boundaries of Nepal and Bhutan to the coast of the Bay of Bengal, and included the entire Ganges Plain to as far west as Gorakhpur. Buchanan divided the area into districts, and spent a year in each, beginning in the eastern regions, then travelling to Purnea for 1809–10, Bhagalpur on the Ganges during 1810–11, upriver to Patna and then south to Gaya in 1811–12, and finally he journeyed westwards to Mirzapur and Gorakhpur in 1812–13.

During the cooler months he travelled continually, questioning the leading people at each place where he camped, and making daily marches, on which he

Grey-necked Bunting

made his own observations and added to his botanical and geological collections. In the hot weather and rainy season he established his headquarters at a town in or near the district concerned, completed his enquiries and wrote his reports. He had to devise his own methods of investigation as there were no previous accounts to draw upon, and the only existing maps, of 11 or 12 miles to the inch, often failed to show the roads and tracks, such as they were. Usually he travelled by elephant, sometimes on foot, and as his health began to deteriorate he longed to return to Scotland, but was unable to receive permission. In 1814 he was at last relieved of his surveying appointment, and granted a position by then better suited to his disposition and diminished energies, that of Director of the Botanical Garden in Calcutta to which he had so often contributed. The detailed reports on which he had laboured for seven years were strangely neglected by the Honourable East India Company, and they were not published until nine years after his death, when portions were collected together under the presumptuous title of *Martin's Eastern India.*

After two years at the Gardens, Buchanan was at last able to plan his final departure and with great care packed all the collections and drawings which he had made during the Bengalese survey, with the intention of preparing many of the accompanying notes and descriptions later, in Scotland. He was deeply shocked when the Governor-General, now Lord Moira, announced shortly before his departure that the drawings belonged to the Company and must be left in Calcutta. This inexplicable action rendered the 750 drawings of animals, birds, fish and plants almost worthless, although they were safely preserved by Nathaniel Wallich, Buchanan's successor at the Garden. The drawings included 147 birds from the Barrackpur aviary and 231 others from various parts of Bengal. It was in this collection, some years after Buchanan's death, that Blyth discovered the undescribed bunting which he designated *E. [mberiza] Buchanani.*

Buchanan returned to Scotland in the summer of 1816 and two years later, on the death of his elder brother, he inherited the estate which had been his mother's property, and therefore decided to take the additional name of Hamilton. Hating both towns and cities, he was content to remain at Leny for the rest of his life, brightening his gardens there by the introduction of many hardy exotics.

He made occasional trips to Glasgow to visit his friend and fellow botanist Joseph Hooker, and on a rare visit to London he retrieved the Nepalese botanical collection which he had deposited at the Linnean Society. He continued with his great icthyological work, *An Account of the Fishes found in the River Ganges and its branches*, begun twenty years earlier, and it was published in Edinburgh in 1822, with a separate volume of plates. The illustrations, however, were fewer than he had first envisaged, due to Lord Moira's unfortunate decision in India.

In 1821 the Marquis of Wellesley was appointed the Lord Lieutenant of Ireland and invited Buchanan-Hamilton to join his staff, but he declined—perhaps because, at the age of fifty-nine, he was about to be married. His wife, Anne, bore two children. Their daughter died in childhood, but their son John survived his parents and remembered his elderly father as a tall man with a ruddy complexion and white hair. In 1828 Buchanan-Hamilton took much pleasure in becoming the recognized head of the Clan Buchanan and died the following year, at Leny, on the 15 June, aged 67.

BULWER. *NORFOLK CLERGYMAN AND AMATEUR NATURALIST,*
MAINLY INTERESTED IN SHELLS. THE BULWER'S PETREL
WHICH HE COLLECTED OFF MADEIRA HAS A CURIOUS HIS-
TORY. THE PORTRAIT SHOWS HIM OUTSIDE THE CHURCH
DOOR AT HUNWORTH, IN NORFOLK, AT THE AGE OF SIXTY-
SIX.

James Bulwer
(1794-1879)

BULWER'S PETREL *Bulweria bulwerii* (Jardine and Selby)

Bulweria Bonaparte, 1843. *Nuovi Annali di Scienze Naturali, Bologna* 8 (1842), p. 426. Type by monotypy, *Procellaria bulwerii* Jardine and Selby
Procellaria Bulwerii Jardine and Selby, 1828. *Illustrations of Ornithology*, Vol. 2, Pl. 65 and text: Madeira or nearby

"We are indebted to the kindness of Mr. Bulwer, during some years a resident in Madeira, for the subject of this plate which we consider as yet undescribed. It is not to be found in the works of Latham or Shaw, or indeed in any other which we have had an opportunity of consulting; and from its marked characters it is not a species that would be easily overlooked. The length of our specimen is about ten inches; it inhabits Madeira, or the small islands adjacent."

This extract, together with a description of the petrel, appeared in 1828 in *Illustrations of Ornithology* by Sir William Jardine and Prideaux John Selby. They named the species *Procellaria Bulwerii* and gave it its English name. 'Bulwer' now appears in both parts of the scientific name and also appears in the French, Spanish, Dutch and German names, yet the Reverend James Bulwer had few connections with ornithology other than his correspondence with Jardine. Bulwer's Pheasant, of Borneo and Sarawak, is named after Sir Henry Bulwer, one-time governor of Labuan and no relation. The Reverend Bulwer was more interested in conchology and archaeology, and was better known for his association and friendship with the philosopher and traveller Alfred Lyall and the famous landscape artist John Sell Cotman—at his best, one of the finest of all English watercolourists.

James Bulwer was the son of James Bulwer of the Manor House, Aylsham in Norfolk and his mother Mary Seaman was originally from Norwich. He was born on 21 March 1794, educated at North Walsham School and was later at Jesus College, Cambridge, where he obtained his B.A. in 1818 and his M.A. in 1823. As an undergraduate he took drawing lessons from Cotman and became a Fellow of the Linnean Society on the strength of his knowledge and interest in 'Testaceous Mollusca'; one of his three proposers was William Elford Leach.

In 1818 Bulwer was made a deacon and in 1822 a priest. Between these ordinations, and after moving to Ireland, he married Eliza Redfoord of Dublin by whom he had three sons and one daughter. In 1823 he was appointed perpetual curate of Booterstown, Dublin, but by 1831 he was in Bristol and in 1833 he was curate of St James's Chapel, Piccadilly. Between his time in Ireland and London he spent at least two winters, perhaps four, travelling in Spain, Portugal and Madeira. One of these trips is recorded in *Rambles in Madeira and in Portugal, in the early part of 1826*. Written by his companion Alfred Lyall, but for some reason published anonymously, it gives a general account of their wanderings over the island. It was Lyall's first visit and because he knew little about natural history he benefited greatly from Bulwer's company: "I am very happy in my guide—having spent the last spring here, B. is perfectly at home in the country, of which he seems to know every lane and dingle. He is moreover a very quick observer and an ardent naturalist . . ."

Bulwer did less of the rambling than his friend as he often stopped along the way or remained behind in the villages to sketch. Twenty-six of his drawings were published in a supplementary volume as *Views in the Island of Madeira* (1827), and though sometimes very inaccurate due to artistic licence they are well carried out and show considerable talent.

The absence of roads meant that they usually travelled by pony but on one occasion, when on foot, they became lost in the mountains above Funchal. Low cloud had descended and they spent hours struggling over rocks and through dense vegetation until a break in the mist showed that they were going in completely the wrong direction. By late evening as they were approaching Funchal they were met by a party of villagers, with torches and horses, who had set out to look for them, and the two exhausted men were able to ride the last few miles back to their lodgings. Looking back on the incident Lyall admitted that the prospect of having to spend a night in the open had worried him because he knew that Bulwer was "something of an invalid". This supports a suggestion that these winter trips abroad were made on medical advice.

The appendix to Lyall's book is credited to Bulwer and contains a reference to a former visit to Madeira which included a twenty-mile crossing, in a large rowing boat, to a barren rocky island: "A party of us made an excursion to the middle or great Deserta, and passed the night there . . . We slept in a tent which we had brought with us. All night long there was a singular noise, like that of children crying, which we found proceeded from the mother Carey's chickens [petrels]. During the day these birds hide in the rabbit burrows."

Bulwer's Petrel

At present, three species of tubenose are known to breed on that island: Cory's Shearwater, Bulwer's Petrel and Madeiran Storm-petrel; and Little Shearwater and Soft-plumaged Petrel breed nearby. The sound that Bulwer described most probably came from the Cory's Shearwaters, nevertheless, it seems likely that Bulwer's Petrel was first collected on this brief expedition in the spring of 1825.

The second part of *Rambles in Madeira* deals with their return journey. In May 1826, after five months on the island they took passage for England but broke the voyage at Lisbon to make excursions to some of the surrounding villages. Lyall commented that "[We] suffered less from our beds than we had feared—they were clean; and I think we commonly had them to ourselves." One presumes that he was referring to fleas or bedbugs. Bulwer is said to have published *Views of Cintra in Portugal* in 1828 but this cannot be traced. In another winter he visited Spain.

When Bulwer sent his sons to King's College School he was able to rekindle his friendship with Cotman who became the school's drawing master in 1834. Two of Bulwer's sketches from Spain inspired Cotman's watercolours, *Alhambra at Granada* and *Toledo*, and another from Madeira forms the basis for *Cliffs on the North-east side of Point Lorenzo*. The two friends later worked together on drawings of scenery and antiquities in the Minehead district of Somerset which were intended to be bound up as a supplement to James Savage's *History of the Hundred of Carhampton*, but the work seems never to have been completed. Independently, Bulwer contributed to *Scenery in the North of Devon*, a collection of prints published in Ilfracombe, circa 1837.

Although views and antiquities were his usual subjects, Sir Hugh Gladstone had in his possession two sketches of birds by Bulwer "remarkable for their appreciation of detail".

As curate of St James's Chapel, Bulwer was present at the coronation of Queen Victoria in 1838 but a year later, when forty-four years old, he left London to return to Norfolk where he spent the rest of his life in quiet obscurity. At first he was the curate of Blickling with Erpingham, near Norwich, but later he changed curacies and moved to Old Stody Lodge and then the rectory at Hunworth.

The remaining years of his life were spent attending to his parishioners and continuing his interests in sketching, natural history and archaeology. Bulwer owned several hundred drawings and watercolours by Cotman and the year before the great artist died, the two of them spent some time travelling around the county. Many of Cotman's works remained in the Bulwer family until the 1920s but they are now to be seen in the Victoria and Albert Museum, the British Museum and other art galleries in Britain or in North America. As a clergyman naturalist, Bulwer cannot be compared with Canon Tristram or the Reverend Gilbert White; he collected only a few birds and wrote only one short paper related to natural history which concerned some molluscs from the Irish Sea. Nevertheless he gained pleasure from adding to his large collection of shells from time to time and also, between 1847 and 1879, contributed eleven papers to *Norfolk Archaeology* which include 'Gold Torques at Foulsham', 'Wendling Abbey' and a 'Notice on Wells Church'.

In 1945, Gladstone wrote that there were still a few people alive in the parish who could remember Bulwer "as an old man with a very long white beard who was taken about the village in a kind of push chair". He was buried in Hunworth graveyard on the north side of the church, and the cross erected over his grave bears the enigmatic inscription: Sacred to the Memory of/James Bulwer M.A./ of Jesus College/Rector of Hunworth and Stody/from 1848–1879/died 11 June 1879/That by any means I preach to others,/I myself might be a castaway. The last two lines are from I Corinthians Ch. 9 v. 27, and refer to St Paul's hope that after years of preaching the Gospel to others he himself would not have failed to earn his Father's approval and heavenly reward.

After Bulwer's death no obituary appeared in any scientific or archaeological journal, nor in *The Times*. It is also strange that in Jardine's own catalogue of birds there is no mention of the type specimen of Bulwer's Petrel nor of the Reverend James Bulwer. The main collection of over 8500 skins was not sold until several years after Jardine died. The British Museum tried to buy it but their offer was turned down as the sum was considered to be inadequate for so large and so precious a collection and it was eventually dispersed by public auction. As a result of bad organization and limited advertizing the sale was poorly attended and all the birds together fetched only £217 2s 6d—less than the museum's earlier offer. To his surprise, the buyer for the Natural History Department of the British Museum purchased the type specimen of Bulwer's Petrel amongst an unspecified lot of mounted birds for only a few shillings![1]

Edward Arthur Butler (1843-1916)

HUME'S TAWNY OWL *Strix butleri* (Hume)

Asio butleri [Hume], 1878. *Stray Feathers* 7, p. 316: Omara [= Ormara], Makran coast, Baluchistan

Recent observations have shown that Hume's Tawny Owl is not quite so rare as was first thought. Nevertheless very little is known about its breeding biology and distribution. It occurs in some arid parts of the Middle East, Saudi Arabia and Baluchistan; most sightings have been in Israel where it occupies many of the steep-cliffed wadis of the western edge of the Dead Sea depression.

So far there are only about ten specimens of this owl in museums throughout the world. The first and easternmost example was obtained in the latter part of the nineteenth century on the Makran coast of Baluchistan by Mr G. Nash of the Telegraph Department at Ormara.[1] Nash passed the bird on to Captain Butler who, in turn, forwarded it to Allan Hume. For many years the species was known only from this single skin and it became known as Hume's Tawny Owl despite the fact that Hume had honoured his friend Butler in the bird's scientific name. Hume named it, not so much for Butler's association with this particular bird, but because Butler had often supplied him with information and other specimens and, more importantly, because of his general contribution to Indian ornithology.

At that time a captain in the Indian Army, Butler was an excellent naturalist and marksman, an untiring walker, and expert at field identification. Hume once described him as the most accomplished taxidermist in India; praise indeed from Hume who was accustomed to receiving specimens from a vast network of collectors from all over the Indian Empire. Hume's opinion was re-affirmed by Bowdler Sharpe, at the British Museum (Natural History), who wrote: "Colonel Butler is one of the most artistic preservers of specimens that I have ever known, every single skin of his collections having been prepared with the most scrupulous care."[2]

Butler spent eleven years in India but army life meant that he was often on the move within and between countries. He was born at Coton House, Warwickshire, on 4 July 1843, the third son of the Honourable Charles Lennox Butler and grandson of the thirteenth Lord Dunboyne. At the age of twenty-one, after an Eton education, Edward Arthur Butler joined the 83rd Regiment

BUTLER. *BRITISH ARMY OFFICER WHO SERVED IN INDIA AND SOUTHERN AFRICA WHERE HE ENJOYED BIG-GAME HUNTING AND STUDYING AND COLLECTING BIRDS. HE WAS KNOWN ESPECIALLY FOR HIS WORK IN INDIA AND FOR HIS SKILL AS A TAXIDERMIST.*

and spent the next three years based at Gibraltar, where he quickly made contact with the ornithologist Howard Irby. It was Butler's first opportunity to collect birds abroad and on being transferred to India he began to collect in earnest. Many of his experiences and observations are recounted in Hume's *Nests and Eggs of Indian Birds* (1873) and in the short-lived journal *Stray Feathers*. To the latter Butler contributed an account of his voyage to the Gulf of Oman, which seems to have been his only excursion into the breeding range of *Strix butleri*.

Through the influence and instigation of Hume, Butler joined the Telegraph Steamer *Amberwitch* at Karachi which then proceeded 500 miles westwards as far as Jashk, near the Straits of Hormuz, and then returned more slowly, making a number of short business stops on the way back to Karachi. Butler collected at every opportunity and at Jashk shot four Desert Larks, one Kentish Plover, one 'English swallow' and enjoyed watching groups of Turnstones feeding amongst large flocks of flamingos. Elsewhere he procured skins of Sooty Gull and Swift Tern which were the two principal objectives of the voyage as far as Butler was concerned. On 29 May, as arranged, the steamer stopped for the entire day at Astola, a barren, uninhabited, waterless, rocky islet less than two miles long and less than a mile across. It was usually only visited by natives who came to collect turtles and their eggs. Butler had other ideas and wrote excitedly about the bird life there:

> "The cries of Larus hemprichii and Sterna bergii were almost deafening as we climbed the steep cliff side leading to the summit of the island, and with the exception of one or two Crested larks and a solitary swallow (Hirundo rustica) there was not another bird to be seen."[3]

Unfortunately for Butler he had arrived too soon. None of the gulls were yet laying and apart from the addition of thirty more skins he brought back 'only' ninety-three of the tern eggs, each one beautifully marked as though written upon in Arabic script. Butler teased his native helpers who believed him when he explained that the terns wrote on the eggs with their bills, so that when the birds returned from feeding out at sea they could each recognize their own clutches!

Later Butler managed to get more tern eggs through Mr Nash, who sent a boat out to the island from Ormara in mid-June; but still the gulls had not laid. The *Amberwitch* had called at Ormara during the voyage but in his account Butler only reported that he had collected some tropic birds there. Nash may have given Butler the Hume's Tawny Owl skin on this visit or he may have sent it on later; either way, Hume had received and named it by the following year, 1878.

Before being transferred southwards from Deesa to Belgaum, near Bombay, Butler managed to write his 'Last Notes on the Avifauna of Sind', for *Stray Feathers*. Amongst some other exploits he recounted how he and a friend, accompanied by some natives towing egg-boxes, had swum naked out to a huge heron colony in a tamarisk thicket and collected eggs from the nests of White Ibises, Darters, Purple Herons and cormorants. Butler claimed that he had never seen a more imposing sight than this great concentration of wetland birds. Other publications by Butler include a 'Catalogue of the Birds of Sind, Cutch,

Kathiawar, North Gujarat and Mount Aboo' and 'A Catalogue of the Birds of the southern portion of the Bombay Presidency', both of which appeared in the *Bombay Gazetteer* (1879 and 1880).

At the end of 1880, trouble flared up again in southern Africa between the Boers and the British who had annexed the Transvaal, and Butler was among those troops that were quickly dispatched to the Cape. He served with the Royal Irish Rifles in the Natal Field Force and for most of 1881 was stationed at Newcastle in the north-east of Natal. His ornithological interests continued unabated, however, and he sometimes managed to team up with the noted collector Captain Savile Reid and another character, Major Henry Fielden, who had studied birds in China and the Arctic (and who by a strange set of circumstances later served with the Confederate Army in the American Civil War). Together they wrote notes to *The Zoologist* and *The Ibis*, one to the latter being of special interest at the time as it helped to elucidate the remarkable variations in the plumage of the Mountain Chat.

At the end of the Transvaal Campaign Butler's regiment returned to Britain and was stationed at Alderney and then at Belfast. Soon afterwards, in 1884, Butler retired as a Lieutenant-Colonel at the age of only forty-one. He had served exactly twenty years in the army.

He went to live in the south-east of England, moving around between Bury St Edmunds, Bilderston and Lowestoft before finally settling at Winsford Hall at Stokesby, near Great Yarmouth. The hunting lodge there was bedecked with many of his big game trophies and some of his ornithological mementoes. He continued to busy himself with his collections although the bulk of his Indian specimens had gone to Hume, and his birds from Natal had been added to the Shelley collection. Butler then set about developing his interests in horticulture but after his wife died, in 1912, and as his own health began to fail he became increasingly reclusive and he took his own life, on a sudden impulse, on 16 April 1916, while in his seventy-third year.

Back in 1872, two years after his promotion to Captain, Butler had married Clara Francis, the second daughter of Major-General Francis of the Bombay Staff Corps. The first of their three sons, Arthur Lennox Butler, was born at Karachi in February 1873 and became Curator of the Selangor State Museum in Malaya and was afterwards Superintendent of Game Preservation in the Sudan from 1901 to 1915. He was a first-rate ornithologist and taxidermist and more

Hume's Tawny Owl

than 3000 of his beautifully prepared skins are at the British Museum (Natural History). A number of birds with the specific designation *butleri*, including the Nicobar Shikra *Accipiter butleri*, are named after the younger Butler, who from his earliest days had been instructed and encouraged by his father.

CANUTE. *KING OF ENGLAND, NORWAY AND DENMARK,
SHOWN HERE REBUKING HIS COURTIERS.*

Canute, or Cnut the Great (c. 995-1035)

KNOT *Calidris canutus* (Linnaeus)

Tringa Canutus Linnaeus, 1758. *Systema Naturae*, 10th edn, p. 149: Sweden

Immediately after the death of Canute's father Sweyn, King of England and Denmark, the English recalled their old king, Ethelred, from Normandy. Nineteen year old Canute was forced to leave England, but he returned in the summer of 1015 with a large Danish army and began to take possession of much of the country. Ethelred died and Canute fought five pitched battles with Ethelred's son, only managing to subdue the English army during a sixth encounter. Thereafter Canute showed himself to be an especially just and beneficial ruler, enforcing the old English laws and creating wise new ones. During his reign of twenty years the internal state of England was one of unprecedented peace and order. He died at Shaftesbury at the age of forty, and such was his personal influence that his large empire which comprised England, Denmark and Norway fell into disarray.

The connection between King Canute and the shorebird can be traced back to the 1607 edition of William Camden's *Britannia*.[1] Camden thought that the word 'knot' alluded to the well-known story concerning Canute, who rebuked his flattering courtiers by physically demonstrating that despite his huge empire he had no power to stop the incoming tide. Camden was only expressing his opinion that the Knot, which often frequents the tide edge, could be connected

Knot

with Canute, but later authors determinedly repeated the idea and Linnaeus compounded the theory by giving the bird the scientific name *Tringa Canutus*.

The word 'knot' is more likely to be derived from the sound of the bird's grunting call; while another idea suggests that the dense wintering flocks of the birds, at a great distance, sometimes resemble clouds of gnats. Either way, the scientific name refers to Canute, but 'knot' does not.

Francesco Cetti
(1726-1778)

CETTI'S WARBLER *Cettia cetti* (Temminck)

Cettia Bonaparte, 1834. *Iconografia della Fauna Italica*, Vol. 1, text to Pl. 29. Type, by original designation, *Sylvia Cetti* Marmora [= *S. cetti* Temminck] *Sylvia cetti* Temminck, 1820. *Manuel d'Ornithologie*, 2nd edn, Vol. 1, p. 194: Sardinia

Francesco Cetti was born in Mannheim, in southern Germany, on 9 August 1726, but his parents were both natives of Como, in northern Italy. He was educated in Lombardy and at the age of sixteen he entered the Jesuit College at Monza, where he took his solemn vows in February 1760. As well as being a good mathematician, he was highly regarded as a philosopher and theologian. Through the combination of study and writing, worship and teaching Cetti expressed his great love for God and man, and all creation, with an intellectual ability and a deep enthusiasm which impressed all who knew him. When the King of Sardinia, Charles Emmanuel III, invited the Jesuits to help improve the standard of education on the island, Cetti was one of a party of distinguished men who were sent there in 1765. The following year he was appointed to the Chair of Mathematics at the University of Sassari and he held that position until his death more than twenty years later.

Sassari was a small town in the north-west corner of the island, its university, cathedral and maze of narrow alleyways and piazzas still surrounded by medieval walls. Whenever he could, Cetti escaped from the confines of the town and made lengthy journeys into the mountains and along the coast. He constantly made new discoveries which he collated in his great work *Storia naturale della Sardegna* [Natural History of Sardinia]; succeeding volumes of which were published in 1774, 1776 and 1777. The first dealt with the quadrupeds so well that seventy-five years later J. W. Tyndale considered that it was still, by far, the best work on the zoology of the island. Cetti's second volume was devoted to ornithology and covered most of the Sardinian birds, including the rusty-coloured warbler which Marmora later dedicated to him. It also contained observations on the Greater Flamingos which the priest had often delighted in watching on the marshes at Cagliari, where they arrived about September in spectacular flocks of two or three thousand, and over-wintered until April.

CETTI. *JESUIT PRIEST WHO MADE THE BEST EARLY NATURAL HISTORY STUDY OF SARDINIA. NO AUTHENTIC PORTRAIT EXISTS. THIS PAINTING IN THE LUXURIOUS ASSEMBLY HALL OF SASSARI UNIVERSITY SHOWS CETTI AND G. G. MORIS, ANOTHER NATURALIST. THE ARTIST HAD TO RELY ON HIS IMAGINATION AND IT IS NOT KNOWN WHICH OF THEM REPRESENTS CETTI; BUT HE IS BELIEVED TO BE THE MAN WITH SPECTACLES.*

Icthyology was the subject of the next volume. The fourth described the insects and fossils, but Cetti became ill while he was nearing its completion and he died, at Sassari, on 20 November 1778, at the age of fifty-two.

Forty years later, Alberto della Marmora travelled extensively in Sardinia collecting both Eleonora's Falcon and Cetti's Warbler there. He found the warbler at Iglesias (and also on the mainland near Nice), and named the species *Sylvia Cetti*, in honour of the Jesuit priest who had pioneered research into the natural history of the island and who had first alluded to the warbler. Marmora's account of Cetti's Warbler appeared in *Memorie della Reale Accademia delle scienze di Torino* for the year 1820. However Temminck is credited as the first to fully describe the species because his description (from one of Marmora's specimens) was published earlier in the same year.[1] The English name was given soon afterwards by John Latham, in 1823.

At that time the breeding range of Cetti's Warbler was limited to the Mediterranean area, but at the beginning of the twentieth century it began a gradual progression northwards through France. The first reliable record of a Cetti's Warbler in Britain occurred in 1961 and since then numbers have increased with remarkable rapidity. They now breed in many southern counties as well as in Belgium and The Netherlands.

Cetti's Warbler

CLOT. *HIGH-RANKING FRENCH PHYSICIAN AND SURGEON IN EGYPT.*

Antoine-Barthélemy Clot (1793-1868)

THICK-BILLED LARK *Rhamphocorys clotbey* (Bonaparte)

Melanocorypha clot-bey Bonaparte, 1850. *Conspectus Generum Avium*, Vol. 1, p. 242: "ex Deserto Egypt"

The Thick-billed Lark is found in some stony desert regions of North Africa and the Middle East. The males have the unusual habit, during courtship, of carrying small pebbles in their curiously stout bills and presenting them to the females and these pebbles then pile up on the ground around the nest. The scientific name for the species is derived from Dr Clot who lived and worked in Egypt for over twenty-five years, and who first sent a specimen to Europe.

Clot was born at Grenoble on 5 November 1793, the son of Louis Clot, a sergeant-major in the Engineers. At the age of fifteen the young Clot went to Brignoles where he worked for four years under the supervision of a surgeon and a pharmacist. He had little formal training but he was intelligent and resourceful and after a period at the Marseilles Hospital he qualified as a doctor in 1820, and as a surgeon three years later.

In January 1825 he set sail for Alexandria to take up an appointment as physician to Mohammed Ali, the Viceroy of Egypt. Clot was soon also engaged in reorganizing both the civil and military health services there. In 1827 he founded and supervised the running of the medical school at Abou-Zabel Hospital, and despite serious religious objections he prevailed upon some of the Muslims to study anatomy by means of dissection. Clot was promoted to Public Health Inspector in 1833, became Director-General of the Egyptian Medical Services two years later and was frequently kept busy by outbreaks of cholera and other epidemics.

He took the opportunity to accompany [Sir] John Bowring to Syria in 1838 and together they visited Antioch, Aleppo and Damascus. In the Hauran (an area east of Galilee) Clot collected a number of rare books of the Druse, which he later presented to the King of Bavaria. Dr Bowring, commenting on Clot, said that "Wherever he went in Syria he was regarded as a public benefactor, and followed by crowds to be healed. I never saw such marks of popular confidence and affection." On Clot's return to Egypt in the following year he was sent on an unofficial mission to the French Government, and whilst in his home country published *De la peste observée en Égypte* (1840) and *Aperçu général sur l'Égypte* (1840). In the first of these he stated his conviction that the plague was not a contagious disease. The latter work was a concise and methodical review of the physical, social and political state of Egypt in which the natural history section dealt with the minerals, plants, mammals and birds as well as the different human races that were to be found there. However, the zoology and botany were written by other specialists who lived in Egypt.

In August 1840, shortly after his marriage, Clot returned to Egypt but following the deaths of Mohammed Ali and his son Ibrahim in 1848 Clot was obliged to give up his medical position and he returned to France. French nationals were out of favour with the new viceroy, the traditionalist Abbas I, but in 1854 he was succeeded by Sa'id Pasha who reversed the policy towards the French and granted them concessions concerning the construction of the Suez Canal. Under the new regime Clot was recalled to direct the health service once more and he continued to do so until his retirement. He settled at Marseilles and died there on 20 August 1868 at the age of seventy-four. An edited version of his memoirs appeared for the first time in 1949.

In the Thick-billed Lark's scientific name, and sometimes elsewhere, Dr Clot is referred to as Clot-Bey. The honorary title Bey was conferred upon him by Mohammed Ali in 1832, for his services during the terrible cholera epidemic of the preceding year.

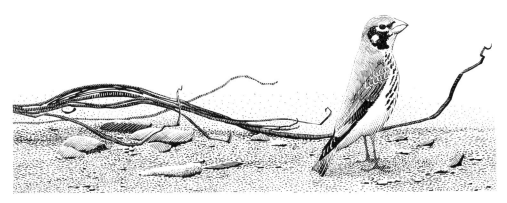

Thick-billed Lark

Charles Barney Cory
(1857-1921)

CORY'S SHEARWATER *Calonectris diomedea* (Scopoli)

Procellaria diomedia Scopoli, 1769. *Annus 1 Historico-Naturalis*, p. 74: No locality = Tremiti Islands, Adriatic

When the game of golf arrived in the United States Charles Barney Cory was among the first to take it up, becoming a skilful player and the champion of Florida. Soon he was designing golf clubs and writing articles for golfing magazines. He also excelled at billiards and was one of the best pistol shots in America, a favourite trick of his being to use a visiting card as a target—edge on. He took all of his sporting activities very seriously and most of his close personal friends were sportsmen. But he never allowed any of these interests to restrict his ornithological activities, in the pursuit of which he enjoyed a somewhat unusual advantage: a seemingly unlimited supply of money. This allowed him to go wherever he wanted, whenever he wanted, without the time-consuming handicap of having to earn a living.

Both sides of Cory's family had arrived in North America in the first half of the seventeenth century and had settled in New England. His father, Nathaniel B. Cory, had been apprenticed at the age of fourteen to a large import business and had amassed a huge fortune after becoming a partner in the firm, which dealt in fine wines, silks and other luxury items. Charles B. Cory was born on 31 January 1857 at his parent's imposing residence in Boston. When he was eleven he secretly bought a pistol and with another boy went off shooting birds. On hearing of this, far from being angry, his father encouraged him and had him expertly tutored in shooting as well as boxing, fencing and riding. When Cory was only sixteen he set off on his first expedition, with a friend, to the woods of Maine. The trip confirmed his passion for ornithology for within a year he had started a skin collection, later to grow to enormous proportions. After only a few years his collection of the birds of the Caribbean and the Gulf of Mexico was the best in existence, and Cory became the leading authority on the birds of that region.

When he was eighteen he went with his mother on a tour of England, France, Italy and Egypt. At Florence he met another American, Martin Ryerson, who became a lifelong friend with whom he journeyed up the Nile collecting specimens. About a year afterwards, Cory and Ryerson were room-mates at

CORY. *AMERICAN MILLIONAIRE, ORNITHOLOGIST, SPORTSMAN AND AUTHOR. HE TRAVELLED MAINLY IN THE EASTERN UNITED STATES AND THE CARIBBEAN AND BECAME A LEADING AUTHORITY ON THE BIRDS OF THOSE REGIONS.*

Harvard. Cory did less well academically, chiefly because his work was interrupted by the numerous excursions which he continued to indulge in. For example, in November 1877, he went on a trip to Florida for a few months, hunting, fishing and bird-collecting, and afterwards wrote an account of his exploits in *Southern Rambles*, a diary in peculiar nonsense style.

He never finished his studies at Harvard and lasted only a few months at the Boston Law School because he persisted in his life of travel. His trips were usually of short duration but they were frequent and intensive. He mainly concentrated on the eastern portion of North America, the islands of the Caribbean and the adjacent parts of Central America. In July and August of 1878 Cory made a trip to the Magdalen Islands in the Gulf of St Lawrence, wrote *A Naturalist in the Magdalen Islands* (1878), and by December he was in the Bahamas. He stayed until July, six months later his *The Birds of the Bahamas* was published and he went to Europe buying books and bird skins. By February of the following year he was collecting in Haiti, where he was a guest of the President for a brief period.

In 1882 Cory's father passed away and when his mother and sister also died he became the sole heir to the family fortune. In May 1883, a few months before becoming a founder member of the American Ornithologists' Union, Cory married Harriet Peterson who was a woman of charm and character with similar interests to his own. They had two children and to his wife's lasting credit she remained loyal and devoted to him when their circumstances were later to change so drastically.

Shortly after their marriage Cory had a summer house built on a 1000-acre estate near Hyannis on Nantucket Island. The grounds were stocked with large mammals such as elk and deer, and it was probably the first bird sanctuary in the United States.

Life for Cory seemed to continue much as it had done beforehand except that Harriet now often went with him on his expeditions. In the winter of 1884 they were in Florida and over the next twenty years spent at least part of every winter in the state. Cory was now employing collectors who either went with him or acted independently, and at Palm Beach he established the Florida Museum of Natural History where he took on a caretaker and taxidermist. It was a great local attraction but most of the birds were destroyed in a fire in 1903 and Cory often expressed regret at the unfortunate loss of so much of his early work. He also used Florida as a departure point for many of his trips to the West Indies, Cuba, Mexico and the south-west United States. Sometimes he went further afield: to Alberta big-game hunting, to Manitoba duck shooting with Ryerson, or to Europe for an International Zoological Congress.

By the age of thirty-five, Cory had amassed over 19,000 bird specimens which took up three large rooms of his Boston home. When the house was sold, the collection was moved to the museum of the Boston Society and afterwards to the Chicago Field Museum of Natural History where Cory became the Curator of Ornithology. The post was created especially for him by the trustees of the museum who included, amongst other friends, Martin Ryerson. It was really an honorary position which gave Cory some recognition by professional ornithologists, but at the same time allowed him to continue his way of life unhindered.

Although well known as a bird collector Cory had a reputation as an amateur and a playboy. Once when he was in Florida with Harriet, on his sloop, he met up with some of America's most noted professional ornithologists, but they thought him too unreliable and not single-minded enough to work with. Frank Chapman wrote to C. S. Allen: "Did you ever see such an uncertain man? He spends the greater part of his time in making plans, only to change and rechange them."[1] And William Brewster in a letter to Chapman commented: "The working part of the trip will hardly be to his taste and we are going for WORK, not merely to have a pleasant time."[2] Nevertheless, Cory got on well enough with Chapman to introduce him successfully to golf, and he considered Chapman, Brewster and Robert Ridgway to be among his few ornithological friends.

Suddenly, at the age of forty-nine, Cory lost his entire fortune. He was forced to sell all his property and was left with only a few personal effects. He renounced many of his former friends and moved his family to Chicago, where a salaried position had been found for him as Curator of Zoology at the Field Museum. Deskbound, he worked there untiringly for the rest of his life. He never really recovered from his losses which had been brought about by poor advice and heavy speculation, though he concealed any bitterness and managed to retain his wonderful sense of humour. He also continued to play golf but his club was far less exclusive.

At Chicago he added to his publications. *The Birds of Illinois and Wisconsin* (1909) was followed by a companion volume on the mammals. The latter work was produced partly to allay criticism that he was only an ornithologist in a zoological post; the book was well illustrated with maps and line drawings and remained one of the best works on mammals, for a particular region of the United States, for many years. His earlier publications had included *Birds of Haiti and San Domingo* (1885) and *The Birds of the West Indies* (1889). He had also devised a series of identification guides for the increasing number of interested people. In 1897 the *Key to the Water Birds of Florida* was followed by *How to know the Ducks, Geese and Swans* and *How to know the Shorebirds*. Each key was dichotomous and brief with a woodcut of a head, bill, wing pattern or other distinguishing feature set into the text, and they eventually led to the *Key to the Birds of Eastern North America* (1899–1900), mostly bought by wildfowlers.

His last major work was the four-part *The Birds of the Americas*. Assistants from the museum who were sent to Central and South America were instructed

Cory's Shearwater

by Cory to devote a good proportion of their time to collecting birds. By 1913, the museum finances were suffering and this ambitious fieldwork was discontinued, but Cory kept working and by December 1919 the second part had been published. The third part was ready shortly afterwards and Cory devotedly struggled on with the final part even though he had become partially paralysed. He was just able to continue his work at home if skins and books were brought to him and he pathetically strived to complete the work before his end came since he had been told to expect death at any time.

Cory died in late July 1921, while on a visit to a resort in Ashland, Wisconsin, where it had been hoped that his health would improve. A museum colleague later wrote in *The Auk*:

> "It has been said, that to him Ornithology was a game—the greatest and best game he played. If so he played it like other games, to win, and none knew better than he that winners never quit."

Responsible, directly or indirectly, for a great deal of exploration Cory discovered many new species. Among the mammals, the Florida Cougar *Felis coryi* is named after him and among the birds the rare melanisto-erythritic form of the North American Least Bittern is known as Cory's Least Bittern. The name Cory's Shearwater applies, strictly, to only one Atlantic race of the Mediterranean Shearwater. Cory's Shearwater breeds on Madeira, the Azores and the Canary Islands but Cory never saw them breeding. Towards the end of October they disperse and some birds reach north-east America between Cape Cod and Cape Hatteras. Somewhat unsuitably, Cory gave the sub-specific designation *borealis* to a specimen that he obtained at Chatham Island, Cape Cod, on 11 October 1880. The enthusiastic twenty-three year old showed it to some fishermen who returned in the afternoon with several more, shot from a flock which had flown close to their boat.[3] The term Cory's Shearwater was first coined by Herbert K. Job in the *Bulletin of the Nuttall Ornithological Club* in 1883, but since 1948 it has been used as a general name to also include the races of this shearwater that breed on the Cape Verde Islands and in the Mediterranean because they are indistinguishable in the field.

CRETZSCHMAR. *FOUNDER OF THE SENCKENBERG NATURAL HISTORY SOCIETY IN FRANKFURT. HE WROTE UP THE ORNITHOLOGY FOR SOME OF RÜPPELL'S TRAVELS.*

Philipp Jakob Cretzschmar (1786-1845)

CRETZSCHMAR'S BUNTING *Emberiza caesia* Cretzschmar

Emberiza caesia Cretzschmar, 1826. *Atlas zu der Reise im nördlichen Afrika von E. Rüppell—Vögel*, p. 17, Pl. 10, Fig. b: Kurgos Island, Nile River, Sudan

Cretzschmar was born on 11 June 1786 in Sulzbach (now in West Germany), where his father Otto was a minister; his mother was a seamstress and like her husband was originally from Frankfurt, about 100 miles to the north. The young boy showed an early interest in natural history by exploring the surrounding countryside, by keeping and taming animals, and by starting his own small zoological collection. At the age of eighteen he was studying at Würzburg and he then went to Halle to study medicine. In 1807, because of the Napoleonic Wars, he was forced to return to Würzburg where he finally obtained his medical degree. At the age of twenty-two he entered medical practice in Frankfurt, but was recruited as a doctor by the French army and after serving in military hospitals in Germany he did surgical work at Vienna, Paris and in Spain. When he was at last able to leave the army he returned to Würzburg and studied obstetrics under Elias von Siebold. He soon moved to Frankfurt where he took up medicine again and also started courses in anatomy, and instruction in field dressing for assistant surgeons in military hospitals; as a result of which the Senckenberg Medical Institute gave him a teaching post in anatomy and later in zoology.

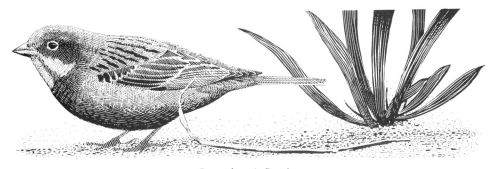

Cretzschmar's Bunting

On 22 November 1817 Cretzschmar founded the Senckenberg Natural History Society and presided over it for the next twenty-eight years. He worked tirelessly to augment its collections, until his death on 4 May 1845, in Frankfurt, at the age of fifty-nine.

Frankfurt-born Eduard Rüppell was one of the founder members of the Senckenberg Society and was its main early contributor of exotic specimens. In later years Rüppell disassociated himself from the society but to begin with the two naturalists co-operated well. Cretzschmar wrote the foreword and made various contributions to *Atlas zu der Reise im nördlichen Afrika von E. Rüppell* [Atlas of Rüppell's Travels in Northern Africa] (1826–30). The ornithological section, published in 1826, contained the descriptions of some thirty or so of Rüppell's newly-discovered birds, including Meyer's Parrot, Nubian Bustard, Goliath Heron, Scrub Warbler and the grey and rufous bunting that now commemorates the name of Cretzschmar. Compiled while Rüppell was still in Africa, the descriptions represent Cretzschmar's most significant written contribution to ornithology but they were said to be the initial cause of disharmony between the two men. All the birds had been collected during the course of Rüppell's 1822–25 travels through Egypt, Sinai and the Sudan. The type specimen of Cretzschmar's Bunting was a wintering bird obtained in the region of Kurgos Island, on the Nile, just north of Khartoum. Cretzschmar speculated that their breeding grounds would be found in the mountains of Ethiopia, but in fact the species breeds only in Greece and Turkey and some adjacent areas.

Other written works by Cretzschmar were two volumes on 'Religion and Freemasonry' (1838–44) and two volumes entitled 'Contributions to Studies of Life' (1840–43). The Cretzschmar medal is still awarded to deserving naturalists by the Senckenberg Foundation in Frankfurt.

Dixon Denham
(1786-1828)

DENHAM'S BUSTARD *Neotis denhami* (Children)

Otis Denhami Children, 1826. In D. Denham, *Narrative of Travels and Discoveries in Northern and Central Africa*, Vol. 2, App. xxi, p. 200: near Lake Chad

The existence of the River Niger, near Timbuktu, had been known in Europe for the greater part of the eighteenth century but its course was largely unknown. Some thought it flowed into a large inland sea, while others considered it to be a tributary of either the Congo or the Nile. When Mungo Park proved conclusively, in 1796, that the river's general direction of flow was eastward, John Barrow became convinced that the Niger was a tributary of the Nile and for several years he took a great interest in this portion of Africa. It was Barrow who was responsible for ensuring that Denham's travels in Africa were published; and it was Barrow, as Second Secretary to the Admiralty, who later encouraged the organization of at least two expeditions to ascend the Niger when its outlet into the Gulf of Guinea had finally been identified.

After Napoleon's defeat in 1815, Major Denham toured in Europe for a while and then, to further his taste for adventure, he requested a place on the Bornu Mission together with Walter Oudney and Hugh Clapperton. The expedition's objectives were manyfold but Oudney had been instructed to set himself up as British vice-consul at Bornu "with a view to the extension of commerce in that region"; and Denham "was to explore the country to the southward and eastward of Bornu, principally with a view to tracing the course of the Niger . . ."

It is not unusual for ill-feeling to develop during the course of expeditions but unfortunately, before this party of travellers had even met, a good deal of resentment already existed. Oudney and Clapperton were well underway when Denham was suddenly instructed to join them as expedition leader. This privileged position may have been bestowed upon Denham because of influential friends. Letters prove a connection between Denham and none other than the Duke of Wellington, though it is not clear how the connection began or the nature of its extent. It may possibly have dated from the time when Denham served as a Lieutenant in Wellington's army in Portugal and Spain, and in France where he had distinguished himself in the Battle of Toulouse of 1812 by carrying the severely wounded Sir James Douglas out of the line of fire.

DENHAM. *BRITISH ARMY OFFICER AND AFRICAN EXPLORER.*
HE CROSSED THE SAHARA FROM THE MEDITERRANEAN TO
LAKE CHAD AND BROUGHT BACK A SMALL NATURAL HISTORY
COLLECTION.

The expedition was to approach the Niger from the Mediterranean and after landing at Tripoli Denham made his way southwards across the desert to Murzuk. But, when he failed to gain the support of the local sheik, Denham set off back towards England leaving his companions without any orders. He had travelled as far as Marseilles when a message reached him informing him that if he returned an armed escort would be provided by the sheik to accompany him southward. Meanwhile, Oudney and Clapperton had decided to make good use of their time and had successfully explored an area west of Murzuk. Denham never forgave them for doing so without him and, but for the insistence of Barrow, Denham would have omitted many of their discoveries from the expedition narrative.

The three explorers and their attendants all eventually arrived at Kuka, near Lake Chad, in the early part of 1823 and from there they made several long excursions, Denham apparently enjoying his many adventures: he sanctioned a sortie to steal camels after his own had nearly all died in the desert, but on another occasion he only just escaped with his life when his own force of Bornuese were routed by an opposing force of natives. Denham partially explored Lake Chad and visited other areas to the south but in failing to circumnavigate the lake he failed to prove conclusively that no large river flowed out of it eastwards. He could not be blamed because the tribes on the shores and on the islands in the lake were more than unusually hostile; so much so that Denham considered that "50 men each with firearms would stand but a bad chance".

For much of this time, Oudney and Clapperton were exploring an area to the westward where they thought they had a better chance of finding the Niger. Oudney died of pneumonia and the general weakness of his condition. Clapperton reached a point only about five days travel from the river but was misled and prevented from reaching it by an obstructive chief. He retraced his route back to Kuka for a rendezvous with Denham, after which they began to plan their return homewards.

Denham's narrative of the whole expedition is often written as though he travelled alone and there are but few references to natural history. Near Tripoli, before he had really got underway, he took part in a falconry hunt and, much later, he reported that a large 'guana' and young crocodile were brought to him.

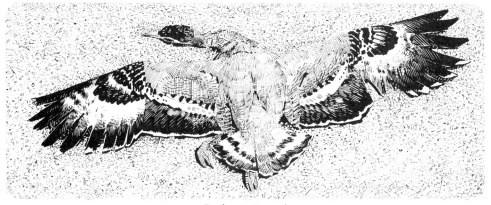

Denham's Bustard

He skinned them and dried them "and although this was a matter I had never before had the least experience in, or taste for, yet I became every day more and more interested in the collection and preservation of our specimens of birds and other animals".[1] Unfortunately, because of the obvious difficulties, only the horns of the larger mammals were brought back and not all the bird specimens survived the return journey intact. To prepare and preserve the skins, Denham had only a penknife and a small amount of arsenical soap left over from the stores of the Ritchie–Lyon expedition (see Dupont). The twenty-four species mentioned in the ornithological appendix by J. G. Children (and N. A. Vigors) included the Spur-winged Goose, White Pelican, Spoonbill, Darter and three species new to science: the Black-headed Heron, Clapperton's Francolin and Denham's Bustard. The latter was from the environs of Lake Chad, where, as Denham related, "a man brought a large bird, called oubara, or African bustard . . . this was exceedingly large, weighing as much as twelve pounds; and we gave him about two shillings for his present, in coarse cloth; and before breakfast this morning, he brought another still larger; but finding we had spoiled the market, for this I only gave him half as much. These birds are peculiar for the brilliancy of their large eyes, which exceeds that of the gazelle, and the flesh very much resembles our pheasants in flavour."[2]

At Kuka, Denham also began to surround himself with a small menagerie which included five parrots, four Ostriches, two monkeys, a civet cat, a young hyena and a young mongoose. Somehow, he managed to take the Ostriches and some of the other animals back to England alive. They were presented to King George IV and ended up in his majesty's zoological collection at Windsor!

Denham and Clapperton had arrived back in England, via Tripoli, after what can only be described as three years of hardship and ill-health, marred still further by a series of bitter disagreements between the two principal survivors. There is no doubt that Denham was supremely self-confident, arrogant and dictatorial but the blame is unlikely to have been his alone. Clapperton was a rebellious, fiery, one-handed adventurer who had once deserted his ship at Gibraltar.

Despite the limited success of the expedition, Denham's arrival in his home town of London was triumphant and within a year he was elected a Fellow of the Royal and Zoological Societies. He had little time to enjoy his new found prestige because he soon left England to take up an appointment as Superintendent, and later, Governor-General of Sierra Leone, arriving there in January 1827. Amongst his former travelling companions Denham had generally been the least affected by fever. Oudney was already dead and in 1827, whilst Lieutenant-Colonel Denham was on an official trip to the island of Fernando Po, Richard Lander brought the news to him that Clapperton, once more back in the Niger region, had died of fever and dysentery. Within a year, on 8 May 1828, Denham too died of fever, aged forty-two.

Five years later a traveller to Sierra Leone reported that: "He lies in the new burial ground behind the barracks under a young plum tree [palm tree?] . . . Poor Denham, after long braving the climate of Africa, said that his fate was sealed when he was appointed here. He then imprudently exchanged his residence from the government-house to a wooden building beside a creek, the mud of which, at low water, was most offensive. He also took to physicking himself, became soft and fleshy, and gradually sank under the fever. His grave is covered almost entirely with grass and bushes; and I was obliged to remove them before I could see the simple superstructure of brick and lime, raised over the mouldering remains of a traveller of first-rate enterprise."[3]

DUNN. BRITISH ARMY OFFICER, BIG-GAME HUNTER AND BIRD-COLLECTOR. HE SERVED IN SUDAN, ABYSSINIA, INDIA AND FRANCE. DUNN (ON LEFT, WITH HELMET ON KNEE) WAS PHOTOGRAPHED AFTER SHOOTING HIS FIRST ELEPHANT, NEAR THE WHITE NILE, IN DECEMBER 1899.

Henry Nason Dunn[1] (1864-1952)

DUNN'S LARK *Eremalauda dunni* (Shelley)

Calendula dunni Shelley, 1904. *Bulletin of the British Ornithologists' Club* 14, p. 82: Kordofan, Sudan

George Ernest Shelley, a nephew of the famous poet, was well known for his love of African birds; he produced the standard works, *The Birds of Egypt* (1872) and *The Birds of Africa* (1896–1912). Among the many new species which he designated were three African species of lark: Stark's Lark, Sclater's Lark and Dunn's Lark. Dr Stark had already been killed by a shell during the siege of Ladysmith, and W. L. Sclater was mortally wounded when a flying bomb hit his London home in 1944. Dunn only just escaped a similarly violent end when he was severely wounded in France, during the Great War.

The son of a doctor at Kinsale, County Cork, Dunn was born on 7 September 1864 and educated at Trinity College, Dublin, where he obtained a medical degree. He then joined the Royal Artillery Medical Corps and served with the British Army in Egypt and Sudan from 1896 to 1903. In his first year there he was involved in operations in Dongola and in the three following years he took part in army expeditions further up the Nile. He saw action on a number of occasions and was several times mentioned in dispatches.

Whenever time would allow, Dunn hunted big-game or collected birds. He shot his first elephant in December 1899 and his other trophies included a hippopotamus and a wide variety of horned ungulates. The pursuit of bustards

Dunn's Lark

and sandgrouse was also a favourite pastime. On a hunting trip to the Zeraf River, an extremely remote tributary of the upper Nile, there was an amusing incident. After a morning's shooting, Dunn and his Sudanese soldier-servants returned to camp and were astonished to find it occupied by another European. The stranger later recorded their phlegmatic greeting:

"Capt Dunn.   'How do you do?'
I.   'Oh, very fit, thanks; how are you? Had any sport?'
Capt Dunn.   'Oh, pretty fair, but there is not much here. Have a drink? You must be hungry; I'll hurry on lunch. Had any shooting? See any elephant?'
     Then we washed, lunched, discussed the war and eventually Dunn asked where the devil I had come from . . ."[2]

The weary traveller was Ewart Grogan who had arrived overland from Cape Town, over three thousand miles away! The chance meeting with Dunn assured Grogan of a safe passage downriver and he eventually completed his journey to Cairo, thereby becoming the first person to traverse the continent from south to north.

About four years later, on a similar hunting foray, Dunn came upon a new species of lark. Still of uncertain status within the Western Palearctic, Dunn's Lark was first found at Ogageh Wells in Western Kordofan, in November 1902. In all, Dunn contributed 234 specimens of birds and eggs from the regions surrounding Khartoum and the White Nile to the British Museum (Natural History). There were many interesting species, and in 1906 Bowdler Sharpe commented that anyone writing on the ornithology of the Eastern Sudan should examine them. From 1903–04 Dunn served with the Abyssinian Expeditionary Force in Somaliland but sent only six birds to the museum. His African collection of ninety mammals presented to the museum included the types of twelve new species.

In 1908 he was transferred to India, where he was based on the North-west Frontier and continued to enjoy his customary hunting activities. He trekked way up into the mountains of Kashmir to search for bear and ibex, and on the plains of the Punjab he shot snipe, duck, quail and other gamebirds. On one occasion, near Multan, his bag included twenty brace of Black Francolins and twenty-six brace of Indian Grey Partridges.

During the Great War Dunn served in France as Assistant Director of Medical Services for the 8th and then the 25th Divisions. After the war, and after recovering from his wounds, he was with the 10th Army Corps of the British Army of the Rhine. By the time he left the service in 1923, Dunn had been awarded both the C.M.G. and the D.S.O., and had risen to the rank of Colonel. During his long retirement he lived at Bath, in Somerset. He was a keen angler and gardener, and belonged to the Bath Golf Club besides being on the board of Governors of the Royal National Hospital for Rheumatic Diseases and the Eye Infirmary. When the Second World War began he insisted on joining the Home Guard, even though he was then in his late seventies.

In his last few years, blindness eventually forced him to give up his many activities and he died at home, on 21 October 1952, in his 89th year. He was survived by his wife, Maud, a daughter and his son Colonel Henry G. M. Dunn.

Léonard Puech Dupont† (1795-1828)

DUPONT'S LARK *Chersophilus duponti* (Vieillot)

Alauda Duponti Vieillot, 1820. *Faune Française*, p. 173: Provence

When Louis Vieillot first described this interesting and unusual lark he simply stated that it had been made known to him by Monsieur Dupont, a naturalist who had found the bird in Provence. The collector's forenames were probably omitted because Dupont was so well known in French natural history circles that no further identification was necessary. The most likely candidate would therefore appear to be Léonard Puech Dupont.

L. P. Dupont was born at Bayeux, in Normandy, in 1795. As a youth he showed a distinct taste for natural history and often took time off from his modest employment to collect insects and other animals in the surrounding countryside. He later frequented the Jardin des Plantes at Paris where he discussed his recent finds, attended a variety of courses given by eminent scientists and then began to concentrate on anatomy and surgery. With the fall of Napoleon in 1815, Dupont lost his position with the Minister of Finance and was unable to support his studies.

At around this time the English surgeon Joseph Ritchie, Private Secretary to the British Ambassador in Paris, began making plans to penetrate southwards across the Sahara to search for the Niger; the impetus for the venture apparently

Dupont's Lark

†No portrait traced.

coming from Sir John Barrow. In 1817, Ritchie hired Dupont "for the purpose of collecting and preparing objects of natural history". They sailed from Marseilles and in September arrived at Malta, where George Francis Lyon, then a Royal Navy Lieutenant, and John Belford, a shipwright, both volunteered to join them. At the end of November they were all assembled in Tripoli and were forced to remain there for several weeks because of various delays. In preparation for their journey they all adopted full Moorish dress, had their heads and beards shaved, and each of them also took an Arab name—Dupont calling himself Mourad. By the end of the following year Ritchie had died at Murzuk 450 miles to the south while Lyon and Belford managed to struggle only a little further into the Libyan desert before returning homewards.

Unfortunately, Lyon's full account of the expedition (*A Narrative of Travels in Northern Africa in the years 1818, 19, and 20*) gives us little information about Dupont's activities since he is not mentioned beyond page twenty! Just before the party left Tripoli, on 7 February 1818, Dupont resigned, "influenced, as we had reason to think, by the advice and suggestions of some of his supposed friends". Nevertheless, when Dupont returned to Paris after an absence of fifteen months he had with him a large collection of birds, reptiles and insects, over 200 of which were said to be new to science.

Little is known about Dupont during the next few years and it is unclear whether or not he set himself up as a commercial dealer in natural history specimens. He certainly modelled wax faces and figures for foreign collectors and two of his busts, of Laplace and Linnaeus, were both placed in a Paris museum. He died in the city in 1828.

The supposition that Léonard Dupont is the person after whom Dupont's Lark is named is supported by the fact that Vieillot's description of the bird was published in 1820, the year after Dupont's return from Tripoli, an area where Dupont's Lark is known to be a resident breeder. However, Vieillot clearly stated that the specimen he described had been found in Provence, in southern France, where the species is only occasionally recorded. There could have been a mistake about the specimen's origin or, alternatively, Dupont collected the bird in Provence either on his outward or return journey through Marseilles. In the absence of any positive link between the lark and Léonard Dupont the possibility remains that the new species was collected there by another naturalist by the name of Dupont.

Dupont's Hummingbird *Tilmatura dupontii*, native to Mexico and Nicaragua, was so named in 1829 but the dedication by Lesson relates only that Monsieur Dupont was a Parisian natural history dealer. Mulsant and Verreaux in their book on hummingbirds say that this man died in July 1873 at the age of seventy-five.[1] When Dupont's Lark was named this other Dupont would have been about twenty-two years old and could instead be the person after whom the lark is named. He might even have been a relative of Léonard Dupont carrying on a family tradition.

Eleonora of Arborea
(c.1350-1404)

ELEONORA'S FALCON *Falco eleonorae* Gené

Falco Eleonorae Gené, 1839. *Revue Zoologique*, p. 105: Sardinia

This remarkable falcon bears the name of a remarkable princess. Eleonora's Falcon is dark, slim and rakish, similar to the Hobby but with longer wings, body and tail. It is the only European raptor which has adapted its breeding cycle to coincide with the autumn migration. The eggs are not laid until late July or August, so that by the time the young falcons hatch, millions of small birds are streaming southwards to their winter quarters.

Surprisingly, in view of the long tradition of falconry in Europe, Eleonora's Falcon was not described until 1839, despite the fact that it breeds in colonies on many of the Mediterranean islands. The Italian naturalist and historian, Alberto della Marmora, shot several specimens in 1833 or earlier when he visited the little island of Toro, at the south-western extremity of Sardinia, six miles beyond Cape Sperone. The falcons frequent the high, sandstone cliffs which rise precipitously out of the sea on the eastern side. Where the ground slopes in open terraces, Herring Gulls and Audouin's Gulls nest among the yellow flowers and Shags gather together on the sea-beaten rocks to the lea of the island. The falcons here are well placed for catching Swifts, Swallows, Redstarts, Wheatears, Whinchats and other migrants. When there is a shortage of prey, they and their neighbours from Vacca Island raid the nearest portion of the Sardinian mainland for Cirl Buntings, Goldfinches, Woodlarks and other small passerines. Marmora sent his falcon skins to the zoologist Giuseppe Gené, in Turin, who named the species after Eleonora of Arborea, the Sardinian *giudicessa* (ruler or judge) who is still the islanders' greatest heroine.

Eleonora gained fame, not just as a military leader who led her troops into battle, but also as a politician and as the legislatress responsible for the *Carta di Logu*, a code of laws which later earned her Gené's admiration. In 1840 he wrote of "her admirable wisdom in the century of barbarities in which she reigned to protect the honour, the life and the goods of the people".[1] She also protected the hawks and falcons in her dominion by prohibiting the taking of young from the nest.

In the fourteenth century Sardinia was divided into *giudicate* or provinces, each ruled by a *giudice*. Eleonora's father, Mariano IV, had been brought

ELEONORA. *SARDINIA'S NATIONAL HEROINE, FAMED FOR HER*
INFLUENTIAL CODE OF LAWS. HER MARBLE STATUE WAS ERECTED
IN THE PIAZZA ELEONORA, IN ORISTANO, IN 1881. SIDE PANELS
DEPICT HER CIVIL AND MILITARY TRIUMPHS.

up at the Aragonese Court in north-east Spain but in 1346 he became *giudice* of Arborea, and so lived on the west coast of the island. In order to strengthen his local alliances he married Eleonora to Brancaleone Doria, a nobleman from a wealthy and influential Sardinian family. They were singularly ill-matched. Soon afterwards, in a battle in 1368, the cowardly Brancaleone deserted to the Aragonese and it was left to Eleonora's brother, Ugone, to lead the Arboreans to victory. When their father died from the plague eight years later, Ugone succeeded him and continued the war against the Aragonese, but in March 1383 there was an uprising: Ugone and his daughter were murdered. The insurgents tried to destroy the entire reigning family with the intention of forming a republic and Brancaleone fled to Aragon for safety. Bearing arms, Eleonora rode out at the head of those troops who were still faithful to her and speedily defeated the rebels. Her eldest son Frederick was officially declared *giudice*, but as he was only an infant, Eleonora had the population swear their allegiance to the young boy and she became regent.

During the next four years Eleonora successfully waged war until she was in a strong enough position to negotiate a favourable treaty with the Aragonese. However, before a treaty could be concluded the King of Aragon and young Frederick of Arborea both died. The new king continued negotiations and she was persuaded to give up some towns, including Sassari and Villa Ecclesia, but Arborea was independent and remained so until 1410.

Brancaleone had spent the last few years in close confinement at the southern port of Cagliari but on his release he at last supported his wife and son, now Mariano V. Together they formed an alliance with the Genoese and with the aid of their fleet subdued nearly the whole of Logudoro. When the King of Aragon died, his brother proposed a truce which Eleonora accepted and which secured the prosperity and honour of Arborea during her lifetime.

Despite the repeated warfare, Eleonora had found time during those years to compose the *Carta di Logu*, named after her lands in Logudoro, and it became effective in April 1395. John Warre Tyndale, who produced a detailed three-volume survey of Sardinia in 1849, considered that, "The framing of a body of laws so far in advance of those of other countries, where greater civilisation existed, must ever be the brightest ornament in the diadem of the *Giudicessa*."

Eleonora's Falcons off Toro

The ideas had been proposed by her father but it was Eleonora who composed the comprehensive laws designed to solve the problems of her day. For example, to deter sheep stealing, the *Carta* ruled that anyone possessing a sheepskin had to be able to prove its origin. Because the consequences of fire could be so serious on such a dry and windswept island, the laws against arson (or even carelessness) were severe. If anyone lit a fire anywhere in the countryside in the summer he had to pay a large fine; if the fire caused damage he lost an ear. If it was proved to be arson the fine was so stupendous that he was unlikely to be able to pay it and so lost his right hand. Urban arson was punished with death by burning. The laws which protected hawks and falcons were similar to those elsewhere in Europe and were intended to preserve falconry for the nobility. The penalty for most crimes was a fine; the wives and children of offenders were never punished and possessions and property were never confiscated. It was widely recognized as a humanitarian code which greatly benefited the people, and as a remarkable achievement for those times.

By 1422 the *Carta* had become effective throughout almost the whole island and was still in use when Marmora collected the type specimens of Eleonora's Falcon. It was only superseded on Sardinia's unification with Italy in 1861. The original *Carta* now rests in the University Library of Cagliari. It is in bound form and contains 198 chapters in fine, close script.

In either 1403 or the following year, Sardinia's national heroine died of the plague. She is said to have been buried in Oristano, in the Church of Santa Chiari.

Eduard Friedrich Eversmann (1794-1860)

YELLOW-EYED STOCK DOVE *Columba eversmanni* Bonaparte

Columba eversmanni Bonaparte, 1856. *Comptes Rendus de l'Académie des Sciences de Paris* 43, p. 838: western and central Asia

EVERSMANN'S REDSTART *Phoenicurus erythronotus* (Eversmann)

Sylvia erythronota Eversmann, 1841. *Addenda ad celeberrini Pallasii Zoographium Rosso-Asiaticum*, Pt 2, p. 11: Altai

The Yellow-eyed Stock Dove and Eversmann's Redstart were both first discovered by Eduard Eversmann. The stock dove is a native of northern India and Afghanistan but has occasionally been recorded in the Soviet Union, around the Aral Sea. The redstart is slightly larger than the better known Redstart of western Europe and the male has a dark rufous back and a grey head with an almost white forehead. It is a rare passage migrant and winter visitor to Transcaspia and southern Iraq, and breeds outside the Western Palearctic from the mountains of Kashmir to western China.

The name of Eversmann will probably be more familiar to older birdwatchers, since Eversmann's Warbler was a name in common usage until about thirty years ago, when it was changed to Arctic Warbler.

Born on 23 January 1794 in the village of Hagen in Westphalia, Eduard Eversmann was later educated at the Universities of Marburg, Halle, Berlin and Dorpat. In 1814, at Halle, he received his degree of Philosophy and Master of Liberal Sciences and not long after he went to Russia to join his father, who was then the director of the Imperial Ordnance Factory at Slatovsk, in the Urals. Eduard completed his education at Dorpat, graduated in 1817 as a Doctor of Medicine and Surgery, and practised for a time at his father's house in Slatovsk. Over the next three years Eversmann made frequent trips into the southern Urals collecting mammals, birds, insects, plants and geological specimens, most of which he sent to Hinrich Lichtenstein, the director of the Berlin Museum.

EVERSMANN. *GERMAN NATURALIST WHO BECAME WELL RESPECTED FOR HIS STUDIES IN SOUTH-EAST RUSSIA. IN HIS YOUTH HE MADE A PARTIALLY SUCCESSFUL EXPEDITION TO BUKHARA WHICH RESULTED IN THE DISCOVERY OF SEVERAL NEW BIRD SPECIES.*

Interested in natural history since his youth, Eversmann had ambitious plans. As early as 1813, when only nineteen, he had devised a scheme to travel as a naturalist eastwards into central Asia. To this end, although mineralogy and entomology were his chief interests, he made an effort to study mammals, birds and plants; he also studied the languages, customs and Muslim religion of the peoples whom he expected to come into contact with, and through meeting sundry Khirgiz and Bukhara traders in Russia, he learnt about the various trade routes to the East that were then in use. By combining the callings of doctor and merchant he hoped to travel into areas never before penetrated by European naturalists. He applied for, and received, both practical and financial help from Germany, and through the influence of the Military Governor of Orenburg he obtained the backing of the Imperial Russian Government, which appointed Eversmann official doctor to the Negri Mission to Bukhara.

Eversmann's Redstart

In the autumn of 1820, disguised as a merchant and accompanied by several traders, he set off for Bukhara, famous then, as now, as a trading point for exotic rugs and carpets. The results of the expedition appeared in *Reise Orenburg nach Buchara* (1823), with a thirty-seven-page natural history appendix by Lichtenstein, in which are described such new discoveries as the White-tailed Plover, Desert Finch and Booted Warbler. Eversmann's own account was at first in diary form and mainly gave details of the distances travelled, the stops that were made along the way, and some geological information. Once at Bukhara, he described the city's sordid narrow streets and its 360 mosques, many of which still stand despite numerous earthquakes, and which are currently being restored; their tiled domes of azure-blue adding colour to the otherwise drab metropolis. Eversmann went on to give a most unflattering account of the Khan, his tyrannical regime and the various sexual vices of his subjects. Several sections are devoted to the countryside surrounding the city, where the cultivation and irrigation of the fields was mostly carried out by slaves, the majority from Persia. More than half the section on natural history, however, is taken up by a crude eye-witness description of copulating camels. Of the three engravings in the book, one depicts the two camels in action, "drawn from nature"; the others show the tomb of a famous Khirgiz and a plan of the city.

After three months in Bukhara Eversmann prepared to join a caravan about to travel eastwards to Kashgar, in the westernmost part of China. Unfortunately, he was denounced as a Russian spy to the Khan, who issued instructions that he was to be murdered as soon as he was well away from the city. Hearing of this, Eversmann promptly headed as fast as possible back towards Russia. By now it was spring and when he felt safe to do so, he paused to collect specimens.

Thirty years before, Pallas had commented on the uniform appearance of the steppe country and Eversmann also found it similarly uninspiring:

> "The journey through the everlasting Steppes is, I agree, somewhat tedious to read about and I can sympathise with the gentle reader who ploughs through the following pages. I can however assure him that the reality is a great deal more tedious. You can read through my book in an evening but we had to trudge through the weary wastes for two months and nine days. Tough travelling."

On his return, despite the blow to his plans, Eversmann was able to console himself by marrying the daughter of a Tartar aristocrat. The marriage provided him with financial independence, allowing him to give up his medical practice at Orenburg each summer, and to spend the time on his estate or on journeys to neighbouring provinces. In 1825 he joined the armed expedition of Colonel Berg to Khiva, 250 miles north-west of Bukhara, but after that he settled upon a more academic career although he continued to travel occasionally. (For example, he was in Provence and Algeria in the winter of 1852–53.) He was appointed ordinary Professor of Zoology and Botany at Kazan University in 1828. Of his fifty-five publications more concern entomology than any other subject but two University publications, in Russian, outline his early activities there: 'A Journey from Kazan to various places in the Provinces of Orenburg and Astrakhan, and along the shores of the Caspian' in 1829, and, a 'Report to the Council of the University of Kazan after completing a Journey to the Caucasian Mountains' in 1830. For the next thirty years Eversmann specialized in the natural history of the Ural–Volga region, and the elaboration of the flora and fauna of the steppe in the neighbourhood of Kazan is primarily due to his efforts.

Dr Eversmann was a member of ten learned societies including the Moscow Naturalists, the St Petersburg Academy of Sciences, the Senkenburg in Frankfurt and the Stettin Entomological Society. When he died, after a prolonged illness, on 14 April 1860, he was still Professor at Kazan. A colleague declared that he had earned "one of the most honourable places in the history of science of our country".

His most extensive ornithological work appeared in his 'Natural History of the Orenburg Region', published between 1840 and 1850. The first volume consisted of a general introduction and review, the second concerned the mammals, while the ornithology, in the third part, consisted solely of a

Yellow-eyed Stock Dove

description of each of the species. For many years it was the only work on the identification of birds that was widely available to Russian readers. An earlier, and better work on the subject, was his *Addenda ad celeberrini Pallasii Zoographium Rosso-Asiaticum* which was published, again in three parts, in 1835, 1841 and 1845. Originals of this work are extremely rare because a fire at the publishing house destroyed most of the stock. When Dresser reprinted it in exact facsimile in 1876, he stated that he knew of only one complete copy of the original. This belonged to Hugh Strickland and was given to Cambridge University after Strickland was knocked down by an express train. Examination of the work, however, throws little light on the circumstances surrounding Eversmann's discovery of the redstart that now bears his name. Apart from the classical description and some measurements, he adds only that it was "killed 5 March, in the rocky mountains of the Altai, near the village district of Uimon".

The Yellow-eyed Stock Dove was one of the birds brought back from Eversmann's youthful venture to Bukhara but Lichtenstein thought that it was only a variant of the Stock Dove. Bonaparte gave it specific status and chose to name the bird after Eversmann.

FINSCH. *IMPORTANT PRUSSIAN ORNITHOLOGIST, CURATOR, AUTHOR, TRAVELLER AND COLLECTOR. HE IS BEST REMEM-BERED FOR HIS MONOGRAPH ON THE PARROTS AND HIS WORKS ON THE BIRDS OF EAST AFRICA AND POLYNESIA.*

Friedrich Hermann Otto Finsch (1839-1917)

FINSCH'S WHEATEAR *Oenanthe finschii* (Heuglin)

Saxicola Finschii Heuglin, 1869. *Ornithologie Nordost-Afrika's*, Vol. 1, p. 350: "Siberia", specimen probably mislabelled [Syria is suggested by Meinertzhagen, 1930. Nicoll's *Birds of Egypt*, p. 273]

Dr Otto Finsch was one of the great ornithological explorers of the nineteenth century. A Prussian, he was born in Silesia (now mainly in south-west Poland) on 8 August 1839. His father expected him to enter the family business as a tradesman and painter on glass, but after his apprenticeship Finsch left his home town of Warmbrunn and travelled to Bulgaria where he worked as a private tutor for over a year. Already a keen student of natural history, he taught himself all that he could on the subject and at the age of twenty published his first paper, in the *Journal für Ornithologie*, on the birds of Bulgaria. It was to be followed by important works on birds from every quarter of the globe: New Guinea and Polynesia, Japan, Australia and New Zealand, Siberia, California and Alaska, Lapland and many other countries.

Shortly after his return from south-east Europe, Finsch became assistant curator at the Dutch National Museum in Leyden, where he gained a much wider knowledge of ornithology and became acquainted with the techniques of museum work under Professor Hermann Schlegel, who had just recently taken over the directorship after the death of Temminck. In 1864 Finsch moved to Germany where he was the Curator of the Bremen Museum for the next fourteen years, a period of prolific writing and extensive travel.

In 1867 he published the first of two volumes of *Die Papageien*, a monograph on the parrots of the world, one of the best pieces of systematic work of that period and which earned him an honorary doctorate from the University of Bonn. With Dr Gustav Hartlaub he produced *Beiträge zur Fauna Central-Polynesiens* (1867), chiefly on the ornithology of Polynesia. Three years later they collaborated again on *Die Vögel Ost-Afrikas* [The Birds of East Africa] (1870), an exhaustive study of the collections and observations made by Baron von Decken which became the standard reference for the area for many years. Finsch also collated systematic lists of the birds of Australia, New Zealand and

Samoa from studying museum skin collections. Around 1870 he began to contribute regularly to *The Ibis*, having made the acquaintance in 1864 of various English ornithologists on his visits to the Natural History Department of the British Museum, to study parrot skins, and at the age of thirty-two he was elected an Honorary Member of the British Ornithologists' Union. Soon afterwards he went to California and then, in the summer of 1873, he crossed Lapland from the Altafjord to the Varangerfjord.

In 1876 he made a zoological exploration of western Siberia accompanied by Alfred Brehm and Count Karl von Walburg-Zeil-Trauchburg. They left Nishni-Novgorod (Gor'kiy) on 19 March and for the next month travelled along appalling roads until they came to Omsk. From there they pushed on to Semipalatinsk, noting on the way that Hooded Crows and Magpies were building their nests just a few feet above the ground in bushes, as there were few large trees. Rose-coloured Starlings were plentiful, occurring in flocks of up to a thousand birds, so that on one occasion a single shot brought down twenty-five of them. Early in May Finsch led his party into the Altai, on the Russo–Mongolian border, where they explored high into the mountains until they reached the snowline. There they enjoyed hunting both mammals and birds, including the largest race of wild sheep, the Altai Argali *Ovis ammon ammon* with their large strangely curved horns, and the aggressive, noisy little Bluethroat, which Finsch was interested to discover was of the red-throated form. Around the shores of one large lake he watched more kites and eagles than he had ever seen before, counting fifteen Black Kites perched in one dead tree.

By late June the explorers had reached Barnaul, and from there they turned their attentions northwards and headed for the Arctic Ocean, travelling by boat down the River Ob, their plan being to explore some of the low-lying land between the Ob and the Urals before they reached the coast. Unfortunately, they were plagued by an abundance of mosquitoes and a dearth of food and fuel. Much precious time had to be spent hunting Willow Grouse and waders for sustenance, and the only White-fronted Goose which they obtained was a welcome addition to their diet. Common breeding birds of the areas that they traversed were Arctic and Pomarine Skuas, Temminck's Stints, Ruffs and Great Snipe. They also found ground-nesting Peregrines on the tundra, while other pairs used the cut banks of the river, most having three or four young still in the nest. Altogether, Finsch obtained specimens of 283 species during the course of the expedition, a brief but rather turgid account of which later appeared in *The Ibis* (1877).

Just two years later, at the age of thirty-nine, Finsch resigned his curatorship so that he could travel again. During the next four years, accompanied by his first wife Josephine, he visited the Polynesian Islands, New Zealand, Australia and New Guinea, seeing many of the birds which he had hitherto only studied as skins. After crossing the Atlantic he visited Professor Baird at the Smithsonian Institute in Washington. He then travelled to San Francisco, from whence he sailed to Honolulu and on to the Marshall Islands, an archipelago with a rather limited avifauna, but which he long remembered as a result of almost being shipwrecked there. The only moment of ornithological excitement occurred when King Kabua and his family visited the collector, bearing a very rare bird which they had never seen before; Finsch, however, was singularly unimpressed when they presented him with a Wigeon!

On Nawado, one of the Phoenix Islands, Finsch found that some of the natives kept Brown Noddies and Turnstones as pets. The latter were kept singly, or in pairs, in cup-shaped cages and were highly esteemed by the villagers who set the pugnacious little waders to fight against each other, much as Europeans then used fighting cocks for sport. Finsch spent the next seven months investigating the birds of New Britain and acquired 102 of the 112 species known to occur there at that time. Shortly after he left, another German collector, Theodor Kleinschmidt, was killed there by the natives.

Finsch moved on to New Zealand where he stayed for eleven weeks travelling extensively on both islands, through woods, swamps, plains, lakes and the alpine regions. It was outside the breeding season and he was disappointed in the bird life with regard to both variety and density, seldom seeing more than a dozen species in a day. Many of the commonest birds (House Sparrows, Skylarks, Greenfinches, Goldfinches, Chaffinches, Starlings, Indian Mynas and Pheasants) had been introduced, and were still being released in great numbers, although societies dedicated to the extermination of *Passer domesticus* were already beginning to develop. Finsch naturally took a particular interest in the parrots, especially the hardy Kea which he first saw amidst the wild and icy terrain below Mount Cook. He expected their rapid extinction, partly because of their palatable flesh, and more particularly because of their unpopular habit of attacking sheep and eating the fat of their kidneys, but fortunately, his pessimistic prediction has not been fulfilled.

On leaving New Zealand Dr Finsch sailed to Sydney and after a while collecting in the north of Australia on Cape York, he crossed over to Port Moresby and made many trips along the New Guinea coast. He was delighted to meet another German collector there, Carl Hunstein, who guided him into the interior where he found many exotic species.

In November 1882 he returned to Germany, but two years later he disappeared rather quietly from Europe. In February 1885 he wrote to *The Ibis* from Duke of York Island, omitting to mention his exact business there, but commenting that he had "travelled a good deal in New Guinea, and visited parts of that

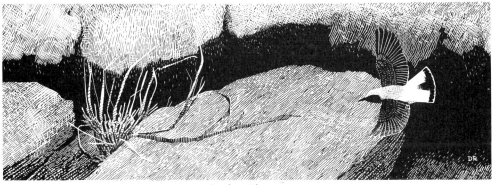

Finsch's Wheatear

island where scarcely any white men have been before". For once, the collector was not on an ornithological expedition; through his efforts and negotiations, as Bismarck's Imperial Commissioner, the north-eastern portion of New Guinea, together with New Britain and New Ireland became a German protectorate and were renamed Kaiser Wilhelm's Land and the Bismarck Archipelago. Finsch's own name is still retained in Finschhafen, the capital of the colony. Characteristically, Finsch did find some time for his more usual pursuits and he returned with two sensational new species of birds of paradise. Sadly, during the next five years of German colonial rule, more than 50,000 bird of paradise skins were exported from New Guinea for the millinary trade, and their exploitation continued until a ban was at last imposed in 1924.

Finsch quickly became disillusioned with politicians. Their principles and ambitions were very different from his own, and less than a year after returning to Berlin he forsook his advisory post and tried to pick up the traces of his old way of life. In 1886 he married again but for many years had to be dependent on the income from his travel writings, including an account of his last journey, *Samoa Fahrten* [Voyage of the *Samoa*] published in 1888.

In 1899 he was offered the curatorship of the bird collections at the Rijkmuseum in Leyden, where he worked for the next six years, but when he was given the chance to accept a modest post as head of the ethnographical department of the Municipal Museum at Brunswick, he willingly returned to Germany, drawn there by homesickness as much as by his growing interest in ethnology. For the last twelve years of his life Finsch abandoned the study of birds in favour of his fellow man, and worked at the museum until his death at the age of seventy-seven. In his last years, Finsch was described by a friend as "a stately figure even then, upright and proud, content simply to know the value of his own achievements". Fortunately, he died (on 31 January 1917) before it was obvious that his country would lose her huge colonial empire, including the islands where Finsch himself had raised the German flag.

As an ornithologist, Otto Finsch's most valuable work concerned birds that occur well beyond the confines of Europe, and though perhaps best remembered for his work on parrots, in all, Finsch described 14 new genera and about 150 new species of birds. He was highly regarded by his own generation of ornithologists and was honoured by them when they named such species as the Amazon Parrot *Amazona finschi* (Sclater), the Grey-headed Parakeet *Psittacula finschii* (Hume), Finsch's Imperial Pigeon *Ducula finschii* (Ramsay), Finsch's Flycatcher-thrush *Stizorhina finschii* (Sharpe) and Finsch's Wheatear *Oenanthe finschii* (Heuglin). Theodor von Heuglin chose the complimentary name for the wheatear because Finsch had already provided an unpublished description of it from a specimen in the Bremen Museum. The origin of the type specimen is uncertain.

Johann Gotthelf Fischer von Waldheim (1771-1853)

SPECTACLED EIDER *Somateria fischeri* (Brandt)

Fuligula (Lampronetta) Fischeri Brandt, 1847. *Novam Avium Rossicarum Speciem*, pp. 1–18, Pl. 1: St Michael, Alaska

J. G. Fischer was the son of a linen weaver, born on 13 October 1771 in Waldheim, Saxony. He would probably have followed in his father's trade if his intellectual brilliance had not won him the aid of various benefactors who provided for his general education and sent him to Leipzig in 1792 to study medicine.

Five years later Fischer travelled to Vienna and then on to Paris with his friend, the scientist and geographer, Alexander von Humboldt. In Paris he studied comparative anatomy under Baron Cuvier translating many of his lectures for publication in German and he then took up a professorship at Mainz, on the Rhine. In 1804 he was called to be Professor of Natural History and Director of the Natural History Museum at the Moscow Academy, and in August of the following year he founded the Société Impériale des Naturalistes de Moscou. He continued to study zoology and during this period he was primarily engaged in the classification of invertebrates. Between 1820 and 1851 the fruits of his entomological studies were published in the five-volume work, *Entomographia*

Spectacled Eider

FISCHER. *ZOOLOGIST AND PALAEONTOLOGIST AT THE MOSCOW ACADEMY, HE TOOK AN INTEREST IN BIRDS DURING THE LAST YEARS OF HIS LIFE.*

Imperii Rossici. He was also engaged in studying the fossils from the wooded countryside around Moscow, his zoological and palaeontological investigations earning him the title of 'Russia's Cuvier'. Many fossils were called after Fischer but his wide-ranging interests also included mineralogy, and his labours in that branch of science were honoured in an aluminium phosphate known as Fischerite.

In September 1812 Moscow was occupied by the French until the Russians started a great fire which forced Napoleon to withdraw, but which destroyed many of the city's finest buildings, including the Natural History Museum and Fischer's own library. After the war Fischer and his fellow scientists immediately planned a new museum and the acquisition of collections for it.

In 1835 Fischer was elevated to the nobility, adopting the title of von Waldheim because of his great and lasting affection for his native town. That same year he also became a privy councillor.

It was only in later years that he turned his attention to ornithology. He pursued this new activity with such success and enthusiasm that when a new species of eider was sent from Alaska to St Petersburg, J. F. Brandt, the director of the Academy's zoological museum, decided to name the bird in recognition of Fischer's many and varied contributions to the study of natural history. The type specimen of this extraordinary-looking bird was a drake which had been collected by I. G. Vosnesensky at the Russian settlement of St Michael, near the Yukon delta. After they have wintered at sea along the edge of the pack-ice Spectacled Eiders breed sporadically along this coast and in north-eastern Siberia, arriving in pairs as soon as the ice melts on the river deltas and on the shallow tundra pools.

Six years after Fischer's name was given to this Arctic duck, of which we still have only a very limited knowledge, the naturalist died in Moscow in October 1853, at the age of eighty-two.

FORSTER. *UNDERRATED GERMAN NATURALIST, AUTHOR AND TRANSLATOR WHO MADE CONTRIBUTIONS TO THE EARLY ORNITHOLOGY OF NORTH AMERICA AND CENTRAL EUROPE. BEST KNOWN AS THE NATURALIST ON COOK'S SECOND PACIFIC VOYAGE, HE IS DEPICTED HERE, IN TAHITI, WITH HIS SON, GEORGE.*

Johann Reinhold Forster (1729-1798)

FORSTER'S TERN *Sterna forsteri* Nuttall

Sterna forsteri Nuttall, 1834. *Manual of the Ornithology of the United States and Canada*, Vol. 2, p. 274. New name for *Sterna hirundo* Richardson, 1831. *Fauna Boreali-Americana*, Vol. 2, p. 412 (*nec* Linnaeus): Banks of Saskatchewan between Cumberland House and Lake Winnipeg

Forster's Tern breeds in the interior of North America on salt and freshwater marshes, and has only occasionally straggled to Europe. It is very similar in appearance to the Common Tern and for a long time was overlooked as a distinct species. It was first described in the journals of Lewis and Clark, but the early publications concerning their 1804–06 expedition from the Missouri to the Pacific failed to include all of their scientific work. Some years later, on the banks of the Saskatchewan, Dr Richardson obtained the specimen which is considered to be the type of the species although he and Swainson had both believed it to be a Common Tern. Thomas Nuttall, in his *Ornithology of the United States and Canada* (1834) described the differences between the two species and named the new tern *Sterna forsteri*, "from the eminent naturalist and voyager who first suggested these distinctions".

Nuttall was honouring one of the earliest naturalists to study the fauna of North America. In 1771 Forster had compiled a *Catalogue of the Animals of North America*, published in London by Gilbert White's brother, Benjamin. His information was gleaned from the works of Catesby, various other authors, and from collections brought to England from Newfoundland and elsewhere. It was an early attempt to correlate the research that had been carried out up until then. He opened the introduction to the ornithological section with a somewhat unnecessary definition:

> "A bird is an animal covered with feathers; furnished with a bill; having two wings, and only two legs; with the faculty, except in a few instances, of removing itself from place to place."

In the following year he presented *An account of the birds sent from Hudson's Bay* to the *Philosophical Transactions of the Royal Society*.[1] It contained the first scientific description of the now extinct, or almost extinct, Eskimo Curlew, which then occurred in enormous numbers. Among the other species was a Forster's Tern which he described as a "variety" of "the greater Tern". It was this description that Nuttall alluded to when he named the species.

Although Forster wrote about the birds of North America he never visited the continent. His early life was spent in eastern Europe and he afterwards achieved fame, though not fortune, as the naturalist on James Cook's second Pacific voyage.

Johann Reinhold Forster, an only child, was born about twenty miles south of Danzig at Dirschau (Tczew) where his father was the mayor. The male line of the family was descended from a George Forster who had been born in Yorkshire but who was of Scottish descent—Forster being a corruption of Forrester. His mother was also related to a number of Scottish emigrant families. The young Forster spent some of his formative years on a farm and his interest in natural history probably stems from this period. At first, his education was neglected but he showed obvious talent and distinguished himself at schools in Dirschau and Berlin and later moved on to Halle University. His father wanted him to study law and would not support his desire to study medicine. Instead, Forster chose theology and his natural history interests lay dormant.

For twelve years, until he was thirty-six years old, Forster was the minister in a country parish a few miles south-east of Danzig. During this time he married a cousin, Justina, who produced three sons and four daughters, whom he considered to be a terrible financial burden throughout his life. However, his lavish taste for buying books lay behind many of his financial troubles. He read widely, specializing in languages, geography and Egyptology. When the time came for him to preach he was often very tired, having spent all night pursuing his own interests and preparing for the sermon only at the last minute.

His interest in natural history was aroused again by his precocious first child, George. The lad showed such an interest in the subject that the elder Forster resolved to teach his son, and himself, everything that he possibly could. Their first major expedition together took place when George was only eleven years old. In 1765 his father seized an opportunity to leave the Church to report on the new German colonies that were being set up near the banks of the Volga in south-west Russia. The authorities hoped that Forster would allay the rumours filtering back into Germany that the new settlements were not the havens of peace and plenty that they were claimed to be.

Travelling south from St Petersburg, the Forsters visited Saratov and Volgograd and then crossed the river onto the Kalmuck Steppe. Continuing eastwards as far as Lake Elton he discovered the magnificent Black Lark *Alauda yeltoniensis*; one of sixty-four bird species he recorded from the area. Young George eagerly helped his father, particularly with the plant collecting. They quickly completed their official duties and by the end of October they were back at St Petersburg, having covered over 2500 miles in just a few months. True to character, Forster produced an uncomplimentary but accurate report with little thought of the consequences; any chance of a career at the prestigious Academy of Sciences disappeared and although he repeatedly asked for payment he never received the full amount owed to him. Arranging for the rest of the family to follow on later, the two Forsters left the city in August and sailed through the Baltic to

London, where the scientific results of the Russian expedition were published. Twenty-eight years later the work received some unnecessary criticism. Pallas visited the same area and complained about Forster's meagre results even though Forster had admitted that it was only an attempt towards a natural history of the region and had explained that many of the botanical specimens had been lost whilst re-crossing the Volga.

In England, with at first scarcely a word of the language, Forster established himself in eminent scientific circles, began corresponding with Linnaeus, Pennant and other naturalists, and within a year was chosen to replace Joseph Priestly at the influential Dissenter's Academy at Warrington, in Lancashire. He stayed for three years as a lecturer but after a while his relationship with the governors broke down and he resigned, glad of the change. Within three more years he was sailing towards Antarctica.

Despite some statements to the contrary which have appeared from time to time, Forster had excellent qualifications for being appointed as naturalist to Cook's second Pacific voyage. He was knowledgeable on a great many subjects besides natural history, and his son, who went with him, was already a capable botanist and a talented artist. Their chance arose when the wealthy Joseph Banks, who had been with Cook on his previous voyage, forfeited his place through an argument with Cook over the number of his assistants and the large ungainly superstructure that he wanted added to the *Resolution* in order to house them all. When they set off in July 1772, Forster had reached the age of forty-two; George was not yet eighteen years old.

By the time that the *Resolution* reached southern Africa Forster had realized that he would need another scientific assistant and he persuaded Cook to let him employ Anders Sparrman, a young Swedish student of Linnaeus who happened to be at the Cape. They divided the work load and thereafter Sparrman and George concentrated on the botany while the elder Forster described the animals and the native peoples. With this motley trio of naturalists, Cook visited a multitude of Pacific islands including Tonga, Tahiti and Easter Island, choosing New Zealand as his main base. He penetrated further south into the snow and ice of Antarctica than any previous ship had done and returned home after three years by way of Cape Horn, the Falkland Islands and South Georgia. It was Cook's greatest voyage, yet few accounts have been written without some scathing reference to the humourless, disgruntled and fiery-tempered Forster. It

Forster's Tern

is true that he was rash and proud, with a temper that often led him into trouble, and he may not have been a particularly likeable man. But it would have been strange if he had not grumbled about the conditions on board. The Forsters' cabin was badly situated next to a hatchway and sometimes they could not enter or leave because of the equipment piled up outside. The cabin was so cramped that many of the expensive books had to be stored in the hold where they were ruined by salt water. For some of the time there were cattle housed on one side and goats on the other, and in heavy rain, or rough weather, water leaked into the room and ruined papers and specimens alike. Furthermore, of the 1100 days of the expedition only 290 were spent at anchor or ashore and the collecting forays were necessarily brief and hurried. While Cook may have been content to zig-zag across the seas, in any conditions, for weeks on end, secure in the knowledge that he was mapping vast sections of the globe, it was of little consolation to Forster.

Forster's character defects have also led some writers to dismiss his scientific achievements but a recent biographer (Hoare, 1976) gives a fairer assessment of his contributions and acknowledges Forster as one of the earliest anthropologists of the Pacific and a pioneer ornithologist of Antarctica, New Zealand and many Pacific islands. Inevitably, most of the birds he encountered were coastal or pelagic. He described five new species of penguins, a number of petrels, and, in *Mémoire sur les Albatros*, written years later, in 1785, he gave fresh details about three kinds of albatross. It was unfortunate that his *Descriptiones animalium* was not also published sooner. It contained a mass of original material and was almost complete within a month of returning to England but partly due to Forster's disagreements with publishers it was not issued for another seventy years when an edited and annotated version was brought out by Lichtenstein in 1844. One of the most interesting birds mentioned in it is the Mysterious Bird of Ulieta, from the Society Islands, which is now only known from descriptions by Forster and Latham and from one of George's drawings (now in the British Museum (Natural History)).

After their return to England Forster's financial position deteriorated still further. Most of the £4000 he had been paid had been swallowed up on necessary expenses including the employment of Sparrman. Forster also lost money by wrangling over the rights to publish the expedition narrative. The two Forsters eventually went ahead without the blessing of the Admiralty and from his father's journals George wrote *A Voyage Round the World* (1777). It was published six weeks before Cook's version but Cook was the hero of the day and his two volumes sold much better. In the following year J. R. Forster published *Observations made during a Voyage around the World* and although it was one of his most significant books, it failed to clear his debts and the bulk of George's drawings had to be sold to Joseph Banks. For the next few years Forster undertook a variety of writing and translation work, including (in 1781) a German version of Pennant's *Indian Zoology*. In time the family returned to the Continent, and at the age of fifty Forster became Professor of Natural History at Halle, where he remained for the rest of his life.

As he became older he mellowed considerably and was looked upon more affectionately by his colleagues. He worked almost continuously at translating travel and scientific works and he remained a leading authority on many aspects of the Pacific. His last years were tinged with sadness when his son was exiled from Germany as a traitor. After a promising start as Professor of Natural History at Wilna, and after a successful tour of the Rhine with Alexander von Humboldt, George had taken up the cause of the French Revolution and died a lonely death in a Parisian garret in 1794, probably from pneumonia complicated by scurvy.

The elder Forster died five years later on 9 December 1798 aged sixty-nine after suffering from angina for some time. Paradoxically, because of the value of his books, mineral specimens, herbaria and South Sea artefacts he died a fairly rich man and the proceeds from their sale helped to ease the remaining years for his long-suffering wife.

FRANKLIN. *ROYAL NAVY OFFICER AND ARCTIC EXPLORER. HE MADE TWO OVERLAND CANADIAN EXPEDITIONS WITH THE ZOOLOGIST DR JOHN RICHARDSON AND LED A DISASTROUS EXPEDITION TO SEARCH FOR THE NORTH-WEST PASSAGE, ON WHICH EVERY MAN PERISHED.*

John Franklin (1786-1847)

FRANKLIN'S GULL *Larus pipixcan* Wagler

Larus Pipixcan Wagler, 1831. *Isis von Oken* 24, No. 5 (May), col. 515: Mexico

By the time John Franklin was eighteen years old he had taken an active part in the Battle of Copenhagen, he had sailed around part of Australia with his uncle Matthew Flinders and had been shipwrecked on the Great Barrier Reef. By the time he was thirty-two years old Franklin had survived the Battle of Trafalgar, he had been wounded at New Orleans and had captained a ship that had sailed northwards in an attempt to reach the North Pole.

The unsuccessful Arctic voyage afterwards brought him into contact with many senior naval officers with an interest in exploration and science. They were quick to see that Franklin had the qualities of a first-rate expedition leader: he was cool in the face of danger, he was an excellent seaman and navigator, he was interested in the promotion of science for its own sake, and he had a buoyant temperament maintained by a deep faith in God which was able to see him through the most difficult circumstances.

Not long after his return from the Arctic, with a view to furthering the exploration of the North-west Passage, Lieutenant Franklin was therefore given command of a small group of men and instructed to travel from Hudson Bay to the Arctic coast. The party consisted of midshipmen George Back and Robert Hood, a sailor by the name of Hepburn and Dr John Richardson. The latter was almost the same age as Franklin, had also seen active naval service in Europe and North America and had also had experience of extreme cold weather. They became lifelong friends, Richardson later marrying Franklin's niece.

The expedition landed at York Factory, on Hudson Bay, on 30 August 1819. The trip inland was slow and difficult because of rapids and waterfalls and it took them nearly two months to cover the 650 miles to Cumberland House, where they spent most of the first winter. In January it became so cold that Franklin later wrote: "our tea froze in the tin pots before we could drink it, and even a mixture of spirits and water became quite thick by congelation". It was a small hardship compared with the events which occurred later.

Franklin, Back and Hepburn set off at the beginning of the year for a trading post where they hoped to collect fresh supplies and hire French-Canadian *voyageurs* who would paddle them northwards in large canoes. Travelling by dogsled and snowshoe they arrived at their new winter quarters at Fort Chipewyan where Franklin noted, rather vaguely, that the only resident birds to be seen were "ravens, magpies, partridges, crossbills and woodpecker". Richardson caught up with Franklin in July but little progress had been made with supplies because of the lack of local co-operation from the Indians and *voyageurs*. At last, they got underway again and when they arrived at Old Fort Providence they met the Copper Indians who were supposed to be their hunters for their second winter and the following summer. They travelled north up the Yellowknife River and built Fort Enterprise as their next winter quarters. When spring came they moved northwards once more, the coniferous trees becoming increasingly stunted and sparse as they neared the Arctic coast, until, at the mouth of the Coppermine River, the only wooded vegetation was a few small willows. Seeing before them the partially thawed ocean the Copper Indians refused to accompany Franklin any further and returned homewards to the Great Slave Lake.

The remaining explorers paddled their two large canoes into the sea and proceeded eastwards, carefully surveying the coast as they went. At first they lived well because they shot some Musk Oxen, two Brown Bears, several Sandhill Cranes, some Long-tailed ducks and grey geese. On 18 August they camped

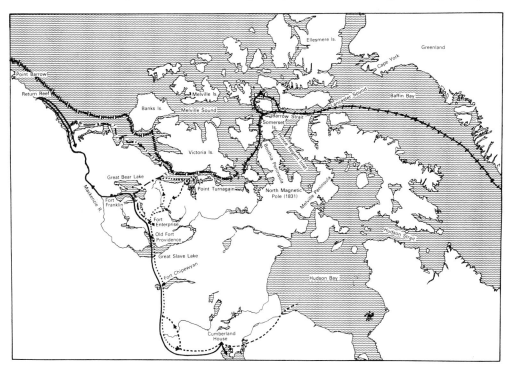

THE SEARCH FOR THE NORTH-WEST PASSAGE:
- - - - - - FRANKLIN 1819–22
———————— FRANKLIN
- - — - - RICHARDSON'S PARTY } 1825–27
+++ +++ +++ FRANKLIN, 1845–47
╫╫ ╫╫ ╫╫ COLLINSON'S OUTWARD VOYAGE, 1850–55, WITH ADAMS

at Point Turnagain and, before heading south, Franklin, Richardson and Back walked a further twelve miles east and examined the land beyond by telescope.

The only way back to Fort Enterprise was a long and arduous overland trip across the open tundra. There were almost twenty men under Franklin's command: the four Britons, plus eleven *voyageurs*, two Indian and two Eskimo interpreters. Their late start in the summer was now aggravated by the early arrival of winter. They were soon trudging through deep snow and for this reason abandoned everything that was not essential, including the canoes and, by a tragic mistake, all their fishing equipment. After some tough travelling they came to a deep river which had to be crossed. They built a small raft of willows but a strong bitterly cold wind prevented them from launching it. Richardson volunteered to swim across with a line around his middle and despite cutting his foot to the bone on a knife left lying on the ground he plunged into the icy waters. He did not get far before his arms seized up and so he turned over on his back and kicked with his legs. He had almost reached the far bank when he sank. The others hauled him out more dead than alive but he recovered slowly after a fire was lit. Eventually they got across one at a time in a small canoe constructed out of birch and canvas, but it was much precious time wasted.

Franklin realized that at least some of them would not survive and he sent Back and two *voyageurs* on ahead, to get help from the Indians at Fort Enterprise. After six days without any fresh meat, the main party managed to shoot a Musk Ox, eating the stomach contents at once and then the raw intestines. When the meat was finished, game once more proved hard to come by and they were soon reduced to lichen and ptarmigan boiled together. They eventually had to resort to boiled leather and lichen or, on some days, nothing at all. The snow became deeper as the explorers moved off the tundra and into the spruce forest but only in these later stages did Richardson abandon his small and cherished collection of plants and geological specimens.

Hood was now in a pitiful condition and could proceed no further. Richardson and Hepburn volunteered to stay with him and were later joined by the Iroquois Indian, Michel, and the French-Canadian, Bélanger, both of whom had failed to keep up with the main party and had been sent back by Franklin. One day, Bélanger and Michel went off to hunt for game but only Michel returned. A few days later Hood was found shot in the back of the head. Michel, who was with Hood when the shot was fired, insisted that Hood had accidently shot himself but Richardson could see from the length of the barrel and the position of the wound that the shot had not been self-inflicted. Now relieved of the burden of Hood, they started walking again, but Richardson and Hepburn thought that Michel had not only killed Hood but had also murdered the missing Bélanger. They now even believed that some of the meat that Michel had brought back to camp had been cut from Bélanger's body! After consultation with Hepburn and fearing for their own lives, Richardson shot and killed Michel at the first opportunity.

The two survivors of this group eventually caught up with Franklin at Fort Enterprise on 29 October, where they saw "the ghastly countenances, dilated eyeballs and sepulchral voices of Capt. Franklin and those with him". When Franklin had arrived at the fort he had found it deserted. All he found in the way of food were some discarded bones and Caribou skins which they boiled together for a watery soup. Two of Franklin's party had died on the way to the fort and two more men now died. The rest were so weak that they could hardly haul wood for the fire or hunt for lichen beneath the snow. Death seemed inevitable for them all. Franklin still managed, as usual, to hold prayers and a daily service until finally, on 7 November, the Copper Indians arrived with fresh Caribou meat. George Back, by superhuman effort, had struggled on to Fort Providence but had travelled still further to track down the Indians.

By December the survivors were fit enough to move on once more and the following October the Britons arrived back in England to a tremendous welcome. Despite their 5500 mile overland journey, only 550 new miles of Arctic coast had been surveyed. Nevertheless it was another small step towards charting the possible course of the North-west Passage. Franklin was elected a Fellow of the Royal Society, and in 1823 married his first wife Eleanor (who died two years later). His excellent *Narrative* of the expedition contained a number of scientific appendices: there were observations on the Aurora Borealis by the unfortunate Hood; sections on the geology, botany and icthyology by Richardson; and accounts concerning the mammals and birds by Joseph Sabine, compiled from Richardson's field-notes. During the long Canadian winters there had been only a few resident birds present and in the short spring and summer, despite the arrival of migrants, there had been little opportunity for collecting and preserving skins, because most of their time was then occupied by travelling. Even so, Richardson made notes on about 110 bird species and succeeded in shooting examples of many of them. The specimens did not all survive the journey to Britain. Sabine restricted his ornithological account to the sixty-seven species of which he was able to examine specimens and as a result it is rather disappointing. Although Sabine gives details on, for example, Passenger Pigeons, Whooping Cranes, Hudsonian Godwits and Wilson's Phalaropes (see Wilson) there is no mention of the first-ever Eskimo Curlew nest that Richardson had discovered and described, nor of the adult birds obtained.

Franklin's Gull

Only three years after enduring such terrible privations, and apparently undaunted by them, the thirty-nine year old Franklin returned to Canada with a second naval expedition. Richardson and Back joined him again, along with twenty volunteer naval ratings, Midshipman Kendall and Thomas Drummond (a civilian) as the assistant naturalist. They reached Cumberland House in June 1825 and a month later arrived at Fort Chipewyan. Drummond was left behind here, as arranged, to pursue his own botanical interests while the main party pressed on in order to build their winter quarters at Fort Franklin on the shores of the Great Bear Lake. This time Franklin's organization was much better; with fifty people gathered at the fort it was vital that the supply of game and fish was continually maintained. In the spring the expedition paddled quickly down to the mouth of the Mackenzie River and split up. Franklin and Back went westwards in two boats hoping to meet Lieutenant Beechey in HMS *Blossom* approaching from the Bering Straits. Richardson sailed eastwards as far as the Coppermine River in the hope of meeting Captain Parry approaching from Hudson Bay. In the event, none of the explorers met up and the two groups of the Franklin expedition had to make their own way back to Fort Franklin.

Richardson was the first to return, and leaving a message at the fort he continued southwards to reconnoitre the Great Slave Lake by canoe before heading down the Saskatchewan River where he made contact with Drummond. The botanist, travelling alone, summer and winter, had reached the Rocky Mountains and collected more than 1500 plant species, 150 kinds of birds, fifty mammals and a considerable number of insects. The two naturalists met Franklin at Cumberland House in June 1827, eleven months after Franklin and Richardson had parted company at the mouth of the Mackenzie.

Franklin had reached as far as Return Reef, some 160 miles from Point Barrow and although he had had confrontations with some Eskimos, he had handled the situations skilfully and there had been no loss of life. The combined total of new Arctic coastline surveyed by Franklin and Richardson exceeded 1500 miles and all that was now needed to complete the North-west Passage were 400 miles between Franklin's Point Turnagain and Parry's Cresswell Bay. For his achievements on this second expedition Franklin was knighted, partly, one suspects, because of the poor showing by the other naval expeditions and the Government's desire for a popular hero.

The *Narrative* for his second expedition was quickly completed but there were too many natural history discoveries to place them in an appendix. And so, at Government expense, two important works were published: W. J. Hooker's *Flora Boreali-Americana* (1833–40) and Richardson's *Fauna Boreali-Americana* (1829–37). For the latter work Richardson co-wrote the volume on quadrupeds with J. E. Gray; the second volume on birds was written with William Swainson; the third on the fishes was by Richardson alone; and the fourth on insects was by William Kirby. The combined works on both animals and plants represented a real step forward in the study of Arctic biology and Richardson's efforts established him as one of the greatest naturalists of his time.

The important volume on birds contained descriptions of several new species and many others already described and named elsewhere. But so great was the work's influence that it succeeded in giving us such vernacular bird names as Barrow's Goldeneye, Bonaparte's Gull, Franklin's Gull, Franklin's Spruce Grouse and, indirectly, Swainson's Thrush. (Richardson's Skua, an alternative name for the Arctic Skua, has been obsolete only since the 1950s.) "Franklin's Rosy Gull *Larus Franklinii*" was described from a male killed on the Saskatchewan River on 6 June 1827.[1] Although the name of Franklin has been retained in the common name, another scientific description was published earlier in the same year by Johann Wagler. His description originated from an even earlier account by Francisco Hernandez who had collected in Mexico from 1570 to 1577 and who had amassed many pictures and descriptions of animals, many of which he furnished with Aztec names—hence *Larus pipixcan* as the scientific name for Franklin's Gull.

While others strove to complete the scientific results of the expedition Franklin tried in vain to persuade the Admiralty to continue the search for a North-west Passage. The Government now had neither the money nor the inclination to support any more expeditions to the area, realizing, at last, that it would never prove a useful route to the Far East. Franklin married a second time, to Jane Griffen, and was afterwards posted to the eastern Mediterranean as the senior Naval Officer. From 1836 to 1843 he served as the Lieutenant Governor of Tasmania which was then a penal settlement. When Franklin eventually returned to England the climate of opinion had changed, national pride was at stake and the Government were again considering an attempt on the North-west Passage, determined that it would be completed by the British Navy. Franklin volunteered immediately and although he was now almost sixty years old he secured a certificate of good health (from Dr Richardson!) and persuaded the reluctant Admiralty to give him command. On 19 May 1845 Franklin set sail with the hardy *Erebus* and *Terror* and a full complement of 134 officers and men, none of whom survived.

After several belated search expeditions, Leopold McLintock returned with documents found at a stone cairn that reported the death of Sir John Franklin aboard the *Erebus* on 11 June 1847. The winter of 1845–46 had been spent at Beechey Island, then, turning southwards, the two ships had become stuck in the ice for two whole winters until they had been forced to abandon ship. The 105 surviving officers and men had struggled southwards on foot over the ice with perhaps about forty reaching the mainland. By doing so they had "forged the last link [of the North-west Passage] with their lives".

In his first two Canadian expeditions Franklin had traversed a large proportion of the Passage between Point Barrow and Hudson's Bay and had contributed considerably to the world's geographical knowledge of the Arctic. By dying and disappearing in those regions it could be said that he added to it still further. More than a dozen expeditions were sent out to search for the two missing crews, with the result that more than 7000 miles of coastline were surveyed and charted, far sooner than would otherwise have been the case. However, apart from the surveying, scientific work was often meagre because of the difficult conditions in the extreme high latitudes where the search was carried out.

Zoologically and botanically nothing was achieved to compare with Franklin's two overland expeditions: the discoveries made in the boreal forests of Canada were the most ornithologically significant of all the northern expeditions of the period. Franklin is therefore better commemorated by Franklin's Gull, which breeds in Saskatchewan, than by any species of the high Arctic, the area with which historians and geographers more usually associate him.

GENÉ. *ITALIAN NATURALIST WHO LIVED IN NORTHERN ITALY, WHERE HE BECAME PROFESSOR OF ZOOLOGY AT THE UNIVERSITY OF TURIN.*

Giuseppe Gené
(1800-1847)

SLENDER-BILLED GULL *Larus genei* Brème

Larus Genei Brème, 1840. *Revue Zoologique* for 1839, p. 321: Sardinia

The son of humble parents, Giuseppe Gené was born on 7 December 1800 at Turbigo in Lombardy. After attending local schools he went to the University of Pavia where he gained his Ph.D. During the following years he studied natural history with notable success and published a number of papers, particularly on entomology. At the age of twenty-seven he became an assistant lecturer in natural history at the University and a year afterwards he went on a trip to Hungary, returning with an impressive collection of insects.

When Franco Bonelli died in 1830, Gené succeeded him as Professor of Zoology and Director of the Royal Zoological Museum at Turin. He soon became known as an inspiring lecturer, and the museum also flourished under his supervision. He continued to write widely about the insects, reptiles and birds of the region and as his fame spread many naturalists sent him specimens. Count Alberto della Marmora dispatched a new falcon which he had shot as it soared above the high sea-cliffs of southern Sardinia. Gené presented a scientific description of the species at a meeting of the Royal Academy of Sciences of Turin on 5 May 1834, and chose to name it after Eleonora of Arborea.

In turn, Gené enjoyed the honour of having a bird named for himself in 1839. His friend the Marquis de Brème published a description of a new species of gull, very similar to the winter plumaged Black-headed Gull but with a longer neck and bill. It had hitherto escaped attention because of its comparative rarity and its sporadic breeding distribution in the Mediterranean and central Asian regions. Brème named it *Larus Genei* in recognition of the professor's contribution to zoology, especially his work on the fauna of Sardinia. Eight years later, on 14 July 1847, Gené died at Turin.

Slender-billed Gull

GODLEWSKI. *POLISH FARMER AND AMATEUR NATURALIST,*
EXILED TO SIBERIA.

Wictor Witold Godlewski (1831-1900) [1]

BLYTH'S PIPIT *Anthus godlewskii* (Taczanowski)

Agrodroma Godlewskii Taczanowski, 1876. *Bulletin de la Société Zoologique de France* 1, p. 158: Argun River, south Dauria

The widespread insurrection that occurred in Poland in January 1863 had been brought about by plans to press the revolutionary youth into the Russian army. Ethnic groups united in a common cause against the Tzar but after fifteen months the uprising was put down and was followed by confiscation, executions and deportations, thereby ending all hopes of a Polish state for the next fifty years. Wictor Godlewski, a farmer near Warsaw with an interest in natural history, and Benedict Dybowski, Professor of Zoology at Cracow, were amongst those banished to Siberia.

Godlewski was an exceptionally astute observer and, under Dybowski's tutelage, he became an excellent field collector taking part in a number of expeditions to Lake Baykal, Dauria, the Amur and Ussuriland. Because of the lack of proper facilities, neither of the two

Blyth's Pipit

exiles were able to do much work on the main bulk of their collections which they sent back to the Warsaw Museum, to be examined by Ladislas Taczanowski. The material that they had collected, including many new species, later formed an important part of Taczanowski's two-volume *Faune ornithologique de la Sibérie Orientale* [Birds of East Siberia], issued by the Imperial Academy of Sciences of St Petersburg in 1891 and 1893. Many of Godlewski's field observations are quoted in the work.

In 1877, after almost fourteen years in Siberia, both Godlewski and Dybowski were pardoned and they returned to Poland. They had already collaborated on four accounts of the fauna of Lake Baykal and after their return Godlewski busied himself in writing up his field notes. Thereafter he seems to have been content to remain in Poland and he died there in 1900, in the village of Smolechy, at the age of sixty-nine. Dybowski, on the other hand, later returned to eastern Siberia of his own free will, visiting Kamchatka and Bering Island. As Professor of Zoology at Lemburg he became well known as an authority on the birds of Dauria.

The nomenclature of Blyth's Pipit has had a complicated history. It is enough to record here that it was Edward Blyth who first described the species fully but his scientific name, and those put forward later by several other naturalists, were afterwards considered to be invalid.[2] We are left with Taczanowski's name for this pipit, *Anthus godlewskii*, which he gave to a specimen obtained from the steppe country along the Argun River in southern Dauria.

John Edward Gray
(1800-1875)

INDIAN POND HERON *Ardeola grayii* (Sykes)

Ardea Grayii Sykes, 1832. *Proceedings of the Zoological Society of London*, p. 158: Dukhun [= Deccan], India

George Robert Gray
(1808-1872)

GRAY'S GRASSHOPPER WARBLER *Locustella fasciolata* (G. R. Gray)

Acrocephalus fasciolatus G. R. Gray, 1860. *Proceedings of the Zoological Society of London*, p. 349: Batjan, Molluccas

The Gray family had a remarkable association with natural history which extended through six generations for over two hundred years; no less than seven members of the family were employed at the British Museum. Among the more notable was the botanist Edward Whitaker Gray who was Keeper of the Natural History Department from 1787 to 1806. His elder brother, botanist and pharmacologist Samuel Frederick Gray, was the father of the two noted zoologists J. E. and G. R. Gray who served together at the museum for many years.

John Edward Gray was born at Walsall, Staffordshire, in 1800, but moved with the family to London where he later studied for the medical profession. He was much more interested in botany and helped considerably towards his father's 1821 publication *The Natural Arrangement of British Plants*. Unfortunately John's involvement with the work caused him to be blackballed from the

J. E. GRAY. *KEEPER OF ZOOLOGY AT THE BRITISH MUSEUM. DURING HIS FIFTY YEARS OF SERVICE HE ADDED OVER A MILLION SPECIMENS TO THE COLLECTION.*

G. R. GRAY. *YOUNGER BROTHER OF J. E. GRAY. HEAD OF THE BIRD SECTION AT THE BRITISH MUSEUM. HE IS PERHAPS BEST REMEMBERED FOR HIS* GENERA OF BIRDS.

Linnean Society for many years; allegedly because he and his father had referred to Smith and Sowerby's *English Botany* as Sowerby's *English Botany*. The President of the Linnean Society, Sir J. E. Smith, is said to have objected strongly to this omission. Disenchanted with botany, and botanists, John Gray turned his attention to zoology.

Through his position as Secretary of the Entomological Society he became well acquainted with William Leach at the British Museum, and was allowed to help John George Children to catalogue the reptile collection. No zoologist himself, Children gave Gray almost complete freedom to work at the museum and on Children's retirement in 1840 Gray took over as Keeper of the Zoological Branch of the Natural History Department.

In 1826 John Gray married Maria Emma Gray, widow of a cousin, who herself was an able conchologist and algologist, and she helped her husband by illustrating some of his numerous works. During the fifty years that her husband was employed at the museum he wrote 497 papers, the titles of which occupy 28 columns in the Royal Society Catalogue, while a privately printed list of books, memoirs and miscellaneous papers lists just over a thousand publications. He was an original member of several London societies and was respected as a scientist both in Britain and on the Continent, where he often made visits to study museum displays and systems of arrangement. He spent much of his life striving to increase the collections, sometimes at his own expense and often against opposition from the directors who considered the Natural History Department less important than some of the others. By 1858 he had managed to introduce the idea of separating the specimens for study and research from those on public view; up until then every specimen was usually on display to the public. John Gray did not specialize but busied himself with all branches of zoology. He published some short ornithological papers and described over forty new species of birds, but otherwise this subject was left almost entirely to his younger brother who was appointed Assistant Keeper of the Zoology Branch in 1831.

George Robert Gray started work at the museum by cataloguing insects and he published an *Entomology of Australia* (1833) as well as contributing the entomological section to an English edition of Cuvier's *Animal Kingdom*. When he took over the ornithological section (a position he retained for forty-one years), a large proportion of his time was spent cataloguing the ever increasing

Indian Pond Heron

number of specimens in the bird collection. Between 1844 and 1849 G. R. Gray produced his most important work, *Genera of Birds*, which was issued in three volumes and was very well illustrated by D. W. Mitchell and Joseph Wolf. It contained 46,000 references and brought the number of species recorded in the world up to 11,000. Although of little use today, at the time of publication it was extremely useful to working ornithologists everywhere.

Hardly any less prolific than his brother, he issued a number of catalogues and often contributed to scientific journals. His original description of the warbler now known as Gray's Grasshopper Warbler appeared in the 1860 *Proceedings of the Zoological Society*. The type specimen had been collected by Alfred Russell Wallace in the Molluccas, between Borneo and New Guinea; the species is only an accidental visitor to the Western Palearctic from its Asiatic breeding grounds. The first description of the Indian Pond Heron appeared in an earlier volume of the same journal, in 1832, but Colonel W. H. Sykes gave no indication as to which Gray he was referring to. In 1832 G. R. Gray had only just taken over the ornithological section at the British Museum and unless it was intended as a compliment to both of them,

Gray's Grasshopper Warbler

Ardeola grayii is most probably named after J. E. Gray; especially as the latter was at that time striving to produce *Illustrations of Indian Zoology* (1832–34) from a selection of Hardwicke's drawings, one of the works mentioned in support of J. E. Gray's election to the Royal Society in January 1832.

When George Gray died on 6 May 1872, at the age of sixty-four, the obituary in *The Ibis* commented that: "Mr Gray's works are concise to a fault . . . Few men have written so much in so few words." In this respect he was ahead of his time—in today's scientific publications there is no place for the wordiness that *The Ibis* and other journals then enjoyed. He was outlived by his elder brother who died three years later, on 7 March 1875.

Although both Grays had married neither had any children of their own. Neither did they live to see the long-planned transfer of the entire zoological collection from Bloomsbury to the new building at Cromwell Road, at South Kensington, in 1881. By then few of the bird specimens obtained before 1840 remained: there were none from Sir Hans Sloane's collection and only a handful had survived from Cook's voyages and from George Montagu's collection, partly because they had not been looked after well. Most of the specimens had therefore been acquired whilst the Grays worked at the museum. The reputation established by them was later continued and greatly enhanced by Bowdler Sharpe, so that many private collectors bequeathed their collections of a lifetime to the museum, confident that they would now be well catalogued and well cared for. The museum had already obtained the collections of Darwin, Gould and Raffles as well as Hodgson's hoard from India and Nepal, Ross's Antarctic specimens and others from the East India Company. In time, Hume's superb Indian collection, Seebohm's Palearctic collection of 20,000 skins and the smaller collections of Boyd Alexander, the Butlers and John Whitehead were all added, and by 1909 the bird skins numbered almost half a million. In 1972 the bulk of the collection was moved out of London to the Rothschild Museum at Tring. The number of study skins there now exceeds one million and it remains one of the world's most important collections.

In conclusion, confusion should be avoided between John Edward Gray and Sir Edward Grey (Viscount Grey of Falloden) (1862–1933), the famous statesman and naturalist who wrote *The Charm of Birds* (1927), and after whom the Edward Grey Institute of Field Ornithology at Oxford is named. And neither should George Robert Gray be confused with the noted ornithologist Robert Gray (1825–1887), who wrote the *Birds of the West of Scotland* (1871) and was co-author, with T. Anderson, of *Birds of Ayrshire and Wigtownshire* (1869).

Johann Anton Güldenstädt† (1745-1781)

GÜLDENSTÄDT'S REDSTART *Phoenicurus erythrogaster* (Güldenstädt)

Motacilla erythrogastra Güldenstädt, 1775. *Novi Commentarii Academiae Scientiarum Imperialis Petropolitanae* 19, p. 469, Pls 16, 17: Caucasus

When Pallas set out in 1768 on his first great expedition to explore Catherine the Great's vast empire, Güldenstädt was among the complement of naturalists. While Pallas concentrated on exploring in the Urals, the Altai and eastwards beyond Lake Baykal, Güldenstädt travelled southwards to the Caucasus and did not return to St Petersburg for seven years. A further six years later he was dead; struck down by an epidemic on 23 March 1781, while carrying out his duties as a doctor within the city.

During his short life of only thirty-six years Güldenstädt became well known as a zoologist and botanist, and also gained fame as the founder of soil science in Russia. Wherever he travelled he noted the underlying rocks and the soils that covered them. He was the first to report on the black earth of the steppe which extends on a broad front from the area north of the Black Sea to the Urals—a quarter of a billion acres of farmland which owes its fertility and colour to layers and layers of grassy humus and has since become the centre of Soviet agriculture. To ornithologists, Güldenstädt is remembered for being the first discoverer and describer of a small number of birds; with the exception of the Ferruginous Duck they are all very distinctive species.

He was born at Riga on 26 April 1745, and at eighteen started his medical career at Berlin, later transferring himself to Frankfurt University where he obtained his doctorate in 1767. His father had been Secretary to the Imperial Cabinet and it was probably through this connection that the young Güldenstädt was invited to take part in the expedition that set out from St Petersburg in the following year. Although the naturalists (Pallas, Lepechin, Falk, Georgi, S. G. Gmelin and Güldenstädt) sometimes travelled together and occasionally met for a pre-arranged rendezvous, most of the time they led separate branches of the expedition which enabled each of them to pursue their own lines of enquiry.

†No known portrait.

Güldenstädt travelled south to Moscow and thence successively to Voronetz, Volgograd and Astrakhan. As he slowly journeyed further southwards he came to the Terek River which has its source in the mountains of the Caucasus. It issues from the base of a small glacier, rapidly descends to the lowlands and, joined by several tributaries, flows for more than 200 miles through a tract of marshy wilderness to the Caspian Sea. In these lower regions of the river, well stocked in spring and autumn with birds on passage, Güldenstädt first obtained and later described that curious small wader with the tip-tilted bill, the Terek Sandpiper.

Up in the mountains he had the privilege of being the first naturalist to observe the almost thrush-sized Caucasian or Great Rosefinch; the dark red males contrasting markedly with the drab, grey-brown females. Another of his high altitude finds was a new large redstart which he recorded along the banks of streams, adding that it was restless but not at all shy. After two hundred years surprisingly little has been added to his observations on Güldenstädt's Redstart.[1] Two populations exist: one is restricted to the Caucasus, while the main range extends from Afghanistan, Kashmir, Nepal and Sikkim to Mongolia. Very few nests have ever been found but it can breed as high as 15,000 feet.

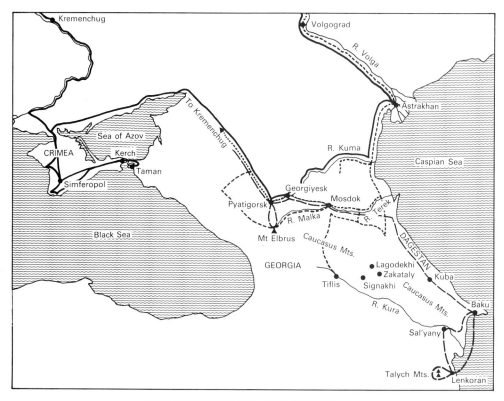

THE CAUCASUS AND THE CRIMEA:
- - - - - - - - - - - *GÜLDENSTÄDT, 1768–75*
―――――――   *PALLAS, 1793–94*
― ― ― ―   *MÉNÉTRIES, 1829–30*

One nineteenth century traveller, Dr Henderson, on his way from northern India to Chinese Turkestan saw this hardy bird in the Himalayas at 17,800 feet.

Moving down from the mountains in September 1771, Güldenstädt continued his explorations in Georgia, which like the rest of the Caucasus, had not yet been completely conquered by the Russians and was still occupied by hostile tribes. He saw here many other marvellous birds. He noted, for example, wintering flocks of Black Larks which had moved down from their breeding areas north of the Caspian Sea, and he enjoyed the spring arrival of Black-headed Buntings from the south-east.

At the end of the summer of 1772 he resolved to leave Georgia and with an escort of three hundred men he headed northwards for Mosdok on the Terek. He had difficulty crossing back into Russia because of a large band of rebels but with the arrival of soldiers and cannons from the north, Güldenstädt eventually reached the comparative safety of the northern slopes of the Caucasus, the area where the greater part of his expedition was spent. He continued his examination of the region by visiting various mines, ascended the River Malka to its source near Mount Elbrus and later travelled north-westwards to investigate the shores of the Sea of Azov. He passed the sixth winter at Kremenchug, on the Dneiper, but in July he received the order to return to St Petersburg. He arrived back there in March 1775, more fortunate than Gmelin and Falk who both failed to return. In the preceding year Gmelin had been travelling homewards after exploring the southern shores of the Caspian Sea, but as he neared the safety of a Russian fort on the Terek he was seized as a hostage by marauding Tartars and died afterwards as a result of his imprisonment. Falk, a student of Linnaeus, suffered from depression and he killed himself in March 1774 while at Kazan.

Güldenstädt lived long enough to publish several zoological and botanical papers in the Transactions of the Academy of Sciences at St Petersburg. Unfortunately, he was over-conscientious and did not wish to publish a full account of his work until he considered it to be perfect, with the result that he never finished it. A summary of his achievements was not completed until ten years after his death when Pallas issued two sturdy volumes entitled *D[r]. J. A. Güldenstädt . . . Reisen durch Russland und im Caucasischen Gebürge* [Travels in Russia and the Mountains of the Caucasus] (1787–91), which had been compiled from Güldenstädt's notes and his journal.

Güldenstädt's Redstart

Friedrich Wilhelm Hemprich† (1796-1825)

SOOTY GULL *Larus hemprichii* (Bruch)

Adelarus Hemprichii Bruch, 1853. *Journal für Ornithologie* 1, p. 106, *ex* Bonaparte MS: Red Sea

The names of Hemprich and Ehrenberg are inseparably linked in the minds of ornithologists who are familiar with the birds of north-east Africa and the Middle East. Travelling together up the Nile, across the Sinai desert, through the Lebanon and along the coasts of the Red Sea, the two young scientists were the first to discover and describe many of the birds which occur there, as well as numerous other indigenous species of plants and animals.

Hemprich was born in the Prussian town of Glatz (Klodzko, Poland), on 24 June 1796, the son of the district surgeon. On leaving school he worked as a medical attendant in the army and at the age of eighteen he moved to Breslau to study medicine. After a year there he gained practical experience as an army surgeon in France, then resumed his studies, this time in Berlin, where he obtained his doctorate. It was here that he formed a close friendship with Christian Gottfried Ehrenberg who was just one year older and a fellow medical student. Their passion for the study of natural history was mutual, Ehrenberg being primarily interested, at that time, in the reproductive methods of fungi, the subject of his thesis. They dreamed of taking part in some great scientific expedition together, ideally to Madagascar, but in the meantime each was forced to earn a living. Hemprich lectured at Berlin University on comparative physiology, wrote *Grundriss der Naturgeschichte* [The Rudiments of Natural History] (1820), and in his spare time studied reptiles and amphibians at the Zoological Museum under M. H. C. Lichtenstein. Ehrenberg took up a lectureship at Königsberg in Prussia (Kaliningrad, U.S.S.R).

Both young men instantly resigned their posts when they were invited to join an expedition to Egypt, in which they were to serve as naturalists on a primarily archaeological venture led by the Prussian General von Minutoli. The Berlin Academy undertook to financially support them. They were both determined to travel slowly through Egypt and Abyssinia, not merely collecting new and

†No known portrait.

exotic specimens, but taking the time to study plant and animal biology in the natural environment. After making thorough preparations in Berlin and Vienna they embarked from Trieste in the late summer of 1820, ahead of von Minutoli, and enjoyed brief forays ashore at several ports. As they sailed through the Greek islands, unaware of the trials that lay before them, Ehrenberg was inspired by memories of Homer to give poetical expression to his hopes and ambitions (as was his wont), and soon they arrived at Alexandria where they awaited the rest of the company.

Once assembled, they all set off south-westwards on the first part of the expedition through the desert to the oasis of Ammon, in Cyrenaica. It was a disappointing introduction to desert travel. Their Bedouin escort fought amongst themselves so that the party became divided, political troubles barred them from Tripoli on the North African coast and the two naturalists returned to Alexandria having achieved little at all. To make matters worse, there was an outbreak of plague in the town and the expedition artist died there. When their zoological assistant also fell ill with fever Hemprich and Ehrenberg took him to Cairo, but the strain of the journey took its toll and he also succumbed.

In accordance with their original plans the naturalists worked independently of the main contingent from this time onwards, but still they were continually beset by problems. In March they left Cairo to travel further up the Nile, but almost immediately Ehrenberg fell ill with typhus and only recovered through his friend's devoted nursing. By late July he was fit enough to travel again but one of their new assistants died soon afterwards. Sailing upriver in the heat of August they at least reached Dongola, the capital of Nubia, and set up a base there. (For a map of Egypt, Abyssinia and the Sinai, see Rüppell p. 319).

For the next two years the two scientists strove to study the natural history of that part of Egypt and they were helped considerably by the interest which the governor of Dongola, Abdim Bey, took in their work. The Egyptian gave them considerable protection and hospitality. On one occasion Ehrenberg moved his camp out into the remote countryside and laboured there while Hemprich returned to Alexandria to send their valuable collections to Europe. The camp was unexpectedly flooded at a time when Ehrenberg and his companions were all suffering from illness; the local inhabitants treated the foreigners with suspicion, and realizing that they were too sick to help themselves, Ehrenberg sent a message to Abdim Bey, who promptly dispatched a rescue party. Hemprich rejoined them in Dongola with the disturbing news that the funds and stores which they had requested from Berlin had not yet arrived.

On another of his disheartening visits to Alexandria Hemprich met the wealthy Eduard Rüppell, who was leading an independent and well-equipped expedition to Nubia after his successful reconnaissance of the Red Sea coast and the Sinai. Rüppell's secure position contrasted sharply with that of Hemprich and Ehrenberg who were forced to pay off their European assistants, in the spring of 1823, after receiving an official rebuke from the Berlin Academy which accused them of sending unsatisfactory balance sheets. Rüppell was delighted when Franz Lamprecht entered his service after gaining much valuable experience while working for his rivals. It was a long time before Hemprich and Ehrenberg discovered that the Berlin Academy had sent them both money and equipment which they never received because the Prussian Consul in Trieste had kept back their supplies and lost all their money gambling.

In the meantime they considered abandoning their plans and returning to Berlin, but the intervention and support of the Austrian Consul in Cairo made it possible for them to carry on and they planned their next journey with renewed enthusiasm. With several companions they sailed across the Gulf of Suez to El Tur on the south-west coast of the Sinai Peninsula, making it their base for the next nine months. From there they travelled on camels up through the arid, rocky mountains to the Monastery of St Catherine at the foot of Mt Sinai. Like many other pilgrims before and since, they climbed the sacred mountain where God had made his covenant with Moses and where the prophet Elijah had sought safety and solitude. From the summit Hemprich and Ehrenberg viewed range after range of hazy, tawny mountains inhabited by only a few hardy desert birds such as Brown-necked Ravens, Sand Partridges and White-crowned Black Wheatears. It was here that they first discovered the lovely Sinai Rosefinch which nests on the steep slopes but which can be seen at the monastery in winter, flitting in and around the various buildings. In the ancient monastery, surrounded by strong high walls and tall dark cypress trees, the naturalists were made most welcome by the Archbishop, and spent some time there examining the botany and zoology, the history and legends of that peaceful place.

Well pleased with their discoveries they rode back through the barren wilderness to El Tur and from there Hemprich sailed alone to Alexandria to send off their recent acquisitions. He was met by further administrative setbacks. While he struggled to improve their financial position and tried to avoid the periodic epidemics, his partner remained at El Tur, one of the first naturalists to study the wonderfully rich and varied marine life of the Red Sea. Ehrenberg particularly studied the coral polyps which thrive in the warm, shallow waters there.

Hemprich joined him again in March 1824 with the gloomy news that they still lacked sufficient funds to travel to the Abyssinia highlands, as they had long planned to do. Such an expedition was extremely expensive, requiring the hire of numerous assistants and extensive provisions. Liberal funds would also be required throughout the journey, as the natives of every plain and mountain pass levied heavy tolls on each and every traveller.

Hoping that it would be possible to sail south at a later date, the two naturalists decided to make a brief and affordable journey to the Lebanon. They went ashore at Beirut, accompanied by three assistants, and early in June the small party set off on foot for the interior, their baggage carried by mules. At first their route took them higher and higher into the mountains but then the track wound downhill again to Zahle and they travelled up the Beqa'a valley to Ba'albek, arriving there on the first of July. After a brief rest they carried on towards the hazy summit of the Jebel Liban and made their base at Bcharre, where they were able to take rooms.

For the next few weeks Hemprich and Ehrenberg revelled in the superb scenery and the abundant wildlife. In the cedar forests they discovered two species new to science, both typical of the montane woodland: the Syrian Woodpecker and the Syrian Serin. In the more open country Scops Owls,

Woodlarks and Orphean Warblers were common and amidst the scree and boulders above the tree-line they watched Rock Nuthatches and procured several. So much time was spent in the pursuit of birds that the collectors ran short of powder and shot and Hemprich had to go to Tripoli for more.

On 24 July they began the return journey, heading for Batrun on the Mediterranean coast, then southwards to Beirut. The mules were laden with bird skins including those of Griffon Vulture, Jay, Alpine Chough, Rock Thrush, Blue Rock Thrush, Wheatear, Black-eared and Isabelline Wheatear, Redstart, Black Redstart, Blackcap, Whitethroat, Upcher's Warbler, Shore Lark, Chaffinch, Crimson-winged Finch, Rock Bunting, Calandra Lark and Yellow-vented Bulbul. There was also a stuffed bear and many montane plants; while gathering the latter, Hemprich had been bitten by a poisonous snake, and for a time Ehrenberg had feared for his friend's life, but he had now fully recovered.

At the beginning of August they boarded a French naval vessel bound for Damietta and landed in Egypt after an absence of three months. They had every reason to be highly satisfied with their pioneering studies of the ornithology, botany and geology of the Lebanon but now found that new problems awaited them. Hemprich felt that he could no longer face further hardships and disappointments and, not surprisingly, favoured their return home, but Ehrenberg persuaded him to stay until they had achieved their primary objective.

The Austrian Consul again gave them invaluable aid and in November, with several assistants, they at last set off southwards. They called at various Red Sea ports, including Jidda from where they journeyed inland and procured a good number of examples of the prized Balm Tree *Commiphora gileadensis*, cherished as a healing agent for wounds, an antidote to snake bite and as an ingredient of perfume. They spent many more weeks exploring the scattered offshore islands and eventually the small party sailed into the harbour at Massawa on the Eritrean coast. For the last four years their cherished goal had been the mysterious highlands of Abyssinia. Fifty years earlier the Scottish explorer, James Bruce, had discovered the source of the Blue Nile there, and had taken an interest in the birds of the area, but Hemprich, Ehrenberg and Rüppell were the first to visit north-east Africa with the fundamental objective of studying the natural history of the region.

Time and time again Hemprich and Ehrenberg had been frustrated by poverty and administrative ineptitude; sadly, they were cheated at the end by death

Sooty Gull

itself. Before they could even begin to strike inland, Hemprich fell ill again with a virulent fever and weakened by discouragement and malnutrition, he died in the arms of his friend on the last day of June, less than a week after his twenty-ninth birthday.

Ehrenberg buried him on the island of Toalul and then sick at heart, weak and ill himself, he abandoned his hopes and sailed back up the coast with his remaining companions. They travelled across the desert to the Nile, Ehrenberg so delirious with fever that he had to be tied on to the back of his camel. On the long sail downriver he began to recover his strength and at Alexandria he was able to arrange and pack the multitude of botanical, zoological and mineralogical specimens for their safe transportation to Europe. He arrived back in Trieste at the end of 1825, exhausted and dispirited, only to be subjected to the rigours of a long period of quarantine. When he reached Vienna he again became seriously ill, but recovered sufficiently to enjoy being honoured and fêted when he arrived at Berlin.

In 1828 Ehrenberg published an account of their discoveries, under both their names, entitled *Symbolae Physicae*. He deposited their massive collections in the Berlin Museum; the whole collection filled 114 chests, each with a capacity of 20–30 cubic feet. There were 46,000 botanical specimens, of some 3000 species; often there were hundreds of examples of each, with the whole plant preserved if it was small enough. There were nearly 4000 animal species represented by 34,000 specimens, including many new species and new races of birds, often represented by both males and females, adults and juveniles.

Many of the birds which they had discovered were described by Lichtenstein, the Director of the Zoological Museum in Berlin, but he also bartered or gave away some of their specimens before the collection had been properly worked out. In addition, he removed many of the original labels and notes, replaced them with his own and in doing so, confused the origins of many specimens. It was a great pity that the results of all their efforts were not handled by a more competent ornithologist.

It was Charles Bonaparte who first attached Hemprich's name to the Sooty Gull, which breeds on islands near Massawa and elsewhere on the Red Sea. Ehrenberg dedicated one of the discoveries to the memory of his friend, calling it *[Tockus] hemprichii*—Hemprich's Hornbill. But not all of Hemprich's friends were as loyal as Ehrenberg. Before he left Berlin, Hemprich entrusted a manuscript on reptiles and amphibians to L. J. Fitzinger, who published it under his own name a year after the writer's death.

HEY. *GERMAN SURGEON EMPLOYED AS A COLLECTOR ON RÜPPELL'S FIRST MAJOR EXPEDITION TO NORTH-EAST AFRICA. HE IMPERILLED THE SUCCESS OF THE WHOLE VENTURE BY HIS DRUNKENNESS AND LACK OF INITIATIVE. THIS ROMANTICIZED PORTRAIT SHOWS HEY STANDING BESIDE RÜPPELL, NEAR THE PYRAMIDS, AFTER SHOOTING A SACRED IBIS AND A YELLOW-BILLED STORK.*

Michael Hey
(1798-1832)

SAND PARTRIDGE *Ammoperdix heyi* (Temminck)

Perdix Heyi Temminck, 1825. In C. J. Temminck and M. Laugier, *Nouveau Recueil de Planches coloriées d'Oiseaux*, Pt 55, Pls 328, 329: Aqaba

Michael Hey was a young surgeon from Rüdesheim, who came to the attention of Cretzschmar while studying medicine at nearby Frankfurt. Cretzschmar, the President of the Senckenberg Natural History Society in that city, suggested to his friend Eduard Rüppell that Hey would be a suitable person to take along as collector and preparator on his expedition to the Sinai, Nubia and Kordofan. Consequently, the two men travelled together for the next six years.

At the end of 1821 they left Egypt and crossed the Sinai Peninsula, spending several months surveying the shores of the Gulf of Aqaba. In the desert near the head of the gulf Hey shot a pair of very pretty partridges. Both birds had yellow bills and feet, but the female was dull and nondescript compared to the delicate hues of buffy-pink and greyish-brown of her mate's plumage, with his white stripe through the eye and chestnut barring on the flanks. Even today, little is known about these Sand Partridges which occur in rocky or stony deserts in the Middle East, up to a height of about 7000 ft.

The two Germans travelled through southern Sinai to Alexandria and dispatched their collection, including the skins of Hey's partridges, to Cretzschmar at Frankfurt. In the accompanying notes, Rüppell suggested that as the species was new to science, it should be called 'Perdix flavirostris', on account of the bill colour. He was not pleased when Cretzschmar sent the specimens to Temminck, who described the partridges in 1825 in his *Planches coloriées d'Oiseaux* under the name *Perdix Heyi*. It was not just the change of name

Sand Partridge

which offended Rüppell, but also Temminck's eloquent praise of Hey's dedication and bravery: the success of the expedition had more than once been jeopardized by Hey's alcoholism, and his drunken behaviour had almost driven Rüppell to despair. Nonetheless they endured four more years together in the Middle East before sailing to Italy, from whence Hey travelled to Frankfurt with the collections. Rüppell remained for a time in Tuscany and wrote a bitter letter to Cretzschmar expressing his regret that he had tolerated his collector's incompetence for so long:

> "O God, why did I not have any useful assistants on my journey! Why did I not send Hey back at the first opportunity (in 1823), when I discovered his vice of drunkenness, which led to his negligence!"[1]

In Europe Rüppell and Hey were regarded as friends and equals, and the Senckenberg Society had circulated prints of an oil painting to its members depicting Rüppell seated near the pyramids, with Hey standing beside him in the dominant pose, slender and smartly dressed, with a dark neat beard. Rüppell suggested that his own image should have been removed and replaced by that of a huge brandy bottle, with the words "Ecce homo!" written underneath.

Hey did not stay long in Germany. He returned to Cairo and worked there as a doctor and veterinary surgeon, sharing his house for a while with another zoological collector, Matthias Lindemann, whom he had travelled with for a time on Rüppell's expedition. When Rüppell next visited Cairo at the beginning of his second great expedition, he was surprised when Hey visited him and even more surprised to find that he enjoyed the visits. Hey told him that he had only once become drunk since moving to the town, but Rüppell was not sufficiently convinced of his reformed character to invite him to work for him again. Instead he re-hired Lindemann, who had recently quarrelled with Hey. Perhaps exhibiting the paranoid tendencies often found in chronic alcoholics, Hey had accused his friend of trying to poison him.

When Rüppell was next in Cairo, in October 1833 after his remarkable journey to the Abyssinian highlands, he was genuinely saddened by the news that Hey had died there the previous year, in his early thirties.

For a more detailed account of Hey's experiences in north-east Africa, see Rüppell, pp. 317–322.

Brian Houghton Hodgson (1800-1894)

OLIVE-BACKED PIPIT *Anthus hodgsoni* Richmond

Anthus trivialis hodgsoni Richmond, 1907. In E. Blackwelder, *Research in China,* Carnegie Institute of Washington, publ. No. 54, p. 493: [Calcutta], India

The three great pioneers of Indian ornithology were Thomas Jerdon, Edward Blyth and Brian Hodgson. The latter achieved this distinction despite the fact that he was primarily an ethnologist; birds were just one of his many interests.

Hodgson was born on 1 February 1800 at Prestbury in Cheshire, the second child and eldest son, and was followed by five other brothers and sisters. Unfortunately, by the time that the family was complete, Brian's father had lost all his income through an unwise investment. Their comfortable home had to be sold and the household thereafter moved from place to place. At the age of sixteen, Brian entered Haileybury College in preparation for a career in the East India Company's Civil Service.

The following year he passed out as medallist and head of term and sailed to Calcutta, where he studied native languages and Indian law for a year at the College of Fort William. Although troubled by ill-health he distinguished himself in the study of Persian, and gained a good grounding in Sanskrit, but it was the beginning of his long struggle against the liver disease and the fevers that were to assail him for the next forty years until he returned to live in England. At the end of his first year in India, he wrote: "My medical advisor recommended me to throw up the service, and go home. 'Here', said he, 'is your choice—six feet underground, resign the service, or get a hill-appointment.'" To return home an invalid seemed to Hodgson to be a worse alternative than death, for the financial burden of both his parents and his brothers and sisters now rested on his shoulders. But a hill-appointment was almost an impossibility for such a young and inexperienced civilian. Fortunately, his academic successes and the friends he had made led to a posting at Kumaun, a mountainous area of some 11,000 square miles, north of Delhi.

Hodgson found himself surrounded by some of the most magnificent scenery in the world. Warm, luxuriant valleys only two or three thousand feet above sea level lay between mountains clad in pine, oak and rhododendron forests below peaks of perpetual snow. Over the next year his health greatly improved and he began to learn his business as assistant to the Commissioner, G. W. Traill.

HODGSON. *SELF-TAUGHT NATURALIST WHO MADE AN ENORMOUS CONTRIBUTION TO INDIAN ORNITHOLOGY WHILE PURSUING A BRILLIANT CAREER IN THE CIVIL SERVICE. ESTEEMED FOR HIS ORIGINAL RESEARCHES INTO BUDDHISM, HE WAS A MAN OF MANY PARTS AND A PRODIGIOUS WRITER. HE DONATED HIS BIRD COLLECTIONS FROM KATMANDU AND DARJEELING TO THE BRITISH MUSEUM.*

The country had been ravaged by invading Gurkhas for twenty-four years and had only recently been conquered by the British. The two officials spent much of their time marching from one village to the next, assessing and classifying each community. They often travelled along narrow footpaths and ledges cut out of sheer cliffs, sometimes having to scramble up or down the rocks if they met a file of sheep or goats. Traill's love of enquiry, his respect for the hill peoples, his enthusiasm and efficiency all had an inspiring effect on his younger colleague, but, less than two years later, Hodgson was transferred to Katmandu where he found himself in a narrow world of Residency routine, forbidden to stray further than a morning's walk from the town.

In 1822 he was glad to be promoted to the Foreign Office in Calcutta as acting Deputy-Secretary in the Persian Department. It was one of the most prized posts in the junior service, offering unlimited career opportunities, but the following autumn he again became so ill that he had to be sent back to the healthier climate of Katmandu; for the next twenty years he remained in Nepal.

The long isolation from family and friends and the monotonous routine of his duties spurred Hodgson to adopt new interests. Although he had no scientific training, he began to investigate the natural history of the area by sending out native collectors who brought him birds and animals. Some of these he drew himself, but he also employed and trained three native artists to paint the specimens with extreme accuracy, under his careful supervision. The collection eventually comprised 1241 sheets of birds, accompanied in many cases by drawings of their nests and eggs with detailed notes on the colours of the bare parts, measurements, food (discovered by dissection), breeding habits, behaviour and distribution. Always generous with his collection, Hodgson lent most of the illustrations to Allan Hume, and then donated them to the Zoological Society of London together with 567 sheets of mammals and fifty-five of reptiles.

Within two years of returning to Katmandu, Hodgson had discovered a new species of antelope, the Tibetan Antelope *Pantolopus hodgsoni*. He sent a specimen to Dr Abel (Lady Amherst's personal physician) who named it after him. Hodgson built up a very fine collection of mammal skins which he later gave to the British Museum. It was undoubtedly the most important donation of mammals which they ever received from an individual, due to its size (more than 900 specimens), the accompaniment of many skeletons and, above all, to the very great number of type specimens. Between 1830 and 1843 Hodgson contributed over fifty papers on the Himalayan mammals to various scientific journals. His first ornithological paper appeared in 1829, describing the huge Rufous-necked Hornbill which inhabits the northern evergreen hill forests. Although he worked only from Katmandu (and later from Darjeeling), he added 150 species to the Indian avifauna and such was his thoroughness that few new birds have since been discovered in these areas. The 9500 bird skins which Hodgson amassed in India also went to the British Museum. After the curator had made a selection he forwarded the rest to the museums of Edinburgh, Dublin, Leyden and Paris.

Many species of birds and many more races have been named in his honour, including Hodgson's Frogmouth *Batrachostomus hodgsoni* by G. R. Gray and the Rustybreasted Blue Flycatcher *Muscicapa hodgsonii* by Jules Verreaux. The

Whitebellied Redstart or Hodgson's Shortwing, which breeds in the Himalayas above the timber-line, belongs to the genus *Hodgsonius*, so designated by Charles Bonaparte. The Olive-backed Pipit *Anthus hodgsoni* is a common breeding bird in the Himalayas and winters over practically the whole Indian continent, commonly in coffee and cardamon plantations. Also known as the Indian Tree Pipit, *Anthus hodgsoni* is a new name for the *Anthus maculatus* of Hodgson which appeared in J. E. Gray's *Zoological Miscellany* in 1844.

Allan Hume, the leading Indian ornithologist of the next generation, in appreciation of Hodgson's enormous influence declared that:

> "Hodgson combined much of Blyth's talent for classification with much of Jerdon's habit of persevering personal observation, and excelled the latter in literary gifts and minute and exact research. But with Hodgson ornithology was only a pastime or at best a *parergon*, and humble a branch of science as is ornithology, it is yet like all other branches a jealous mistress demanding an undivided allegiance; and hence with, on the whole, higher qualifications, he exercised practically somewhat less influence on ornithological evolution than either of his great contemporaries . . . there is no Indian ornithologist living to whom the memories of these three great pioneers are not dear and sacred, and that so long as this fascinating study has any votaries in our Indian Empire, so long will the names of Blyth, Hodgson, and Jerdon be remembered, cherished, and revered."[1]

Hodgson derived much pleasure from his zoological studies, but his primary interest was in the Nepalese people whom he constantly sought to understand better, both as tribes and as individuals. He produced a constant stream of papers, the titles of which give an idea of his diverse interests; for example: 'On the Languages, Literature and Religion of Nepal' (1828), 'Sketch of Buddhism, derived from the Baudda Scriptures of Nepal' (1828), 'On Trans-Himalayan Commerce' (1831), 'On the Paper of Nepal' (1832), 'On the Law and Legal Practice of Nepal' (1834) and 'On the Wool of Tibet' (1846). He particularly devoted himself to collecting Sanskrit manuscripts relating to northern Buddhism with which he endowed the libraries of Europe and India. Many scrolls were of extreme age, some dating back as far as the eleventh century AD. Hodgson did not merely preserve and disseminate the precious manuscripts; he was the first to give a clear and intelligible explanation of Buddhism to Europe, thus earning the enduring respect of Orientalists.

Olive-backed Pipit

In 1833 Hodgson became the British Resident in Katmandu and for the next ten years he strove to maintain peace with the Nepalese, a task in which he succeeded only because of his deep empathy with the people and his intimate knowledge of the striving factions within the Nepalese Court. Part of Hodgson's extraordinary influence with the native people was due to his reputation among them as a man of ascetic life (always abstemious, he had given up drinking wine and had become a strict vegetarian after his severe illness in 1837) and he won the friendship of the Grand Lama, the Tibetan over-lord, through his Buddhist learning.

Throughout his years in Nepal, Hodgson regularly sent money to his parents, but he was unable to go home on furlough because of his financial responsibilities. The separation was a great source of sorrow to him but his ailing younger brother William, who served in the Indian Army, was his guest for nearly two years during 1828 and 1829. After William recovered and married Samuel Tickell's sister, Brian hoped that his brother would be transferred to Katmandu to command his escort but William died in 1838 and the post was later filled by Tickell. Edward, the youngest brother, had also died in India three years earlier, after catching a fever while snipe-shooting in the marshes.

Hodgson found solace in his marriage, which, though not amounting to such in the legal sense, was regarded by both himself and his Muslim wife as a binding relationship for as long as she lived. Their children brought him much joy and satisfaction and they were later educated by his sister Frances, in Holland.

In 1844 Hodgson suddenly resigned from the Service after being censured by the newly appointed Governor-General, Lord Ellenborough. Hodgson had chosen to disobey his misguided orders, realizing that to have carried them out would have negated all the good effects of previous long-held policies. When Hodgson returned to England he was sympathetically received by the East India Company's Court of Directors and enjoyed the long-awaited reunion with his surviving family, but he was unsuited for idleness. He decided to return to India the next year in order to continue his researches in a private capacity. From his new home in Darjeeling he spent the next thirteen years investigating the peoples of northern India, the physical geography of Himalaya and Tibet, and the zoology of Sikkim.

It was a reclusive existence, partly due to his poor health. He only left the house when he went down to the plains each winter. In the spring of 1848 he was visited by Joseph Hooker who delighted in the warm hospitality he received over the next two years between his numerous botanical excursions. Hodgson's keenest energies at that time were directed towards extending the benefits of vernacular education for the Indians. More than ten years earlier, it had been Hodgson who had first proposed that the Indians should be taught in their mother tongue, at a time when all others debated whether education should be in English or the classical languages of India. It was for this far reaching influence that Hodgson was best known to the ordinary people of India.

While visiting England and Holland in 1853 he met and married Miss Anne Scott, who returned to Darjeeling with him. Several years later Mrs Hodgson's health broke down and she sailed home to England, followed the next year by her husband and they settled in the Cotswolds. After her death in 1868, Hodgson married again, at the age of sixty-nine, yet lived to celebrate his silver wedding anniversary! For many years he enjoyed the pleasures of a country gentleman, hunting with the hounds until the age of eighty-six, annually visiting London or the Riviera and delighting in the company of his much younger wife. He rarely made public appearances but enjoyed the company of many famous visitors. One of the last to visit him was his old friend Hooker, who complained to him about unfinished work. Hodgson chided him, "Do not complain of work! Thank God you have got it to do, and can do it. The hardest work of all is idleness." It was a telling comment, for most men would have been highly satisfied to have made just one of Hodgson's contributions: in Public Service, to ethnology or to zoology.

Hodgson passed away on 23 May 1894 and was buried in the shade of an ancient yew tree in the quiet churchyard at Alderley, between Bristol and Gloucester, on the edge of the Cotswold Hills.

Jens Wilken Hornemann (1770-1841)

ARCTIC REDPOLL *Acanthis hornemanni* (Holböll)

L[inota] Hornemanni Holböll, 1843. *Naturhistorike Tidsskrift* 4, p. 398: [Ameralikfjord], Greenland

The Arctic Redpoll has the distinction of often being the most northerly wintering passerine. The differences between this species and other redpolls were first noticed by Carl Peter Holböll, who wrote of the birds that he had seen in Greenland:

> "It is decidedly a resident and during the winter frequents the fells of the interior of the country, but is commoner north of 66° than south of that latitude. In February 1826 I saw several flocks on the fells . . . the Reindeer-hunters also see large flocks when they penetrate far into the interior in the winter."[1]

They are able to over-winter only where strong winds sweep the ground bare of snow, enabling them to feed on exposed seeds. Their digestive tracts are especially adapted to take in large amounts of food during the short days which can then be digested slowly through the long nights.

Holböll was a Danish zoologist whose long association with Greenland lasted from the 1820s until his death in 1856, when a ship that was taking him from Copenhagen to Greenland sank and disappeared without trace. During his visits to the north he travelled extensively and took every opportunity to collect for the Royal Natural History Museum at Copenhagen. In 1840 he wrote (in Danish) 'Ornithological Contributions to the Fauna of Greenland' which appeared in the *Naturhistorike Tidsskrift* (1842–43). It contained his description of the Arctic Redpoll which he named *L[inota] Hornemanni* after J. W. Hornemann, the Director of the Botanical Gardens at Copenhagen, where Holböll's father was the head gardener.

Jens Wilken Hornemann was born on 6 March 1770 in Marstal on the small Danish island of Aerø, which lies quite close to the Baltic coast of Germany. He was educated by his father until he was thirteen years old when he was sent to live on the much larger island of Fyn with an uncle, Pastor Morten Bredsdorff, from whom he evidently derived his interest in natural history. After three years he was sent from the beautiful countryside that surrounded the manse to Copenhagen to study under Jens Bindesböll. Hornemann matriculated at the

HORNEMANN. *DANISH BOTANIST. AUTHOR OF THE* FLORA
DANICA *AND FRIEND OF THE HOLBÖLL FAMILY. HE WAS
SIXTY YEARS OLD WHEN THIS PORTRAIT WAS PAINTED.*

University in 1788 but by then his father had died and he had to supplement his income by teaching.

When a natural history society was founded in the city in 1789, Hornemann attended the lectures and became closely associated with Martin Vahl, the principal instructor, with whom he developed a lifelong friendship. There seemed to be little hope of earning a living from his interests and so Hornemann decided to study medicine; he changed his mind in 1793 when he won an essay competition with *Forsøg til en Dansk økonomisk Plantelaere* which concerned the economic importance of Danish plants. It was a youthful work, incomplete and unoriginal, but was useful as a travelling flora and so gained a wide circulation; many of today's Danish plant names stem from its first publication in 1796. It went into a second and third edition which was completely revised and expanded to cover the whole Danish Kingdom and so included plants from Norway, Iceland and Greenland.

In 1798, aided by public and private funds, Hornemann visited Germany, the Pyrenees, the south of France and Paris, and in 1800 he spent five months studying the various herbaria in London. On his return to Denmark, through the influence of Vahl who was then Professor of Botany at Copenhagen University, Hornemann was appointed Lecturer at the Botanic Gardens. Not long after this, in October 1801, he married Marie Judithe, the daughter of Professor Claus Hornemann. Vahl died two years later and Hornemann not only took over his lectures but also continued with Vahl's *Flora Danica* and in 1808 became Professor of Botany. In later years many of his students admitted that he had not been an original or inspiring teacher, but his friendly and obliging nature made him a popular figure at the University among both students and colleagues and on his sixtieth birthday they paid him the unusual compliment of organizing a torch-light procession. His wife died only two months later and Hornemann himself was in poor health for the last five or so years of his life. Eventually he had to abandon his duties entirely and died on 30 July 1841, at Copenhagen.

For thirty-five years he had been the leading Danish botanist. His most important contribution, for which he had collected most of the specimens, was the *Flora Danica, or Differences of the Vegetation in the Danish Provinces* (1824). In eighteen parts, with 1100 plates, it was especially good for the vascular plants

Arctic Redpoll

but the section on the non-flowering plants was considered to be poor. It was later translated into German and English.

Hornemann had few connections with ornithology but he was deeply interested in the exploration of Greenland. He supplied a list of the plants of that island to W. A. Graah, one-time travelling companion of C. P. Holböll, and this was added to Graah's 'Narrative of an Expedition to the east coast of Greenland', published, in Danish, in 1837. Hornemann also took a keen interest in the exploits of Holböll for he knew the young man and his family well. F. L. Holböll, his head gardener, had worked with him for many years and together they had brought the Botanic Gardens up to a very high standard.

Hornemann was long remembered in the vernacular name Hornemann's Redpoll but this is now rarely used. In 1946 it was proposed that the name Arctic Redpoll be adopted as a collective term to include both Hornemann's and Coues's Redpolls, because they are indistinguishable in the field.[2] Rather confusingly, Holböll's Redpoll is a race of a different species, the Mealy Redpoll *A. flammea holboellii*.

Allan Octavian Hume
(1829-1912)

HUME'S TAWNY OWL *Strix butleri* (Hume)

Asio butleri [Hume], 1878. *Stray Feathers* 7, p. 316: Omara [= Ormara], Makran coast, Baluchistan

HUME'S WHEATEAR *Oenanthe alboniger* (Hume)

Saxicola Alboniger Hume, 1872. *Stray Feathers* 1, p. 2: "Stony hills which divide Kelat from Sindh . . . and Mekran coast"

HUME'S LESSER WHITETHROAT *Sylvia althaea* Hume

Sylvia althaea Hume, 1878. *Stray Feathers* 7, p. 60: Kashmir

The Indian National Congress was founded in 1885 in order to increase Indian involvement in the formation of British policy in India, but by 1905 the view within Congress, which had become the main political party of the Hindu, was that the country should have complete independence. Mahatma Gandhi, one time leader of Congress, dominated the campaign of civil disobedience and passive resistance to British rule from 1915 until Independence Day in August 1947. Congress became the ruling party of India and maintained power until the 1977 elections. The founder and long-serving first Secretary of the Indian National Congress was Allan Octavian Hume.

For over thirty years, between 1849 and 1882, Hume worked in the Indian Civil Service, firstly as an excellent District Officer and later as Secretary to the Government. He was a truly remarkable man. He made close contact with the people, travelled over much of the country, knew about its forestry, mineralogy, art and history, and as a naturalist studied its many plants, mammals and birds. Hume believed that he knew India, *as a whole*, better than anyone and that few loved the country more. He achieved social, educational and agricultural reforms as well as far-reaching political changes. But for an unfortunate incident his ornithological contribution would have been monumental.

His father, Joseph Hume, a well-known radical politician in Britain who had campaigned for the repeal of the Corn Laws, had also spent time in India and it seems that Allan was destined for the Indian Civil Service from his earliest days. At thirteen, as part of his schooling he served as a junior midshipman on

HUME. *BRITISH CIVIL SERVANT IN INDIA, POLITICAL REFORMER, BIG-GAME HUNTER, ORNITHOLOGIST AND BOTANIST. CREATOR OF THE JOURNAL* STRAY FEATHERS, *HE DOMINATED INDIAN ORNITHOLOGY FOR DECADES AND AMASSED THE LARGEST PRIVATE COLLECTION OF INDIAN BIRDS EVER KNOWN.*

the frigate *Vanguard*, mostly in the Mediterranean. He continued his education at Haileybury Training College (founded by the East India Company for the very purpose of providing India with administrators), and he then went to University College Hospital where he studied medicine and surgery. When he was twenty he sailed for India and joined the Bengal Civil Service at Etawah; a town of 34,000 people situated between Delhi and Cawnpore.

Hume started his career as a junior clerk but soon rose to be the chief civil officer for a district of 16,000 square miles. He began a programme of popular education, police reform, the establishment of juvenile reformatories and the control of alcohol and even created a local vernacular newspaper. In 1853 he married Mary Anne Grindall and they had one daughter. In fact all was progressing well until, nine years after Hume's arrival, the Indian Mutiny erupted at Meerut 250 miles to the north of Etawah.

Rebels soon arrived in Hume's district and some were found secure in a nearby Muslim temple. Hume went to the scene at once but did not order the local militia to attack because he knew that many of them were sympathetic to the mutineers. Instead, with only his assistant and one native policeman he stormed the building. Two rebels and the policeman were killed. Hume's assistant was severely wounded but Hume managed to drag him to safety. In a storm in the night the remaining mutineers escaped. Returning quickly to Etawah he found that the local troops were still loyal to the British but he

Hume's Tawny Owl

feared that this would change if the mutiny spread. He therefore decided to evacuate all the British civilians to Agra and then served in its defence on several occasions by manning the batteries. He was laid low by cholera for a few months but recovered and returned to Etawah with fifty men and occupied the town without difficulty. Hume later became involved in some minor skirmishes and even pitched battles. On one occasion, although the British were vastly outnumbered, Hume led such a ferocious charge into the rebels that he forced them to retreat and he captured their artillery. The regular army officers commended his bravery and in 1860 he was made Commander of the Bath for his services during the mutiny.

When order was restored Hume ensured that few severe punishments were carried out in his district. Only seven mutineers were hanged on Hume's judgements and he himself devised the gallows to ensure that death was swift. He was accused of an "excess of leniency" but he knew well that only a small minority were strongly anti-British, indeed throughout the mutiny he had kept up a correspondence with several of his loyal employees and associates. His one desire was to return to peace and to carry on with his projects for improving the lot of the common people. Over 180 schools were established in his district catering for about 5000 pupils—only two of which were girls. The paper which he started, *The Peoples' Friend*, was for the benefit of these newly literate pupils. It was very cheap, accessible to all and gained a circulation well beyond the district it was intended for and was even shown to Queen Victoria.

In 1867 Hume's period as a District Officer ended and he became Commissioner of Customs for the North West Provinces. His principal achievement here was to begin the gradual abolition of the great salt barrier. Two and a half thousand miles long, it was designed to protect the Government's salt monopoly from cheap salt produced in the Rajputana States but it was a great expense to maintain and a source of endless corruption. At the same time Hume became Director-General of Agriculture and had to travel throughout India learning about the country's forestry and farming. It was during this period that Hume established a network of over fifty bird collectors who supplied him with specimens from all parts of India and even Burma. To cope with the ever increasing amount of material he employed William Davison to assist in preparing and cataloguing skins, and to collect fresh specimens; Davison himself being supplied with a staff of taxidermists and, for his travels, a number of horses and elephants.

Although Hume showed a particular concern for the poor in rural India he was often frustrated in his plans for reform by the ruling powers at Simla, who saw no need to educate the people nor to change their economic position—the Government invariably supported the *status quo*. Hume encountered even more problems when he moved to Simla. As Secretary to the Government under the Viceroyalty of Lord Mayo, Hume and other staff were encouraged to put forward their opinions and points of view. The next two viceroys failed to see how anyone else's ideas could differ from their own and they discouraged such independence. Eventually Hume, too busy and not anyway inclined to cultivate favour in high places, over-reached his mark and was dismissed with no official explanation. Hume's biographer, Sir William Wedderburn, called this a gross act of injustice. But changes of staff at Simla were frequent and part of accepted policy; by serving there for over nine years Hume had been particularly honoured and the fact that he was later offered a Lieutenant-Governorship (which he declined), supports the view that he was not harshly treated. All the same it appears to have been a surprise to him and it was a blow to his ornithological pursuits because it was impossible for him to take his huge collection and library to Allahabad where he worked for the next three years on the Revenue Board.

During the preceding years Hume had spent £20,000 on building up a museum and library and had accumulated the largest collection of Asiatic birds in the world. In order to house the collection he had added special rooms to *Rothney Castle*, his home at Simla. All the materials and the workmanship were of the best quality and the neatly labelled specimens were arranged superbly for ease of access and were only a few steps from the working library, which also housed the egg cabinets.

In 1872, at his own expense, he started the quarterly journal *Stray Feathers—A journal of ornithology for India and dependencies*. Printed at Calcutta, Hume established himself as editor and became the principal contributor. A review in *The Ibis*[1] sneered at his motives since Hume had complained earlier that several of his new discoveries and their original descriptions had previously taken so long to appear in print that by then others had established priority. The reviewer was nevertheless forced to admire the contents and expressed the hope that the high standard could be maintained. In the first year Hume contributed the results of his sailing trip down the Indus and analysed his collection of the birds of Sind and the Makran coast. His expedition had gathered 1200 bird skins of 250 species, eighteen of them new to the Indian avifauna. One of his discoveries was Hume's Wheatear, found in "the stony hills which divide Kelat from Sindh". A subsequent issue of 1878 contained his new descriptions of Hume's Lesser Whitethroat, from Kashmir, as well as Hume's Tawny Owl obtained at Ormara on the Makran coast and sent to him by Captain Butler. In time Hume acquired Butler's collection and those of a number of others including Cripps, Chill, Brooks, Bingham and Eugene Oates in Burma.

Hume continued to go on expeditions whenever time would allow. One year he hired a steamer and with Davison and several friends visited the Andaman and Nicobar Islands; in another year Hume made a trip to the Lacadives off the south-west coast of India. In 1879, on what proved to be his last major expedition, he spent seven months collecting in Manipur in Burma where he made a discovery which he considered to be among the most interesting and important of his ornithological career. A Manipuri official who had been sent to assist him arrived wearing some feathers in his head-dress which Hume at once realized belonged to an undescribed species of pheasant! After numerous enquiries and much searching by native hunters he subsequently received some live examples. Often referred to as Hume's Pheasant it should more correctly be called Mrs Hume's Pheasant as he specifically named it *humiae* after his wife.[2]

In 1873 Hume published *Nests and Eggs of Indian Birds* and followed this in 1879 with the well-illustrated *Game Birds of India, Burma and Ceylon*. This latter work was so expensive to produce that it was limited to only a thousand copies. It was co-written by C. H. T. Marshall, who described Hume as "beyond all doubt the greatest authority on ornithology of the Indian Empire". This was soon to be confirmed by a massive publication incorporating all the birds of India. At the age of fifty-three Hume retired from the Civil Service and returned

Hume's Lesser Whitethroat

to Simla to finish work on what should have been his greatest project. As the winter of 1884 approached, Hume and the other Europeans moved down onto the plains, as usual, and he left his house in the care of his servants. On his return the following spring he found, to his horror, that his manuscripts, additional papers and correspondence for the book (weighing several hundredweights), had all been sold in the bazaar as waste paper. Twenty-five years work had been lost at a stroke.

Hume said little about the tragedy but it killed his interest in ornithology. His book could never be published and no more volumes of *Stray Feathers* appeared after 1888. Only eleven volumes of the journal were ever issued and they remain a substitute memorial to the industry and co-ordinating powers of Allan Hume who had inspired the best out of his contributors.

Since it was obviously impossible for him to replace the lost manuscript Hume decided to dispose of his collection. Although he could have sold it to the United States for £10,000 he generously bequeathed it to the British Museum (Natural History). In the intervening period before Bowdler Sharpe arrived to supervise its packing and transportation 20,000 items had to be thrown out because of moth and damp, and a landslip carried away one end of the museum. Nevertheless there were still 18,500 eggs, 500 nests and 63,000 bird skins in the collection! This vast array of the Indian avifauna included 2830 birds of prey, 1155 owls, 813 parrots, 2120 sandgrouse, 2415 waders and nearly 2000 sunbirds and white-eyes. Two hundred and fifty-eight of the skins were type specimens. Sharpe, who was made most welcome after his long voyage, wrote:

Hume's Wheatear

> "It did not take me many hours to find out that Mr. Hume was a naturalist of no ordinary calibre . . . it is doubtful if such a combination of genius for organisation with energy for the completion of so great a scheme, and the scientific knowledge requisite for its proper development, will again be combined in a single individual."

It was no easy task to transport the forty-seven half-ton packing cases from Hume's museum, 7800 ft up in the mountains, down to the nearest railway station but it was accomplished without serious mishap and eventually they arrived safely in London. Later, the British Museum also acquired the whole of Hume's magnificent hoard of big-game trophies.

Indian politics helped to take Hume's mind off the loss of both manuscript and collection. In 1883 he wrote an open letter to the graduates of Calcutta University calling upon them, as the most important source of all "mental, moral, social and political progress in India", to form their own national movement. Hume declared that:

> "If fifty men cannot be found with sufficient power of self-sacrifice, sufficient love for and pride in their country, sufficient genuine and unselfish patriotism to take the initiative and if needs be devote the rest of their lives to the Cause—then there is no hope for India."

The movement had the approval of the Viceroy, Lord Dufferin, and the Congressmen were at first, as Hume intended, loyal to the British Crown. Unfortunately the moderates were replaced by extremists and within sixty-five years the rule of the British had ended and Pakistan was separated from India.

In 1890 Hume's wife died and four years later he returned to England to settle at Upper Norwood in London. He still maintained an active interest in Indian politics and remained Secretary to Congress until 1908. In Britain he became involved in Liberal politics for over twenty years but though he campaigned in several elections no Liberal candidate that he supported was ever elected. Perhaps to compensate for his disappointment in ornithology, Hume, now over sixty years of age, turned to botany and after a few years founded and endowed the South London Botanic Institute. He hoped that its libraries and collections of plants would be used especially by amateur botanists. His assistant, W. H. Griffen, once commented that garden escapes and accidental introductions wasted much of his own time because he found them difficult to identify, so Hume decided to include all quasi-wild species in their collections; they even planted such exotic species in the Institute's gardens to be sure of obtaining perfect specimens. Later they began a collection of seedlings in various stages of development for mounting, even though they both knew that they would die before their project was finished; it was an idea unique in Europe.

Four young women were employed to help with the work and Hume insisted that this should be done in an artistic way. Every one of the 40,000 sheets of specimens passed through his hands for critical examination and approval before mounting. As one might expect Hume was intolerant of idleness or any display of lack of interest in the work but he was a considerate employer, especially at times of sickness, and he continued to be financially generous in many ways.

Although eminent botanists were later inspired to bequeath their collections to the Institute, much of the initial work was done by Hume and Griffen. In 1901 Hume spent April to October hunting for plants in Cornwall; in 1903 he was in Yorkshire and Upper Teesdale and in 1905 he went to Wales. Thereafter he usually made shorter trips of only one or two months, often to the south coast around Eastbourne and Folkestone. Once again Hume combined his skills as field-worker, organizer and writer to good effect. As he became more elderly his capacity for work eventually decreased and he died on 31 July 1912, at the age of eighty-three. The funeral at Brookward cemetery was a simple one and there were few words on his tombstone.

Yet few Britons ever had so many mourners. The tributes to Hume flowed in from all around India. In Etawah, where Allan Hume had served as a District Officer for almost eighteen years, the people were genuinely grieved: as a mark of respect all the shops in the bazaar closed, even though it was forty-five years since Hume had left the town.

JOUANIN. *FRENCH PHARMACIST, ORNITHOLOGIST AND CONSERVATIONIST. PHOTOGRAPHED IN JULY 1963 BY HIS FRIEND FRANCIS ROUX ON SALVAGEM GRANDE, WHERE HE CONTINUES TO BE INVOLVED IN SEABIRD STUDIES.*

Christian Jouanin (born 1925)

JOUANIN'S PETREL *Bulweria fallax* Jouanin

Bulweria fallax Jouanin, 1955. *L'Oiseau* 25, p. 160: at sea, approx. 12° 30′ N, 55° E. Northwestern Indian Ocean

Man's capacity for inflicting change upon the environment has accelerated remarkably since the heyday of the eighteenth and nineteenth century naturalists. While each succeeding generation of ornithologists has benefited from an overall increased mobility, they have also had to accept more and more reductions in the extent and variety of unspoilt habitats. Consequently, the attitudes and ambitions of today's ornithologists are often radically different from those of their predecessors. Christian Jouanin is an excellent example of the modern professional: well educated, trained as a pharmacist and zoologist, he has served as an assistant at the Paris Natural History Museum and is also a good field-worker. More importantly, he is active in the protection and conservation of threatened species and vulnerable habitat.

He was born on 10 July 1925, at Paris. By the age of fifteen he was already frequenting the ornithological department of the Paris Museum where he was greatly encouraged by Jacques Berlioz. Jouanin developed a special interest in seabirds and became well acquainted with the museum's two famous specimens of the black petrel of Réunion Island (off Madagascar), of which only two other examples were known to exist. The species had not been seen alive since the last century and was considered to be, almost certainly, extinct. Then the English ornithologist W. B. Alexander reported that three new specimens of the petrel had been collected in the northern part of the Indian Ocean: one in 1946 and two in 1953, though unfortunately only one of them had been preserved.[1] In the same area, on 20 June 1954, G. Cherbonnier, a specialist in echinoderms from the Paris Museum, was at sea off the island of Socotra when a petrel flew on board, attracted by the lights of the boat.

When this last bird was examined at Paris it was clearly of the same species as those birds referred to by Alexander, but it was not the Réunion Petrel. Subsequently Jouanin went to Leiden, Oxford and Cambridge to examine and compare notes on all the known study skins of the Réunion Petrel and the other petrels from the Indian Ocean. He concluded that none of the petrels from the Arabian coast were Réunion Petrels and that the bird from near Socotra was a new species! It was described by Jouanin under the name *Bulweria fallax*, and has become known in English as Jouanin's Petrel.

There have only been a few records of this species within the Western Palearctic, but as the bird now appears to be common off the coast of Oman it may well occur regularly in the Gulf of Aden and northwards into the Red Sea. The location of its breeding grounds are still unknown.

Although Jouanin was pleased to have distinguished a new species, he had discovered no new information on the black petrel of Réunion. Accordingly, he wrote to Armand Barau, an ornithologist living on Réunion, who placed sketches and articles concerning the bird in the local press, promising a reward for any positive information received. Sometime afterwards, when a petrel was caught on the beach at St Denis it was forwarded to Jouanin. This bird was obviously not the long-lost petrel as it was grey and white; but neither was it a petrel of any other known species! Jouanin was therefore able to describe a second new species, to which he gave the name *Pterodroma baraui*—Barau's Petrel.

In 1964 Jouanin travelled to Réunion to search for the breeding grounds of this second new petrel, and to try to track down the Réunion Petrel of which there was still no recent news. He pinpointed the nesting sites of Barau's Petrel on steep cliffs in the mountains of the interior and found places where he could watch them returning to their inland nesting sites at dusk. He also found their discarded bones in caves where runaway slaves had long ago feasted on them. There was no sign of the Réunion Petrel and Jouanin began to believe that it really was extinct until Armand Barau's newspaper advertisements at last paid off: a dying bird was brought in by Barau's own dog! Although a second fresh specimen was also found, Jouanin suspects that the petrel is very nocturnal in its movements and is not a colonial nester, which could mean that its status and its breeding sites will remain unknown for years to come.

Jouanin has also described a new subspecies of Audubon's Shearwater which occurs on the Seychelles. He named it *Puffinus lherminier nicolae* after his wife Nicole Berge whom he had married when he was twenty-two years old, the year before he graduated in Paris as a pharmacist. Although pharmacology was his chosen career his deep interest in ornithology led him to become more and more committed to conservation.

In 1956, with the late Michel-Hervé Julien, Jouanin carried out a census of Grey Herons in France which showed that there were less than 2000 pairs in the entire country. They successfully campaigned for a change in legislation so that the birds gained a degree of protection from shooting during the nesting season, and by 1974 the number of Grey Herons had increased to 3300 pairs.

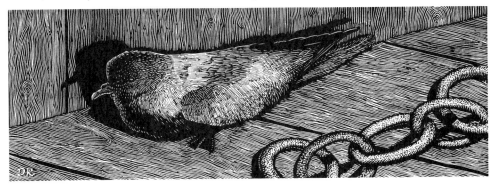

Jouanin's Petrel

They are fully protected today and in 1987 there were more than 12,000 pairs.

The enquiries about herons made Jouanin particularly aware of the decline of their natural habitat. In 1961, in view of the MAR Conference to be held at Saintes Maries-de-la-mer in the Camargue, he compiled an inventory of the more interesting and valuable wetlands in France. Later on, following a proposal from Luc Hoffman and with the support of the World Wildlife Fund, the Bureau MAR was founded to conserve and manage wetlands, with Jouanin as its director. Since then many important steps have been taken towards promoting the value of wetlands and for the preservation of important sites.

Jouanin is particularly proud of the reserve of Chanteloup in the Marais d'Olonne on the west coast, between Nantes and La Rochelle, a small but very attractive reserve. The preserved area, formerly a saline lagoon belonging to an industrial company, had very few birds when it was purchased by the Conseil Supérieur de la Chasse following a suggestion from Jouanin, but by controlling the water levels large numbers have been attracted to winter and to breed. It is now one of only a few Avocet breeding sites on the Atlantic coast.

Meanwhile, Jouanin continued to study seabirds by visiting the Salvagems, a small group of islands near the Canaries.[2] For centuries, Portuguese fishermen from Madeira harvested young Cory's Shearwaters from this barren rocky archipelago with no marked decline in the overall numbers, even though as many as 20,000 birds were taken each season for food, oil and down. The adults were always left unmolested and sufficient numbers of young always survived on the more inhospitable cliffs to maintain the population. Jouanin first visited the islands in 1963 with Francis Roux, his friend and frequent colleague who is now director of the French bird-ringing office. The expedition was organized by the Museu Municipal of Funchal and included Alec Zino who is resident on Madeira. Zino became more and more interested in bird study and conservation and was alarmed by later reports which told of the wholesale destruction of eggs and adults by poachers, causing a sharp decline in the number of shearwaters on the Salvagems. He therefore decided to lease the islands to stop the annual slaughter and to restore the bird population. In addition, Jouanin planned a long term study of the shearwater biology and population dynamics, which was initiated by ringing thousands of chicks in 1968, with the help of J. R. dos Santos Junioz, head of the Portuguese bird ringing centre at Porto. The private owner of the islands was contacted and arrangements began to be made for their purchase by an international conservation body but the Portuguese Government stepped in, bought the islands and made them a national nature reserve. Now the islands are guarded all the year round, the seabirds are fully protected and the Cory's Shearwater colony is recovering.

Jouanin has recently retired from pharmacy and is now able to return to the Salvagems every year to take part in the field-work there. He has served on a number of conservation-based organizations and continues to be active in these circles. From 1966 to 1981 he was Secretary General of the Société Nationale de Protection de la Nature (which is in charge of the famous Camargue reserve) and he was its president in 1981. From 1978 to 1981 he was President of the Société Ornithologique de France; and from 1970 to 1975 he was Vice-President of the International Union for Conservation of Nature and Natural Resources. Jouanin still lives in Neuilly, near Paris, with his wife Nicole, but their two daughters have now left home, are both married and have presented them with six grandchildren.

KITTLITZ. *ORNITHOLOGIST AND ARTIST, BEST KNOWN FOR HIS DISCOVERIES DURING THE ROUND-THE-WORLD VOYAGE OF THE RUSSIAN CORVETTE* SENJAWIN. *THE PROGRESS OF HIS CAREER WAS RUINED BY ILL-HEALTH AND MISFORTUNE.*

Friedrich Heinrich von Kittlitz (1799-1874)

KITTLITZ'S PLOVER *Charadrius pecuarius* Temminck

Charadrius pecuarius Temminck, 1823. In C. J. Temminck and M. Laugier, *Nouveau Recueil de Planches coloriées d'Oiseaux*, Pt 31, Pl. 183: Cape of Good Hope

Baron Heinrich von Kittlitz was born on 16 February 1799 in Breslau (now Woctaw, Poland). His father was a Lieutenant-Colonel in the Prussian army and his maternal grandfather had been a Major-General with the Russians, so the young Kittlitz was following the family tradition when he became a soldier. At the age of sixteen, shortly after Napoleon's defeat at Waterloo, Kittlitz marched into Paris with his regiment. He was soon promoted to Lieutenant and stationed at Mainz, near Frankfurt, where his interest in natural history was encouraged by Eduard Rüppell, who became a close friend.

In 1821 Rüppell set off on his first expedition to north-east Africa and the Sinai Peninsula and for the next six years he periodically dispatched impressive collections to Dr Cretzschmar in Frankfurt. Cretzschmar produced an 'Atlas' (1826) of Rüppell's travels while he was away and he gave Kittlitz the task of providing some of the illustrations from their friend's zoological specimens. Encouraged by this, Kittlitz began to investigate the possibility of abandoning his army career in favour of ornithology and an opportunity arose when he was in his mid-twenties. Through family connections on his mother's side he succeeded in gaining a place on a Russian expedition to Kamchatka, under the leadership of Captain Lütke.

The round-the-world voyage began in 1826 and Kittlitz is now best remembered for the many important ornithological discoveries which he made en route. On board the Russian corvette *Senjawin* he called at Tenerife and Rio de Janeiro, then rounded Cape Horn and headed northwards. In March 1827 he spent some time ashore on the coast of Chile near Valparaiso. Most of the nearby countryside was bare and burnt, as it was the driest time of year, but the damp valley bottoms contained many interesting birds and he discovered a number of new species which he later described in *Über einige Vögel von Chili* [On some Birds from Chile] (1830). It had been suggested at St Petersburg that as many sketches as possible be made of the different types of vegetation, and although Kittlitz was not a botanist, he was an exceptionally careful artist. At every opportunity throughout the voyage he sketched the landscapes and drew the larger plants to be found there, making a rough draft of the illustrations as soon as possible, before his memories faded. He welcomed criticism from Dr Mertens, the expedition's botanist, and learnt a good deal about this branch of natural history from his friend.

By mid-summer they were off south-east Alaska, sailing between dark, spruce-covered islands sparsely inhabited by groups of Tlingit Indians. They called at the small Russian port of Sitka, where the settlers employed Aleuts to hunt up and down the coast for Sea Otters, then sent the precious pelts to St Petersburg. Between 23 June and 21 July Kittlitz spent as much time as he could ashore, walking along the rocky coastline and in the woods, often in heavy rain. In the coniferous forests near Sitka he collected Steller's Jay, the American Robin, the Varied Thrush and Chestnut-backed Chickadees; he was delighted to find the beautiful little Rufous Hummingbird which summers there and he stalked the Great Blue Heron as it hunted in the shallows.

The *Senjawin* continued north-westwards into the Gulf of Alaska sailing past great snow-covered peaks and massive blue glaciers, some of which Steller and Bering had first glimpsed nearly ninety years earlier. In August they cruised down the opposite coast beyond Kodiak and the Shumagin Islands to the sheltered harbour at Unalaska, where another small group of Russians lived among the sod dwellings of the Aleuts. Kittlitz and Mertens had just over a week to explore the misty, rain-shrouded mountains of the island and they delighted in the colourful alpine flora. As autumn approached, Captain Lütke left the northern seas for the warmer waters of the Pacific Ocean and for the next nine months they cruised among many of the scattered archipelagos of the Marianas and the Caroline Islands.

In May 1828 Kittlitz landed at Port Lloyd on Peel Island, one of the Bonin Island group some 700 miles south of Tokyo. Peel Island had never been permanently inhabited by humans and had only been given its name in the previous year by Captain Beechey of HMS *Blossom*. Kittlitz was the first to describe the Bonin Island Thrush which he often saw near the harbour and he collected four skins. He was also the last naturalist to see the Bonin Island Finch alive. Two years later, American, British and Polynesian colonists arrived, bringing cats and dogs with them. Whalers thereafter called in to replenish their stores and careen their ships on the beaches, and rats were inevitably introduced. The lovely metallic-hued Bonin Woodpigeon which Kittlitz discovered here was likewise extirpated before the end of the century, shot and trapped by the settlers who were often threatened by famine.

Kittlitz's Plover

From Peel Island the *Senjawin* sailed northwards and the summer was spent exploring the Kamchatka Peninsula. Compared to South America and the Pacific Islands, Kittlitz found the whole area botanically and zoologically disappointing, for the fauna especially was very similar to that of central and northern Europe. On the other hand, the scenery impressed him deeply and he considered the area to be of great geological interest. A long chain of snow-capped volcanic peaks stretched down through the interior, pine forests covered the steep slopes and on the flatter west coast the party crossed grassy plains and boggy heaths dotted with birch and willow. The naturalists travelled upstream into many of the forests, and often at night they lay listening to great trees falling into the river as the banks of loose sand or clay were undermined by the strong currents.

Many of the birds which Kittlitz collected on the peninsula later went to his friend Rüppell, but one of the species from Kamchatka which he took back to St Petersburg was Kittlitz's Murrelet, about which little is known, even now. It breeds along the coast of Alaska and in parts of eastern Siberia and winters in the north-west Pacific, but the type specimen was collected way off course, at Sans Blas in Mexico, by Captain Beechey's expedition.

When winter drew near, the Russian explorers turned southwards again and visited the Philippines, sailed down the long coast of Sumatra, passed through the straits into the Indian Ocean, continued round the Cape of Good Hope and then made the long journey northwards to the Baltic. Kittlitz returned to Germany in 1829, but he had been troubled by bouts of illness since visiting the Pacific and as a result he was slow to write up many of his observations. He consequently lost the opportunity of being the first describer of numerous species and also suffered financially.

Eduard Rüppell was now planning another expedition to north-east Africa and despite the poor state of his health Kittlitz arranged to join him in Alexandria at the beginning of 1831. The two friends travelled together along the coast to Rosetta, collecting a number of specimens of Mediterranean fish on the way. During the leisurely sail up the Nile to Cairo Rüppell and his assistant Theodor Erckel procured many Egyptian birds, including some of the Pied Kingfishers which flew in noisy flocks past the boat and hovered above the river. Black-winged Kites and a Caspian Tern fell to their guns and even the shy and secretive Senegal Coucal was soon added to the collection of corpses whose skins and skeletons had to be quickly and yet carefully prepared because of the high temperatures. Unfortunately Kittlitz was of little assistance during these exciting days. His health deteriorated rapidly after his arrival in Egypt and he spent most of the time lying on his bunk, dribbling saliva, suffering from diarrhoea and fits of vomiting, becoming increasingly weak and depressed. Eventually, Rüppell had to persuade him to return to Germany to seek medical help, and with much reluctance Kittlitz left Rüppell in Cairo at the beginning of April and started back. Rüppell's kindness in later dedicating his 'Systematic Revue of the Birds of North East Africa' (1845) to Kittlitz must have been of little consolation to him.

While he waited for a ship to take him back to Europe, Kittlitz summoned sufficient strength to collect a little around Alexandria and shot several small, neat plovers which he assumed were passing through on their spring migration.

In fact, they were part of the resident Egyptian population of Kittlitz's Plover which, though common in some other parts of Africa, breed nowhere else in the Western Palearctic. The plovers had already been described by Temminck (from specimens collected by Levaillant) but Kittlitz illustrated them upon his return in *Kupfertafeln zur Naturgeschichte der Vögel* [Engravings Illustrating the Natural History of Birds]. The association between the artist and the little wader was thus established. This book was another cause of misfortune, for due to a lack of money only a few copies were ever produced, although some of the other eighty species described were being shown for the first time.

Kittlitz had intended his habitat illustrations from the *Senjawin* expedition to compliment a botanical account of the voyage by Dr Mertons, but after the doctor's sudden death, Kittlitz had to furnish his own text for *Twenty-four Views of the Vegetation of the Coasts and Islands of the Pacific*. It was not published until 1844 and although it was well received and later translated into English it was another financial failure.

Kittlitz continued to contribute to illustrated German journals such as *Isis*, *Natur* and *Zoologisch Garten*, gaining a reputation as an exciting writer and a masterly illustrator, but due to his recurrent poor health he was unable to join any other expeditions. At the age of forty-five he married the daughter of a forester, who gave him two sons and a daughter. She died in 1865 but Kittlitz lived on until the age of seventy-five and passed away on 10 April 1874, at Mainz.

Wilhelm Heinrich Kramer †
(died 1765)

RING-NECKED PARAKEET *Psittacula krameri* (Scopoli)

Psittacus krameri Scopoli, 1769. *Annus 1 Historico-Naturalis*, p. 31: No locality
= Senegal

Feral populations of this noisy and gregarious pale-green parakeet are now
well established in Great Britain, The Netherlands and West Germany. In
England the parakeets often come to bird-tables and nest in holes in trees,
mainly in parks and large gardens. It also occurs in Israel and Egypt but it is
likely that even these Western Palearctic populations have originated from
escaped cage-birds or deliberate attempts at introduction. In Africa and India
these beautiful birds are considered by both farmers and gardeners to be serious
pests because of the damage they cause to cereal crops, fruit and flowers.

The Ring-necked Parakeet was first described and named by G. A. Scopoli.
He failed to mention which Kramer he had chosen to immortalize, but there is
every likelihood that the eponym was a tribute to Wilhelm Heinrich Kramer,
the Austrian naturalist who had died just four years earlier. The first description
of *Psittacula krameri* appeared in *Annus 1 Historico-Naturalis* [First Annual of
Natural History] (1769), in the preparation of which Scopoli had studied at the
Imperial Vivarium in Vienna.

The young W. H. Kramer went to school in Vienna and after training as a
doctor of medicine he lived and worked for at least fourteen years in Bruck,

Ring-necked Parakeet

†No known portrait.

some ten miles east of the Austrian capital. It was while Kramer was living in Bruck that he completed his most important book, *Elenchus Vegetabilium et Animalium per Austriam Inferiorem Observatorum*: a flora and fauna of Lower Austria which was published in Vienna in 1756. The work followed Linnaeus's system of nomenclature and was remarkably detailed and reliable, although Gilbert White expressed the opinion that Kramer's Latin was very much inferior to Scopoli's.[1] Even so, it was Kramer who coined the name *pratincola*, which was introduced into the English language as pratincole, by Thomas Pennant in 1773. The term was derived from the Latin *pratum* (a meadow) and *incola* (an inhabitant), referring to the pratincole's association with open grassland.[2]

Little else has been recorded about Kramer's life. His date of birth is unknown, but he is believed to have been born in Dresden. He died in 1765 and early the following year his second wife gave birth to a daughter in Bruck, but the naturalist himself appears to have been buried elsewhere. There is not even enough information to speculate about Kramer's age at the time of his death.

Theobald Johannes Krüper (1829-1921)

KRÜPER'S NUTHATCH *Sitta krueperi* Pelzeln

Sitta Krüperi Pelzeln, 1863. *Sitzungsberichte der Mathematisch, Naturwissenscafliche Klasse der Akademie der Wissenschaften, Wien* 48, Pt 1, p. 149: Smyrna [= Izmir]

When Theobald Krüper died, just a few weeks before his ninety-second birthday, he was widely known as the leading authority on the birds of Greece where he had lived for more than fifty years. He wrote well on a number of aspects concerning birds and for much of his life supplied museums and private collectors with eggs and skins obtained in the eastern Mediterranean. He was still collecting with enthusiasm and going on expeditions in his sixties and seventies.

His earliest ornithological studies, however, were carried out in more northern areas. He was born on 30 June 1829 at Uckermünde, on the Baltic coast of what is now East Germany, and attended Stettin Grammar School and afterwards the University of Berlin. An early interest in raptors was shown by the content of his doctoral thesis which concerned the geographical distribution of the falcons of Europe (never formally published) and by his first paper, about the various species of eagle occurring in Pomerania, which appeared in *Naumannia* in 1852. From this time onwards Krüper dedicated his whole life to the study of numerous branches of ornithology and other subjects of natural history. Scarcely a year seemed to pass without Krüper embarking on at least one arduous collecting expedition.

In 1855 he visited Lapland, in 1856 he was in Iceland, and in the following year he was collecting in Gotland, off the east coast of Sweden. In 1858 Krüper turned his attention southwards and went to stay with a friend in Athens; that year he investigated the Ionian Islands and in subsequent years he went on to explore a large part of mainland Greece as well as most of the major islands of the Aegean. In 1862 and 1863 he visited western Turkey, and it was while he was near Smyrna (Izmir) that he discovered the new species of nuthatch that has been named after him. It was described initially by August von Pelzeln, at Vienna, to whom Krüper had first sent specimens.

After several seasons spent collecting in various parts of Greece, Krüper returned to Turkey. In June 1872 the British ornithologist Henry Seebohm

KRÜPER. *GERMAN ORNITHOLOGIST AND BIRD-COLLECTOR WHO WAS THE FOREMOST FIELD-WORKER IN GREECE AND WESTERN TURKEY DURING THE LATTER PART OF THE NINETEENTH CENTURY.*

called upon Krüper at a house at Nimfi, about twenty-five miles over the mountains east of Smyrna. From the balcony they were able to look out onto the red-tiled roofs of the other houses and could see, that summer, thirteen White Storks' nests each with young. Seebohm described the scene, and his own first encounter with the new nuthatch, with enthusiastic detail:

> ". . . on each side of the valley is a range of lofty hills, very rocky, full of caves, apparently mountain-limestone, and sparingly planted here and there with pines. The pines in the valley are often in the possession of a colony of Spanish Sparrows, and sometimes a Woodchat Shrike forsakes his favourite olive-tree and breeds among the Sparrows. The pines on the mountains, on the other hand, are the favourite resort of the Great, Blue, and Sombre Titmouse and of Krüper's Nuthatch . . .
>
> The day after I arrived we took a long stroll on the mountain side to a small pine-forest on a shoulder of the rocky hills. On one tree there was a large nest of the Imperial Eagle tenanted by half-fledged birds. In a hole in a dead or dying stump a Middle Spotted Wood Pecker was rearing her young bird; and flitting from pine to pine, like Titmice, were two pairs of Krüper's Nuthatch. We sat down on an old pine-stump and watched them through a pocket telescope. The deep-chestnut ring on the breast was very distinct below the almost white throat. They were most active little birds . . ."[1]

It was generally considered remarkable that such a distinct species should have only just come to light. So surprising, that it prompted Philip Sclater to write in *The Ibis*, a few years after its discovery:

> "It shows us that the fauna of Asia Minor is by no means so fully worked out as has been supposed, and that novelties of the most attractive character still await the researches of the naturalist at a very short distance from the civilisation of Europe . . ."[2]

Sclater, and indeed Krüper, would have been amazed at the discovery, more than a hundred years later, in 1975, of the Kabylie Nuthatch which has been found only in a tiny area of forest in northern Algeria (see Ledant).

On Krüper's return to Athens from Smyrna, in 1872, he was promoted to Conservator and Director of the Museum of the University of Athens but the position was poorly paid and he was obliged to supplement his income by continuing to supply specimens to other museums and collectors. His efforts in this direction led to the rediscovery of the Cinereous Bunting, a species that

Krüper's Nuthatch

breeds commonly in Iran but in Europe is confined to only a few localities in the eastern Aegean. It had been found near Smyrna by Hugh Strickland in April 1836 and for some time afterwards was known as Strickland's Bunting. Until Krüper managed to obtain specimens the species had not been seen since its original discovery. Together with the nuthatch it was a speciality that Krüper collected and distributed widely.

By now in his mid-forties Dr Krüper showed no sign of cutting down on his exploratory trips and he relentlessly investigated the region, making further excursions to the Aegean and northern Greece and even went as far as the Balkans. He thereby contributed considerably to the early zoology of Greece and by his example did much to encourage other naturalists to explore the south-eastern parts of Europe. Under his direction, despite only a modest endowment, the ornithological section at the Athens Museum developed into a truly remarkable collection, while his own personal egg collection of the birds of Greece was unsurpassed.

Krüper's written works appeared from time to time in German ornithological publications, especially *Naumannia* and the *Journal für Ornithologie*. He contributed thirteen articles to the latter, two of the more important being 'Ornithologische Notizen über Griechenland' [Ornithological Notes from Greece] (1862) and 'Beitrag zur Ornithologie Klein Asiens' [Contributions to the Ornithology of Asia Minor] (1875). Three other papers to the journal showed that his interest in raptors had continued. One concerned the status of Bonelli's Eagle in Greece (1860), while the two others (both published in 1872) contained his observations on the Booted Eagle and the Levant Sparrowhawk which he had observed breeding near Salonica. In his later years he decided to give up writing and his last major work was an exhaustive and detailed check-list of the birds of Greece, including passage migrants. Although it superseded the works of all earlier authors it was unfortunately hidden away in the depths of A. Mommsen's *Griechische Jahreszeiten* [Greek Seasons] (1875) and never received the recognition it deserved.

In his retirement Krüper turned some of his attention to the study of insects and molluscs but his network of collectors continued to supply him with birds' eggs and skins which he forwarded to his worldwide circle of friends. He was a member of the German Ornithological Society for over sixty years and was elected an Honorary Member in 1908, thirteen years before his death, on 23 March 1921, in his adopted city of Athens.

William Elford Leach †
(1790-1836)

LEACH'S STORM-PETREL *Oceanodroma leucorhoa* (Vieillot)

Procellaria leucorhoa Vieillot, 1817. *Nouveau Dictionaire d'Histoire Naturelle, Nouvelle édition*, Vol. 25, p. 422: coast of Picardy

> "Lot 78—an undescribed Petrel with a forked tail, taken at St Kilda in 1818; the only one known (with egg)."

In the summer of 1819 dealers from all over Europe flocked to an important auction in London. Bonelli, Lichtenstein and Temminck were there but the petrel was knocked down for £5 15s to Dr Leach of the British Museum. He also bought a Great Auk and an egg for just over £16.[1]

The owner of the collection, and the man who had obtained the petrel, was William Bullock. He described himself as "Silversmith, Jeweller, Toyman and Statue Figure Manufacturer" but he was also a naturalist, collector, traveller, antiquary and showman. Towards the end of the eighteenth century he established a museum at Sheffield and, encouraged by public interest, moved it to Liverpool and in 1809 transferred it to London, establishing himself at 22 Piccadilly and later at Egyptian Hall nearby. The museum was a truly miscellaneous assortment of items which included works of art, armoury, curiosities from the South Seas, Napoleonic relics and various birds of which Bullock had become an avid field-collector. He made several expeditions to Scotland and in the autumn of 1812 took part in a notorious chase, in a six-oared boat off Papa Westray, after one of the last known Great Auks in British waters. The bird managed to escape its pursuers but was killed in the following year and came into Bullock's possession; it was this bird that eventually found its way to the British Museum (Natural History).

In those days Bullock's museum was a well-known and popular attraction in central London, and his bird specimens were so well mounted that his competitors were forced to improve their standards. Even though the museum was still attracting a large number of people Bullock decided to sell his collection under the hammer, acting as his own auctioneer. It comprised 32,000 curiosities and over 3000 bird specimens and in May 1819, after the sale had been underway for five days, William Leach made his famous purchase.

†No known portrait.

Not long after, whilst on a visit to the British Museum, Temminck asked to examine the petrel and in 1820 in his *Manuel d'Ornithologie* he named it *Procellaria Leachii*.[2] The almost inevitable English name soon followed, along with a protracted debate (which is still resurrected from time to time) over Leach's eligibility for such an honour. To counteract Temminck the Reverend John Fleming proposed that the petrel be called *Procellaria Bullockii*, "in order to do an act of common justice to the individual who had energy to undertake a voyage of enquiry, and sagacity to distinguish the bird in question as an undescribed species".[3] Bullock had already published *A Concise and Easy Method of Preserving Objects of Natural History* (1817), he was a Fellow of the Linnean and Wernerian Societies and would therefore seem to have been capable of writing his own scientific description of the bird. Had he done so it would have been of little consequence as far as the species' present *scientific* name is concerned because, despite the claims of the auction catalogue, there were already three known examples of the petrel in Europe. One was at the Paris Museum, a second was in the possession of Meiffren Laugier and a third, which had been taken in Picardy, was owned by L. A. F. Baillon; the latter being the type specimen which Vieillot described in 1817—the year before Bullock obtained the first British specimen.

An examination of Leach's career shows him to be as well qualified to be commemorated as many another naturalist. He probably achieved more than Bullock in advancing British ornithology and more than most in promoting the study of marine biology. William Elford Leach was born at Plymouth in the family town-house near the Hoe Gate, the youngest of four children. His father, George Leach, was a prosperous solicitor and his mother, Jane Elford, was from a well-known Devon family. From the age of twelve William went to a school in Exeter which was attached to the Devonshire and Exeter Hospital where he first started his studies in anatomy and chemistry. He showed an early interest in collecting marine samples in Plymouth Sound and is known to have visited the Kingsbridge estuary with his friend Charles Prideaux, but whether or not he met George Montagu who was then living nearby does not seem to be recorded; he certainly knew him later.

At seventeen Leach began to study medicine at St Bartholomew's, London, but three years later moved to Edinburgh University and then, in 1812, he was given permission to take his M.D. at St Andrew's University. He then returned to London but gave up his new profession in favour of his zoological interests. In 1813 he edited the Reverend George Low's *Fauna Orcadensis* and in the same year was employed initially as an assistant librarian in the Zoology Department at the British Museum which was then at Montague House. Leach found the zoological collections shockingly neglected. Many of the specimens were unlabelled and unarranged and others had been left to decay in the basements. Sometimes helped by his friend William Swainson, Leach managed to salvage some of the items but was forced on occasions to have evil-smelling bonfires to dispose of those which were considered beyond redemption.

Leach lived in two rooms at the museum, one of which had various skulls placed around it and another which happened to be decorated with some stuffed bats—the 'skullery and battery' as Leach liked to call them. He was extremely agile and active, almost always running up the stairs in leaps and bounds. One of his exercises involved "leaping over the back of a stuffed zebra which was placed in the centre of a large room . . . over which we [Swainson] have seen him vault with the lightness of a harlequin". There is no known portrait of Leach but Swainson considered him to be: "Of a slight form and delicate habit . . . with a naturally nervous and irritable temperament".[4] He was also warm, frank and generous and appears to have been well respected and well liked in Britain and abroad.

In addition to sorting through the collections Leach involved himself in arranging the displays and also carried out research, exchanged and purchased specimens or collected them in the field himself. Somewhat surprisingly, in view of his achievements, he was only employed at the museum for about eight years and even then was not always present: in July 1816 he obtained leave for two months but did not return until after the New Year. Nevertheless, he always worked hard, perhaps too hard. His written works for his period at the British Museum include: a *Zoological Miscellany, being descriptions of new and interesting Animals* published in three volumes (1814–17); a *Monograph on the British Crabs, Lobsters, Prawns and other Crustacea with pedunculated eyes* (1815–17); a *Systematic catalogue of the Specimens of the Indigenous Mammalia and Birds that are preserved at the British Museum* (1816); a *Synopsis of the Mollusca of Great Britain* (circulated in type in 1820, but not published until 1852); and the zoological appendices for a number of Arctic and African expeditions of the period. Other contributions by Leach include articles in the *Encyclopaedia Britannica* and numerous papers in the *Philosophical Transactions of the Royal Society* and the *Zoological Journal*. Apart from some crucial entomological work his main accomplishments were his studies of Crustaceans and Molluscs; after the death of Montagu in 1815, few people in Britain could have known more about the latter two subjects than Leach.

His nomenclature was later heavily criticized. Leach brooded upon the death of his friend John Cranch, on *HMS Congo*, naming in his honour no less than twenty-seven species which Cranch had collected in Africa. Some of Leach's generic names were thought to be irrational and were afterwards declared to be invalid until it was pointed out that they had either Biblical, Classical or Oriental connotations. Leach also showed a preoccupation with the name 'Caroline' and nine genera all dated 1818 concern this name, or anagrams of it. It has been

Leach's Storm-petrel

suggested that the lady in question was the unfortunate Queen Caroline but a more personal contact is perhaps more likely.

Leach began to work at night to catch up on the task he had set himself; his main scientific endeavour now being the creation of his natural system of arrangement and classification, especially of Crustaceans. The work was always laborious and often tiring and eventually his health gave way. In 1821 he became paler and thinner, suffered a complete breakdown, and formally resigned his position as Assistant Keeper on 9 March 1822. The Trustees of the Museum held Leach in high esteem and personally subscribed £850 for an annuity, in addition to paying £995 for his own zoological collections.

His elder sister took him away to the Continent for a prolonged period of rest. They stayed at various villas in the south of France and near Lake Como in northern Italy and they may also have travelled more widely, to Greece and other parts of the eastern Mediterranean. On 26 August 1836, while back in Italy, Leach died suddenly of cholera at the Palazzo San Sebastiano, near Tortona, north of Genoa.

In contrast, the date and place of death of William Bullock is unknown. In 1823 he returned from Mexico with a great collection of curiosities and natural history specimens which he exhibited at his hall. He published an account of his adventures in *Six Months Residence and Travels in Mexico* (1824), followed, with the help of Swainson, by *A Synopsis of Mexican Birds discovered in Mexico* (1827). Two years later Bullock returned to Central America, also spent time in the southern United States and afterwards is said to have lived in South America. His death was reported at a council meeting of the Geological Society in 1849 but there are no further details. The startling orange and black Bullock's Oriole which breeds in the western United States and south into Mexico, commemorates his colourful character. And so neither Leach nor Bullock need be forgotten.

Jean-Paul Ledant
(born 1951)

KABYLIE NUTHATCH *Sitta ledanti* Vielliard

Sitta ledanti Vielliard, 1976. *Alauda* 44, pp. 351–352: Djebel Babor (Petite Kabylie), Algeria

The Corsican Nuthatch is endemic to the pine forests of Corsica where it was first discovered by the twenty-two year old English collector John Whitehead, in 1883. The very similar Kabylie Nuthatch is even more limited in its range. Only about eighty pairs survive in the Kabylie Mountains in northern Algeria, just twelve miles from the Mediterranean coast. The discovery of this new species of nuthatch by the twenty-four year old Belgian ecologist, Jean-Paul Ledant, in 1975, startled the ornithological world.

In October of that year, Ledant took part in an expedition to the Kabylie Mountains. As soon as the party had set up camp near the summit of Djebel Babor, Ledant left his companions, carried on a little further and then sat down to write amongst the mixed evergreen and deciduous trees.

Jean-Paul Ledant had been born in Namur, thirty-five miles south-east of Brussels, on 14 July 1951. He had begun to study natural history in his early teens, successively pursuing interests in rocks, flowers, lichens, mosses and birds. On leaving school, he studied forestry and agriculture at the nearby Faculté des Sciences Agronomiques de l'Etat at Gembloux. In 1974 he left Belgium to work in Algeria at the Institut National Agronomique as an assistant in the forestry department. Subsequently, Ledant was on Djebel Babor on 5 October 1975 to study the montane forest, particularly the Algerian Fir. Sitting among the trees, many of which had stood for more than a hundred years, Ledant was distracted by the tapping of a bird and stopped writing so that he could watch it. He immediately noticed that it was a nuthatch with a black cap and an eyestripe resembling that of the Corsican species. When he rejoined his colleagues, Dirk Raes and Paul Jacobs, they could hardly believe his account, as no nuthatch of any species was known to inhabit Algeria!

Next day he showed the nuthatch to the others but there was no time to study the birds and he was unable to return until Christmas. The summit of the mountain is 6575 feet above sea level and in winter, conditions there are extremely severe with snow lying more than six feet deep. Ledant and his two friends were poorly equipped for an ascent but nevertheless succeeded in reaching

LEDANT. *BELGIAN ECOLOGIST RESPONSIBLE FOR THE SEN-
SATIONAL DISCOVERY OF A NEW SPECIES OF NUTHATCH, IN
ALGERIA, IN 1975. THE PHOTOGRAPH WAS TAKEN IN 1976.*

the edge of the woods. After briefly sheltering from the icy wind they were forced to retreat, exhausted and numb, without even seeing a nuthatch.

In April, Ledant and Jacobs made another attempt to find the birds and although the ground was still covered by heavy snow they camped on the summit. For two days the mountain was shrouded by thick cloud and their search was fruitless, but on the third day the sky slowly cleared and they were able to observe some nuthatches and describe their plumage and calls. Ledant played a tape recording of the song of the Corsican Nuthatch and to his delight one of the Kabylie Nuthatches sang in response. Three months later, at the height of summer, Ledant climbed the mountain again, this time with Jacques Vielliard who took some specimens. The first proclamation of the news of this exciting discovery was made in *Le Monde* on 28 July 1976.

Surprisingly, although the Kabylie Nuthatch had existed undetected until the second half of the twentieth century, it was discovered twice within less than a year. In June 1976, a Swiss naturalist named Eric Burnier ascended the Djebel Babor and while walking through the woods, heard a loud bird-call which was new to him. When the bird appeared he was astounded by the realization that it was a strange nuthatch, being quite unaware of Ledant's discovery just eight months earlier. He made careful sketches and notes which were published in *Nos Oiseaux* in December 1976.

The Kabylie Nuthatch was by then known to be restricted to less than 3500 acres on Djebel Babor, inhabiting the parts of the forest which have the highest diversity of tree species. Algerian Fir, Portuguese Oak, Atlas Cedar, Mediterranean Italian Maple, Aspen, Yew, Common Whitebeam and Wild Service-tree provide food, cover and nest sites for the nuthatches and many other hole-nesters. Pied Flycatchers are the most abundant, but Great Tits, Coal Tits, Moussier's Redstarts, Hoopoes, Tawny Owls and Great Spotted Woodpeckers all commonly occur there. The Kabylie Nuthatch feeds on both seeds and insects and during the second half of June lays its eggs in a tree-hole, most often in the Algerian Fir.

A number of scientific papers concerning the bird and its habitat were quickly produced. Vielliard gave the classical description of *Sitta ledanti* in a special supplement to *Alauda* in 1976, and followed it two years later with another article, in the same journal, on the Djebel Babor. Ledant published three papers

Kabylie Nuthatch

in *Aves* (1977, 1977 and 1978), one of which was a comparative study of the Kabylie and Corsican Nuthatches. Several other naturalists have now also studied the bird and its fragile ecosystem.

In 1977 Ledant left Algeria and since then he has followed a varied career in France, Belgium and the Ivory Coast, also carrying out ornithological research in north Cameroon and Peru. Many of his publications have been about birds, on such diverse subjects as 'The water-birds of the Reghais marshes in Algeria' *Aves* 1979; 'The status and conservation of the Woodlark in southern Belgium' *Gerfaut* 1980; and 'Observations on the ecology of wintering Blue-headed Wagtails, Wheatears and Whitethroats in north Cameroon' *Gerfaut* 1981. Ledant considers that his most important works are 'Contributions to the Algerian Avifauna' *Gerfaut* 1981, and his book on 'The threatened animals of Wallonie. Protection of birds', published at Gembloux in 1983.

In May 1982 Ledant returned to Djebel Babor to carry out a nuthatch census and to assess the dangers affecting the viability of the small and vulnerable population. He found that favourable conditions for the birds are diminishing through the reduction of the forest by fire and by over-grazing; the mixed forest is gradually being replaced by cedars alone. There is also a new threat posed by selfish and irresponsible bird collectors.

Since 1984 Ledant has been working at Brussels at the Institut Royal des Sciences Naturelles de Belgique, and since January 1986 he has been involved part-time at the European Environment Bureau, as a Development Affairs Officer. However, he maintains his active interest in the welfare of the Kabylie Nuthatch: his conclusions and recommendations following the 1982 expedition were published, in French, in *Biological Conservation* (1985).

Jean-Baptiste-Louis-Claude-Théodore Leschenault de la Tour (1773-1826)

GREATER SAND PLOVER *Charadrius leschenaultii* Lesson

Charadrius Leschenaultii Lesson, 1826. In Levrault (Ed.) *Dictionaire des Sciences Naturelles*, Pt 42, p. 36: Pondicherry, India

The Greater Sand Plover breeds in desert and semi-desert regions to the north of the Himalayas, from China westwards to the Caspian Sea, with only small numbers actually breeding within the Western Palearctic, in central Turkey and parts of Jordan. The species was first described from a specimen collected by Leschenault de la Tour from the south-east coast of India at Pondicherry, where the species commonly occurs in winter in association with the similar Lesser Sand Plover. Lesson named the bird after Leschenault who was by then famous as a traveller and naturalist, and who is now remembered especially for his botanical explorations in Java and the southern portion of the Indian sub-continent.

Leschenault was born in Châlon-sur-Saône on the 13 November 1773, the second son of Théodore Leschenault, a judge at the court of Châlon. After his father died, in 1798, Leschenault moved north to Paris where, through his interest in natural history, he came into contact with many eminent scientists and quickly succeeded in being appointed chief botanist to Nicolas Baudin's expedition to Australia.

The two ships *Le Géographe* and *Le Naturaliste* left Le Havre in October 1800, rounded the Cape of Good Hope and spent two years exploring the coastal regions of Australia. There were nine zoologists and botanists on the expedition but four of them, including Bory de St Vincente, were landed at Mauritius on the outward voyage. In June 1801 the two ships arrived at Geographe Bay in south-west Australia and they later negotiated the west coast up to Shark Bay. Among the numerous shore excursions was a boat journey on the Swan River on which Leschenault collected many living plants and seeds

LESCHENAULT. *FRENCH EXPLORER AND NATURALIST KNOWN ESPECIALLY FOR HIS BOTANICAL DISCOVERIES IN JAVA AND INDIA. HE COLLECTED A LARGE NUMBER OF NEW BIRD SPECIES.*

destined for the Empress Josephine's garden at Malmaison. In the autumn they sailed northwards for hundreds of miles to the island of Timor where they spent most of the rest of the year. As they returned southwards there was an outbreak of dysentery and the expedition zoologist and the ornithologist were amongst those who died. The coastlands of Tasmania were then explored to some extent, but afterwards the *Naturaliste* was sent home with the weaker members of both crews.

In April 1802 as the *Géographe* proceeded along the country's southern coast Baudin met Matthew Flinders in Encounter Bay. Leschenault's counterpart on board the British ship was the equally distinguished Scottish botanist Robert Brown, and among the ship's company was a very young John Franklin. The two captains exchanged information, but, distracted by the meeting, they both missed their chance to discover the Murray River. The following April the French ship was again at Timor where the unfortunate Leschenault was left behind because he was so ill. However, he soon recovered sufficiently to make his way to Java where he was unable to find a ship to take him to France because of the Napoleonic Wars. He was forced to remain on Java for the next three years. He used the time profitably by making the first thorough botanical investigation of the island, unexplored by naturalists except briefly by Carl Thunberg thirty years previously. Towards the end of 1806 he was at last able to leave and he arrived back in France in July of the following year with a tremendous collection of plants and birds, much valuable information on the island's flora and fauna, and the basis for a dictionary of the Malay language which he later had published.

Captain Baudin had died at Mauritius in September 1803 as the *Géographe* returned to France, but the natural history material that reached the Paris Museum was the richest it had ever received. There were over 100,000 specimens, including about 2500 species new to science. The ornithological results of the expedition were never properly worked through, and though Vieillot gave some attention to the collection, Lesson in 1831 and Swainson in 1838 were still able to find new species among the material! Leschenault's Javanese birds were described by Cuvier and Vieillot, and Leschenault also generously made his notes and skins available to a young and enthusiastic Dutch collector—Coenraad Jacob Temminck. Leschenault's plant collection from Java was so impressive that the Government rewarded him with a large pension and a lump sum of 10,000 francs for his expenses and as compensation for the considerable hardships he had endured. Meanwhile Leschenault busied himself by arranging his notes from his six years of exploration and published three long articles in the *Annales du Musée d'Histoire Naturelle*, the most notable entitled 'De la Vegetation de la Nouvelle-Hollande [Australia]'.

At the age of forty-three, after a few years of comparative inactivity, Leschenault went to India to collect living plants of economic potential and to establish a botanical garden at the French colony of Pondicherry. The Napoleonic Wars had just ended and relations with Britain had been restored to such an extent that Joseph Banks was able to give him letters of introduction and arranged for him to receive plants from the Calcutta Botanical Garden. The British authorities also gave him permission to travel freely in Madras, Bengal and Ceylon. He set sail from France in May 1816 and was away for a full six years. After studying the environs of Pondicherry he travelled down the coast to Karakil and Tringebar and in 1818 went inland to Salem. In October he crossed the mountains to Coimbetore, barely surviving an attack of cholera which killed many others in his party, and he returned to Pondicherry still extremely ill but with a valuable collection of plants, as well as an elephant which later survived for a number of years at the Jardin des Plantes, at Paris. Undaunted by his privations Leschenault returned to Coimbetore and gathered more plants and bushes many of which he sent to the French colony on Bourbon Island (Réunion), off the east coast of Madagascar.

In September 1819 he sailed north to Bengal for a brief visit and then turned his attentions southwards and explored the regions beyond Pondicherry to the southernmost tip of India. He took a ship to the jungle-covered island of Ceylon, which he investigated thoroughly for six months penetrating far into the interior. He returned to Pondicherry and then sailed to Bourbon Island where many of his seeds and specimens had been grown, some for the benefit of the colony and others to acclimatize them before he took them to France, or sent them on elsewhere. Shortly after Leschenault's arrival in his home country he was awarded the Legion d'Honneur for his services to France.

Only eight months later Leschenault was off to South America and he visited Brazil, Dutch Guiana (Surinam) and French Guiana and successfully introduced tea bushes to Cayenne, the capital of the French colony. Once more he arranged for his plant collections to be shipped to Europe. Unfortunately despite his robust constitution his health broke down and after eighteen months he was forced to return homewards. He enjoyed only a brief rest among his family and friends, dying a year and a half later at Paris, on the 14 March 1826, at the age of fifty-three.

Various branches of natural history interested him, including mineralogy and ornithology, but Leschenault's main preoccupations were botanical, especially any plants which could be of economic importance to the French Colonies. He

Greater Sand Plover

successfully introduced more than a hundred new species to Bourbon Island including two varieties of sugar cane, six varieties of cotton, the cinnamon tree from Ceylon and coffee plants from Bengal.

LEVAILLANT. *FAMOUS FRENCH EXPLORER OF SOUTHERN AFRICA. ACCOUNTS OF HIS TRAVELS INSPIRED A WHOLE GENERATION OF NATURALISTS. HE FABRICATED SOME BIRDS AND INVENTED JOURNEYS TO SUPPORT HIS CLAIMS FOR NEW SPECIES, THUS DISCREDITING SOME OF HIS REAL ACHIEVEMENTS. THE PORTRAIT WAS DRAWN FROM LIFE IN 1820.*

François Levaillant
(1753-1824)

LEVAILLANT'S GREEN WOODPECKER *Picus vaillantii* (Malherbe)

Chloropicus Vaillantii Malherbe, 1847. *Mémoires de l'Académie Royale de Metz* 28, p. 130: near Bône, Algeria

Levaillant's Green Woodpecker occurs in the warm and open woods of the hillier parts of Morocco, Algeria and Tunisia. The type specimen was shot in the extreme north-east of Algeria in the mountains of Edough near Bône and it was sent to Metz in east central France. In the following year, a detailed description of the new bird appeared in the *Mémoires de l'Académie Royale de Metz* (1847), in which Alfred Malherbe dedicated it to the "celebrated explorer-naturalist who had lived at Metz for a longtime".

The Levaillants had been lawyers at Metz for several generations, but François was born at Paramaribo in Dutch Guiana (Surinam), where his father had been appointed French Consul. In 1763 the family returned to Metz and ten year old François continued to devote his life to collecting birds, at first locally but later in Alsace and Lorraine, particularly around Lunéville. He married at the age of twenty-three and soon afterwards moved to Paris where he began to examine the bird collections of wealthy private collectors. In 1780 he went to Holland where Jacob Temminck (father of C. J. Temminck) was so impressed by his ability as a hunter and taxidermist that he gave him the necessary finances for a voyage to the southern tip of Africa.

Shortly after his arrival, while he was ashore collecting at Saldanha Bay, the Dutch ship carrying all his equipment was blown up. Levaillant was left with the clothes he wore, his rifle and ten ducats. He managed to borrow more money until new funds arrived from Europe and between April 1781 and July 1784 he made two lengthy expeditions within the Cape Colony. At first he went eastwards to the Great Fish River and then afterwards went north to Namaqualand. His discoveries included Klaas's Cuckoo which he named after one of his servants, and the Narina Trogon which he dedicated to a lovely Hottentot girl with whom he is said to have formed a "romantic attachment". In all, he discovered about fifty new species and made many new observations regarding bird behaviour in general. When he returned to Europe he took with him over 2000 bird skins, many of which passed from the elder to the younger

Temminck and later helped form the nucleus of the Dutch National Collection at Leyden.

Levaillant's imaginative and dramatic accounts of his two expeditions brought him instant fame and recognition; so much so that in 1796 he was able to follow up his initial publications by simultaneously issuing three different-sized editions of his best known work: *Histoire naturelle des oiseaux d'Afrique* (1796–1808). He did not approve of the Linnean system of classification and only gave his discoveries French names. Other naturalists therefore had to redescribe and name the birds in the approved manner. In time, two francolins, a cuckoo and a barbet were dedicated to his memory in their scientific names. The Bateleur and Chanteur are two examples of his common bird names still in use.

Five years after his return to France, Levaillant married his second wife, Pierrette Foyot, by whom he had four children. From 1796 the family lived at La Noue, near Sézanne, some sixty miles east of Paris, although an apartment was also maintained in the capital for his convenience. He did not live again at Metz. Over the next few years Levaillant produced lavishly illustrated works on the birds of America and the West Indies (1801), a natural history of parakeets (1801), a natural history of birds of paradise, rollers and toucans (1803–06) and another miscellaneous bird book published in 1807. No one had examined as many different species of birds and for a while François Levaillant was the most famous naturalist in Europe.

The sixth volume of *Oiseaux d'Afrique* was issued in 1808 but public interest in Levaillant and the demand for his works thereafter declined. By mixing his accurate observations with other details which he had invented to enhance his fame he succeeded in denying himself a more honoured position amongst early ornithologists. He had even fabricated "new species", with feathers from several different species, in order to support an account of a journey across the Orange River which he never made! Married for a third time around the turn of the century, he died in relative obscurity at La Noue on 22 November 1824, at the age of seventy-one.

In 1862, a vault was built over his grave from contributions by his four surviving sons. One of these sons had a deep interest in ornithology and has connections with the early discovery of the North African green woodpecker.

Jean-Jacques-Rousseau Levaillant, the eldest son from the second marriage, was born at Cambrai on 5 October 1790 but spent his childhood at La Noue, his father having left Metz by this time. A German naturalist who visited the

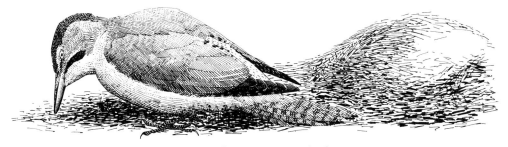

Levaillant's Green Woodpecker

household in 1802 remarked that in François Levaillant's company "everyone must enjoy natural history . . . the older boy loves it already, and may perhaps some day follow his father". Jean might well have become a famous naturalist but the Napoleonic Wars intervened. He enlisted in the French army and at twenty-two years of age took part in Napoleon's disastrous winter retreat from Moscow. He fought at the battles of Lutzen, Bautzen and Leipzig but was captured at Dresden and imprisoned in Hungary until the end of the war. After a short period in Paris with a firm of publishers, he rejoined the army and saw active service in Spain from 1823 to 1828. In 1838, having risen to the rank of Lieutenant-Colonel, he was transferred from France to Algeria where he spent the next ten years.

Because of his biological interests, Jean Levaillant was made battalion commander of the Mission d'Exploration Scientifique de l'Algérie and was responsible for supervising the collection of mammals and birds for the Paris Natural History Museum. Fifteen coloured plates of birds were executed under his direction and issued in 1848–49. One of the plates depicted the new woodpecker and the male specimen from which it was drawn was forwarded to Paris. Unfortunately, it is not now clear to what extent he was involved with the type specimen sent to Metz. It had been collected in 1846 in the same part of Algeria but Malherbe, who undoubtedly dedicated the bird to François Levaillant, does not say whether or not Jean Levaillant had sent it to him.

The younger Levaillant was initially charged with supplying the text for the fifteen plates as well as full accounts of the other birds and mammals collected by the Mission, but he was unable to carry out the task, as he was promoted to General in 1848 and recalled to Europe in late 1849. He took part in the siege of Rome and commanded the city's occupying forces until 1853. In his absence, his *Introduction à l'histoire des mammifères et des oiseaux du nord de l'Afrique* (1851) was printed at Philippeville, on the Algerian coast, but this does not appear to have been part of the work of the Scientific Mission. He retired from the army in 1854 and spent the next twenty years living the life of a country gentleman at Sézanne. On his death, on 13 January 1876, he was buried at La Noue beside his father.

Levaillant's younger brother, General Jean-Charles Levaillant (1795–1871), also served in Algeria and collected innumerable insects for the Mission, chiefly from the western part of the country around Oran. In 1853 Captain Victor Loche took command of the Mission. Under his impetus a *Catalogue des mammifères et des oiseaux observée en Algérie* was brought out in 1858. The full results of the whole survey which included historical, geological, botanical and other zoological subjects was finally completed in 1867, some years after Loche himself had died of fever at Bône.

LICHTENSTEIN. *GERMAN ZOOLOGIST WHO SPENT HIS EARLY YEARS IN SOUTHERN AFRICA. HE RETURNED TO BECOME THE LONG-SERVING DIRECTOR OF THE BERLIN ZOOLOGICAL MUSEUM. ACCORDING TO SWAINSON, THIS PORTRAIT FROM* LICHTENSTEIN'S TRAVELS IN SOUTHERN AFRICA *IS "A LIKENESS, BUT CERTAINLY NOT A FLATTERING ONE".*

Martin Hinrich Carl Lichtenstein (1780-1857)

LICHTENSTEIN'S SANDGROUSE *Pterocles lichtensteinii* Temminck

Pterocles lichtensteinii Temminck, 1825. In C. J.Temminck and M. Laugier, *Nouveau Recueil de Planches coloriées d'Oiseaux*, Pt 60, Pls 355, 361: Nubia

Professor Temminck (1778–1858), one of the most influential and enduring of the museum directors of Continental Europe during the first half of the nineteenth century, named this species of sandgrouse[1] in honour of Hinrich Lichtenstein who was almost his exact contemporary and another of the great museum directors. Under Lichtenstein's guidance the Zoological Museum of Berlin became one of the largest and finest in existence.

Lichtenstein was an all-round naturalist who specialized in birds, though during his youth in southern Africa he claimed that the collection of insects had been his main preoccupation. Born at Hamburg on 10 June 1780, he took his degree in medicine at Helmstedt at the age of twenty-one and the year after became the personal physician to General Janssens, the newly appointed Dutch Governor of the Cape of Good Hope. The colony had just been restored to Holland by the treaty of Amiens, six years after its capture by British forces. Together with the Governor and his family, Lichtenstein set sail from Europe in July 1802 and after a prolonged call at Tenerife, and another period of four weeks during which they waited for a favourable wind, they at last arrived at Table Bay on Christmas Eve.

General Janssens wanted to know as much about the colony as possible, and in October a group of more than forty people set off, under the protection of a squadron of dragoons, to investigate the country's topography, mineralogy, natural history and tribal inhabitants. Janssens' thirteen year old son, the youngest daughter of the Commissary-General, her female friend and two female servants were amongst the party which Lichtenstein accompanied in his role as a Commissioner and as physician, surgeon, naturalist and tutor to the children. He took with him the works of Sparrman, Thunberg and Barrow and enjoyed being alternately critical or full of praise for Barrow's *Account of Travels into the Interior of Southern Africa in 1797–98* (1801–04). Indeed, Lichtenstein's own contribution, published in German under the title *Reisen in suedlichen Africa* [Travels in southern Africa] (1810–12), is in a similar all-encompassing style; every branch of science and every aspect of his surroundings seems to have been remarked upon.

The large wagon-train and accompanying horses and mules headed northwards from Table Bay towards the Bay of St Helena, stopping at Saldanha Bay on the way. This enabled Lichtenstein and some of the others to visit Sheep Island with its many snakes, lizards and seafowl, and allowed them all to feast upon the eggs of the Jackass Penguins. The party then moved eastwards along the borders of the Great Karoo Desert to Mossel Bay and up the south-east coast to Algoa Bay as far as the Great Fish River. After heading inland again to Graaf Reinett they returned to Cape Town. By chance Lichtenstein met an old farmer who recounted how the life of his sick child had been saved, many years earlier, by the botanist Carl Thunberg who had happened to be travelling by. On the natural history side, it was already evident that many of the larger mammals were in decline but they had frequent opportunities to study some of the smaller mammals, the reptiles and birds; Lichtenstein's notes about the Ostrich being one of the best early accounts. He had also managed to gather some 700 species of insects, 340 of which were entirely new.

During the course of the expedition they had traversed hundreds of miles and Lichtenstein marvelled that the party had never once been held up by the female contingent! Only a fraction of the colony had been visited but in the next few years Lichtenstein was able to undertake many more expeditions, including a botanical trip to the Zwelandan Mountains, a visit to Bushman country and excursions to the Roggeveld Mountains and Tulbagh. The results of these latter investigations were all incorporated into the second volume of his travels along with more comments on the earlier written accounts of other south African explorers.

When the Cape was retaken by the British in 1806, Lichtenstein had no option but to return to Europe with his patron and he spent most of the next few years in Brunswick, Göttingen, Jena and at his home in Hamburg. When the University of Berlin was founded in 1810, he was awarded the Chair of Zoology even though he still had only a superficial knowledge of many of its branches. Shortly after his appointment his reputation was greatly enhanced by the publication of his African travels and in 1815 he was also appointed the first Director of the Berlin Zoological Museum. He quickly brought out the first of a series of

Lichtenstein's Sandgrouse

catalogues listing the specimens housed at Berlin which frequently contained descriptions of newly discovered species, many of which were birds. Lichtenstein, M. H. C. (sometimes M. H. K.) should not be confused with his father Anton August Heinrich Lichtenstein (1753–1816) who gave descriptions of some southern African bird species in the *Catalogus Rerum Naturalium Rarissimarum* (1793).

The younger Lichtenstein's major works include an appendix to Eversmann's journey to Bukhara (1823); a poorly edited version of J. R. Forster's long-awaited, and previously unpublished, *Descriptiones animalium* (1884)—from Cook's second Pacific voyage of 1772–74; zoological commentaries on the American collections of the explorers Marcgrave, Piso and Hernandez (1823); a monograph on the gulls (1838) and yet others on the ornithology of California and the Sandwich Islands (1838). His last important work, published three years before his death, was a hand-list of all the bird specimens in the Berlin Museum. It gave the distribution of each species as it was then known, the number of birds in the collections and a price at which duplicates could be sold.

In those days museums often acquired material by funding their own collectors and sending them off to various parts of the world, afterwards recouping some of their expenses by selling off any surplus. Another common way of adding to their stocks was to buy up private collections, or parts of them, and for this reason Lichtenstein had gone to London in 1818 to be present at the sale of the Bullock Museum. The connections that he built up in England and throughout the rest of the world enabled him to amass a collection which even rivalled the hoard at the Leyden Museum. Unfortunately the systematic evaluation of this stock of birds was not Lichtenstein's strong point; he tended to ignore anatomical criteria and he even bartered or sold specimens before they had been thoroughly investigated—the birds that Sellows had gathered in Brazil, and Hemprich and Ehrenberg's hard-won Syrio-African collections suffered especially. Rather confusingly, Lichtenstein also refused to accept the rule of priority in nomenclature which had been adopted almost everywhere since 1842. On the more positive side, he was friendly with J. F. Naumann and put many bird skins at his disposal, and he made a good choice for the development of German ornithology when he chose Jean Cabanis as his assistant.

William Swainson met Lichtenstein on one of his visits to England and afterwards recorded his impressions of the visitor. "Lichtenstein . . . speaks our language remarkably well. His manners are particularly agreeable. He has a very fine taste in music, and is himself an accomplished performer."[2] In June 1815 Lichtenstein had married twenty-two year old Victoria Hothro, the daughter of a Berlin industrialist who shared his musical interests. The Lichtensteins were both members of the Berlin Choral Academy and they were friendly with the composer Carl Maria von Weber whose son further described the naturalist as small and robust, broad shouldered, with intelligent and somewhat Semitic features, versatile, full of enthusiasm and charm.

Lichtenstein died at sea, on 3 September 1857, at the age of seventy-seven, while returning from a trip to Stockholm, and was buried at Kiel.

Peter McDougall[1][†]
(1777-1814)

ROSEATE TERN *Sterna dougallii* Montagu

Sterna Dougallii Montagu, 1813. *Supplement to the Ornithological Dictionary*, text and plate to "Tern-Roseate" [not paged]: Cumbrae Island, Firth of Clyde, Scotland

The Roseate Tern is chiefly a warm-water species which breeds along the coasts of eastern North America, the Caribbean and north-western and southern Africa; other races frequent the Red Sea, the Indian Ocean, the Pacific and the coasts of Australasia. Because Scotland is at the very northernmost extent of the tern's breeding range, it is not thought of as a characteristically Scottish species and its existence was not even suspected until 1812 when Dr Peter McDougall discovered the tern breeding in the Firth of Clyde.

In 1772, or perhaps a year or two before, Alexander McDougall, a merchant in Kilsyth, married Mary Jeffray. Their first child, Anne, was born in July 1773 and thereafter the McDougalls had six more children of whom Peter was the third child and second son. He was born on 18 January 1777 and grew up in and around Kilsyth, a small town which was then becoming prosperous because of the weaving trade and which was conveniently situated some ten or so miles north-east of the centre of Glasgow. In 1789 Peter matriculated at the University, entered the humanity class and finally graduated as M.D. in 1802. He had been influenced and encouraged throughout his education by his maternal uncle, James Jeffray, who was Professor of Anatomy at Glasgow University from 1790 until 1848. The professor gained fame, and a certain degree of unpopularity, through an experiment carried out in 1818. He passed an electric current through a very recently hanged criminal who immediately sat up and stared about in surprise; Jeffray ended the experiment, somewhat prematurely, and inconclusively, by a swift thrust with his scalpel to the poor man's jugular vein whilst the invited audience either clapped in admiration, or fainted. Jeffray was an early member of the Edinburgh-based Wernerian Natural History Society but his nephew does not seem to have joined.

Two years after McDougall graduated he was to be found in central Glasgow in practice with another physician, called Barrie. The partnership lasted from 1804 until 1809 when McDougall became one of the surgeons at the newly built Glasgow Royal Infirmary. Because of a disagreement over his licence to practise

†No known portrait.

as a surgeon he was not re-appointed in the following year and he returned to his medical practice, now without his former partner. Once again McDougall lived at various addresses immediately to the south of George Square, right in the heart of the city.

Whilst in general practice he occupied his leisure time by actively collecting objects of natural history and occasionally purchasing or exchanging specimens. Captain James Laskey, the Director of the Hunterian Museum, which is attached to the University, was sometimes assisted by McDougall in the Anatomy Department which then housed a particularly gruesome collection of human parts preserved in spirit, many of them diseased or deformed. McDougall also took a great interest in the other sections of the museum which included miscellaneous collections of fish, shells and birds from various parts of the world.

On 24 July 1812 McDougall was with two friends on the island of Great Cumbrae, in the Firth of Clyde. Together they went out to two small islets in Millport Bay, each of which is not much more than a hundred yards across; although generally rocky around the edges they are sufficiently well vegetated to suit the requirements of Roseate Terns. Sadly these birds no longer breed there yet when McDougall visited the islets he reported that he could scarcely walk about for fear of treading on tern eggs. As the parent birds flew excitedly overhead, one of his companions shot one of them and it landed close to McDougall. He picked it up, noticed it was different from the other terns, and asked his friends to shoot some more while he himself began to observe the flying terns more closely:

> "The new species was discerned by the comparative shortness of the wing, whiteness of plumage, and by the elegance and comparative slowness of motion, sweeping along, or resting in the air almost immovable, like some species of Hawk, and from its size being considerably less than that of *Sterna hirundo* [Common Tern]."[2]

Unknown to McDougall, Arctic Terns were probably also present, but the distinction between the Common and Arctic Tern was not made widely known until 1819, seven years after his visit. Several of the Roseate Terns were added to his collection and he mounted three of them, two males and a female, in a glass case together with a 'White House Swallow'. McDougall's friend Captain Laskey was friendly with George Montagu through a mutual interest in

Roseate Tern

conchology and their membership of the Wernerian Society, and Laskey soon informed Montagu of this new addition to the British avifauna. He arranged for a surplus specimen to be sent to Devon and Montagu was thus able to publish the first description of the tern. He gave it the scientific name *Sterna Dougallii* in order "to make our public acknowledgements to Doctor M'Dougall, for the very liberal and handsome manner in which the history of this interesting bird was communicated to us, and more particularly for the specimen that accompanied it".[3] It later transpired that the bird which Montagu received was not McDougall's best example as the doctor later admitted that "the figure in the Supplement to Colonel Montagu's Dictionary was taken from a specimen, which was wounded in the neck, and, in consequence, the bird was placed in an unnatural position to hide the defect".[4] Montagu's *Supplement* was issued in 1813; only a year later, at the age of 37, McDougall was dead.

While carrying out his duties as a doctor he caught a fever, which may have been typhus, and he died on 25 April 1814. The Glasgow papers announced his death with the brief epitaph: "His talents were but beginning to be known—his worth was known to many". He was buried at the cemetery in Ingram Street, which is now much neglected with no obvious memorial to the doctor; many of the headstones are covered in moss or are too badly weathered to be decipherable, while some others disappeared long ago, when the street was widened. McDougall must have died unmarried because on 12 May his entire household contents were offered for sale. They included carpets, rugs, beds, bedding, grates, fire irons, mahogany tables and chairs and kitchen furniture as well as an "electrifying machine" and various natural history curiosities. One such item which was not sold was the "horn of a sea unicorn" (narwhal tooth), which someone, somehow, managed to steal and take away unobserved.

McDougall's fine collection of British and foreign birds was considered important enough to be sold separately and it was dispersed by auction, two months later, on 15 July at Mr Angus's Academy in Ingram Street. The 101 foreign birds, mounted in twelve glass cases, consisted mainly of colourful species such as toucans, parrots and humming-birds. Most of these came from the West Indies and South America while other birds were from India and North America, but there is no evidence that McDougall collected any of them himself. He lived in one of the most prosperous parts of Glasgow surrounded by wealthy merchants who sent ships from the Clyde to all parts of the world. Most of his foreign birds were probably either purchased from contacts within the shipping trade or came from other collectors. However, the 150 British birds which were in twenty-seven cases, along with more than seventy-five other uncased birds, give the indication that they had been collected locally, a good proportion probably by McDougall himself. Most of the birds of prey were represented, including a Sea Eagle, and there were many different species of owls, ducks, seabirds, finches and thrushes as well as his case of Roseate Terns. The only species in the British section not then regularly occurring in Scotland was his single Hoopoe specimen. One extra case contained both British and West Indian birds, and indeed the general arrangement was rather haphazard.

In addition, amongst the miscellaneous assortment of other items on sale, there were three snakes' skins, two snouts of swordfish, an armadillo, an alligator, a bat from Botany Bay, a chest of drawers full of West and East Indian shells, thirty-two numbers of George Graves's *British Ornithology* and five volumes of John Latham's *General History of Birds*. An assortment of over 200 small glass eyes clearly showed that McDougall had done much of his own taxidermy.

William Bullock may have been one of the natural history dealers who attended the sale since McDougall is mentioned as a 'donor' in one of Bullock's catalogues dated 1816, although of course McDougall may have sent him birds long before the sale took place. Apart from the type specimen Roseate Tern which Montagu described and which is now in the possession of the British Museum, it seems most unlikely that any other of McDougall's bird specimens still exist.

Since the death of Peter McDougall his name has been almost forgotten. This must be partly the fault of Montagu who, for some reason, when naming the tern left out the prefix 'Mc', so that the person honoured would appear to have been named 'Dougall'. Indeed, the Dutch and French names for the Roseate Tern are, respectively, 'Dougall's Stern' and 'Sterne de Dougall'. In 1842 William MacGillivray patriotically tried to correct the omission by naming the species 'MacDougall's Tern', but with no lasting effect.

Alberto Ferrero della Marmora (1789-1863)

MARMORA'S WARBLER *Sylvia sarda* Temminck

Sylvia sarda Temminck, 1820. *Manuel d'Ornithologie*, 2nd edn, Vol. 1, p. 204: Sardinia

Alberto della Marmora was the son of the Marchese Celestino and the Marchesa Raffaella Argentera di Bersezio. He was born at Turin in the Piedmont, on 7 April 1789, but studied at the Military School of Fontainebleau near Paris, and graduated there in 1807, as a 2nd lieutenant in the French infantry. He was the second of four brothers: Carlo, Alberto, Allessandro and Alfonso, who all distinguished themselves in their military careers.

Alberto served under Macdonald in the mountains of Calabria and in 1809 joined the army of the Kingdom of Italy, taking part in the campaign in Venetia. At the age of twenty-four he fought at the battle of Bautzen, at which the Russian and Prussian forces were defeated, and he was afterwards decorated with the Legion d'Honneur from the hands of Napoleon himself. When the Emperor was compelled to abdicate, Marmora gave his allegiance to the House of Savoy, which again ruled his native Piedmont and Sardinia.

For a time Marmora served on the island, but the King of Savoy's anti-revolutionary measures stirred up rebellion amongst his subjects and during the insurrection of 1820 and 1821 Marmora's sympathies lay with the rebels. He was forced to resign from active service, but three years later was recalled. Because of his liberal sympathies, his service was thereafter mostly confined to assignments on Sardinia. Nevertheless, he rose to the rank of General and in 1840 he was given command of the Royal School of Marines.

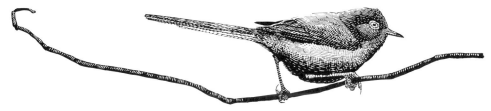

Marmora's Warbler

MARMORA. *PROFESSIONAL SOLDIER WHO BECAME GOVERNOR-GENERAL OF SARDINIA. HE CONTINUED AND GREATLY IMPROVED UPON CETTI'S NATURAL HISTORY STUDIES OF THE ISLAND.*

Marmora's fame, like that of Francesco Cetti, lies in his association with Sardinia. During the eighteenth century Cetti was the first to seriously study the natural history of the island. During the nineteenth century Marmora benefited from Cetti's labours and continued his investigations there. Marmora explored every part of the large, mountainous, sparsely populated island; a land exposed to long, hot, dry summers and persistent, dessicating winds. He studied the archaeology, ethnology and economy of Sardinia, as well as its natural history. The first edition of his minutely detailed observations was published in 1826, entitled *Voyage en Sardaigne de 1819 à 1825, ou descriptione statistique, physique et politique de cette île*. His early efforts to produce a geological map were frustrated by the discovery that previous cartographers had not been sufficiently accurate, and so he had to carry out his own surveys, which he began in 1834. His maps were engraved in Paris, published in two volumes in 1845 and were used for more than half a century. On modern maps, the highest peak on Sardinia is the Punta la Marmora which, at over 6000 feet, dominates the remote deforested highlands of the Barbagia.

Marmora was aided in his faunistic studies by Franco Bonelli, Professor of Zoology at Turin University, to whom he sent many of his discoveries, including Bonelli's Eagle. He later corresponded with Bonelli's successor, Giuseppe Gené, who described and named the specimens of Eleonora's Falcon which Marmora sent to him. Marmora rediscovered Cetti's Warbler and also found a new species of warbler which he named *Sylvia Sarda*, the scientific name being indicative of its origins. Known in English as Marmora's Warbler it closely resembles the Dartford Warbler but is darker, even more skulking in its habits, and tends to frequent the more mountainous maquis of the island.

Marmora's description of the new bird was read to the Turin Academy on 28 August 1819 but it was not published until after Temminck's version appeared in 1820. As with Cetti's Warbler, Temminck is credited as the first describer—from Marmora's specimens!

An exceptional naturalist, Marmora, through his acute observations and numerous discoveries, made an important contribution to the development of European ornithology. Other ornithologists besides Temminck were indebted to his field-work and collections. Though most of his work was done on Sardinia, Marmora also visited the south of France, the Balearic Islands and Gozo, off Malta. In 1849 he became Commander General of Sardinia, eventually retiring to Turin, where he died at the age of seventy-three on 18 March 1863.

Ernesto Mauri [†] (1791-1836)

WESTERN SANDPIPER *Calidris mauri* (Cabanis)

Ereunetes Mauri Cabanis, 1857. *Journal für Ornithologie* 4, No. 24 (1856), p. 419: South Carolina

The Western Sandpiper is named after an Italian Professor of Botany, has South Carolina as its type locality and breeds only on the open tundra of western Alaska and the Chukotskiy Peninsula; this curious piece of ornithological history therefore deserves some explanation.

Ernesto Mauri was born in Rome on 12 January 1791. He became the director of the botanical gardens there and the author of several papers on early Roman botany. One of his close friends was Charles Bonaparte, who was engaged in producing the *Iconografia della Fauna Italica* (1832–41) with which Mauri gave much valuable assistance. However, Mauri died before the third volume was published and Bonaparte consequently described a new species of fish (*Smaris maurii*) in volume three, dedicating it to the memory of "my dear professor of practical botany". Shortly afterwards, in 1838, Bonaparte also named the sandpiper in his friend's honour when he compiled a comparative list of the birds of Rome and Philadelphia.

In autumn, most Western Sandpipers migrate down the Pacific seaboard, wintering all along the coast to as far south as Peru; it also commonly occurs on the eastern coast of the United States, some moving southwards through the

Western Sandpiper

†No portrait traced.

West Indies to Guyana and Surinam. Although Bonaparte noted that the birds occurred in Philadelphia, he did not give a description of the little wader, and this task was later undertaken by the German naturalist, Jean Cabanis, from an American specimen. Only a few months before Bonaparte died, he visited Cabanis in Berlin and persuaded him to adopt his earlier appellation, which Cabanis then published in the *Journal für Ornithologie*.

Edouard Ménétries (1802-1861)

MÉNÉTRIES'S WARBLER *Sylvia mystacea* Ménétries

Sylvia mystacea Ménétries, 1832. *Catalogue raisonée des objets de Zoology récuillis dans un voyage au Caucase*, p. 34: Sal'yany, lower Kura River, eastern Transcaucasia

At the age of nineteen Edouard Ménétries was invited to join a Russian-backed expedition to Brazil led by Baron von Langsdorff. They arrived in March 1822 at a time when Brazil was undergoing great political upheaval and Langsdorff therefore decided to return to Europe. The young Ménétries was left to explore and collect, as best he could, in the provinces of São Paulo and Rio de Janeiro.

Two years later, as the political situation began to stabilize, Langsdorff returned to Brazil and, together with Ménétries and an artist called Rugendas, he made an eight-month excursion four hundred miles northwards from Rio de Janeiro to Tejuco (Diamentina). On their return to the coast Langsdorff's mental condition began to deteriorate and after several disagreements with Ménétries and Rugendas he replaced them both with new personnel. The disappointed Ménétries then made his way to Europe, arriving back after an absence of four years. His time in Brazil had nevertheless been an important and valuable period. It had given him the practical experience of collecting under difficult circumstances, the challenge of attempting to arrange and classify new species without the necessary facilities and also allowed him to develop close links with scientific establishments in Russia.

Born in Paris on 2 October 1802, Ménétries decided at first to study medicine. After a while, stimulated by vivid accounts of Alexander von Humboldt's tropical explorations, he abandoned his original career in order to work at the Jardin des Plantes under the supervision of Cuvier and Latreille. He was particularly drawn to the study of insects and it was not long before he was nominated by the Paris Museum as a suitably competent zoologist to accompany Langsdorff to Brazil. The expedition had been instigated by the Czar of Russia, Alexander I, and on his return Ménétries was rewarded with the Curatorship of the Zoological Collection at St Petersburg. He remained in the Russian employ for the remainder of his life.

After taking up his new appointment Ménétries began to arrange, classify and catalogue the existing collections and added to them by means of exchanges with

MÉNÉTRIES. *FRENCH ENTOMOLOGIST WHO COLLECTED IN SOUTH AMER-ICA BEFORE BECOMING CURATOR OF ZOOLOGY AT THE ST PETERSBURG ACADEMY OF SCIENCES. HE TRAVELLED THROUGH THE CAUCASUS TO THE CASPIAN SEA AND AFTERWARDS PRODUCED THE FIRST GOOD CHECK-LIST OF THE BIRDS OF THOSE REGIONS.*

foreign museums. But his work at St Petersburg was soon interrupted: at the age of twenty-six he was sent by the new Czar, Nicholas I, on an eighteen-month exploratory trip to the Caucasus, in south-west Russia. (For a map of Ménétries's route in the Caucasus, see Güldenstädt, p. 180).

He left St Petersburg on 7 June 1829 with three other Academicians and eighteen days later arrived at Pyatigorsk, in the northern foothills. On the same day they left to explore the region surrounding Mt Elbrus, accompanied by a large military escort which had been waiting for them. Russia was still in the process of subjugating the various hill peoples of the Caucasus and it was unsafe for Ménétries and his companions to travel anywhere unless they were joined by a group of Cossacks. After less than four weeks they had completed their objectives and were back at Pyatigorsk, where Ménétries and another scientist received instructions to explore the shores of the Caspian Sea down to the frontier with Persia. With a succession of escorts they began by travelling eastwards along the River Terek, Ménétries successfully acquiring a number of wetland birds at Mosdok (which had been visited almost sixty years earlier by Güldenstädt). Although they had some trouble finding suitable pack-horses to carry their equipment and were delayed by the lack of adequate roads they eventually reached Baku on the west coast of the Caspian Sea on 9 December. They found themselves in a remarkably arid and sterile region where the winds blew constantly, whipping up sand and dust to add to the torment provided by the glare from the bare ground. Despite the additional hardship of often finding only brackish water with which to quench his thirst, Ménétries seized every opportunity to collect. It was the poorest time of year to search for insects but he encountered large wintering flocks of Little Bustards, some pelicans and a great variety of wildfowl.

At the end of April they left Baku on horseback and followed the edge of the sea to Sal'yany. Ménétries was glad to leave the arid steppe country behind and, in comparison, found the areas on either side of the River Kura very lush and teeming with birds and insects. Near Lenkoran it was equally rewarding and from the end of May, for almost a month, they explored the Talych Mountains; a superbly verdant range being humid and well wooded up to about 4000 ft. When they returned to Lenkoran they were alarmed to discover that cholera was raging through the town but quickly managed to take a small ship to Baku. Here too there was an epidemic and they left overland as soon as possible for Kuba and then made their way homewards, arriving back at St Petersburg on 19 December 1830.

Although insects had been his main preoccupation, ornithology benefited considerably from Ménétries's investigations because he fortunately possessed the discerning eye of the good field-collector. Some of his most important discoveries were made on the south side of the Caucasian Range, near the Caspian Sea. On a saline lake near Lenkoran Ménétries obtained the first specimens of that curiously mottled fawn-grey duck, the Marbled Teal, of which rather unusually, the two sexes are alike. Here too he observed large numbers of the Isabelline Wheatear, a large wheatear with the most upright stance of all their kind; for several years, even though he was not the first to discover the species, it was known as Ménétries's Wheatear. The only bird by which he is now remembered in the English language is Ménétries's Warbler: similar to the perhaps more familiar Sardinian Warbler of the Mediterranean region, except that the males possess lovely dull pinkish-coloured breasts. It is now known to breed in the plains and lower mountain slopes of eastern Turkey eastwards through Transcaucasia to Afghanistan. Ménétries first found this splendid warbler on the lower reaches of the Kura River where he obtained a fine series of skins. Later on, 6000 feet up in the Talych Mountains he discovered another new bird and named it *Melanocorypha bimaculata*; the specific name means 'two spotted' and refers to the two thin dark neck-patches of the Bimaculated Lark.

Despite the fact that the Caucasus had been traversed by naturalists of the calibre of S. G. Gmelin, Güldenstädt and Pallas, ornithological accounts from the region were still very meagre. Edouard Ménétries was the first to make a reasonably comprehensive list of Caucasian birds. Although it was his only major contribution to the subject, his *Catalogue raisonée des objets de Zoology récuillis dans un voyage au Caucase et jusqu'aux frontières actuelles de la Perse* (1832) included notes on 175 species of birds and provided a sound basis on which a host of later nineteenth century naturalists were able to build. The brief visits of Eversmann in 1830 and Nordmann in 1836 were followed by the more lengthy investigations of Radde from 1864 and Bogdanov from 1871; the latter being responsible for naming a race of Buzzard *Buteo buteo menetriesi*, the common buzzard of the northern Caucasus, south Crimea and northern Iran.

At St Petersburg Ménétries continued with some of the tasks that he had commenced before his departure, and entomology remained his principal interest from then onwards. He established and maintained good relations with such naturalists as Christian von Steven, Fischer von Waldheim and Count Mannerheim and worked hard to develop a correspondence with many scientists abroad, using the collections which he had gathered himself as a precious nucleus of exchange material with which to augment the collection at St Petersburg. Within a short period the entomological section grew into one of the most extensive in Europe and Ménétries became the leading Russian entomologist of his day.

In 1829, his first paper, 'Observations on some Lepidoptera of Brazil' was published at Moscow and thereafter a steady stream of entomological papers appeared in a variety of journals. Of the twenty-eight papers credited to Ménétries some dealt with insects from such places as the West Indies, the Balkans, Turkey and Chinese Mongolia but he devoted his attentions mainly to

Ménétries's Warbler

the entomology of Russia and her dominions, which then included Russian America (Alaska). He analysed the various insect collections made in Siberia by Middendorff and Stupendorff, and from the Amur by Carl Maximowicz and Leopold von Schrenck.

In his last years Ménétries delighted in the company of his fellow entomologists, both professional and amateur, and the library where he worked was often a meeting place and forum for discussion on insects and other topics of natural history. He died at St Petersburg, at the age of fifty-eight, on 10 April 1861, a victim of "a severe emphysema". He had only recently founded the Russian Entomological Society and had been working at the museum until just a few months before his death.

MŁOKOSIEWICZ. *POLISH AMATEUR NATURALIST WHO SERVED IN THE RUSSIAN ARMY. HE LATER WORKED AS A FORESTER IN THE MOUNTAINS OF THE CAUCASUS WHERE HE EXPLORED EXTEN-SIVELY.*

Ludwik Franciszek Młokosiewicz (1831-1909)

CAUCASIAN BLACK GROUSE *Tetrao mlokosiewiczi* Taczanowski

Tetrao mlokosiewiczi Taczanowski, 1875. *Proceedings of the Zoological Society of London*, p. 267, Figs 1–2, 4: Lagodekhi, eastern Caucasus

Ludwik Młokosiewicz (pronounced Mwok'ō'she'vitch) was born in Warsaw on 25 August 1831. He was from a wealthy and aristocratic family and joined the Caucasian Division of the army of Russia at the age of twenty-two. While stationed on the south-eastern slopes of the Caucasus at Lagodekhi, his botanical talents were employed in laying out and planting a regimental park, orchard and water garden. In 1861, after less than ten years of army life, frustrated and wearied by various intrigues, he resigned and travelled southwards "to seek oblivion . . . in the deserts of Persia". On his return, however, he was arrested and charged with inciting a revolt amongst the Poles in the Caucasus. Although innocent he was sentenced to six years enforced residence in the province of Voronetz and his botanical collections were taken from him and eventually lost.

When restrictions upon him were lifted in 1876 Młokosiewicz continued his explorations in the mountains of Dagestan and two years later went again to

Caucasian Black Grouse

Persia, travelling as far as Baluchistan. He returned the following year and was appointed Inspector of Forests for the Signakhi District, basing himself at Lagodekhi, where he remained for the rest of his life—apart from his numerous exploratory trips into the mountains. His work gave him an excellent opportunity to tramp through the woods on the lower slopes but being a fit and agile man he also liked to explore high above the tree-line. An outstanding field-naturalist he supplied many foreign museums with both botanical and zoological specimens and became highly regarded in Polish and Russian scientific circles.

The botanical finds made by Młokosiewicz include *Gentiana lagodechiana* and *Paeonia mlokosewitschii*, one of the loveliest of all paeonies. He had a large family and enjoyed taking them on field excursions even when some of them were so young that they had to be carried; it was his daughter Julia who discovered *Primula juliae*.

His discovery of the Caucasian Black Grouse was made on Mt Bogosch near Zakataly, not many miles east of Lagodekhi. "With the exception of the shepherds", observed Młokosiewicz, "no one in the country is acquainted with these birds; and the native hunter does not care to expend his powder on such insignificant game, preferring to save it for deer and ibex . . . This bird is in their eyes of no more value than a sparrow; and their astonishment was great indeed at seeing us so earnestly occupied in the pursuit of such game."[1] He sent a pair of specimens to Ladislas Taczanowski, for many years the Director of the Zoological Museum of Warsaw. Taczanowski gratefully named the species in honour of the collector, "who, with perseverance worthy of admiration continued amongst a thousand difficulties to collect everything that could enrich the natural history of Russian Georgia and has so justly appraised, after discovering it, the specific characteristics of this fine bird . . ."

The species is confined to the upper parts of the Caucasus where it usually frequents the high forests, rhododendron thickets and alpine meadows, though Młokosiewicz even found some solitary males of this rather confiding game-bird in the snows at 11,000 ft, well above the tree-line. The general remoteness of its breeding habitat no doubt contributed to its comparatively late discovery.

Młokosiewicz died, at the age of seventy-eight, whilst enjoying one of his customary forays into the mountains of Dagestan. His only ornithological publication was a report on the biology of the new species of black grouse.

George Montagu
(1753-1815)

MONTAGU'S HARRIER *Circus pygargus* (Linnaeus)

Falco Pygargus Linnaeus, 1758. *Systema Naturae*, 10th edn, p. 89: Europe [= England, *ex* Albin]

George Montagu has been characterized as a "peculiar man" with "peculiar tastes" and as a "decidedly commonplace individual, clever but not intellectual, industrious but not very brilliant". The following account is also rather contradictory: he led an unusual, controversial and indeed scandalous life and at the same time carried out a slow, methodical and exact study of natural history, of which birds and inshore marine life were his particular interests.

He was descended from two distinguished families. His father James Montagu was related to the first Earl of Manchester and his mother, Elioner, was the daughter of William Hedges of Alderton House, Wiltshire, whose father, Sir Charles Hedges, had been Secretary of State to Queen Anne. Born at the family home of Lackham House in Wiltshire, George Montagu had twelve brothers and sisters. The Register of Baptisms at Lacock Church notes his christening on 9 July 1753 and the presumption that he was also born in this year is supported by the parochial church register of Kingsbridge, in Devon, which gives his age at death as sixty-two and the date of his burial as 24 June 1815.[1]

George's childhood home, since destroyed by fire, had been visited by Henry VIII and was surrounded by extensive woodland. A prestigious career, such as could be obtained in the army was probably expected of him and so before he was seventeen, on 22 June 1770, he was enrolled as an Ensign in the 15th Regiment of Foot. Over the next five years he moved around Britain with his regiment being mainly stationed in northern England and Ireland. In 1773 he was promoted to Lieutenant and thereafter he rose steadily through the ranks; but it was not a particularly distinguished career and he later caused the family much embarrassment.

When he was about twenty he married into an illustrious family but seems not to have had the blessing of either set of parents. His wife, Ann Courtenay, was the eldest daughter of William Courtenay of London and Lady Jane Stuart whose brother John, Earl of Bute, had been Prime Minister to George III. The date of the marriage has been given as 1773 but there is no confirmation of this. Between 1945 and 1948 Sir Hugh Gladstone instigated a search for the details

MONTAGU. *LIEUTENANT-COLONEL IN THE WILTSHIRE MIL-
ITIA. FOLLOWING HIS COURT-MARTIAL HE SPENT THE REST
OF HIS LIFE WITH HIS MISTRESS IN DEVON. HIS* ORNITHO-
LOGICAL DICTIONARY *WAS THE FIRST ACCURATE SUMMARY
OF THE BIRDS OF BRITAIN. HE WAS ALSO A PIONEER MALACOL-
OGIST AND MARINE BIOLOGIST.*

of the marriage amongst the family papers in Wiltshire, London and Bute, in Diocesan and Church papers, in London Marriage Licences and at the Royal College of Arms. The search was unsuccessful but it led to the discovery of three curious paragraphs in the London *General Evening Post* of 1773:

"On Sunday evening a young lady of very large independent fortune, niece of a nobleman near South-Audley Street, set off on a matrimonial expedition to Scotland, with one of her uncle's domestic chaplains."

29–31 July 1773

"Not many days since the youngest daughter of the E — of B —, walking in her father's park at L — H —, with only a maid attendant, a postchaise appearing, she ordered the maid to walk on, and she would overtake her, but the maid having walked some considerable while, and looking back, had just time to see the last of her lady, then going with an officer northwards, with a view to consummate a matrimonial contract."

7–10 August 1773

"We are informed that the daughter of a northern nobleman, who lately took a trip to Scotland with a young officer, has no more than £2000 independent of her much offended father, nor her intended spouse more than his bare commission."

12–14 August 1773

Sir Hugh Gladstone summed up the accounts as follows:

"The first extract is perhaps not so material as the other two. It might read either that the young lady was eloping with one of her uncle's domestic chaplains, or that she was taking him with her to perform the marriage with a third party. It is known that the 3rd Earl of Bute lived at South Audley Street; he died there on 10 March 1792.

When reading the second extract it is to be remembered that the E[arl] of B[ute] lived at L[uton] H[oo] in Bedfordshire. Ann Courtenay was not his daughter but his niece but she might have been staying, with her uncle, at Luton Hoo.

The third extract is confirmatory of the second. 'A northern nobleman' might well be the Earl of Bute but, as already stated Ann Courtenay was not his daughter but his niece.

In view of the fact that the date of the marriage of George Montagu to Ann Courtenay cannot be found in the usual records it would seem permissible to 'read between the lines' in the extracts from the *General Evening Post* and assume that the marriage was clandestine."[2]

About a year after their marriage George was sent overseas with his Regiment where he served in the war against the American Colonies. His stay abroad was short, perhaps not much more than twelve months, but while he was there he is said to have collected birds and preserved them as gifts for his wife. On 1 December 1775 he was promoted to Captain but two years later he retired from the Regiment of Foot and afterwards joined the Wiltshire Militia in which he rose to the rank of Lieutenant-Colonel.

George and Ann lived at various manor houses in Wiltshire, settling for a time at Easton Grey near Malmesbury where the last of their four sons and two daughters was born. On the death of his uncle, Thomas Hedges, in 1782, George was left the estate of Alderton House and other property in Wiltshire. There must have been some sort of reconciliation between the Montagus and Courtenays for when George and his family transferred to Alderton House his mother-in-law, Lady Jane Courtenay, moved in with them. Eight years later George's father died and left the estates and Lackham House to George's elder brother James Montagu. It was around this time that George Montagu's marriage and career began to disintegrate. Lady Holland, a well-known political hostess of her day, met Montagu at a dinner party at Saltram in September 1799:

> "Colonel Montagu I saw but once . . . and during a three hours assemblage of people at and after dinner he gave the natural history of every bird that flies and every fish that swims. He is a man of bad temper, nor does it sound creditable to him that none of his officers speak to him, and they are on the eve of bringing him to Court-martial. He is separated from his wife, and might inherit an estate of his brother's if he would be united to her; but the condition is too hard, and he renounces the possession of a benefit *so* encumbered."[3]

Her account of the birds and fishes is no doubt exaggerated but the rest of her gossip was sadly true. When James Montagu died unmarried in 1797 he left his brother George the family estates and Lackham House, provided that he resided in one of the Manor Houses together with his wife. Not only did George fail to comply with this but in the following year he had moved to Devon and was living at Knowle House, near Kingsbridge, with Mrs Elizabeth Dorville, wife of John Dorville, a London merchant! It was an unusually flagrant act for a man of Montagu's position. On 30 April 1800 his eldest son, George Conway Courtenay Montagu, filed a suit in Chancery against the trustees of the estate because of his father's failure to comply with the terms of the will. In addition, although the exact circumstances do not now seem clear, it appears that James Montagu had borrowed £25,000 to allow him to complete the purchase of Pewsham Forest adjoining Lackham and there was provision in the will for clearing the debt. The bitter legal battle that developed between father and son partly concerned these debts; the prolonged litigation led to £70,000 worth of timber being cut down and the fine libraries, collections of coins and medals were sold off by decree of the Court.[4] The years of legal wrangling, coupled with the son's extravagance, led to the eventual loss of most of the family estates.

On top of all these troubles Lieutenant-Colonel Montagu underwent a court-martial, held between 28 September and 15 October 1799 at Plymouth Dock. There were several charges arising from his personal dislike of three fellow officers and his subsequent extraordinary attempts to align the remaining officers against them.[5] Some disparaging remarks concerning Montagu, made by the wives of two of the officers, were said to be the cause of the initial disharmony. Montagu was found guilty on almost all the charges and was sentenced to be "displaced". This meant that he was expelled from the Militia but was free to join any other regiment—though it seems doubtful that this would have been possible.[6]

In Montagu's defence it could be said that he had married too young and was in a career that, at least latterly, neither suited nor agreed with him. From the natural history point of view the court martial was perhaps the best thing that could have happened to him; it allowed him to concentrate all his energies to one purpose. At Knowle House he did the bulk of his marine research and wrote his best ornithological work. Just four years after moving to Devon his two-volume *Ornithological Dictionary; or Alphabetical Synopsis of British Birds* was published and Eliza Dorville was responsible for most of the illustrations. One can guess that she had similar interests to his own for he bequeathed to her his library, his cabinet collections of natural history specimens, and all his manuscripts and publications. When he wrote in the *Dictionary* using the royal 'we' he was heavily criticized, but he may only have been acknowledging Eliza, his helpful co-worker. There is no reason to suppose that they were otherwise than happy and well matched to each other during the seventeen or more years that they were together.

Although George Montagu confined most of his ornithological studies to only part of southern England, he contributed significantly to our early knowledge of British birds. Most of his work on the subject appeared in the aforementioned *Dictionary* of 1802 and its *Supplement* which was published in 1813. In them he adopted a factual approach and showed many hitherto accepted species to be invalid. He showed that the Greenwich Sandpiper was the Ruff in winter plumage and the Ash-coloured Sandpiper was the same bird as the Knot. His care was demonstrated by his unwillingness to accept the Black Woodpecker as a British species because he had not seen it for himself.

Until the beginning of the nineteenth century it was generally believed that the brown 'Ring-tail Hawk' and the predominantly grey male Hen Harrier were different species. Montagu, by taking young birds from the nest and keeping them in captivity until a single young male, in the first moult, changed from brown to grey, proved conclusively that brown and grey birds were the same species. He then went on to discover a second species of harrier with a similar diversity of plumage.

The first specimen of the 'Ash-coloured Falcon'—as he called it—was shot on 10 August 1803 not far from Montagu's Devon home; the bird was an adult male and had the remains of a Skylark in its stomach. He gave the harrier the

Montagu's Harrier

scientific name *Falco Cineraceus* but Eleazor Albin had already published a coloured plate of the species in 1734,[7] and Linnaeus had used this picture when he described the bird under the name *Falco Pygargus* in 1758. Because of the law of priority concerning nomenclature Montagu's scientific name is not now used, although it was Montagu who really cleared up the general confusion that existed relating to these two harrier species and the difference between the sexes. Two continental ornithologists, Vieillot and Temminck, acknowledged Montagu's achievements by using the vernacular name 'Le Busard Montagu' and not long after, in 1836, MacGillivray first used the term Montagu's Harrier which was thereafter generally adopted in Britain.

A similar situation arose with the Cirl Bunting. In the winter of 1800 Montagu had noticed the species among flocks of Yellowhammers and Chaffinches and he obtained several specimens of both sexes and then in the following spring he found them breeding near Kingsbridge. It was a first record for Britain, but Linnaeus had again already named and described the buntings.

Montagu was also involved with the first British records of the Cattle Egret, Little Gull and Gull-billed Tern. The gull was killed on the Thames, near Chelsea, by·a Mr Plasted who sent him the body; the egret was shot near Kingsbridge where it "suffered a bungling marksman to fire twice before he could kill it"; and the tern was obtained in 1802 but thought to be a Sandwich Tern. (He only noticed that it was different when he saw Latham's type specimen of the Sandwich Tern a few years later.) All these species had previously been described elsewhere. He was eventually in luck when Dr Peter McDougall of Glasgow sent him a tern that had been shot in the Firth of Clyde: Montagu wrote the first scientific description of the Roseate Tern giving it the name *Sterna Dougallii*. The first description of the American Bittern is also credited to Montagu; the type specimen was shot at Piddletown in Dorset in 1804 and purchased by Montagu from another Devon collector. Only about fifty of these bitterns have ever been recorded in Europe, most of them before 1900.

Montagu's *Ornithological Dictionary* set a new high standard for others to follow. The work later went into other editions, largely rewritten but not greatly improved, by James Rennie and then by Edward Newman. The critical American ornithologist Elliott Coues described it as "one of the most notable treatises on British Birds . . . a vade-mecum [handbook] which has held its place at a thousand elbows for three-quarters of a century".[8] It is now interesting mainly because it enables us to reflect upon the changed status of certain species. For example, Montagu described the Wryneck as "not uncommon in the southern and eastern parts of the kingdom", and for the Red-backed Shrike he commented that although it "appears to be a local species, it is not uncommon in the north of Wiltshire, and part of Gloucestershire and Somersetshire, particularly about Bristol . . .". As breeding birds these two species now maintain, at most, only a tenuous hold in southern England. A third species may have left us forever, unless a current programme of reintroduction is successful:

> "The [Great] Bustard is only found upon the large extensive plains, and are almost extinct, except upon those of Wiltshire, where they are become very scarce within these few years. It is an extremely shy bird, and difficult to be shot. Young ones have frequently been taken by the shepherd's dogs before they are capable of flight; and their eggs are eagerly sought after for the purpose of hatching under hens . . . and the consequence will be a total extinction in a few years".

Only eleven years later, as Montagu had predicted, he recorded in the *Supplement* that "the shepherds with whom we have conversed lately, declare that they have not seen one in their most favourite haunts . . . for the last two of three years".

During Montagu's time in Wiltshire he corresponded with Gilbert White. Two letters have survived, in one of which, dated 29 June 1789, he confessed that he had "delighted in being an ornithologist from infancy, and, was I not bound by conjugal attachment, should like to ride my hobby into distant parts". He went on to ask White questions concerning the three species of 'willow wrens', and requested skins of Nightjar and Crossbill, offering to return the favour in a similar manner. White was apparently surprised by the request for a Nightjar as they were so common around Selborne that he thought Montagu would have little trouble obtaining some closer to his home.

One of Montagu's other pursuits was the study of marine and freshwater natural history, at a time when few other people were interested. His great work, the *Testacea Britannica, a History of British Marine, Land and Freshwater Shells*, which was published in two parts in 1803, was again illustrated by Eliza Dorville. In them he described 470 species of molluscs, 100 of which were new to the British list and for seventy-two species he gave their first ever descriptions. He also supplied several new species of Crustacea to his young friend William Leach at the British Museum and he recorded many species of fish for the first time in English waters, besides discovering new species such at Montagu's Blenny and Montagu's Snapper. Not surprisingly his interests also extended to mammals: at Kent's Hole, near Torquay, among the large colony of Greater Horseshoe Bats he discovered and then described the Lesser Horseshoe Bat for the first time.

Montagu was an early member of the Linnean Society and contributed several articles including, in 1807, some of his notable work on harriers. To the Memoirs of the Wernerian Natural History Society he gave the first descriptions of several new species of fish. He also wrote one other book, little more than a pamphlet, that was not entirely related to natural history. In his *Sportsmans Directory, or Tractate on Gunpowder* (1792) he recounted the effect of lead shot upon flying birds but mostly he gave instructions to would-be duellists. Besides providing details about the weapons, he emphasized that the left arm should not be used to rest the pistol upon, in order to achieve better aim, as this presented the side of the body unprotected to the opponent. He must have gained his knowledge during his long military service and though it seems quite possible there is no positive indication that he had personal experience of duelling.

Misunderstood by his family and society and poorly represented by his early biographers, Montagu is usually portrayed as a brusque, arrogant and punctual military man. A recent account of his life sees him in a more sympathetic light and describes him as "honest, sincere, responsible, considerate [and] reliable".[9] This reinforces the essential good nature suggested by an acquaintance who knew Montagu, when the naturalist was in his fifties, as a "fine upstanding man, rather stout, very genial, and [with] a good word for everybody".[10]

Despite his contribution to early natural history (and despite his more colourful character) he has failed to achieve the fame of his contemporary, Gilbert White. This is almost certainly because Montagu's writing lacked style and often contained grammatical errors. But considering his non-academic background his accomplishments are remarkable: he described the animals that he observed extremely well and was one of the best naturalists of his generation.

Montagu's final years were not without bitterness. His younger sons, through no fault of their own, caused him much sorrow. During the Napoleonic Wars John was killed in a naval action, James died as a prisoner of war in France and, in 1811, Frederick was hit by a musket ball as he led his men in a charge at Albuera, in Spain. Montagu's own death occurred only four years after the death of Frederick. When alterations were being carried out at Knowle House, some old timber was left lying about; he stepped on a rusty nail and a few days later, on 20 June 1815, he died of tetanus. Before he died he was asked by his old friend and fellow collector, the Reverend Kerr Vaughan, where he wished to be buried and is said to have replied: "Where the tree falls there let it lie" (Ecclesiastes Ch. 11, v. 3). He was buried at Kingsbridge Parish Church but was not left to lie in peace; some years later his coffin was broken open, the lead was removed and his bones were thrown back into the vault.

The surviving and eldest son was never forgiven over the legal wrangle concerning the estates. In his will of 1805, George Montagu specifically demanded, and repeated in his codicil of 1814, that absolutely nothing was to be given to him. Monetary bequests, however, were made to his wife Ann and their two daughters Eleonora and Louisa, who were also to receive some of the property that remained at Alderton House and Lackham. The main beneficiary of his estate was Eliza Dorville and her children by him: Henry, Isabella and Georgiana. Many years later in 1874, Henry Dorville bequeathed the miniature portrait of his father, in the uniform of a Lieutenant-Colonel of the Militia, to the Linnean Society, along with annotated copies of the *Dictionary* and *Testacea Britannica*, and some of his mother's original drawings for the two works.

Montagu's wife survived him by less than eight months and died at Hotwells, Bristol on 10 February 1816. Eliza Dorville died in 1844. Montagu's large collection of birds was bought by the British Museum for £1200. Unfortunately many of the specimens were poorly prepared, were being attacked by mites and were falling to pieces. None the less, 200 of his birds were saved by careful restoration and are now housed at the Tring Museum.

Horace Bénédict Alfred Moquin-Tandon (1804-1863)

AFRICAN BLACK OYSTERCATCHER *Haematopus moquini* Bonaparte

Haematopus moquini Bonaparte, 1856. *Comptes Rendus de l'Académie des Sciences de Paris* 43, p. 1020: Gaboon

Chiefly remembered as a botanist, Alfred Moquin-Tandon has an ornithological connection with the Canary Islands, the only place within the Western Palearctic where the African Black Oystercatcher has been recorded.

He was born at Montpellier on 7 May 1804, and graduated there as both Doctor of Science and Doctor of Medicine. He became Professor of Zoology at Marseilles at the age of twenty-five and remained there until 1833 when he became Professor of Botany and director of the botanical gardens at Toulouse. In 1850 he was instructed by the French Government to take charge of a special mission to Corsica and he afterwards co-authored a *Flore de la Corse*. In 1853 he moved to Paris and took the chair of medical natural history left vacant by the death of Achille Richard. He later directed the Jardin des Plantes and the Académie des Sciences. He became a much respected naturalist and died in Paris on 15 April 1863, in his sixtieth year.

Although most of Moquin-Tandon's written works were of a botanical nature his zoological studies included a dissertation on the eggs of both birds and reptiles, a monograph on the Hirundines, notes on the birds of the south of

African Black Oystercatcher

A. MOQUIN-TANDON.

Lith de Thierry Frères.

MOQUIN-TANDON. *EMINENT FRENCH NATURALIST. CO-AUTHOR OF THE FIRST MAJOR STUDY OF THE BIRDS OF THE CANARY ISLANDS.*

France and a natural history of the terrestrial and river molluscs of his country. He also collaborated with the English botanist Philip Barker-Webb and the French zoologist Sabin Berthelot on the *L'Histoire Naturelle des Îles Canaries* (1835–50). The ornithological section was published in 1842 as the *Ornithologie Canarienne*; much of it written by Moquin-Tandon. The African Black Oystercatcher was featured in the work under the name *Haematopus niger* but this name, and some others, were afterwards judged to be invalid.[1] In 1856 Bonaparte was forced to create a new name for the species and he decided to name it after Moquin-Tandon in recognition of his investigations into the ornithology of the Canaries. However, the specimens that Bonaparte described were from the southern portion of Africa and the race peculiar to the Canaries has been named after an English ornithologist.

Haematopus moquini meadewaldoi has never been known to be common and is now believed to be extinct. Sabin Berthelot recorded it on the small barren island of Graciosa, and Carl Bolle reported several pairs on the peninsula of Handia in 1852, and collected one specimen. Meade-Waldo obtained three of the birds in the Canaries around 1888, and the last skins were taken in June 1913 by David Bannerman. The bird is thought to have finally disappeared from the islands around 1940.[2]

Jean Moussier†
(1795-c.1850)

MOUSSIER'S REDSTART *Phoenicurus moussieri* (Olph-Galliard)

Erithacus Moussieri Olph-Galliard, 1852. *Annales des Sciences Physiques et Naturelles de la Société Impériale d'Agriculture de Lyon*, Ser. 2, Vol. 4, p. 101, Pl. 2: Province of Oran, Algeria

"While one race of man after another has rushed like a flood over North Africa, and left the faint traces of each invasion in a few stranded ruins on the shores, or in the tide marks of some wreck of humanity of the mountain-sides—long before the Phoenician galley had entered the Bay of Tunis and treated with the Numidian king, before either Roman, Vandal, or Saracen had disturbed his retreats, Moussier was here, never disturbed by a restless state of emigration . . ."[1]

So wrote Canon Tristram, in characteristic style, concerning not the man but the delightful and distinctive Moussier's Redstart, resident across North Africa from Morocco to the western parts of Libya. The species was first described by Léon Olph-Galliard on 2 April 1852, at Lyon, at a meeting of the Société Nationale d'Agriculture, d'Histoire Naturelle et des Arts. Olph-Galliard noted that Moussier had "met with the present species in February in the Province of Oran where it is rare. It is more shy than the Stonechat with which species it consorts. Perched on an *Asphodelium* plant it perceives danger from afar, and generally disappears before the sportsman can get within shot-range."[2] Despite

Moussier's Redstart

†No portrait traced.

the difficulty, Moussier must have succeeded in securing at least two birds since an engraving of a stuffed pair of redstarts accompanied the description of their plumage.

Unfortunately, Olph-Galliard gave little information about Moussier. And it is doubtful if Tristram, who was in North Africa for the winters of 1855–56 and 1856–57, could have added much to the following brief account.·

Jean Moussier was born on 5 November 1795 at Sainte Colombes-lès-Vienne, a small town about twenty miles south of Lyon, in the Rhône valley. In April 1813, before he was seventeen years old, he joined Napoleon's *Grand Armée* as a surgeon's assistant. After Napoleon's defeat in 1815, Moussier studied in the south of France at Montpellier and qualified there as a civil doctor in 1818. Between 1823 and 1826 he had a series of temporary enlistments at various military establishments. After this, nothing is known about his activities until 1840 when he began another series of military appointments as a surgeon. On 10 April 1846 he signed on (as *Chirurgien Aide-Major*) with the First Battalion of the French Foreign Legion in Algeria, and remained with them for the next year and a half. During this period he found time to pursue his interest in birds but he was forced to resign from the Legion because of ill health and he returned to France soon after 28 October 1847. He then took employment on the tiny prison island of Sainte Marguerite (off Cannes) where he was entrusted with the welfare of Arab prisoners until August 1849. This was the last of his military postings and his subsequent movements are unknown.

The description of Moussier's Redstart was not published until some five years after Moussier returned from North Africa. Perhaps Moussier retired to the Lyon area around 1852 with a small collection of birds which he showed or presented to the local authorities. Enquiries at Lyon and at his home town have provided no additional information and Moussier's manuscript notes for the year 1846, which are referred to by Olph-Galliard, have not been traced. Jean Moussier's date and place of death, and his degree of interest in ornithology, therefore remain a mystery.

Johann Andreas Naumann (1744-1826)

NAUMANN'S THRUSH *Turdus naumanni* Temminck

Turdus naumanni Temminck, 1820. *Manuel d'Ornithologie*, 2nd edn, Vol. 1, p. 170: "Les parties orientales; se montre en Silésie et en Autriche; plus commun en Hongrie"

Johann Friedrich Naumann (1780-1857)

LESSER KESTREL *Falco naumanni* Fleischer

Falco Naumanni Fleischer, 1818. In C. P. Laurop and V. F. Fischer, *Sylvan, ein Jahrbuch für Forstmänner, Jäger und Jagdfreunde für das Jahr 1817–18*, p. 174: "scarce visitor to southern Germany and Switzerland" [error for Sicily according to Stresemann MS]

Johann Andreas Naumann was a German farmer whose land lay near the town of Halle, about 100 miles south-west of Berlin. The fields were often wet and boggy and yielded disappointing crops, but they were rich in breeding waders and wintering ducks. It was therefore not surprising that Naumann was a keen hunter, wildfowler and trapper. Although poorly educated he was continually learning about the wild birds which frequented the surrounding countryside and he began to write about his observations and discoveries. At first he intended only to describe the birds of the region of Anhalt, where he lived, but it swelled into an ornithology of northern Germany and the neighbouring countries and was completed in 1804.

In November of that year a gamekeeper brought Naumann a thrush which he had caught in a wood near the farmer's home.[1] Although it was a juvenile

J. A. NAUMANN. *GERMAN FARMER WHO LACKED ANY SCIEN-
TIFIC TRAINING, BUT WHO PRODUCED AN IMPORTANT AND
INFLUENTIAL GUIDE TO THE BIRDS OF GERMANY.*

J. F. NAUMANN. *THE SON OF J. A. NAUMANN, HE ILLUSTRATED AND UPDATED HIS FATHER'S WORK AND SUPERSEDED HIM IN IMPORTANCE. PORTRAYED IN HIS STUDY, NAUMANN IS HOLDING THE THRUSH WHICH HE DREW FOR HIS FATHER.*

bird, Naumann recognized it as being different from the regular wintering thrushes and named it *Turdus dubius*. In 1820 Temminck first described the lovely brown and rufous adults and renamed this vagrant from eastern Siberia, *Turdus naumanni*.

Naumann had two sons who shared his passion for hunting and trapping. The elder was Johann Friedrich, born on 14 February 1780. He was sent to school in Dessau, but left at the age of fourteen so that he could help his father on the farm and illustrate his book. His artistic talent had been encouraged from a very early age, and for the next ten years he painted the birds of Germany.

His early efforts reflected his immaturity but his later drawings were beautifully executed; whenever possible he drew from living birds or used specimens which one of the family had shot, with the result that the plates were exceptionally good for their time.

Eight supplements to Naumann's work were published between 1804 and 1817, and a new edition was soon required. The text for the *Naturgeschichte der Vögel Deutschlands* (1820–

Naumann's Thrush

44) was almost entirely rewritten by Johann Friedrich and thirteen supplements to this work were produced between 1846 and 1860. The fact that the Naumanns lacked any scientific training was, in one way, something of an advantage, for the resulting simplicity of their style made the book highly attractive to the general public, and their observations resulting from their intimate knowledge of wild birds appealed also to the serious ornithologist. 'The Natural History of German Birds', in twelve volumes, was both popular and highly influential, stimulating many others in Germany to take up ornithology.

Lesser Kestrel

From 1818 to 1828 J. F. Naumann and D. A. Buhle published *Die Eier der Vögel Deutschlands* [The Eggs of German Birds]. The year 1818 also saw the publication of Fleischer's description of the Lesser Kestrel, which he named in honour of Johann Friedrich, who was by then recognized as the founder of scientific ornithology in central Europe. Other tributes followed and in 1837 the Duke of Köthen made him a Professor of Natural History, while two years later the University of Bresel granted him the title of Honorary Doctor.

By the middle of the nineteenth century the name of Naumann was so inseparably associated with birds that when the 'German Ornithological Society' founded their magazine in 1849 they called it *Naumannia*. Johann Friedrich was a frequent contributor to its pages, but in 1853 its name was changed to the *Journal für Ornithologie*. J. F. Naumann died at Ziebigk in Anhalt on 15 August 1857, three years after the death of his younger brother, Carl Andreas.

Carl Andreas Naumann was born on 14 November 1786. Like his brother he was first entrusted with a gun at the age of eight, and was entirely educated at home, accompanying his father on all his hunting expeditions with great enthusiasm. He quickly absorbed the necessary skills and became an outstanding hunter and trapper with a truly exceptional knowledge of the habits and behaviour of his quarry. When he was a young man the French occupied Anhalt, but he escaped the danger of being called up through the intervention of the Duke of Köthen, who made him his gamekeeper for the next few years. Afterwards he worked as a forester near Aken and provided his father and brother with whatever specimens they required, including numerous rare birds which he had shot in the marshes of the Elbe and nearby.

His records for the years 1816 to 1844 reflect the unquestioned attitudes of his time towards wild birds, when waders, ducks and geese were eaten whenever possible and most raptors were considered to be vermin. During those years his tally included 4000 snipe, 648 Woodcock, over 100 Bar-tailed Godwits, nearly 2000 ducks, over 1000 birds of prey, 167 owls, 84 Ravens, more than 9000 Partridges and nearly 300 Quail. He also captured another 27,000 birds which he sold for food or for falconry.

Carl Andreas was not a writer, but he made an enormous contribution to German ornithology by sharing with his brother his experiences, observations and discoveries in the field.

In 1880 a statue of the three Naumanns was erected in the grounds of Köthen Castle. Unfortunately it was destroyed during the Second World War, but it has since been replaced. In 1915 the Naumann Memorial Museum was founded in Köthen Castle. It now consists of three little halls and six exhibition rooms, housing 1186 stuffed birds collected by the Naumanns, as well as many of their books, drawings, letters, manuscripts, guns, traps and other items of much interest. A biography of J. F. Naumann, published in 1957, contains portraits of the three Naumanns and much additional information about all of them.[2]

Franz Neumayer †
(died 1840)

ROCK NUTHATCH *Sitta neumayer* Michahelles

Sitta Neumayer Michahelles, 1830. *Isis von Oken*, col. 814: Ragusa [= Dubrovnik], Dalmatia

The Rock Nuthatch reaches the western edge of its range in Yugoslavia, and though very similar in appearance to its British congener, its habits are rather different. The bird does not breed in woods and forests but in gorges and on rugged mountain slopes where it nests in rocky crevices which it walls up with mud, or else builds a remarkable bottle-shaped nest underneath a projecting rock. It winters at lower altitudes and may then occasionally be observed feeding in trees.

Dr Karl Michahelles was a German naturalist who travelled extensively in Dalmatia and Croatia and became well known for his work on Yugoslavian birds. At the age of twenty-three, he published a description of a new species of nuthatch which had been sent to him by Franz Neumayer, a natural history dealer who lived in Ragusa (Dubrovnik). Neumayer had labelled the specimen *Sitta syriaca* and mentioned that it was a not uncommon resident. It seems likely that it was obtained in winter as he shot the bird amongst some cypresses.

Four years after the description of the Rock Nuthatch appeared in *Isis*, Michahelles sailed to Greece as the doctor to a Bavarian regiment which had been sent to quell an uprising. Soon afterwards, while caring for the sick and injured, he contracted a fever and dysentery, and died there. Much less has been recorded about the naturalist after whom the nuthatch was named. Neumayer's date and place of birth are unknown and there are only a few scant details about his activities. He died on 18 September 1840, in the small village of Kuna on the Peljesac Peninsula, some fifty miles north of the city around which he had collected. A few plants were also named in his honour.

Rock Nuthatch

†No portrait traced.

NORDMANN. *FOR MANY YEARS HE WORKED AS A NATURALIST ON THE
SHORES OF THE BLACK SEA. HIS NUMEROUS EXPEDITIONS IN THE REGION
INCLUDED VISITS TO THE CAUCASUS AND THE CRIMEA.*

Alexander von Nordmann (1803-1866)

BLACK-WINGED PRATINCOLE *Glareola nordmanni* Fischer

Glareola Nordmanni "Fisch." Nordmann, 1842. *Bulletin de la Société Impériale des Naturalistes de Moscou* 15, p. 314, Pl. 2, Fig. 2, a–c: Steppes of southern Russia *ex melanoptera* Nordmann MS

When Nordmann first obtained the Black-winged Pratincole he sent it to the Imperial Society of Naturalists at Moscow under the manuscript name of *Glareola melanoptera*, but when his original description was published the bird appeared under the name *Glareola Nordmanni*. It had been altered by de Fischer von Waldheim, the editor of the society's publication, with the full approval of the Society, and so, rather unusually, the scientific name commemorates both first discoverer and first describer.

Alexander von Nordmann spent more than fifteen years on the shores of the Black Sea at Odessa, where he was Professor of Zoology and Botany at the Richelieu Lyceum. During his time there he made almost annual expeditions to Bessarabia, the area around the mouth of the Danube, to the Crimea and, in 1830, to the Caucasus. It was whilst traversing the steppes of southern Russia that he first differentiated the Black-winged from the Collared Pratincole; two very similar species, not easily distinguished unless seen very well whilst in flight or, of course, in the hand, when the very dark underwing of the Black-winged Pratincole contrasts with the chestnut underwing of the other species. Both of them are birds of arid steppe country and their breeding ranges overlap slightly in the environs of the Black Sea. Although Nordmann spent many years in this area, and was familiar with such birds as pelicans, egrets, bustards and Rose-coloured Starlings, Nordmann was in fact a native of Finland and had developed his natural history interests in the boreal forests of the Baltic coastlands.

He was born on 24 May 1803 in the fortress of Svenskund where his father, David Anton von Nordmann, was the Russian Commander-in-Chief. Alexander's early education was by private tutor and he then attended schools at Frederikshamn and Vyborg, until, at the age of fifteen, he went to the Academy at Porvoo (Borgä). In 1820 he started at the University of Åbo (Turku) where he was greatly influenced by the entomologist Sohlberg. Nordmann took his degree in 1827, just before a great fire destroyed the University and he was forced to move elsewhere. He crossed over the Gulf of Finland and went to Berlin where he studied zoology as a pupil of Ehrenberg, the former travelling companion of the ill-fated Hemprich.

In 1832 Nordmann published a paper, in German, entitled 'Micrographical Contributions to the Natural History of the Invertebrates', which was well received in zoological circles. He later contributed the chapter on birds in Erman's *Reise um die Erde* [Journey round the World] (1835), in which Nordmann described 143 birds, some of which were new—for example, Nordmann's Greenshank.

Meanwhile Nordmann had moved further south to Odessa to take up his professorship, and in the following year, 1833, he was also appointed Director of the Botanical Gardens. Plants from Japan and North America had already been acclimatized there and some trees grew so well that thousands of saplings were sold to offset the garden's other expenses. However, the harsh climate restricted the development of the gardens and instead Nordmann concentrated on the practical instruction of young gardeners who trained there.

Among his various field trips Nordmann took part in the latter half of Count Anatoli Demidoff's lavish 1837 expedition across southern Russia. Demidoff had travelled from Paris to Vienna and then down the Danube to Bucharest, through Moldavia and Bessarabia to the Black Sea and Odessa. Demidoff recounted later how "The collections in the department of natural history, made from this interesting country, and shown to us by M. Nordmann, excited the enthusiasm of our naturalists to such a degree, that they already began to lament over the few days of rest we had spent . . ."[1] Nordmann was also fired by their enthusiasm and despite five previous excursions to the Crimea he could not resist an invitation to go back again and he sailed with the expedition to Yalta. They covered much of the peninsula and explored eastwards across the Straits of Kertsch and later to the lower reaches of the River Don before finally returning to Odessa.

Ten years later, in the hot summer months of 1848 a cholera epidemic swept through the city and Nordmann's wife died. In October he returned to Finland with his four children, determined to start a fresh life, and because of his international reputation he had little difficulty in obtaining an appropriate position. In the next year he was made Professor of Natural History at Helsingfors (Helsinki) University, which had been established there in 1828, a

Black-winged Pratincole

year after the fire at Åbo. He held this position until 1852, when the chair of natural history was divided into zoology and botany, whereupon, despite his skill as a botanist, he chose to become Professor of Zoology and generously contributed his own collection to the Zoological Museum.

Nordmann had spent so many years abroad that he had developed a slight German accent and he found it difficult to adapt again to life in Finland; he never exerted any great personal influence upon his students. He travelled occasionally on the continent and in 1850 visited England, but he never went on any more adventurous collecting expeditions. His son Arthur took part in an expedition to the Amur in the 1850s, sometimes travelling in company with the botanist Carl Maximowicz.

Whilst at Odessa the elder Nordmann had collected and studied fossils and he was now able to use the material he had gathered in his treatise, *Palaentologie Sued Russlands* (1858–60), published by the Finnish Society of Sciences. Other scientific publications appeared in Finnish and foreign journals, including the prestigious Transactions of the Academy of St Petersburg. In January 1866 he was decorated by the Czar with the Order of Vladimir but he died at Helsingfors only a few months later, on 25 June, at the age of sixty-three.

PALLAS. *THE MOST EMINENT EXPLORER-NATURALIST OF HIS DAY. BORN IN BERLIN, HE LATER MOVED TO ST PETERSBURG WHERE HE COMPILED MUCH OF HIS IMPORTANT WRITTEN WORK. HIS SIX-YEAR EXPEDITION ACROSS RUSSIA TO BEYOND LAKE BAYKAL WAS FOLLOWED BY A SHORTER ONE TO THE CRIMEA.*

Peter Simon Pallas
(1741-1811)

PALLAS'S FISH EAGLE *Heliaeetus leucoryphus* (Pallas)

Aquila leucorypha Pallas, 1771. *Reise durch verschiedene Provinzen des Russischen Reichs*, Vol. 1, p. 454: lower Ural River

PALLAS'S SANDGROUSE *Syrrhaptes paradoxus* (Pallas)

Tetrao paradoxa Pallas, 1773. *Reise durch verschiedene Provinzen des Russischen Reichs*, Vol. 2, p. 712, Pl. F.: Tartary desert

PALLAS'S GRASSHOPPER WARBLER *Locustella certhiola* (Pallas)

Motacilla Certhiola Pallas, 1811. *Zoographia Rosso-Asiatica*, Vol. 1, p. 509: Transbaikalia

PALLAS'S LEAF WARBLER *Phylloscopus proregulus* (Pallas)

Motacilla Proregulus Pallas, 1811. *Zoographia Rosso-Asiatica*, Vol. 1, p. 499: Transbaikalia

PALLAS'S ROSEFINCH *Carpodacus roseus* (Pallas)

Fringilla rosea Pallas, 1776. *Reise durch verschiedene Provinzen des Russischen Reichs*, Vol. 3, p. 699: Transbaikalia

PALLAS'S REED BUNTING *Emberiza pallasi* (Cabanis)

C [ynchrames] Pallasi Cabanis, 1851. *Museum Heineanum*, Pt 1, p. 130, *ex* Pallas's *Emberiza schoeniclus* var. B, 1811, *Zoographia Rosso-Asiatica*, p. 48: Transbaikalia

The death of Georg Steller in 1746, at only thirty-seven years of age, deprived the Academy of Sciences at St Petersburg of its most promising naturalist. No one of comparable stature replaced him until twenty years later when Peter Simon Pallas arrived from Germany to become Professor of Natural History. Though brilliant in his own right, he was able to benefit considerably from the notes and discoveries which Steller and J. G. Gmelin had made in their explorations across Siberia to Kamchatka. Pallas retraced some of their route as far as Lake Baykal and claimed to have covered that area in more detail than either. Considering the wide scope of Pallas's interests this was probably true, yet the accounts of his two remarkable expeditions have gained a long-standing reputation for being both lifeless and dull.

The English translator of one of Pallas's German books commented on the author's "uncouth and almost barbarous style". In these early translations the present day reader is further confronted by the use of the old-fashioned long 's', as in this extract: ". . . innumerable flocks of ſmall birds which feed on ſeeds particularly ſiſkins and greenfinches, that ſwarm about the ſtacks . . .". Nevertheless, Pallas rightly deserves his status as one of the greatest of all eighteenth century naturalists, in the broadest sense of the term; zoology, botany, geology, ethnology and philology all received his attentions.

Most of Pallas's ornithological discoveries relate to Eastern Palearctic species. Five such birds bearing his name only occasionally occur in Europe, wanderers from their Siberian breeding grounds. A sixth bird, Pallas's Fish Eagle, formerly bred on the north shore of the Caspian Sea but it is also now mainly confined to central and southern Asia.

The most famous of the birds named in his honour is undoubtedly Pallas's Sandgrouse. For many years it had the distinction of appearing in almost all books about British breeding birds even though breeding was only proved to have occurred in 1888 and 1889; two instances were at Culbin Sands, Morayshire, and one in Yorkshire. They all followed the spectacular irruption of 1888 when hundreds if not thousands of the birds arrived in Britain. These mass movements were believed to be due to food shortages caused by deep snow, or a crust of ice upon snow, and not due to sudden overpopulation. The movements took place towards both the east and the west and were known to be unpredictable even in Pallas's day.

Pallas's Fish Eagle

Peter Simon Pallas was born on 22 September 1741 at Berlin, where his father was a Professor of Surgery; his mother was of French extraction. He had an elder brother and at least one sister. He was instructed in Latin, French, English and German by private tutors and his interest in natural history was evident long before he was fifteen, for by then he was studying entomology and devising his own system of animal classification. In the autumn of 1758 he attended Halle University but in the following spring transferred to Göttingen University where he was often confined to his room because of illness. However, he took the opportunity to read avidly and continued his intensive studies of animals. In July 1760, attracted by its eminent professors, Pallas moved to Leyden University and passed his doctor's degree at only nineteen years of age.

He travelled throughout The Netherlands visiting all the more important hospitals and museums and then, in July 1761, he went to London for ten months to improve his medical and surgical knowledge. Here, after working all day, "he would frequently employ the greater part of the night, or often whole nights together, in devouring some new publication, which either awakened

Pallas's Sandgrouse

his curiosity, or which bore upon his more immediate researches". He found time to visit Sussex and later spent a few days studying the shore near Harwich, collecting marine samples because his ship to The Netherlands had been delayed by strong winds.

Pallas's father had recalled him to Berlin so that he could serve as a surgeon in the Prussian army but by the time he arrived the Seven Years War was over. He persuaded his father to let him settle at The Hague, where he continued his studies. His new system of animal classification earned him the praise of the distinguished Baron Cuvier. Pallas had already written an account of the insects in the March of Brandenburg, near Berlin, and in 1766 followed this with his *Miscellania Zoologica*. In the latter work of 200 pages, he described several vertebrates new to science which he had discovered amongst the vast Dutch museum collections, while another part of the book concerned his original observations on worms and molluscs. The whole publication again earned the admiration of Cuvier, and ensured for Pallas a position as the foremost young naturalist in Europe.

At around this time Pallas met Thomas Pennant who was making a tour of the Continent. In later years the two men corresponded frequently and often exchanged information and specimens. It was Pallas who supplied most of the Russian material for Pennant's *Arctic Zoology* (1784–87).

Plans for a voyage to southern Africa and the East Indies were proposed to the Prince of Orange by Pallas, but before this idea could be developed his authoritarian father once more recalled him to Berlin to continue his medical career. During this period at Berlin, Pallas commenced his *Spicilegia Zoologica* (1767–80), which was brought out in successive issues of thirty to forty pages, but only four issues came out under his own direct supervision. The work was brought to a temporary close by an invitation from Catherine II to join the Academy of Sciences at St Petersburg. In June 1767 Pallas left Berlin accompanied by his new wife, despite his father's opposition to the move.

Catherine II wanted to know as much as possible about her vast new Empire. Almost at once, Pallas began to prepare himself for an ambitious expedition, various branches of which were to travel southwards to the Caucasus, northwards to the Arctic Ocean or eastwards beyond Lake Baykal to Mongolia. Like Captain Cook's first voyage to the Pacific, the expedition had been timed to coincide with the transit of Venus across the sun in 1769.

One of the anomalies of travel in Russia at this time, was that progress was often quickest and easiest in winter, when the opportunities for collecting were at a minimum. Most travelling was therefore done in early winter or early spring

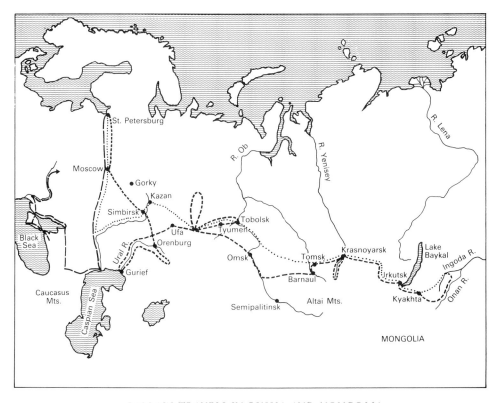

PALLAS'S TRAVELS IN RUSSIA AND MONGOLIA:
----------   *OUTWARD* ⎫
....   *RETURN*   ⎬ *1768–74*
——————   *1793–94* ⎭

whilst the rivers were frozen and daylight hours were longer than in mid-winter. Travel during the spring thaw was generally impossible, while in summer progress was slow and laborious unless the luxury of floating down a river was convenient. Pallas set off in June with seven astronomers and mathematicians, a great number of assistants and several other naturalists: Lepechin, Georgi, Falk, S. G. Gmelin and Güldenstädt. Winter was spent at Simbirsk on the banks of the Volga and five more winters passed before Pallas returned to St Petersburg. Not all the others survived and Güldenstädt died not long after his return. Throughout the expedition the Academicians repeatedly separated in order to complete their different tasks and to cover a greater area of the country. For this reason Pallas was not present when Falk killed himself at Kazan nor when Gmelin was captured by Tartars in the Caucasus.

Early in 1769 Pallas made the journey to Orenburg and then descended the Ural River to Gurief for a rendezvous on the north shore of the Caspian Sea. After the meeting he moved northwards to spend the second winter at Ufa, close to the Ural Mountains. The following season he made extensive studies of the geology and mineralogy of the mountains and proposed startling new theories on their formation. In December as he travelled towards Tobolsk, where the third winter was spent, he paused at Tyumen to visit Steller's grave on a high bank above the river. He then made his way eastwards through the Altai Mountains, visited the silver mines at Kolivan and wintered at Krasnoyarsk on the Yenisey. He crossed Lake Baykal and explored the region to the east beyond Kyakhta as far as the Onan and Ingoda Rivers, near the Mongolian border. This is the area of Transbaikalia where Pallas discovered the grasshopper warbler, leaf warbler, reed bunting and rosefinch that all now bear his name. It was the furthest east that he penetrated. For his fifth winter he returned westwards to Krasnoyarsk and then rapidly retraced his route to the Urals before moving south-westwards to the lower reaches of the Volga where he passed the final winter before returning to the Academy.

During the course of this tremendous six-year expedition Pallas had sent a series of reports to St Petersburg which were gathered together and published in three volumes as *Reise durch verschiedene Provinzen des Russischen Reichs* [Journey through various provinces of the Russian Empire] (1771–76). For once

Pallas's Grasshopper Warbler

Cuvier criticized his work because he felt that more life could have been injected into the text to relieve the "long and dry enumeration of mines and forges, and often repeated catalogue of common plants and birds he encountered, which do not supply agreeable reading". Cuvier went on to excuse Pallas by describing the arduous conditions under which he had been forced to work:

> "Long winters of six months duration, spent in a miserable cabin, with black bread and brandy for his only luxuries, at a temperature which froze mercury, and a summer's heat almost insupportable the few weeks it lasted; with his time fully occupied in clambering rocks and fording morasses, in pioneering a road through thick forests, amid myriads of insects which darken the air, and almost devour you, amongst people who bear the stamp of all the miseries of the country, generally disgustingly dirty, often frightfully ugly, and always dreadfully stupid,—all this could but damp the liveliest imagination."[1]

Pallas's accounts covered an amazing diversity of subjects; little escaped his attention. Besides the geology and mineralogy, he reported on the native peoples and their religions; he discussed the origins of an undecayed extinct rhinoceros found in permafrost near the River Lena; he gave classical descriptions of plants and animals (including Pallas's Cat, native to the desert and mountain regions of southern Siberia); he recorded his observations on the habits and mode of hunting of the Dipper and Dalmatian Pelican; he commented on the Kirghiz tribesmen who hunted wolves and foxes with Golden Eagles; and he gave all-embracing summaries of the changes in the seasons and the effect upon the mammals and birds. Amongst this miscellany, Pallas's Sandgrouse, Pallas's Fish Eagle and Pallas's Rosefinch were first remarked upon. He obtained the sandgrouse in the "Tartary desert", the eagle from the lower Ural River near the

Pallas's Rosefinch

Caspian, and the rosefinch from the banks of the Uda and Selanga Rivers of Transbaikalia.

More or less content to remain at St Petersburg, Pallas settled down to enjoy the patronage of Catherine II and became one of her favourites, their friendship no doubt aided by their shared Germanic origins. He was instructed to teach natural history and physics to the Grand Dukes Alexander and Constantine. The Empress also ordered all the herbaria collected by other naturalists to be made available to Pallas who was engaged to complete the *Flora Rossica* (1784–1815), at her expense. For financial reasons this extravagantly illustrated work was never finished; only the two volumes on trees and shrubs were issued. Yet some years later, when Pallas considered selling his own large collection of plants the Empress raised his asking price from 1500 roubles to 2000 and then let him keep his collection during his lifetime.

While at St Petersburg Pallas started on his great three-volume *Zoographia Rosso-Asiatica* (1811–31), a work that was to occupy him until he died. It is here, amongst its varied contents that he gave the first details of Pallas's Grasshopper Warbler and Pallas's Leaf Warbler, obtained many years earlier in Transbaikalia but hitherto undescribed, such was the extent of his zoological collection. At around this time Pallas set himself the task of salvaging material from the notes and specimens of Güldenstädt, publishing in 1787 and 1791 a two-volume account of Güldenstädt's travels in the Caucasus.

Suddenly, at the age of fifty-two, Pallas decided to go on another expedition, financed by himself. In a letter to Pennant he confessed that he wanted to get away from the "incessant bustle, as well as the artificial society prevailing in the metropolis . . .". He took with him his daughter (by his first wife who had died in 1782), his new wife, an artist, various servants and a military escort. In February 1793, the party went overland to Saratov and then travelled downriver, on the ice, to Volgograd. In the spring Pallas and his escort explored the country to the east, causing him to acclaim: "In the course of my travels I have met with few countries with

Pallas's Leaf Warbler

so uniform an appearance as the steppe in these regions of the Volga . . . it was almost devoid of vegetable productions except a few peculiar and rare plants." Among the birds which he saw in these arid regions were Great and Little Bustards, Black and Crested Larks and the Glossy Ibis; the latter species frequenting the shallow edges of the numerous saline lakes. Although Pallas was seemingly unafraid and undeterred by the general lack of fresh water he had great trouble persuading his unadventurous escort commander to penetrate any further eastwards with him.

At the beginning of August they rejoined the women at Astrakhan and they all travelled south along the Caspian coast to the River Kuma which they ascended as far as Georgiyesk. Pallas spent three weeks exploring the mountains of the Caucasus collecting mainly plants and seeds; one of the better known being *Azalea pontica* which grew abundantly just above the tree-line. In September the whole party journeyed to the Crimea by way of the north shore of the Sea of Azov and wintered at Simferol. Because of ill health Pallas did little work until March when he explored south-east across the Straits of Kerch to Taman. On 18 July, after many successful excursions, the entire party set off homewards up the Dneiper River valley and arrived at St Petersburg in mid-September 1794, less than two years after leaving the city. (See map p. 180.)

Pallas immediately set about compiling an account of his journey: *P. S. Pallas*

Bemerkungen auf einer Reise in die Südlichen Statthalterschaften des Russischen Reichs, in den Jahren 1793 und 1794 was published in 1799 and 1801. It was followed in 1802 by an English edition entitled *Travels through the Southern Provinces of the Russian Empire*, which was in a similar style to the account of his earlier expedition. Meanwhile Pallas had privately described the recently annexed Crimea to Catherine II in such glowing terms that, wishing to honour him, she gave him a large estate near Simferol. Obliged to accept the offer, he spent the next thirteen years in the Crimea regretting the move. Although his estate was beautiful, it was swampy and unhealthy and much of the surrounding countryside had been ravaged by soldiers. In addition he missed the fine libraries and collections which he thrived upon. However, he was not entirely isolated for he had a series of eminent visitors, one of whom, Dr E. D. Clarke, unsuccessfully tried to persuade him to move to England. Instead, Pallas sold him a collection of plants knowing that it would be more appreciated at Cambridge than in the Crimea.

When Pallas's second wife died he left Simferol and moved to his widowed daughter's estate to be near his grandchildren. Not long after, in 1810, he was granted permission to leave Russia by the Emperor Alexander and after a separation of forty-three years he was reunited with his brother in Berlin. Pallas died there in the following year on the 8 September, just before his seventieth birthday.

Pallas's Reed Bunting

Undoubtedly hard working and with an astonishing encyclopaedic knowledge, Pallas has also gained a reputation for being uninteresting himself; it is indeed difficult to deduce much about the character of the man. He is known to have had a quiet, even disposition and was well respected by his colleagues. Somehow, because Pallas often travelled with an escort and servants he does not come across as a great field naturalist comparable to Steller or Wilson, both of whom often worked alone. Yet to have survived at all in Siberia he must have been a rugged and adaptable individual. Above all he possessed those essential qualities which have spurred countless naturalists to explore and investigate unknown regions under extreme hardship: motivation and an enquiring mind. His letters to Pennant, of which those written between 1777 and 1781 have survived, offer few insights into his personality but tell us that his stay in Russia does not appear to have been a happy one. He admitted to Pennant that he longed to return to Germany; he had not unpacked some of his collections (sealed with tar within great chests), "partly because I expect every year to leave this Country".

There is little comparison between the letters of the Reverend Gilbert White and those of Peter Simon Pallas. White's letters to Pennant, combined together as part of *The Natural History of Selborne* (1788), have become a literary classic of countless editions; whereas Pallas's letters to Pennant, only recently published in a limited edition, are full of grammatical errors, weird use of capitals and punctuation, and are in stilted English. But there is no reason why Pallas's letters should have been otherwise. They were mostly business transactions, written in an alien language, dealing with the exchange of papers, books and specimens from which both Pennant and Pallas benefited. Pallas, for instance, offered such exotic species as Pallas's Rosefinch, Scarlet Grosbeak, Black-bellied Sandgrouse, Red-flanked Bluetail and Azure Tit in exchange for British plants and birds, with a particular request for the Puffin and "the Moorfowl of Scotland"—in this case the Red Grouse.

RADDE. *GERMAN NATURALIST AND EXPLORER. MAINLY KNOWN FOR HIS ORNITHOLOGICAL INVESTIGATIONS IN THE CAUCASUS AND SURROUND-ING REGIONS. DIRECTOR OF THE TIFLIS MUSEUM.*

Gustav Ferdinand Richard Radde (1831-1903)

RADDE'S ACCENTOR *Prunella ocularis* (Radde)

Accentor ocularis Radde, 1884. *Ornis Caucasica*, p. 244, Pl. 14: Kiz Yurdi Mt., Talych

RADDE'S WARBLER *Phylloscopus schwarzi* (Radde)

Sylvia (Phyllopneuste) Schwarzi Radde, 1863. *Reisen im Süden von Ost-Sibirien*, Vol. 2, p. 260, Pl. 9: Tarei Nor and Bureya Mts [Transbaikalia and Amurland]

Tigers once frequented the very borders of the Western Palearctic in the Talych Mountains of Lenkoran, south-east of the Caucasian Range and close to the shores of the Caspian. These warm and humid mountains were also the stronghold of bears, wolves, wild boar, lynx and leopards, chamois and ibex; and it was in these lofty heights (at 8000 ft) that Radde first discovered a small accentor which inhabits the upper, juniper-covered mountain slopes. Radde's Accentor also occurs along the length of the Caucasus and in some parts of eastern Turkey, as well as northern Iran. His description of this secretive species, along with his observations on such birds as Güldenstädt's Redstart, the Snow Finch and Caspian Snowcock, was published in *Ornis Caucasica* (1884), his most important work on the birds of the Caucasus and surrounding regions: an area Radde lived in and delighted in exploring for almost forty years.

Gustav Radde was born in Danzig, the capital of West Prussia, on 27 November 1831. The son of a schoolmaster, he had little academic education and began a career as an apothecary which he continued until he was twenty-one. Increasingly drawn to the study of natural history, he renounced his career and spent two years with the botanist Christian von Steven in the southern part of the Crimea, where he scoured the forests for both plants and animals. He made other trips to south Russia with J. F. von Brandt and K. E. von Baer, and by 1864 he had decided that he wanted to settle in the Caucasus. He thereupon took up residence at Tiflis (Tbilisi), in the central southern foothills.

Radde had no sooner arrived than he set off to explore the region surrounding Mt Elbrus, the highest mountain in the Western Palearctic, and much of that summer and the next was often spent botanizing at more than 6000 ft above sea level. The mountains offered a rich hunting ground for the naturalist but many of the hill tribes were very hostile and he had to take great care of himself, his horse and his equipment. He managed to record the way of life of some of the hill people noting, as best he could, their languages, ballads and customs; but they never really endeared themselves to Radde who wrote of one such tribe:

> "Among the Suanetians intelligent faces are seldom found. In their countenances insolence and rudeness are prominent, and hoary-headed obstinacy is often united to the stupidity of savage animal life. Amongst these people, individuals are frequently met with who have committed ten or more murders, which their standard of morality not only permits, but in many cases commands."[1]

Despite the general air of inhospitality that he encountered Radde loved his mountains and never seemed to tire of exploring and collecting there, each valley or peak offering the possibility of something new and exciting that he could take back to Tiflis where he had quickly established a museum and working library. By 1869 an English traveller, passing through the town, was able to report that "the collection is already most interesting. Specimens of the geology, natural history, the costumes, and household articles of the inhabitants of the neighbouring regions, are grouped together as effectively as the limited space will allow . . . Two very well stuffed tigers from Lenkoran occupy the middle of a room, round which are grouped

Radde's Accentor

bears, chamois, and bouquetins [ibex] from the Caucasus."[2] A botanical garden had also been established in a "wrinkle of the monstrous hill overhanging the town".

Many more expeditions were carried out by Radde who did not confine his attentions to just the Caucasus and Talych Mountains; he visited the east coastlands of the Black Sea and travelled eastwards beyond the Caspian Sea to Askhabad, almost to the very borders of Afghanistan. Scarcely a spring or summer went by without Radde embarking on a major collecting journey. Radde was almost as familiar with the nearby steppe country and desert regions as he was with the mountain slopes, and soon no one could dispute that he was the leading authority on the plants, birds and animals of those regions. As his fame increased he received a steady trickle of visitors whom he delighted in showing the more local fauna and flora. He wrote numerous papers for a great variety of German language journals, mostly published in his home country of Germany with which he always maintained close links. His activities and achievements were also looked upon with great interest by those British ornithologists whose horizons extended eastwards: Henry Dresser being one such enthusiast with whom he often corresponded and exchanged specimens.

In 1884, the same year that saw the publication of *Ornis Caucasica*, Gustav Radde was honoured with the chairmanship of the First International Ornithological Congress which was held at Vienna. In later years he was created an honorary member of the D.O-G., a foreign member of the B.O.U. and the Zoological Society of London, and he received honours from many other foreign institutions. He died at Tiflis, in March 1903, at the age of seventy-one, having just completed half of the intended six-volume *Museum Caucasicum* concerning the collection at Tiflis.

Despite his long and invaluable association with this most interesting portion of southern Russia, Radde had also been on lengthy and important expeditions elsewhere. At the age of sixty-four he had sailed to India and Japan with the Grand Duke Michael and, two years later, again as official naturalist, he accompanied other members of the Russian Imperial Family on a trip to North Africa. Moreover, many years earlier, when only twenty-four, and not long after his first trip to the Crimea, Radde was invited to join a lengthy and arduous expedition which was to travel eastwards across the vast expanse of the Russian Empire to the Amur, which Russia was then in the process of annexing from China.

This East Siberian Expedition stemmed from a proposal put forward to the Russian Geographical Society in 1850, by two wealthy men, who backed their ideas with a generous gift of about £8000. It was originally intended to explore Kamchatka, the Kuril Islands and Russian America (Alaska) but this ambitious plan was abandoned and it was decided to investigate the territories from Lake Baykal eastwards to the coast. Led by the astronomer Ludwig Schwarz, the mixed assortment of scientists and servicemen arrived at Irkutsk in the spring of 1855, and then divided into three groups; one to cover Transbaikalia and the Vitim, a second to explore the upper reaches of the Amur and the third to descend to the middle and lower sections of that great river. Radde, as botanist and zoologist to the expedition, spent much of 1856 on the Argun River close to the Mongolian border where the country was mostly arid and barren, vegetation being very sparse and chiefly confined to the valley bottoms. He afterwards continued along the Daurio–Mongolian border to the mid Amur and the Hing-gan Mountains where thick forests of oak, lime, ash and elm presented a variety of problems to the young explorer and collector:

Radde's Warbler

"In the summer, the eye cannot penetrate the thick foliage of the surrounding forest, and the inhabitants of its boughs are thus secure from the rapacious sight of the collecting ornithologist. Nature in her full virgin strength has produced such a luxuriant vegetation, that it is with the greatest trouble that the copse wood can be penetrated; and when even the barriers of living plants are surmounted, the trunks of dead trees present new difficulties to the traveller, who is thankful if he falls on the beaten track of a bear which he can follow with ease."[3]

To add to this, willing guides were impossible to find because the Chinese had imposed the death penalty for fraternization with the Russians. Tigers, which were common in certain regions of the Hing-gan Mountains, often attacked the horses of the local hunters and this provided an additional deterrent. Travel was therefore mainly confined to the River Amur and its many tributaries which offered the additional benefit, as Radde quickly noticed, of supplying him with one or two sturgeon almost daily.

During the year 1857 Radde collected great quantities of material as he explored from the mouth of the Bureya River downstream some 400 miles to the junction of the Amur and the Ussuri. In the following spring and summer he reconnoitred in the Bureya Mountains until the close of the season, whereupon he returned to Lake Baykal and Irkutsk, arriving back in Europe after an absence of four years.

Although Radde's chief successes were botanical he had also collected mammals and birds of many kinds and over 900 insect specimens, including several varieties of the Apollo butterfly. His ornithological results were published in 1863 in the

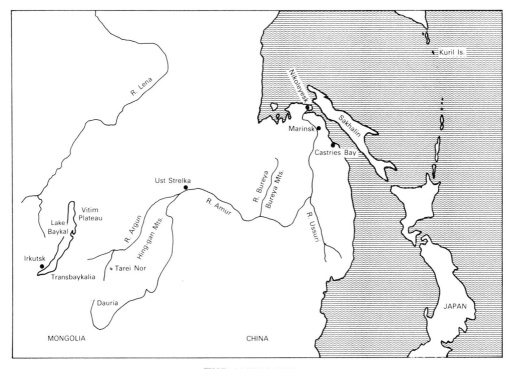

THE AMURLAND

second volume of *Reisen im Süden von Ost-Sibirien in den Jahren 1855–59* [Travels in South and East Siberia]. It was sub-titled *Die Festlands-Ornis* [The Mainland Birds] and was described in *The Ibis* of 1866 as "indispensible to all who busy themselves with the ornithology of any parts of Europe and Asia".[4] New species discovered and described by Radde included Baer's Pochard, the Eastern or Manchurian Red-footed Falcon and a large grey-brown warbler, with a prominent eye-stripe, now known as Radde's Warbler *Phylloscopus schwarzi* (see Schwarz). It was first discovered on 22 September 1856, skulking in a kitchen garden at Kullussutajevsk, near the shores of Tarei Nor in Transbaikalia and was later also found by him in the Bureya Mountains.

Monsieur Richard†
of Lunéville
(c. 1750- c. 1820)

RICHARD'S PIPIT *Anthus novaeseelandiae* (J. F. Gmelin)

Alauda novae Seelandiae J. F. Gmelin, 1789. *Systema Naturae*, Vol. 1, p. 799 (1788 *ex* Latham): New Zealand

Richard's Pipit has a wide distribution. It breeds as far south as New Zealand, where it was first discovered foraging on the shores of Queen Charlotte Sound by the Forsters, during Cook's second voyage. John Latham, using George Forster's drawing, described it as the "New Zealand Lark", hence Gmelin's scientific name.[1] The species also ranges across eastern and central Siberia breeding as far west as the Irtyusk River south of Omsk where it is found on the steppe and in some marshy meadows and river valleys, often associating with Yellow Wagtails.

Some Richard's Pipits wander annually to western Europe, and the first known European specimen was shot in 1805 by Baron Nicolas-Damase Marchant who was, for a time, the mayor of Metz, in Moselle, and a keen collector of local birds.[2] He did not, however, write a description of the pipit. Seven years later, in October 1812, one was netted alive in a field north of London. N. A. Vigors

Richard's Pipit

†No known portrait.

did not exhibit this specimen until April 1824, when he presented it at a meeting of the Zoological Club of the Linnean Society.[3] By this time, it had already been described in France by Louis Vieillot who was unaware that it was the same pipit already described by Gmelin. Vieillot named it *Anthus Richardi* and wrote:

> "This species was obtained at the end of October 1815 by a very zealous advocate for the progress of ornithology, M. Richard of Lunéville, to whom I have dedicated it, by giving it his name, as the first who has made it known and who has made me aware of it to describe in the new edition of the *Dictionaire d'Histoire Naturelle*. M. Richard obtained another in 1816 and at the same season . . ."[4]

Forty years ago Sir Hugh Gladstone made extensive enquiries among French ornithologists and institutions, in an endeavour to learn more about Monsieur Richard, but without success. In 1815 there were two prominent naturalists by the name of Richard: Louis C. M. Richard (1754–1821), and his son Achille Richard (1794–1852). Both were primarily botanists and neither appears to have any connection with Lunéville. It seems certain that neither of them was Vieillot's correspondent.

The great ornithological historian, Erwin Stresemann, described Richard simply as "a collector of native birds". He only adds that around 1775 Richard became acquainted with François Levaillant who collected birds in Alsace and Lorraine, particularly around Lunéville, for a period of seven years prior to his south African travels.[5]

Richard is still a common surname in and around Lunéville, but unless new information comes to light, we shall never know any more about the man from whom Richard's Pipit derives its name.

James Clark Ross
(1800-1862)

ROSS'S GULL *Rhodostethia rosea* (MacGillivray)

L[arus] roseus MacGillivray, 1824. *Memoirs of the Wernerian Natural History Society* 5, p. 249: Igloolik, Melville Peninsula

For over eighty years, one of the great ornithological mysteries of the Arctic was the location of the breeding grounds of Ross's Gull. The bird had been seen only among the pack-ice of the far north so it seemed most likely that it bred in the high Arctic. This belief was perpetuated when a single nest was found on the west coast of Greenland in 1885, but this later proved to be an isolated and unusual record. In 1905, against expectations, the Russian explorer Alexandrovitch Buturlin discovered the main breeding area only just within the Arctic Circle, on the Kolyma River delta of eastern Siberia.[1] These, and subsequent breeding records showed that Ross's Gull bred as far south as 67° N, often in association with Arctic Tern, Spotted Redshank, Snipe and Ruff in well-vegetated marshy areas. Had he been alive, it is unlikely that anyone would have been more surprised than James Clark Ross; the man who shot the first specimen of the gull and who undoubtedly associated the bird only with ice and snow.

In the nineteenth century few, if any, Europeans had as much Arctic experience as James Ross. He had been in the Arctic together with his uncle, John Ross, on several occasions, and these voyages prepared them well for their expedition of 1829–33 when they were forced by ice to spend four consecutive winters in the extreme north; a record at that time for any European.

George Ross was a merchant and entrepreneur who had inherited the family home of Balsarroch near Stranraer in south-west Scotland. He later owned a house in Finsbury Square, London, where his third son James Clark Ross was born on 15 April 1800. The boy's uncle, John Ross, had joined the Navy as a first class volunteer at the age of nine and served with distinction in the Napoleonic Wars, claiming to have been wounded fourteen times and to have been three times in French prisons. When John Ross was sent on naval duty to the North Sea and the Baltic his twelve year old nephew joined him for the first time. James was to follow his uncle from ship to ship for the next six years in

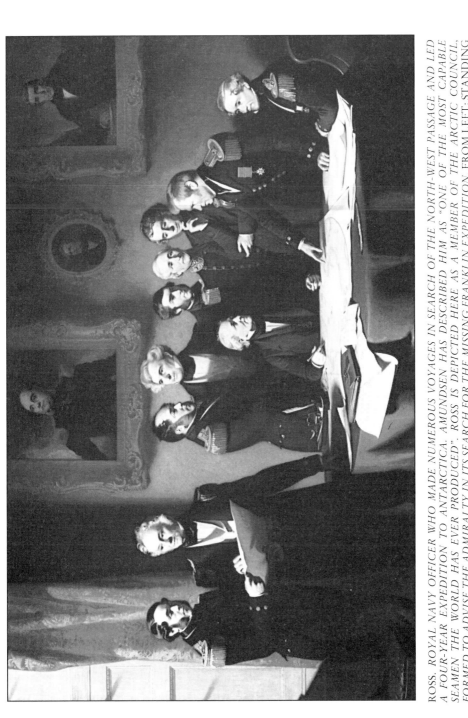

ROSS. ROYAL NAVY OFFICER WHO MADE NUMEROUS VOYAGES IN SEARCH OF THE NORTH-WEST PASSAGE AND LED A FOUR-YEAR EXPEDITION TO ANTARCTICA. AMUNDSEN HAS DESCRIBED HIM AS "ONE OF THE MOST CAPABLE SEAMEN THE WORLD HAS EVER PRODUCED". ROSS IS DEPICTED HERE AS A MEMBER OF THE ARCTIC COUNCIL, FORMED TO ADVISE THE ADMIRALTY IN ITS SEARCH FOR THE MISSING FRANKLIN EXPEDITION. FROM LEFT: STANDING — GEORGE BACK, WILLIAM PARRY, EDWARD BIRD, JAMES ROSS, JOHN BARROW JR, EDWARD SABINE, BAILLIE HAMILTON, JOHN RICHARDSON. SEATED — FRANCIS BEAUFORT, FREDERICK BEECHEY. PORTRAITS — JOHN FRANKLIN, JAMES FITZJAMES, JOHN BARROW.

both Arctic and home waters. In 1814–15 they were in the White Sea, where they surveyed the coast near Archangel. In 1815–17 they were on duty around Scotland and in the next year on the *Isabella*, a hired whaler, they went in search of the North-west Passage. The astronomer on board was Edward Sabine who became a lifelong friend of the younger Ross.

Sailing northwards, accompanied by the *Alexander* under William Parry, John Ross had orders to round the north-east point of America and head for the Bering Sea and Kamchatka. There, he was to hand his journal to the Russian Governor who was to send it overland to London. After that, Ross was to replenish his supplies at Hawaii and then return by the same route. With hindsight, it was an unreasonable prospect. The voyage was the continuation of a series of naval expeditions to search for a northern route to the Far East, which somewhat surprisingly were continued long after it had become obvious that such a route would never be of any commercial or strategic value.

In Baffin Bay, close to the west coast of Greenland, they made the first contact, by Europeans, with the Polar or Thule Eskimos and Sabine obtained a new species of gull (see Sabine). Smith Sound was blocked by ice so they retreated and then headed westwards into Lancaster Sound where John Ross made a fateful decision. There was no current or swell in the sound and when Ross thought he saw the way ahead blocked by a range of mountains, he gave

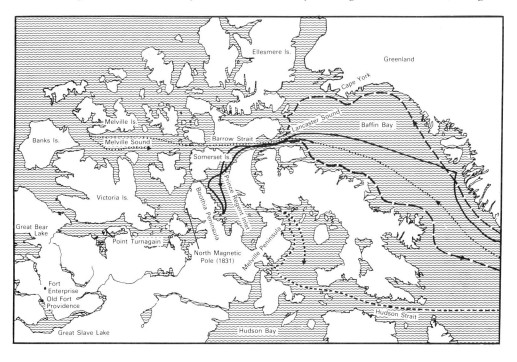

THE SEARCH FOR THE NORTH-WEST PASSAGE:
_ _ _ _   JOHN ROSS, 1818; WITH JAMES ROSS AND SABINE
....   PARRY, 1819–20, WITH JAMES ROSS AND SABINE
- - - - - - -   PARRY, 1821–23, WITH JAMES ROSS
————————   JOHN ROSS, 1829–33, WITH JAMES ROSS

the order to return homewards. The other officers agreed with the decision at the time but later changed their opinions. Back in London John Ross was severely criticized by the Secretary to the Admiralty, John Barrow, for failing to investigate more thoroughly. The long feud that developed between them put a temporary end to John Ross's Arctic expeditions but opened the way for the careers of William Parry and the younger Ross.

In the next season for exploration the *Griper*, with midshipman James Ross and Sabine on board, was led through Lancaster Sound and the non-existent Croker Mountains by Captain Parry on the *Hecla*. They over-wintered on Melville Island at Winter Harbour, cheered by the knowledge that the captains and crews would share the £5000 reward from the Admiralty for penetrating beyond 110° W, in that region. Although it was to be the furthest west that any ship reached for many years, it was too far north to be of use as the North-west Passage; the way westwards was permanent pack-ice. If there was a route it would have to be sought further south, closer to mainland America, where the ice sometimes thawed in late summer.

In 1823 a different approach was tried, through Hudson Strait and the north part of Hudson Bay. Once again, Parry took command of the *Hecla*. George Lyon, after an agonizing journey into the Sahara (see Dupont), suddenly found himself captain of the *Fury*. Together they explored as far west as the junction of Prince Regent Inlet, and Hecla and Fury Straits. They over-wintered at Winter Island and again at Igloolik. In June 1823, as they explored the Melville Peninsula two Ross's Gulls were shot: the first by James Ross who was acting as the expedition naturalist and the other by Joseph Sherer, another midshipman. Parry even recorded the first event in the expedition *Journal*:

> "Our shooting parties to the southward had of late been tolerably successful, not less than two hundred and thirty ducks having been sent in to the ships in the course of the last week. Mr. Ross had procured a specimen of gull having a black ring round its neck, and which in its present plumage, we could not find described. This bird was alone when killed but flying at no great distance from a flock of tern, which latter it somewhat resembles in size as well as in its red legs; but is on closer inspection easily distinguished by its beak and tail, as well as by a beautiful tint of most delicate rose-colour on its breast."[2]

When the two ships returned to Britain, Parry commissioned the zoologist and Arctic explorer Dr John Richardson to describe the natural history material that had been collected during the voyage and presented Richardson with one of the gulls. In January 1824 Richardson read a paper to the Wernerian Natural History Society of Edinburgh in which he named the new species the Cuneate-tailed Gull *Larus Rossii*. His description appeared in the zoological appendix to the *Journal* of Parry's voyage, not published until 1825. In the intervening period a gull had been given to the Edinburgh University Museum, where William MacGillivray called the species Ross's Rosy Gull *Larus roseus*, and, because his description was published before Richardson's, MacGillivray has gained the credit as the original describer. He said that he had named the bird "pro tempore", but he obviously did not like Richardson's nomenclature.[3] Whether this move was intentional or otherwise, Richardson was sufficiently piqued to comment upon it six years later in his *Fauna Boreali-Americana*,[4] noting that there were two different scientific names and two different common names for a bird for which only two specimens were known to science!

Meanwhile Parry had spent the winter planning another Arctic expedition and had set sail in the spring of 1824. He failed to penetrate very far westwards and in the following July, after a long severe winter in the north, the *Fury* was blown ashore and wrecked in Regent Inlet. Second Lieutenant Ross, the other officers and all the men were safely transferred to the *Hecla* but there was no room for all the stores which had to be left stacked upon the beach. These supplies proved to be providential for John and James Ross a few years later.

Parry instructed James Ross to compile the zoological appendix to the *Journal* of this last voyage but despite Ross's enthusiasm for collecting birds and other natural history specimens his ornithological remarks were extremely brief. This was excused by the statement that "The Natural History of the Arctic Regions has lately received so much attention, and has been so ably and copiously illustrated, that little is now left to be said on the subject"! He would never have made that kind of remark about polar exploration.

Ross's fourth expedition with Parry was of a different nature as it was an attempt to reach the North Pole from Spitzbergen. The idea was to sail the *Hecla* as far north as possible and leave her with a skeleton crew while the main party made their way further northward across the ice with small "sledge boats". The conditions were difficult and the work was excessively hard, even by their standards, and progress was frustrated by the southward drift of the ice. By the 23 July they were at 82° 45′ N, a record for that time, but Parry was forced to abandon all hope of success and they were back in England by October 1827, Ross having encountered Ross's Gulls for the second time, about 100 miles north of Spitzbergen.

At around this time, John Ross, unable to travel in the Arctic supported by the Government because of Barrow's opposition, was seeking private backing from a friend, the wealthy gin-distiller Felix Booth. Ross put £3000 of his own money towards the £17,000 that Booth supplied for buying and equipping the *Victory*, the first steamship to be used in Arctic exploration. James Ross was invited by his uncle to join him again in a search for the North-west Passage, and, in the middle of June 1829, the elder Ross had the galling experience of sailing through Lancaster Sound and the provocatively named Barrow Straits. In Prince Regent Inlet they inspected the stores that had been left on the shore

Ross's Gull (with Arctic Terns)

after the wreck of the *Fury* and, despite the ravages of Polar Bears, most were still intact although some bird skins left by James Ross had vanished. They took some of the supplies and proceeded westwards, with frequent engine trouble, and spent the winter at Felix Harbour on the Boothia Peninsula. The crew made contact with some friendly Eskimos who were greatly impressed when James Ross shot a Musk Ox and even more so when he downed a brace of ptarmigan with "a left and a right". Indeed the younger Ross appears to have been the main provider of fresh meat throughout, shooting several bears and many birds. In May James Ross sledged further west to Cape Felix on King William Island where he was only 220 miles from Point Turnagain which Franklin and Dr Richardson had reached seven years previously approaching from the other direction. Ross was also close to the Arctic breeding grounds of Ross's Goose. This species, however, was named by John Cassin after a Hudson's Bay Company Factor, Bernard R. Ross, who collected and sent bird specimens to the Smithsonian Institute at Washington.

Breakup that summer was late and after a tremendous effort they managed to move the *Victory* only three miles; they were forced by ice to spend a further two winters at Felix Harbour! This meant that they could explore only the tiny fraction of the Arctic that they could reach on foot or by dog-sled. Nevertheless James Ross succeeded in locating the North Magnetic Pole, then at 70° 50′ N and 96° 46′ W on the Boothia Peninsula. At the end of their third winter John Ross decided that they had to make a move if they were to survive and in May, for the first time in thirty-six commands, he abandoned his ship. They planned to head for Fury Beach to pick up the remaining supplies and then hoped to sail to Baffin Bay in small open boats; an overall distance of about 500 miles.

They set off on 29 May but could not find open water and were therefore compelled to leave behind the boats that they had been dragging. Eventually they arrived at Fury Beach where there were more small boats, all in need of repair. By the beginning of August they were ready to continue but after dragging these boats for several days they had still not reached any open water into which they could launch them and so, leaving the boats, they retraced their steps to Somerset House—the name they had given to their collection of huts built from the remains of the *Fury*. In the middle of their fourth winter the carpenter died of scurvy and they were scarcely able to bury him because of the severe conditions. In April James Ross made four trips to the abandoned boats to provision them with supplies and in July the whole party, numbering about thirty, went out to the boats but yet another month passed before they could be launched. Finally, on 26 August, after only eleven days of rowing and sailing they reached Baffin Bay. It says much for the number of whaling ships operating in the area that a sail was sighted on the same day, which made away from them, but they caught up with another ship. By an ironic twist of fate it was the *Isabella*, the very ship that the two Rosses had first sailed to the region in 1818 and upon which John Ross had made his unfortunate decision to turn back from Lancaster Sound.

The explorers had all been assumed dead for over two years (in fact only three men died) and consequently there was great excitement when they reached England. They had shown that it was possible for Europeans to survive in the

Arctic for an extended period and James Ross had discovered the North Magnetic Pole; but they had explored little new territory and found no route westwards.

In 1836 James Ross returned to Baffin Bay to relieve some ice-bound whalers but he spent most of the next few years nearer to home as he became involved in a magnetic survey of Britain, partly instigated by his old friend Edward Sabine. This experience in making magnetic observations and his record eight winters and fourteen navigable seasons in the Arctic now made Ross the ideal choice to lead a four-year expedition to the Antarctic. The main objectives were the systematic observation of the earth's magnetic field wherever they went and the attainment of the South Magnetic Pole. When Ross left Britain virtually nothing was known of the vast Antarctic Continent. Apart from some islands near South Georgia and a few others elsewhere which had already been charted, the map was blank.

In August 1840, a year after setting out, Ross and Crozier arrived at Tasmania in their respective ships, the *Erebus* and the *Terror*. When they met the Lieutenant Governor, Sir John Franklin, Ross was told that the more obvious approach to the Antarctic had already been tried by French and American ships and so, because of this, Ross chose another route between 170° and 180° E where, as it turned out, the pack-ice is most easily penetrated. Next January, land was sighted and Ross named the highest mountain after Sabine, and other features after Franklin and Barrow. Barred from the Magnetic Pole by the first range of mountains Ross now found the way to the South Pole blocked by the Great Ice Barrier—the Ross Ice-shelf. They sailed 400 miles eastwards along the 200–300 ft sheer face of the ice wall but there was no way through. Even so, they had sailed further south than any previous ship and their record of 77° 46′ S was unbroken for fifty years.

In marked contrast to Ross's other polar voyages they were able to return to warmer climates as winter set in and during the course of the expedition, in which they circumnavigated the Antarctic Continent, they spent time in New Zealand, the Falkland Islands and Tierra del Fuego as well as Tasmania. On board Ross's ship serving as naturalists and surgeons were Robert McCormick (an old friend from Ross's time north of Spitzbergen with Parry) and Joseph Hooker. Despite his youth, Hooker was by far the greater naturalist and became one of the leading botanists of the century. McCormick concentrated on geology and the incessant shooting of birds which Ross often helped to turn into study skins.

When the naturalists visited islands they planted currant bushes and strawberries or seeds of cabbages and turnips so that they "may hereafter prove a benefit to vessels calling there". They often released chickens, sheep, pigs and rabbits "to add somewhat to the stock of useful creatures". It was a common and understandable practice in those days but was no doubt responsible for the extinction of an unknown number of island species, both plants and animals.

Ross's own account of the voyage is scattered with observations on penguins, petrels, sheathbills and other Antarctic birds. His genuine interest shows through, but often from the seaman's point of view that certain species told him of certain sea or ice conditions. On landing on Possession Island to unfurl the Union Jack and drink Her Majesty's health he noted that "there was no vegetation, but inconceivable myriads of penguins completely and densely covered the whole surface of the island". One March, as they sailed in the south Atlantic, Ross recorded that "during the day we observed large flocks of a small dark-coloured petrel, which we took to be the young of the Cape-Pigeon proceeding to the northward: by the length of time they took to fly past us, we estimated some of these flocks to be from six to ten miles in length, two or three miles broad and very densely crowded together, literally darkening the sky during the two or three hours they were passing over and about us".[5] It is a description reminiscent of Wilson's account of the large flocks of Passenger Pigeons that existed in eastern America at the beginning of the nineteenth century.

Ross returned to Britain thoroughly worn out after four and a half years away from home. He was knighted and he married Anne Coulman and wished only to settle down to family life. It was four years before his account of the voyage was completed. In contrast, the natural history collections were never fully worked through. *The Zoology of the Antarctic Voyage of H. M. Ships Erebus and Terror* (1846) was edited by J. E. Gray and Richardson but apart from the latter's section on the fish (mostly collected by Ross) the remainder suffered in one way or another from neglect. For example, Gray's work on the birds was published as *1. The Birds of New Zealand* as though other volumes were intended. Only twenty New Zealand species were brought back by the expedition but when Sharpe issued a revised edition in 1875 he added ten of their new discoveries from elsewhere which had not been included in any other work.

Meanwhile Ross had been offered the command of another Arctic voyage to search for the North-west Passage but he declined, in favour of Franklin, partly because steam ships were to be involved again. After a few years, when nothing had been heard from the expedition it was decided to send three relief parties and Ross felt duty-bound to lead one of them. He was given command of the *Enterprise*, and Captain Bird followed in the *Investigator*. They sailed into Lancaster Sound firing rocket signals at regular intervals and they wintered at the confluence of the sound, Regent Inlet and Barrow Straits so that all three channels could be monitored. During the winter they caught Arctic Foxes and around their necks fastened copper collars engraved with the positions of their ships and supply dumps. They hoped that after being released the foxes would be shot by some member of Franklin's party. In the spring Ross reached Somerset Island by sledge but a few months later, when the two ships only just managed to break free from the ice, Ross decided to head for home. He was bitterly disappointed not to have found his old friends Franklin and Crozier. When Ross arrived in England in 1849 he learnt that the other expeditions led by Captain Pullen and Dr Richardson had also been unsuccessful and although it was not confirmed for many years every member of Franklin's expedition was already dead.

In 1850 James Ross's seventy-three year old uncle made his last voyage to the Arctic, another unsuccessful attempt to discover the fate of Franklin, but James Ross never again sailed northwards. He continued to serve in an advisory capacity as the first authority on polar navigation, but he never fully recovered from the death of his wife in 1857 and he died five years afterwards at his estate near Aylesbury, at the age of sixty-two. Though Ross's main contribution was, of course, as an explorer, he possessed more than a superficial interest in natural history. Throughout his Antarctic voyage he had dredged for marine samples which he was passionately fond of collecting. In New Zealand, the great explorer had often paddled in the shallow waters searching for new specimens. He had intended to work through his discoveries himself but he was diverted by Franklin's disappearance and his wife's death which left him with three sons and a daughter to raise. On the more positive side, the excellence of Hooker's *Flora Antarctica* (1847) owes much to Ross's constant encouragement, his contributions to the collections and the fact that he gave the young botanist space in his own cabin to draw and study the plants.

As the discoverer of the hardy Ross's Gull, the link between man and bird seems particularly appropriate. Strangely, there have been some recent isolated breeding records from the Arctic islands of Canada, well outside the normal breeding range for Ross's Gull but not very distant from the region where James Clark Ross spent so many winters.

RÜPPELL. *OUTSTANDING GERMAN ZOOLOGIST, EXPLORER AND CARTOGRAPHER. HE TRAVELLED EXTENSIVELY IN THE SINAI, EGYPT AND SUDAN, THEN BECAME THE FIRST REAL ORNITHOLOGIST TO COLLECT IN ABYSSINIA. THIS PORTRAIT SHOWS RÜPPELL AGED ABOUT EIGHTY. (FOR RÜPPELL AS A YOUNG MAN, SEE HEY.)*

Wilhelm Peter Eduard Simon Rüppell (1794-1884)

RÜPPELL'S VULTURE *Gyps rueppellii* (A. E. Brehm)

Vultur Ruppellii A. E. Brehm, 1852. *Naumannia*, p. 44: Khartoum, Sudan

RÜPPELL'S WARBLER *Sylvia rueppelli* Temminck

Sylvia ruppeli [sic] Temminck, 1823. In C. J. Temminck and M. Laugier, *Nouveau Recueil de Planches coloriées d'Oiseaux*, Pt 41, Pl. 245, Fig. 1: L'île de Candie [= Crete]

For 500 years, from the end of the Crusades until the early nineteenth century, the waters and shores of the Gulf of Aqaba were under Muslim rule and closed to European exploration. Many westerners tried to get to Aqaba: in 1810 Seetzen attempted to reach it from the Sinai, in 1813 Burckhardt tried to enter after rediscovering Petra, and numerous other travellers tried to approach from Palestine, but all were defeated by fear of the fanatical Wahhabite Bedouin of Aqaba who hated all non-Muslims. At last, in the early months of 1822 the barren, rocky coastline of the Gulf of Aqaba was explored and mapped for the first time by the German scientist, Eduard Rüppell.

Rüppell was born at Frankfurt-on-Main on 20 November 1794, the son of a very prosperous banker. Originally destined to be a merchant, he embarked on a course of study in Italy to prepare himself for business ventures in Africa. During that same year of 1817 he made a trip to the western Sinai, which stimulated his interest in natural history to such an extent that he determined, instead, to pursue a career of scientific travel. Accordingly, he attended lectures on botany, zoology and related subjects at the Universities of Pavia and Genoa.

At the age of twenty-seven, Rüppell set out on his first major expedition, which was financed out of his own considerable resources, and supported by the Senckenberg Natural History Society in Frankfurt, who paid his preparator, Michael Hey, a twenty-three year old surgeon. They travelled together from the end of 1821 until 1827, first in the Sinai desert and later through southern

Egypt, under the protection of Mohammed Ali, the tyrannical ruler of Egypt who had defeated the Wahhabite Bedouin.

Rüppell reached Aqaba by following the Darb-el-Hadj, the Muslim pilgrims' route across the Sinai Peninsula, and then spent the next few months charting the shores of the Gulf of Aqaba and the Peninsula. He would have liked to have sailed along the coast, but the local fishermen had no need of boats, simply casting their nets from the rocks to catch the multi-coloured fish of the coral reefs. The survey was therefore conducted from the land, although Rüppell somehow managed to visit Coral Island, south of Taba and he was intrigued by the old Crusader ruins there. His map was published in 1823, earning him widespread acclaim and the honour of being the first foreigner to receive the gold medal of the Royal Geographical Society of London.

From Nuweiba on the east coast of the Sinai Rüppell and Hey rode inland along a well-vegetated wadi and up through the mountainous desert to the Monastery of St Catherine, at the foot of Mt Sinai, where they stayed for a short time amongst the community of Greek Orthodox monks. After investigating some copper diggings in the vicinity, they returned to the east coast, travelled down to Ras Mahommed, and rode up the west coast through El Tur to the Mediterranean.

They then spent several weeks hunting around Damietta and Lake Manzala, which abounded with pelicans and Greater Flamingos, but they were driven to distraction by swarms of biting insects and both suffered from dysentery, making retreat to Alexandria imperative. From there Rüppell forwarded four packing cases of birds, mammals, fish, insects, medallions, coins and artefacts to Frankfurt. He also happened to meet Friedrich Hemprich who was dispatching his Nubian collections to Berlin.

Rüppell's Vulture

During the summer months Rüppell continued his preparations for the next stage of the expedition, southwards to Nubia and Kordofan, again with the protection of Mohammed Ali. The party donned Turkish army uniforms to increase their safety, but a revolt in southern Nubia against Ali's son compelled them to remain a while longer in northern Egypt. Rüppell took the opportunity to examine and draw some of the ancient figures and tombs at Thebes while Hey collected natural history specimens nearby. At the beginning of 1823 Rüppell heard the news that the rising had been quelled and his caravan of camels and donkeys started southwards.

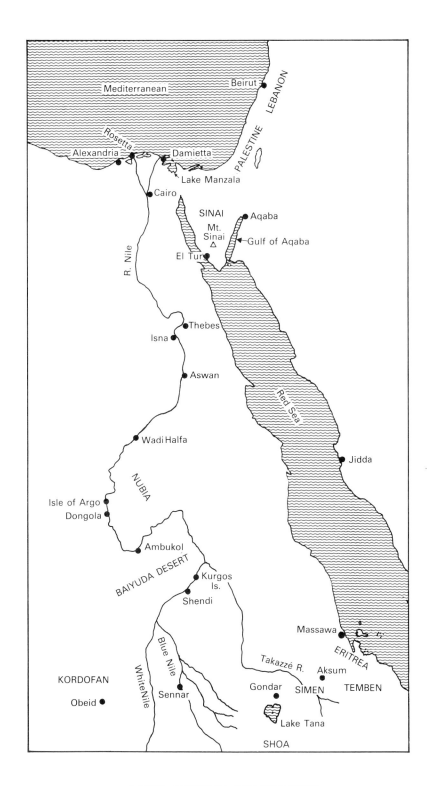

EGYPT, ABYSSINIA AND THE SINAI

At Isna they briefly met up with Christian Ehrenberg, who was on his way from Nubia to Alexandria, to rejoin Hemprich. From Aswan Rüppell travelled by river to the cataracts at Wadi Halfa, while Hey advanced with the caravan by land. They joined forces on the trek to Dongola, the capital of Nubia, where Rüppell first met the governor, Abdim Bey, who had earlier given Hemprich and Ehrenberg much valuable assistance and who now also befriended Rüppell. However, due to the widespread political unrest, Abdim Bey refused him permission to continue southwards, until it would be safer to do so.

In May they were able to set up camp at Ambukol and Rüppell sent Hey into the desert to the south, to hunt there while he collected in the more immediate vicinity, finding a good variety of songbirds and small mammals. When Hey returned a month later, Rüppell was disappointed that he had found little of interest, apart from three Ostriches and a tortoise. The rainy season brought with it hotter weather than the explorers had ever experienced before, and for a time they retreated to Dongola, where it was slightly cooler. Leaving Hey to collect in that area, Rüppell went downriver to Cairo, to send off a second shipment. There he hired Franz Lamprecht, who had hunted for Hemprich and Ehrenberg until their dwindling funds had forced them to pay him off. When Rüppell got back to Dongola in September he was disgusted to find that in his absence, Hey had indulged in an orgy of drinking.

In November Rüppell led his party further south across the Baiyuda desert to Kurgos Island on the Nile, hoping to receive the support of Ali's son-in-law, who ruled Kordofan. Unfortunately the governor was away on the Abyssinian border, seeking to revenge the murder of his predecessor; Rüppell had no choice but to wait for him to return. To make the best of the delay, he hired a barge for Lamprecht and Hey and sent them, with two Egyptian and two Negro servants, to hunt on the White Nile. The two collectors had been travelling up the river for less than three days when the hostility of the local people dissuaded them from going any further, and they retraced their route to where the river joined the Blue Nile, which they ascended as far as Sennar. It was three months before they rejoined Rüppell at Kurgos Island, but their meagre results contained nothing to console their leader for the wasted season. The governor had still not turned up and it was now too late to visit Kordofan that year, so the party returned to Ambukol. From there Rüppell organized an antelope hunt and was rewarded with a number of valuable specimens, but an urgent message from his friend, Abdim Bey, warning him that an army from Darfur had attacked Kordofan and was marching on Ambukol necessitated a hasty retreat to Dongola,

Rüppell's Warbler

where they spent the summer under the Bey's protection. Thirty thousand people died in the widespread violence and Rüppell lost all the contents of a store which he had rented at Isna; a barometer, a spare compass, telescopes, 35 lb of gunpowder and many other precious items were looted by the rebels. However, he was cheered when Abdim Bey presented him with a stuffed sixteen-day old hippopotamus, as his own attempts at hunting them had been unsuccessful.

With the country in such turmoil, Rüppell was disinclined to entrust his next collection for Frankfurt to anyone else, and so, in June, he set off for the Wadi Halfa with a well-loaded camel caravan, and from there transported his treasures by boat to Cairo. He was pleased to find new supplies and equipment awaiting him and in September he commenced the return journey to Dongola where he found that Hey was seriously ill and greatly relieved by his arrival. On 22 September 1824 Rüppell wrote to Cretzschmar, confiding in him that he feared for his assistant's life, but Hey soon recovered and in October and November they went hunting together on the Isle of Argo. Beyond all their expectations, in less than nine days they killed three hippopotami and a crocodile. One of the former was an unusually large male which had not succumbed without putting up a lengthy struggle, during which it had sunk their boat. Hey and Rüppell then had to undertake the tedious process of preparing the skins and skeletons.

At the end of the year Hey was again incapacitated by illness and so Rüppell made a new attempt to enter Kordofan without his help. This time he was successful and reached the oasis of Obeid, afterwards moving southwards and westwards through the desert to hunt for giraffes. He collected several specimens which were added to the many other mammals, birds and amphibians which he and Hey took to Cairo in July 1825.

Rüppell now spent some months making plans to explore the shores of the Red Sea and the highlands of Abyssinia. As he did not intend to return to Europe for another two years, his friend Cretzschmar decided to produce an *Atlas zu der Reise im nördlichen Afrika* [Atlas of Travels in northern Africa] (1826). It was compiled from Rüppell's notes and collections and was illustrated by F. C. Vogel and Kittlitz. Among the many species discovered by Rüppell and described by Cretzschmar are the Arabian Babbler, the Scrub Warbler, the Goliath Heron, and Cretzschmar's Bunting. One of the fine illustrations in the 'Atlas' was of a year-old vulture which Rüppell had acquired near Shendi; Cretzschmar confused it with the superficially similar Cape Vulture, but in 1852 Alfred Brehm realized that Rüppell's bird was a distinct species and named it *Vultur Ruppellii*. This bird is now known to range across the arid and mountainous areas of central Africa from the west to the east coast, and is the dominant vulture in the highlands of Ethiopia, feeding entirely on carrion, particularly the soft flesh and intestines.

Towards the end of 1825 Ehrenberg arrived in Cairo, after a long, slow journey from Massawa, on the Eritrean coast, where his intended expedition to the interior had ended in tragedy. Rüppell hired his Italian artist and his Moravian hunter, being especially glad to acquire the latter as Hey's alcoholism made him increasingly unreliable. But Rüppell's expedition also ended at

Massawa. He was ready to strike inland when several of his companions became gravely ill and his own health began to suffer because of numerous attacks of fever. The party returned to Cairo, with the indomitable Rüppell resolved to make another attempt in the future.

While he was travelling up the coast to Cairo, Rüppell heard that Abdim Bey had been murdered. The Turk had given Hemprich, Ehrenberg and Rüppell enormous help on many occasions, without which both expeditions might have ended much sooner. The central and southern African species, Abdim's Stork *Ciconia abdimii*, preserves his name.

At Alexandria Rüppell dismissed his staff before embarking on an English merchant ship with Hey and twenty-two packing cases containing the precious fruits of their last trip, but their many adventures were not yet over. They had been less than eighteen hours at sea when the ship was attacked and captured by Greek pirates. Six of the pirates then took charge of the merchantman and, escorted by the other vessel, they sailed towards Athens. More than a week later they sighted several strange ships on the horizon, and when the captain of the pirate vessel realized that the distant ships were Turkish, he immediately changed course and abandoned his prize. The six Greeks were quickly overcome by the English sailors, and on the 20 September 1827, Rüppell and Hey once more set foot on European soil, at Leghorn in north-west Italy.

They had to spend the next six weeks in quarantine, and on their release Hey celebrated with such enthusiasm that Rüppell immediately sent him on ahead to the Frankfurt Museum, enraged and embarrassed by his drunken behaviour. As Rüppell was still suffering from the debilitating effects of his Massawa fevers, complicated by jaundice and an inflammation of the throat, he decided to spend the winter in Tuscany. After receiving a copy of Cretzschmar's 'Atlas' of his Egyptian travels, Rüppell wrote to him in a resentful, angry mood, criticizing the standard of his descriptions and the colouring of some of the illustrations and blaming Cretzschmar for selecting Hey as his assistant. Although Rüppell later apologized profusely, the relationship between them continued to deteriorate. Rüppell slowly recovered his health, completed his journey to Frankfurt in March and devoted the next two years to working out the results of his expedition—and planning the next.

Eduard Rüppell celebrated Christmas Day, 1830, by sailing from Leghorn, bound once more for Alexandria, rejoicing in the long-cherished prospect of exploring the mountains of Abyssinia, which he had so far only gazed at from the fever-ridden coast. Now aged thirty-six, he was accompanied by a young man named Theodor Erckel, whom he had already hastily judged to be sadly lacking in both knowledge and enthusiasm—in fact, Erckel soon proved himself to be a conscientious and hard-working collector, whom Rüppell was able to rely upon even in the most difficult and dangerous circumstances. Rüppell had arranged to meet his friend Heinrich von Kittlitz at Alexandria, so that they could travel together, as the latter was an experienced artist and ornithologist who had recently returned from a Russian voyage to Kamchatka and several Pacific island groups.

While they waited for Kittlitz to arrive, the two naturalists studied the marine molluscs of the neighbourhood, then the three of them travelled together to

Rosetta, collecting rare Mediterranean fish en route. From the mouth of the Nile they sailed upriver to Cairo, but it soon became obvious that Kittlitz was still suffering from a most unpleasant illness contracted in the Pacific. This seriously incapacitated him, although when his health allowed, he joined the others on short excursions to visit the pyramids and to hunt for birds. They rode through lush countryside well irrigated by the Nile floods, past plantations of beans and high-stalked hemp and fields of waving corn and dark green clover. The latter provided grazing for buffaloes which were usually followed by little groups of Cattle Egrets feeding on grasshoppers and other insects disturbed by them. Occasionally the naturalists came upon shallow pools and stopped to watch Grey Herons and brilliant Smyrna Kingfishers, while black and white Spur-winged Plovers were often the first birds to take flight in noisy alarm.

Kittlitz was determined to continue with the venture even though his death in Africa seemed to be an inevitable prospect, but his friend persuaded him to return to Europe for medical treatment and they separated in Cairo at the beginning of April. In addition to this setback, Rüppell was forced to postpone his sail to Massawa as the dhows were overcrowded with pilgrims bound for Mecca. After recruiting Matthias Lindemann to help replace the loss of Kittlitz they undertook a brief trip to the Sinai, and from El Tur sailed to Jidda, where Rüppell continued his earlier surveys of the Red Sea coast. In September they embarked on a large Arabian vessel and despite stormy weather they successfully navigated the dangerous shallows and coral reefs on the approach to Massawa.

Before setting off for the highland plateau, Rüppell made an excursion northwards for about twenty-five miles, his primary interest being the birds and animals of the region. He travelled by camel along dusty tracks winding through narrow ravines only scantily vegetated by occasional low trees and stunted thorn bushes. Nevertheless the valleys were inhabited by hyenas, lynxes, leopards and a few lions, as well as by antelopes and small gazelles. Elephants occasionally strayed into the region and were hunted for their ivory. But it was the brilliantly coloured birds which most impressed the naturalist and in one of the more luxuriant valleys he was delighted by their abundance. Parrots chattered through the tops of the trees, swarms of finches pecked seeds from the plant stalks and the fragrant blossoms attracted flocks of tiny sunbirds. Various kinds of bee-eaters hunted everywhere from their perches and in the sandy, dried up river beds Rüppell often flushed coveys of guinea-fowl. In the mornings he sometimes saw seventy species and before the end of the month his hunters had brought him 132 different kinds of birds.

Unfortunately, whilst returning to Massawa during the coolness of the night, one of the camels broke loose and ran off. In giving chase to it, Rüppell's feet were badly cut by the prickly shrubs and sharp splinters of quartz against which his sandals gave only poor protection. It was a fruitless pursuit and for the next six weeks the explorer had to remain in the town until his wounds were healed.

At length a caravan from the mountain capital of Gondar arrived, bringing slaves, musk, wax, coffee and news of the latest ravages and rebellions. Rüppell sent his already substantial collections off to Alexandria and prepared to travel inland. Accompanied by numerous attendants and with his own camels bearing sundry items for barter such as Indian cottons, bands of twisted blue silk, black pepper and drinking glasses, in addition to his usual guns, ammunition and powder, scientific instruments and foodstuffs, Rüppell left the port in the company of 200 other men and forty-nine loaded camels. Most of the merchants were on foot, each dressed in trousers, plaid and shaggy sheepskin with a long curved sabre at his side. Only Rüppell and four of the merchants rode on mules.

After ten days the caravan divided and Rüppell chose to follow those taking the lengthier, but safer route. They were joined by several women who wished to escape the troubles of the area by accompanying them to Gondar, among them a very lovely girl of seventeen who had already been married and divorced seven times and who hoped to find her next husband in the capital. As they passed through the province of Temben towards distant snow-covered peaks they were detained in one town for ten days because of a dispute concerning the dues and tolls to be paid. The naturalists took advantage of the delay to discover as much as they could about the local wildlife, and the Chestnut Weaver was one of the new birds which they added to their baggage.

After they moved off again the villages became more scattered and cultivated ground less common. The caravan had just crossed the Takazzé River when it was ambushed by the inhabitants of the valley who showered rocks down on them, killing one of the mules. In retaliation the party captured three herd boys as hostages, bringing the hostilities to a temporary close. Next morning they were attacked again but after a parley the boys were released and the merchantmen were allowed to continue up into the mountains. From the highland forests Rüppell acquired the first specimens of the Yellow-faced Parrot which often occurred in noisy flocks in the tree tops accompanied by Black-winged Lovebirds.

After four months in Simen, Rüppell pursued his journey to Gondar as part of a much reduced caravan, but just two days away from the capital they were informed that a party of bandits were intending to attack them. Rüppell boldly took charge of the situation and persuaded his companions to overcome their superstitious fear of the dark and to continue travelling at night, an event so improbable that the bandits entirely misjudged their progress and they reached Gondar safely. The town was built on a volcanic hill, the home of about 7000 people, a mixed community of Christians, Muslims and Falasha Jews, who lived in houses of unhewn volcanic stone cemented together with earth and covered by conical roofs of straw.

From Gondar, Rüppell made a number of journeys into the surrounding hills and crossed Lake Tana. On one such trip he came across parties of noisy, agile, black and white monkeys of which he shot several; he had discovered the Abyssinian Colobus, an inhabitant of many mountainous forests in Africa, which feeds mainly on leaves but will also take fruit, buds and flowers. The Gelada, which resembles the baboon in its appearance and which gathers in herds of three or four hundred animals at night to sleep in the safety of high steep cliffs, is another monkey which he discovered here. From Shoa he procured the first specimens of the Abyssinian Blue-winged Goose which occurs nowhere else in the world, and in the rocky, volcanic hills around Gondar he discovered the Freckled Nightjar on the northern edge of its range. Delighted with the rich variety of his collections, Rüppell reluctantly departed for the coast by a more northerly route through Aksum and triumphantly sailed back to Egypt. He had successfully completed a two-year investigation into the natural history of Abyssinia and was the first explorer to traverse the country with that primary objective.

He returned to Frankfurt early in 1834 and between 1835 and 1840 published the zoological results of his expedition in *Neue Wirbelthiere zu der Fauna von Abyssinien gehörig* [New Vertebrate Fauna of Abyssinia]. In 1845 his *Systematischer Übersicht der Vögel Nord-Ost Afrikas* [Systematic review of the birds of north-east Africa] appeared, containing outstanding illustrations by Joseph Wolf and dedicated to the unlucky Kittlitz.

Edward Rüppell donated all of his bird specimens to the Senckenberg Natural History Society (of which he was a founder member) and began to catalogue the collection. However, he never completed the task because of disagreements between himself and Cretzschmar and other members of the society. His stupendous achievements were outlined in his *Reise in Abyssinien* [Travels in Abyssinia] (1838–40); it brought him world fame and recognition, but he found himself unable to work closely with fellow ornithologists and his strong-willed, individualistic temperament which had been a vital factor in the success of his expeditions now led to his gradual alienation from scientific circles. Eventually he ceased all his zoological research and became increasingly suspicious and irascible. During his last years he was dependent on a pension provided by the town of Frankfurt, his own resources having been expended in financing his travels, and his self-imposed isolation only ended with his death, in his native town, on 10 December 1884, at the age of ninety.

Rüppell's Warbler was one of the naturalist's first discoveries, made while he was in his early twenties. Temminck, who described and named the bird, understood that it had been found on Crete, but Hartert considered that the specimen was more likely to have come from Egypt or the Red Sea. One fact beyond any doubt is that if any man deserves to have a bird named in his honour, then Rüppell earned that tribute.

SABINE. *ENGLISH SCIENTIST WHO MADE TWO ARCTIC VOYAGES WITH HIS FRIEND JAMES ROSS. THEY ARE PORTRAYED TOGETHER (IN ROSS) AS MEMBERS OF THE ARCTIC COUNCIL.*

Edward Sabine
(1788-1883)

SABINE'S GULL *Larus sabini* Sabine

Larus Sabini Sabine, 1819. *Transactions of the Linnean Society of London* 12, p. 522, Pl. 29: Sabine Islands, near Melville Bay, west coast of Greenland

Although he was a keen ornithologist Edward Sabine's main interests were terrestrial magnetism and astronomy. It was his capabilities in these latter fields that secured a place for him on Ross's 1818 expedition to search for the North-west Passage (For a map of Sabine's voyages in 1818 and 1819–20, see Ross, p. 309). The *Isabella*, under John Ross, and the *Alexander* under William Parry, set sail from England in the spring and headed northwards to the west coast of Greenland and Baffin Bay, in the hope of penetrating westwards between the islands of the Canadian Arctic to the Pacific Ocean. The Captain's nephew, James Clark Ross, was on board the *Isabella* with Sabine, and the two young men became lifelong friends.

By July the two ships were well beyond the Arctic Circle. On the 25th of the month, not far from Cape York, some low rocky islands, each about a mile across, were sighted about twenty miles offshore. Sabine, James Ross, several of the men and the assistant surgeon set out over the ice to investigate them. Amongst the hundreds of Arctic Terns breeding there, the explorers noticed a number of delicate tern-like gulls with forked tails, dark heads and yellow-tipped black bills. Their task of shooting some of them was made easier by the gulls' vigorous and again, tern-like defence of their newly hatched young. Several adult birds were quickly added to Sabine's collection but were later transferred to a southbound whaler and conveyed to Sabine's elder brother Joseph, in London. Joseph displayed the birds at a meeting of the Linnean Society in mid-December and the gulls, "hitherto unknown and undescribed . . . in conformity with the custom of affixing the name of the original discoverer to a new species", he named *Larus Sabini*.

After the encounter with the gulls the expedition, by chance, made the first contact with the Polar or Thule Eskimos, who had become isolated for generations even from other Eskimos and had lost the art of kayak making. They were astonished by the two ships, believing them to be living beasts because they had seen their 'wings' move. The pig on board the *Isabella* was also a daunting sight for the Eskimos but they were eventually won over by mirrors and other gifts.

Sailing yet further northward, the explorers found the way between Greenland and Ellesmere Island blocked by ice, so they turned south and entered Lancaster Sound. John Ross thought he saw a range of mountains blocking their route westwards and decided to turn about and return home. It proved to be an unwise decision. Ross had concluded that no passage existed because there was no swell from the west and because there was no current with any driftwood. It is probable that all on board agreed with the decision but on the return journey some of the officers changed their minds. In the 'Narrative' of the expedition, published in the following year, John Ross tried to justify his action noting that Sabine had agreed with him at the time. Ross also commented that he had been led to believe that Sabine would assist in compiling the zoological appendices. However, Sabine refused to cooperate and they were written by the surgeon and assistant surgeon, then edited and corrected by William Leach.

Instead, Sabine brought out his own account of the ornithology of the voyage. Entitled 'A Memoir of the Birds of Greenland', it was published in the *Transactions of the Linnean Society* (1819), in the same volume as his brother's description of the new gull. In Edward Sabine's thirty-two page account, he listed the twenty-four species of birds which they had encountered during the course of the expedition, either at sea or on the occasional trip ashore. Besides giving general observations upon the birds he commented on some of the earlier writings, concerning the same species, by such authors as Fabricius, Montagu, Temminck, Pennant and Brünnich; indeed the English name of Brünnich's Guillemot stems from a proposal made by Sabine in this account.

Gyrfalcon, Peregrine, Ptarmigan, Snow Bunting, Glaucous Gull, Fulmar, King Eider and Ivory Gull were among the species that they had met with. At 76° N, hundreds of Little Auks were killed daily for food. Of the waders, they had seen Dunlin, Ringed Plover, both species of Arctic-breeding phalarope, Purple Sandpiper and Knot; failing only to observe the Turnstone and Sanderling amongst the waders known to breed in the areas visited. Sabine examined some tern skins well enough to notice that:

"There is a remarkable difference between the Greenland common Terns and those of the European coasts, in their bills and legs; the bills of the Greenland birds are

Sabine's Gull

one-third shorter than the European ones, and the tarsi of the former are only half the length of the latter."[1]

He was in fact describing some of the differences between the Arctic and Common Tern, but the idea that they were separate species seems not to have occurred to him. He was in good company. The differences escaped the notice of many eminent naturalists until J. F. Naumann, in 1819, made the distinction more widely known.

Some more remarks on Ross's voyage were published in the same year by Sabine but they were of a discordant nature. His criticism of John Ross added still further to the ill feeling between them. But this animosity never extended towards James Clark Ross. When the Admiralty decided on a second expedition to the same area Sabine and the younger Ross gladly joined Parry, who had been selected as leader in preference to the elder Ross. In May 1819, the ships *Hecla* and *Griper* set out for Baffin Bay and sailed right through Lancaster Sound into open water beyond; the Croker Mountains which had been thought to bar the way westwards did not exist.

Although winter was approaching they continued westward extending their season a little longer than perhaps they might otherwise have chosen to do, because they all knew that by passing beyond 110° W, in that region, they would share a £5000 reward from the Admiralty. There was a great celebration on 4 September when they crossed the line, but winter closed in on them almost at once and they found it hard to locate a suitable anchorage. Eventually, with large saws, they managed to cut a 4000 yard channel through the ice and the ships were man-hauled into Winter Harbour, on Melville Island.

It was a long winter. The sun did not show itself from 4 November to 3 February, but they had plenty of provisions and settled in to pass the time as pleasantly as possible. They acted plays and farces (a new one every fortnight), and they sometimes sang and danced to keep their spirits up. Sabine began, and edited, a hand-written weekly journal entitled *The North Georgia Gazette and Winter Chronicle* which ran for twenty-one weeks. When daylight returned they made brief hunting trips and at the beginning of June Parry set out on a ten-day trek to the north shore of the island but he found it utterly desolate, almost devoid of life. In August they sailed fifty miles further west but the ice there was impenetrable. They were too far north to have any chance of finding a passage to the Pacific because of the permanent pack-ice to the west. They returned homewards after this disappointment and arrived in England in November 1820.

Parry's *Journal* of the expedition had natural history appendices on the fish, mammals and birds, all written by Sabine. This time he was able to include the Sanderling which breeds in considerable numbers on the 'North Georgia Islands' and he also mentioned a single Sabine's Gull seen on the wing in Prince Regent Inlet.

The rest of Edward Sabine's life was dominated by his interest in the earth's magnetic field. In November 1821, in connection with this, he sailed on the *Pheasant* to the West Indies, Ascension Island and Sierra Leone on the west coast of Africa. He returned to England in January 1823 but in May of the same year he was back on the *Griper* continuing his magnetic observations in New York, Greenland, Trondheim and Spitzbergen. In 1825 Sabine conducted experiments with Sir John Herschel which involved sending up rocket signals, in order to measure the precise difference in longitude between Greenwich and Paris. Two years later, for a brief period, Sabine was Secretary of the Royal Society but he was determined not to let such responsibilities hinder his own investigations. In July 1833 he was in south-west Ireland and found time to compile a *Notice on the Birds met with on the Coast of Ballybunian*, which appeared as an appendix to William Ainsworth's *Caves of Ballybunian* (1834).

In the following year in conjunction with his friend James Ross and Professor Humphrey Lloyd, Sabine started the first systematic magnetic survey ever made in the British Isles. Starting in Ireland, it was extended to Scotland in 1836 and afterwards to England, Sabine being responsible for most of the written work. Not long after this, Humboldt urged the Royal Society to carry out a world-wide magnetic survey. The plan was quickly approved and a number of nations were invited to participate. Partly because of this, Ross was sent on a four-year expedition to Antarctica. When Ross sighted land there for the first time he named the highest peak Mt Sabine in honour of "one of the best and earliest friends of my youth and to whom the compliment was more especially due, as having been the first proposer and one of the most active and zealous promoters of the expedition."[2]

To enable Sabine to cope with the mass of observations that were sent to him, he acquired a small clerical staff that assisted him at the War Office for the next twenty years. His wife, Elizabeth Leeves of Sussex, whom he had married in 1826, helped him in his scientific work for over fifty years. Eventually Sabine was forced to discontinue his research which, perhaps inevitably, was never completed. He died without issue at Richmond, on 26 June 1883, at the age of ninety-five. He was buried beside his wife's remains in the family vault in Hertfordshire.

Edward Sabine's cheerfulness and attractive personality had made him popular among most of his colleagues. His main scientific achievement was his *Contributions to Terrestrial Magnetism* which he began in 1840. There were fifteen papers on the same subject in the *Philosophical Transactions of the Royal Society*. His contribution to natural history was less significant but as President of the Royal Society (1861–71), he was in a position to advise and direct others. For instance, he was a friend and supporter of the botanist David Douglas and gave him instructions in surveying and in taking geographical observations which Douglas put to good use in his Canadian travels.

Sabine presented some birds which he had obtained on his 1821–23 Atlantic voyages to the Natural History Department of the British Museum, but no record detailing the number of items or the identity of the species has survived. However, the collection almost certainly included Sabine's Puffback Shrike *Dryoscopus sabini* and Sabine's Swift *Chaetura sabini*; birds named by J. E. Gray and both native to the forests of Sierra Leone.[3] Shortly after his visit to West Africa, Sabine is reported to have shot a pair of Sabine's Gulls on Spitzbergen,[4] the only location within the Western Palearctic where the species breeds. There is no confirmation that the pair were breeding, which is unfortunate as proven instances from these islands are few in number.

After ending this brief outline of Sabine's scientific interests it is astonishing to realize that he also conducted an active military career. Edward Sabine was in the Royal Artillery for more than seventy years! When he retired from the army in 1877 he had risen to the rank of General, as his grandfather had done before him.

Edward was the fifth son and ninth child of Joseph Sabine of Tewin, Hertfordshire. Born at Dublin on 14 October 1788 and then educated at Marlow, Edward was no doubt encouraged to embark upon a military career. He entered the Royal Military Academy at Woolwich at fifteen and was made a first lieutenant in the following year. He was based at Gibraltar for a while before serving at various stations in Britain. In January 1813 he was sent to Canada, but the ship was only eight days out of Falmouth when it was attacked by an American privateer. There was a running battle for twenty-four hours during which Sabine and his soldier-servant helped to man the guns until forced to surrender. Not long after, the ship was recaptured by a British frigate and Sabine eventually landed safely in Canada. During that winter, as the American militia advanced on Quebec, Sabine was directed to garrison a small outpost. He later served on the border near Niagara and took part in an attack on Fort Eyrie when the British lost twenty-seven officers and over 300 men. He was again in action whilst on a sortie when the British suffered more heavy losses.

After his return to England in 1816 Captain Sabine devoted himself to his favourite scientific studies, for which he often received leave of absence. In 1830, after his aforementioned Arctic and Atlantic voyages, he was recalled for military duty in Ireland and for the next seven years managed to direct his magnetic surveys from there. In 1865 he was made Colonel Commandant of the Royal Artillery, and then, in the same year, was promoted to Lieutenant-General and later received a knighthood.

SAVI. *ITALIAN NATURALIST AND MINERALOGIST. HE TAUGHT AT THE UNIVERSITY OF PISA AND COMPILED THE* ORNITOLOGIA ITALIANA.

Paolo Savi
(1798-1871)

SAVI'S WARBLER *Locustella luscinioides* (Savi)

Sylvia luscinioides Savi, 1824. *Nuovo Giornale di Letterati* 7, No. 14, p. 341: Pisa

The year 1798 was a very special one for Gaetano Savi who taught botany at the University of Pisa, in Tuscany, for it saw the publication of his *Flora Pisana* as well as the birth of his son Paolo on 11 July. Gaetano's paternal aspirations were more than fulfilled as the boy showed interests similar to his own and at the age of nineteen graduated as Doctor of Physics and Natural Science at the same university. A year later he was appointed assistant to his father in the Chair of Botany, but soon afterwards became seriously ill and was unable to work for twelve months. After his recovery the younger Savi became particularly interested in zoology and mineralogy. He spent much of his time either perfecting his ability to dissect and prepare specimens at the local hospitals, or studying minerals in the university laboratories. At the age of twenty-three, in addition to his teaching post he was entrusted with the care of the Pisa Museum which had been founded by Ferdinand de Medici in 1591. The collections at that time were in no way outstanding and so Savi made it his ambition to develop and extend the museum. To that end he spent many days exploring his beloved Tuscany, studying every aspect of its natural history and collecting diligently in the vine-covered hills, the woods and olive groves and the coastal marshes.

In the autumn of 1821, he first obtained specimens of an unstreaked, dark, rufous-brown warbler with very light underparts, which he realized was different from all other *Sylviidae*: the Savi's Warbler. The following year he noted that it first appeared in local marshes and reedbeds around the middle of April, and in 1824 he published a full description of it under the name of *Sylvia luscinioides*. (Some years earlier a specimen shot in Norfolk had been submitted to Professor Temminck, but even the greatest of ornithologists can make mistakes in identification; he failed to recognize the bird's peculiarity, considering it to be a Cetti's Warbler.)

In 1823 Savi published a catalogue of the birds of the province of Pisa and regularly produced other papers on local birds, animals and insects while working hard on the cataloguing and arranging of his museum's fast-growing collections.

Such was his enthusiasm that in 1826, just five years after his appointment, the museum had to be extended into buildings in an adjoining street. By this time Savi had become full director of the museum as well as Professor of Natural History at the University, where he was extremely popular among his students because of his lucid and enthusiastic teaching.

When Leopold II (who was the same age as Savi) became the ruler of Tuscany in 1824, the two men discovered a shared passion to promote the welfare of their country and became very close friends. For the next thirty-five years the Grand-Duke provided Savi with sufficient financial support for him to travel widely in Italy and abroad, which allowed him to extend his knowledge and to gather additional material for his museum. At the first opportunity Savi visited the area around Naples, the Dolomites and the Tyrol and made the first of many journeys to the Piedmont. In 1828 he spent the summer in Paris with Baron Cuvier, who was an old friend of his father's, and returned home via Geneva and Turin. Two years later he travelled through Bavaria, Austria, Hungary, Saxony and Prussia, bringing back a rich harvest of specimens. However, Paolo Savi was more concerned with the flora and fauna of Tuscany than that of foreign fields and he became intimately acquainted with every part of the duchy. At the Grand-Duke's request he turned his attention to the *maremma*, the malarial marshy coastland, and through his investigations and advice, conditions for the inhabitants were greatly improved. He also tackled the common problem of mildew in vineyards by introducing the custom of spreading sulphur on the vines. From 1827 to 1831 he published his *Ornitologia Toscana*, but later found less and less time for the study of birds.

The Chair of Natural History was divided in 1840 and Savi gave up responsibility for geology and mineralogy. He continued to teach zoology and comparative anatomy, residing within the precincts of the University, as did his brother Pietro who was Professor of Botany. Savi was frequently commissioned by the government, or private individuals, to study and report on quarries, mines and industrial projects, and in 1861, when the Grand-Duchy became fused with the Kingdom of Italy, Savi was one of four jurisconsults chosen to revise the laws dealing with the mining industry.

During the following winter Savi became a Senator of the Kingdom, but, having kept himself apart from politics all of his life, he took no part in affairs of state until Florence became the new capital in 1865. When Savi died on

Savi's Warbler

5 April 1871, he was buried with great solemnity by the City of Pisa in its famous cemetery.

Towards the end of his life Savi had rekindled his passion for ornithology and had endeavoured to finish what was to become his best known work, the *Ornitologia Italiana*. At the time of his death only the final editing remained to be done, and this was ably undertaken by his son Adolpho. The book was published posthumously between 1873 and 1876, fifty years after his earliest ornithological contributions. Savi also achieved his great ambition to elevate the status of the Pisa Museum: in 1844 a new building to house the rich and varied collections had been completed, and by the time of Savi's death his beloved museum was one of the greatest scientific institutions in the whole of Italy.

SCHLEGEL. *EMINENT SINOLOGIST WHO SPENT EIGHTEEN
YEARS IN CHINA. HE WAS A FRIEND OF ROBERT SWINHOE
AND SON OF THE GREAT HERMANN SCHLEGEL, DIRECTOR
OF THE LEYDEN MUSEUM.*

Gustaaf Schlegel
(1840-1903)

PECHORA PIPIT *Anthus gustavi* Swinhoe

Anthus gustavi Swinhoe, 1863. *Proceedings of the Zoological Society of London*, p. 90: Amoy

The Pechora River rises on the western slopes of the Ural Mountains and flows northwards to the Arctic Ocean. As it nears the sea the river leaves the low, larch-covered hills and winds its way through willow thickets inhabited by Bluethroats, Sedge Warblers, Redpolls, Redwings and Bramblings and past lakes where Goldeneye and Oystercatcher nest. It was here, in 1875, a little to the north of the Arctic Circle, that Henry Seebohm became the first to study the Pechora Pipit on its breeding grounds.

Early one morning in the middle of June he moored his boat on a small island which was overgrown with willows, birch and alder and listened to a song, poured forth from high in the sky above him, which he had never heard before. The song began like the trill of a Wood Warbler and then changed to a low guttural warble. Once the bird sang overhead for more than half an hour, then perched on a tree and descended to the ground, still singing. When Seebohm shot one, he saw that it was similar to the Tree Pipit, but more boldly marked, and different from any other species with which he was familiar.

On returning home he presented his friend, Henry Dresser, with five skins and enjoyed the thrill of having the bird described as a new species, the Pechora Pipit *Anthus seebohmi*.[1] Alas for Seebohm, the pipit had already been discovered in south-east China by Gustaaf Schlegel and named *Anthus gustavi*, by Robert Swinhoe.

Gustaaf Schlegel was born on 30 September 1840 in the village of Oegstgêest, near Leyden, the son of Professor Hermann Schlegel who was then working with Temminck at the Leyden Museum and who succeeded him as Director. The museum housed the most important natural history collection in The Netherlands, the botanical gardens at Leyden were then the best in Europe and the position of the town, a little to the south-west of Amsterdam, assured that the museum was visited by many eminent scientists and travellers. Hermann Schlegel was from Saxony, but as well as his native German he spoke Dutch, French and English with equal facility and the young Gustaaf was educated at home until the age of eleven, in what must have been an exciting and stimulating environment. As a child, Gustaaf heard so many fascinating tales of the Far East from visitors to his home that he determined to learn Chinese and began his first lessons in the language at the age of nine! It was a fortunate choice, for the Government needed Chinese interpreters for the Dutch East Indies and from the age of thirteen he was paid 25 florins a month to encourage him in his studies.

In September 1857 he matriculated at Leyden University and sailed for China the following month as a student interpreter. His first few months were spent at Macao, then he moved to Amoy and worked there for the next three years. There were few Europeans living on the small island, but among them was Robert Swinhoe, the English ornithologist, who was just four years older than Schlegel and who was employed as an interpreter at the British Consulate. Their presence at Amoy coincided for one and a half years and they became close friends, often making excursions together, although Swinhoe's knowledge of birds and his passion for collecting was never matched by his companion.

Nevertheless, Schlegel sent his father a few small natural history collections from Amoy; one was chiefly composed of 255 bird skins, another miscellaneous assortment included more than 200 fish and others consisted entirely of invertebrates. In June 1861 Swinhoe wrote to Professor Hermann Schlegel reporting that he and Gustaaf had at last acquired a specimen of the Blue-winged Pitta, a strange, brilliantly coloured bird which had for a long time been known only from the work of Japanese artists.

In 1863 Swinhoe wrote to *The Ibis*, describing some new and little-known Chinese birds, among them *Anthus gustavi*, which his friend Schlegel had procured at Amoy in the middle of May as the pipits were passing northwards along the coast. Swinhoe later obtained many more specimens of the pipit, both males and females together, from an island off Chefoo, and he was also sent a skin from Lake Baykal. By then Seebohm had established that they wintered in the Philippines and Indonesia, and had found them nesting near the Yenisey River; at St Petersburg's Museum he had also identified skins from the Chukotskiy Peninsula and Bering Island. In 1876 Dr Otto Finsch and Dr Alfred Brehm had noted that the birds occurred in the valley of the Ob, so that within the surprisingly short period of just thirteen years since the original discovery of the pipit, its subarctic breeding distribution across Russia, and its migration

Pechora Pipit

route through south-eastern Siberia and east China to south-east Asia had been largely worked out![2]

However, the man whom the pipit commemorates was primarily a sinologist and birds were just one of his interests. During the years in Amoy he devoted much of his spare time to studying the Chinese secret societies, and after he published the results of his research in 1861 the Dutch and the British authorities benefited greatly from his work. At this time he also began to labour on his Dutch–Chinese dictionary, which was eventually published between 1882 and 1891 in four volumes.

At the age of twenty Schlegel was sent to Canton for a year to study the local dialect and afterwards, in June 1862, he left China for the island of Java. He worked at Jakarta for the next ten years, again as an interpreter, and was given the additional responsibility of advising the lawyers who were then drawing up civil laws for the Chinese in the Dutch colonies. He published a number of papers on Chinese law and in 1869, for a dissertation on the customs and pastimes of the Chinese, he earned the title of Doctor of Philosophy from the University of Jena. In June 1872 he was obliged to take some leave because of the poor state of his health and he took the opportunity to travel into central and northern China.

a course for student interpreters of the Chinese language. Two years later the Chair of the Chinese Language was created especially for him and he taught at the University for the rest of his life. A year before his death he made a list of his 256 publications related to the Chinese and their dialects. Unfortunately, he was by this time losing his sight and after a period of illness, ascribed by some of his friends to the consequences of overwork, this remarkable sinologist died at his home in Leyden on 15 October 1903 at the age of sixty-three.

SCHRENCK. *PRUSSIAN NATURALIST WHO INVESTIGATED THE ORNITHOLOGICAL RICHES OF SAKHALIN ISLAND AND THE AMUR.*

Leopold von Schrenck (1826-1894)

SCHRENCK'S LITTLE BITTERN *Ixobrychus eurhythmus* (Swinhoe)

Ardetta eurhythma Swinhoe, 1873. *Ibis*, p. 74. Pl. 2: Amoy and Shanghai

Schrenck's Little Bittern and the Cinnamon Bittern are shy and secretive inhabitants of China and south-east Asia. Their breeding ranges overlap and, broadly speaking, they frequent the same wetland habitats and are of similar size and coloration. Their distinction as separate species was made by Robert Swinhoe while he was attached to the British consular service in China. In 1863 he obtained a Schrenck's Little Bittern at Amoy but having only a single skin he thought that it was probably a hybrid between a Cinnamon and Yellow Bittern. Later he secured several more Schrenck's Little Bitterns that were nesting at Shanghai and realized that they were a new species. When he described the bittern in *The Ibis* of 1873 he acknowledged the species' unwitting first discoverer—Leopold von Schrenck.

Born and brought up in the countryside near Chotenj, south-west of St Petersburg, Schrenck won his doctorate at Dorpat and then studied natural sciences at Berlin and Königsberg, where he specialized in zoology. At the age of twenty-seven he was sent by the Russian Academy of Sciences at St Petersburg to explore the Amurland which had recently been annexed from China. (For a map of the Amurland, see Radde, p. 302). Much of the River Amur, and its tributary the Ussuri, still forms a considerable part of the border between the Maritime Provinces of the Soviet Union and north-east China. Schrenck had instructions to study and collect on the Russian side of the river and eastwards to the then little-known island of Sakhalin, north of Japan.

He left St Petersburg in September 1853 on board the *Aurora* and by mid-April of the following year was off the coast of Peru. French and English warships in the vicinity were waiting for the declaration of war in the Crimea and so the *Aurora* hurried across the Pacific to Kamchatka. Schrenck then joined the *Olivutzu* and proceeded to Castries Bay, where he took a third ship which was heading for the Amur. On the way, the Conservator of the St Petersburg Herbarium, Carl Maximowicz, transferred from a Russian frigate to Schrenck's ship, and the two naturalists arrived together at the mouth of the Amur almost a year after leaving the Baltic independently.

While the botanist continued upriver, Schrenck quickly built himself a log cabin at Nikoleyesk and began to explore locally. In winter he prepared for a visit to Sakhalin and on 8 February 1855, as the daylight hours began to lengthen again, his small sled party set out eastwards, but the natives on the island did not welcome them. The previous fishing season had been so poor that they refused to part with any of their meagre supplies. Schrenck and his party were forced to return to the mainland and instead they ascended the Amur for a few hundred miles before returning to base.

Winter in these regions is long and bitter, and spring does not arrive until the end of May. As the ice cleared from the Amur, Schrenck began to explore upriver again but he fell in with the Governor-General of Siberia who ordered him down to Castries Bay to help in the establishment of the settlement there. Schrenck finally got away again in July and, together with Maximowicz, went upstream branching southwards along the Ussuri to as far as the mouth of the Nor. Unfortunately, the poor health of their rowers and the lack of trading goods forced the party to return to Nikoleyesk in September, though Maximowicz elected to remain at Marinsk.

Schrenck was determined to explore Sakhalin and once more set out in February, accompanied by two Cossacks, a sailor and three sleds of provisions. They soon reached the island but the going was tough because of deep snow and the lack of trails, and, unable to find anyone willing to take them across the island, they set off unguided to traverse three ranges of hills and mountains. They left the tall conifers and leafless deciduous trees of the west coast and soon entered areas where larches predominated, but even these became sparse and increasingly stunted as they approached the opposite coast. In the interior they saw Musk Oxen but throughout the six-week thousand-mile trip they encountered only a few resident birds.

In May of the same year, Schrenck prepared to return overland to Europe although it was a further three months before he had worked his way through the Amur. The return party consisted of about forty Cossacks, a boat with Maximowicz's botanical hoard and three barges with Schrenck's collection of mammals and birds. Whenever possible they tried to add to their discoveries but a great deal of their time was spent struggling against the current and adverse winds; heavy rain and melting snow in the mountains had swollen the river while they themselves toiled in broiling sunshine. When they at last reached Ust Strelka in the upper reaches of the Amur, some 2000 miles from the sea, they

Schrenck's Little Bittern

struck off overland to Lake Baykal and thence to St Petersburg, arriving there some time in 1857.

On his return, Schrenck catalogued his specimens and soon gave a full account of his explorations and the animal life he had seen in the east. He was a skilled writer and through his graphic and imaginative descriptions of the area his reputation quickly spread. Maximowicz went on to become the leading authority on the botany of the Amur and afterwards of Japan; so much so, that any naturalist wishing to study the flora of Japan was, for a long time, recommended to travel instead to St Petersburg, to consult his collections.

In 1884 Schrenck represented the St Petersburg Academy at the First International Ornithological Congress at Vienna. Afterwards his efforts to set up a chain of ornithologists throughout Russia, in accordance with decisions made at the Congress, were unsuccessful. In later years, although he remained at the Academy, he transferred his attention to the study of the native peoples of his country and became Director of the Museum of Anthropology and Ethnography. In this capacity he contributed towards 'Additions to the existing knowledge of the Russian Empire' published in 1886. He died a few years later on 8 January 1894, still engaged in improving and enlarging the museum collections. He was buried on the family estates at Jensel, in Livonia, the region immediately to the south-west of the city where he had spent most of the last years of his life.

The results of Schrenck's expedition of 1853–57 appeared in *Reisen und Forschungen im Amur-Lande* [Travels and Investigations in the Amur]. The first part on the mammals was issued in 1859 and was written in collaboration with other scientists. The ornithological section, which came out in the following year, was the work of Schrenck alone. He was criticized for not giving enough descriptive detail and for lumping species and sub-species together, as it was felt that other taxonomists should have been given the chance to form their own opinions. Nevertheless, Schrenck's work was recognized, in the *Ibis* of 1861, as: ". . . absolutely essential to anyone who wishes to attain a complete knowledge of the birds of Europe, or even of England, as giving details concerning the range of the greater part of our native species, and a fauna of a country whence many of our rarer stragglers are derived".

Along with Middendorf's *Sibirische Reise* (1847–75) and Radde's *Reisen im Süden von Ost-Sibirien* (1862–63) Schrenck's work was, at the close of the nineteenth century, one of the three principal studies on the ornithology of eastern Siberia and remained so for many years. In all, he listed 190 species of birds that he had seen on the lower Amur or on Sakhalin, and he also listed a further 137 species reported from the area by other authors. Schrenck described the typical resident birds of the area such as White-tailed Sea Eagle, Goshawk, Hawk Owl, Nutcracker and Raven, and he tried to delineate their geographical distribution. He explained how the natives often kept eagles, kites, owls and jays as pets, and liked to see swallows using their huts to nest in. He probably gave the first account of the Mandarin in its natural breeding areas, one of the main strongholds for this duck being the marshes, lakes and wooded streams of the lower Amur. Of the heron tribe he listed only the Grey and Green-backed Herons, the large European Bittern and the tiny Cinnamon Bittern. Schrenck's Little Bittern was depicted as the young of the latter species.

SCHWARTZ. *AN ASTRONOMER AT DORPAT, IN RUSSIA, HE TOOK PART IN A LONG EXPEDITION TO THE AMUR.*

Ludwig Schwarz
(1822-1894)

RADDE'S WARBLER *Phylloscopus schwarzi* (Radde)

Sylvia (Phyllopneuste) Schwarzi Radde, 1863. *Reisen im Süden von Ost-Sibirien,* Vol. 2, p. 260, Pl. 9: Tarei Nor and Bureya Mts [Transbaikalia and Amurland]

Ludwig Schwarz was born at Danzig (Gdansk) on 23 May 1822. He sought employment in Russia and at twenty-four years of age became assistant at the Observatory at Dorpat (Tartu). He took part in a number of expeditions into Siberia, chiefly in his capacity as an astronomer. From 1855 to 1859 he led a major expedition eastwards to the Amur, which had recently been annexed from China.

They arrived at Irkutsk, near Lake Baykal, in the spring of 1855 and here Schwarz divided his men into three parties: one to explore north-east towards the River Lena; the second to cover Transbaikalia and the upper reaches of the River Amur; and the third to descend the Amur towards the Sea of Okhotsk. For the next four years each group examined the physical geography of their areas and at the same time tried to assess their economic potential; all aspects of natural history were also, of course, investigated.

After the expedition's return Schwarz continued with his scientific career and in 1872 became Professor of Astronomy and Director of the Observatory at the University of Dorpat. He published a number of works on astronomy during

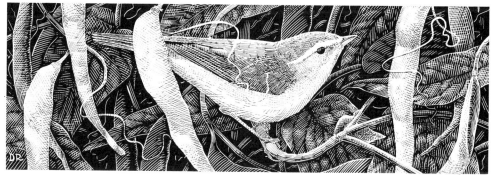

Radde's Warbler

his time there and died at Dorpat, at the age of seventy-five, on 17 September 1894.

When the ornithological details of the Amurland expedition were published in 1863, they contained many new discoveries. One of these was a new species of warbler that Gustav Radde first found on 22 September 1856 in a kitchen-garden near the Tarei Nor, and later in the Bureya Mountains of the middle Amur. Curiously, although Radde named the species in honour of Ludwig Schwarz it has become popularly known as Radde's Warbler. This seems to have been due to Henry Seebohm, who, ever fond of honouring original discoverers, attached Radde's name to the species in the English vernacular, in 1881. In a few European countries it is Schwarz who is commemorated in the common name. In France it is called the Pouillot de Schwarz and in Spain it is known as the Mosquitero de Schwarz.

Georg Wilhelm Steller [†] (1709-1746)

STELLER'S EIDER *Polysticta stelleri* (Pallas)

Anas Stelleri Pallas, 1769. *Spicilegia Zoologica*, Pt 6, p. 35, Pl. 5: Kamchatka

Georg Wilhelm Steller was born on Sunday 10 March 1709, the son of Johannes Jacob Stöhler, a cantor, and his second wife, Susanna. However, despite every attempt of the midwife the baby appeared to be lifeless. After she had tried every trick of her trade, a determined and devoted friend of the mother wrapped the tiny body in hot blankets and kept changing them as they cooled. After several hours, to everyone's amazement, the little one gave a cry and recovered completely.

The family lived at Windsheim, near Nuremberg, now in West Germany. According to one of his brothers, Georg was always interested in natural history, and he doubtless spent many hours exploring the surrounding countryside with his brothers and sisters. He did well at school where only Latin was spoken, becoming head of his class and graduating with a scholarship for the study of theology at the University of Wittenberg. When he took leave of his family in September 1729 he expected to return as a preacher two years later. Instead, he became one of the first white men to stand on Alaskan soil, the pioneer naturalist of that great land and the earliest authority on many of the northern sea mammals.

At University, the outgoing, self-reliant young man began to attend anatomy lectures and studied botany, eventually changing his course from theology to study as a physician, paying for his own fees by teaching at a local orphanage and tutoring. He also gave botanical lectures which attracted a large number of students. At this time many young scientists had already been called to the new Academy of Sciences in St Petersburg, established by the widow of Peter the Great. Frustrated in his attempt to become a Professor of Botany at Halle University, and excited by the idea of travel and exploration, Georg considered the long journey: no easy prospect for an impecunious student. He solved the financial problem by travelling from Danzig as a physician to wounded Russian soldiers who had been besieging the city. He eventually arrived in St Petersburg, despite shipwreck on the way, in November 1734.

As the Russians found his name quite impossible to pronounce, he altered it to Steller and set about learning the language. He was very fortunate in being

[†] No known portrait.

immediately befriended by Archbishop Theophan Prokopovitch, a kindly and powerful benefactor. Steller became his household doctor and spent much of his time botanizing in the nearby countryside if he was not busy at the Academy. During these two happy years the Second Kamchatka Expedition, under Vitus Bering, was much discussed. When it was decided to send out two new members to join the expedition, the influential Archbishop strongly recommended Steller.

Bering's first great expedition was inspired by Peter the Great who naturally desired to learn something of the eastern borders of his vast empire. At that time, none of the land or sea north of Japan or California had been explored and no one knew whether the two continents of Asia and America were joined, or divided by the sea. Fleet-Captain Bering was dispatched to resolve the question and returned during the reign of Empress Anna in 1730, having sailed through the strait which now bears his name, satisfying himself that the two continents were separate. His report met with such scepticism that despite all the hardships he had endured he offered to go back and prove the matter beyond all doubt.

Thus the Second Kamchatka Expedition was born, and Steller was greatly elated when he was accepted as one of its naturalists. Bering, now promoted to Captain Commander, was the head of a quite stupendous undertaking. The objectives were threefold. Firstly, to search for America; secondly, to chart the

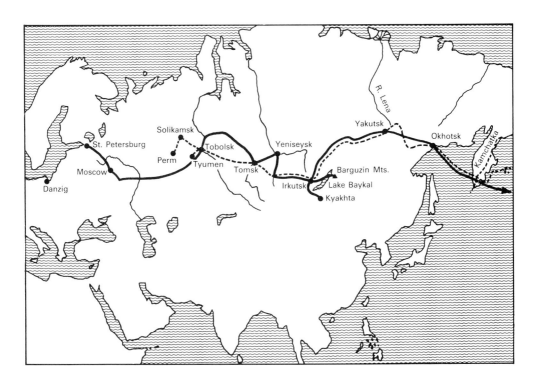

STELLER'S TRAVELS IN RUSSIA:
━━━━━━━━ *OUTWARD*
--------- *RETURN*

Siberian coast of the Arctic Ocean; and thirdly, the Kuril Islands, Japan and other parts of eastern Asia were to be explored.

To join this expedition Steller had to travel right across the Russian Empire to Kamchatka, a journey of well over 5000 miles. Shortly before he set off in January 1738, he married Brigitta Messerschmidt, the young widow of a naturalist who had spent seven years exploring much of Siberia west of the River Lena. Knowing that he would be away for years, Steller was thrilled that his lively, passionate bride was going with him; as Bering and some other participants were accompanied by their families, it was not an unreasonable prospect. In the depths of winter the couple travelled to Moscow among a small caravan of sledges. However, when they arrived there Brigitta refused to go any further; although she had not travelled in Siberia with Messerschmidt, she had heard enough about the dangers and privations to be determined to avoid them, and she insisted that her seven year old daughter needed her more. Steller tried every means of persuasion he knew, but to no avail. After providing her with sufficient money for the next year, he continued eastwards, angry and bitterly disappointed. When he wrote home to his family he did not even mention that he had married.

By the following winter he had reached Tomsk, but before Christmas he suffered such a raging fever that his companions feared for his life. Early in the new year he felt fit enough to move on again and in Yeniseysk he met Müller and the botanist J. G. Gmelin, members of the expedition who were anxious to return to more civilized parts. Gmelin, who like Müller travelled in an enormous caravan with all kinds of servants, well provided with various luxuries, was amazed by Steller's simple needs, recording:

> "He was not troubled about his clothing. As it is necessary in Siberia to carry along one's own housekeeping outfit, he had reduced it to the least possible compass. His drinking cup for beer was the same as his cup for mead and whiskey. Wine he dispensed with entirely. He had only one dish out of which he ate and in which was served all his food. For this he needed no chef. He cooked everything himself, and that with so little circumstance that soup, vegetables and meat were put into the same pot and boiled together. Smoke and smell in the room in which he worked did not affect him. He used no wig and no powder; any kind of shoe or boot suited him."

They were also deeply impressed by his determination and the accuracy of his observations.

Steller spent the summer of 1739 exploring the Barguzin Mountains which lie east of Lake Baykal, returning afterwards to Irkutsk which he made his winter base. From there he sent his carefully packed collections of specimens and manuscripts back to St Petersburg. It was necessary to make extensive preparations for his journey to Yakutsk, including the vital need to replenish his store of paper. For this reason, once Lake Baykal had frozen, he made a round journey of 650 miles to Kyakhta on the Mongolian border, where he procured a good supply. An indefatigable collector whatever the circumstances, he was not deterred by even a Siberian winter and he stopped to gather seeds wherever the wind had blown the ground clear of snow.

In mid-August 1740, more than two and a half years after leaving St Petersburg, Steller at last reached Okhotsk on the east coast. By this time he had become so enamoured of Siberia's attractions that he had written to Gmelin about his wife, saying that "I have entirely forgotten her and fallen in love with Nature". Even so, letters from her requesting more money caused him much anxiety and annoyance.

It was in Okhotsk that Vitus Bering first met Georg Steller. The Dane was now fifty-nine years old, the German thirty-one, but Bering was greatly impressed by the younger man's wide-ranging knowledge and enthusiasm. In August Bering parted from his family, who began the long journey back, and the following month Steller sailed with the small flotilla of four vessels for Kamchatka. Since Steller's original orders had been to explore the Peninsula he was on board the vessel which sailed upriver to Bolsheretsk, the main settlement, while Bering with the other three ships carried on to Avatcha Bay, one of the safest and most scenic natural harbours in the world. Steller spent much time during the long winter gathering information about the 'Great Country' to the east. He wrote of these attempts:

> "Upon my arrival in Kamchatka in the year 1740, I eagerly took pains to obtain such information, questioning all new-comers, traders, cossacks, with the greatest friendliness, and, in case I got nothing out of them by fair means, brought them to confession with brandy as the most pleasant torture."

Steller organized and led an expedition into southern Kamchatka, and took much interest in the local Kamchadals, being very concerned about their material and spiritual poverty. He helped to organize a native school in Bolsheretsk, and unlike many of the others who despised and ill-treated the local people, he had a great deal of respect for them. By this time he was determined to contrive a place on the expedition to America, and as it turned out, Bering was equally keen to have him. His medical skills, his knowledge about every aspect of natural history, and possibly the fact that he was a fellow Lutheran, all commended him. He was officially appointed as the mineralogist but was

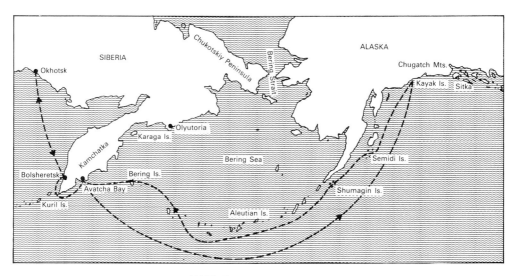

VOYAGE OF THE ST PETER

expected to study all natural phenomena, including local peoples, their appearance and habits.

As a result of his enquiries, Steller was convinced that the American continent lay closest to Asia just opposite the Chukotskiy Peninsula and he therefore suggested that they sail north-eastwards. As Bering had already sailed in the northern waters and seen no land to the east (passing close to the coast while it was shrouded in mist), he could not be so persuaded. On 4 June 1741 the *St Peter* and the *St Paul* set sail east–south-east from Avatcha Bay with Bering and Steller sharing a cabin on the *St Peter*. Six days later Steller was observing Harlequins on the open sea for the first time, though he had previously seen them on some of the fast-flowing rivers of Kamchatka. Towards the end of June the two ships became separated in thick mist, but on 16 July, an overcast rainy day, the clouds suddenly broke to reveal a range of high snow-covered peaks, the Chugatch Mountains of south-east Alaska. After six weeks without sighting land Steller was enraptured at the prospect of so many new and glorious discoveries and was consumed by the desire to explore this virgin territory. In contrast, Bering was weary and anxious, wanting only to find fresh drinking water and to take his men home unharmed.

Steller had to seethe with pent-up excitement for the next four days until he was allowed ashore on Kayak Island with the first watering party. They found a landing beach between high, grey cliffs and Steller set off to explore the dark spruce woods with a Cossack hunter, Thoma Lepikhin. When they found a fireplace and the remains of a recent meal he sent his companion back to warn the crew about the natives, and then carried on alone. Six hours later, loaded with his discoveries, he returned to the landing place and sent word to Bering requesting the help of several men to collect more specimens. While waiting, he brewed up some tea and made written descriptions of his plants. Steller's original notes were always full and detailed; he rarely rewrote or amended his work later.

When Bering's reply came, it was an order to return to the *St Peter* immediately; but first Steller sent Thoma to shoot some birds, as only the Raven and the Magpie had been familiar to him. Thoma shot a blue jay, and though neither the specimen nor the drawing of it ever reached St Petersburg, Steller's detailed description did. In 1788 J. F. Gmelin (not his friend the botanist J. G. Gmelin) named it *[Cyanocitta] stelleri*—Steller's Jay. A more immediate reward came when he returned on board: Bering gave him a rare and expensive luxury, a cup of chocolate.

Early next day they set sail without even refilling the rest of the water casks. To console himself, all poor Steller could do was to hang a hook over the side and he thus caught two new species of sculpins. They made some attempt to examine the coast but foggy weather hindered them and an outbreak of scurvy persuaded Bering to set a course for Kamchatka. Returning by a more northerly route they encountered land several times and among the Semidi Islands Steller was excited by large numbers of Sea Otters, seals, porpoises and sea lions, and a few weeks later he was ashore again with a watering party. Unfortunately he had to spend much of his time collecting anti-scorbutic plants such as gentians and spoonwort. By including them in his diet, Steller was almost the only member of the expedition to escape the ravages of scurvy. He lost more precious time trying unsuccessfully to persuade the others to follow his example and despite his angry protestations the men also filled many of the casks with brackish water; all of which later led to much tragedy. On Nagai Island, Nikita Shumagin was the first crew member to die of scurvy and the island group now records his name.

In foul weather, with many of the men now helpless or dying, they sailed along the Aleutian Islands and on 5 November sighted land to the west. It was a bleak, squally morning with flurries of snow. The *St Peter* had only six barrels of water on board, all of which were contaminated, the rigging was rotten and the mainsail shrouds had snapped; there were not enough healthy men to carry out repairs or to manage the ship. Bering held a council and decided to steer for the land in sight. Just offshore, the ship was caught in a violent squall and was in great danger of being smashed on a jagged reef, but just when shipwreck seemed inevitable, a huge wave carried them over into a quiet channel between the rocks and the beach. By the next morning the death toll had risen to twelve and forty-nine of the surviving sixty-six men were sick.

Steller and a shipmate went ashore, returning with ptarmigan and anti-scorbutic plants. During the next few weeks, when the weather allowed, the crew were gradually moved ashore but there were not enough fit men to weigh anchor and beach the ship. On the night of 28 November a strong north-easterly gale snapped the anchor cable and threw the *St Peter* high up onto the beach, which was generally considered a blessing despite the loss of the rudder and extensive damage to the hull.

The surviving ship's company was now stranded for the winter. Though the optimistic reckoned they were somewhere on Kamchatka, Steller quickly came to the conclusion that they were on an uninhabited island as the Sea Otters and Arctic Foxes showed no fear of man. Throughout their stay these blue foxes were a menace. Great numbers of them roamed around the camp, drawn from all over the island by their presence. Even though up to sixty were shot in one day, they became increasingly aggressive and nothing was safe from them. When Steller was trying to skin animals for food, the foxes tried to tear the meat from his hands and even the corpses of the dead sailors had their noses, fingers and toes bitten off while their graves were being dug.

During the first few weeks, Steller and those others who were able explored the treeless surroundings. The land seemed barren and bleak; snow was already lying but they found deep pits in some sand dunes burrowed out by the foxes. There they excavated a row of five dugouts, made roofs from driftwood and sails and were soon reasonably well sheltered from the elements. Although Bering now had fresh food and water he died of a complication of diseases, including scurvy, on 8 December 1741, half covered by the sand which he would not allow his men to remove, because he said that it gave him a feeling of warmth. They buried him the next day, with Steller performing the rites of the Lutheran Church, near the little camp on what is now known as Bering Island.

Throughout the winter, Steller was occupied with ministering to the spiritual and physical needs of his comrades, gathering firewood and hunting for food. As some tobacco had been saved from the stores he also made pipe-stems from the wing bones of dead albatrosses for himself and the others. Of the seventy-eight men who had set out there were now only forty-six surviving, but when they had recovered their health a little, most spent their spare time gambling for money or Sea Otter pelts. The resulting strife and hatred led Steller to condemn the gambling as a worse epidemic than scurvy and he devoted himself to studying the wildlife of the island.

Off the east shore there were immense flocks of ducks which characteristically dived and surfaced together in tight little bunches. Steller had already collected some specimens at Kamchatka during the previous winter, and from these Pallas named the species *Anas Stelleri* in 1769.

A common bird of the rocky shores was the large, clumsy and almost flightless Spectacled Cormorant. Steller was the only naturalist ever to see them alive, and wrote that they weighed from 12 to 14 lb, "so that one single bird was sufficient for three starving men". Buried in clay and baked in a heated pit, the cormorants made a pleasant change to the usual diet of Sea Otter, seal and ptarmigan meat. Only a hundred years later it had been hunted to extinction.

In the spring Steller watched Pigeon Guillemots, Tufted Puffins, Parakeet Auklets and Red-throated Divers around the coast. As the snow melted Lapland Buntings arrived followed by Skylarks, the most welcome of all the small songsters. Other birds present included Rock Sandpipers, Ravens and Wrens, the latter being quickly nicknamed "the little tobacco quid".

Although Steller shared his primitive dugout with up to nine other men he wrote his most famous work, *De Bestiis Marinis* (1751), while shipwrecked on Bering Island. In it he described the Northern Fur Seal, the Sea Otter, Steller's Sea Lion and Steller's Sea Cow, all unknown to science until then. In May the fur seals began to come ashore and he studied them throughout the breeding season, noting how the adult males arrived first, and how the old, fat bulls fasted for three months before returning, lean and weak, to the sea. In the middle of June Steller built a hide on an elevated part of a rookery and spent the next six days making concise, detailed notes in Latin. He found it quite impossible to assess the total numbers but he recorded the fighting between the harem masters and the remarkable ability of each mother to locate her own, black, big-eyed pup amongst the thousands of other bleating youngsters after she had been feeding offshore.

On 12 July 1742 he dissected a large female mannatee, the Steller's Sea Cow. While he tried to examine it, in cold rainy weather, "packs of most despicable Arctic foxes were tearing with their vile teeth and stealing everything from under my very hands, carrying off my paper, books and inkstand while I examined the animal, and ripping it while I was writing". As with the Spectacled Cormorant, he was the only naturalist to see them alive, watching them almost daily throughout his stay. They swam in family groups at the river mouths, continually browsing on seaweeds while gulls often perched on their backs. They were so unafraid of man that Steller was sometimes able to stroke them. Using a large iron hook, thrown from the ship's boat, the castaways succeeded in dragging some ashore to eat. Only twenty-six years later the species was extinct.

Back in April, the men had decided to break up the ship and build a smaller vessel. Though the three ship's carpenters had all died of scurvy, the new *St Peter* was sound and handled well. Because so many of the men were determined to take bundles of lucrative Sea Otter pelts with them, they imposed a baggage allowance on each individual, including Steller. Touchy at the best of times, he lost his temper, pleaded and coaxed, but was forced to abandon almost all of his priceless collection. He even had to leave the skin of a young sea cow (which he had painstakingly stuffed with dried grasses) and hundreds of other skins, skeletons and dried plants. When they at last set sail, on 13 August, he took only the horny palatal plates of one sea cow, some seeds and his precious manuscripts.

After only thirteen days at sea they sailed into Avatcha Bay where they learned that their sister ship the *St Paul* had reached the Alaskan coast near Sitka. Two small boats had been sent ashore but neither returned and both crews were presumed to have been killed by native Indians. The *St Paul* managed to return safely to Avatcha Bay and later spent some time searching for Bering, but had sailed for Okhotsk with the news that the *St Peter* was assumed lost only a month before Steller and the other survivors returned.

Within two days of landing, Steller set off on foot for Bolsheretsk, a hundred miles away over the mountains, where letters awaited him. He quickly sent his reports off to St Petersburg but he was in no hurry to return to civilization. Instead, he spent the next two years carrying out his original task of exploring the Kamchatka Peninsula. First he travelled to the southern tip and across to three of the Kuril Islands where he made observations on Sea Otter hunting by the natives. He then returned to Bolsheretsk where, as a result of a misunderstood order, seventeen natives were brought to him to be tried as rebels. He set them all free at once, but this act was later to have tragic consequences for him.

In July 1743 Steller and a Cossack set off northwards on foot for a thousand mile journey. Few details of this trip exist but he reached Olyutoria, north of Karaga Island and spent the winter with the natives having observed them hunting whales with nets in the shallow waters. On his return by dog-sled he lost his entire outfit in trying to dash across the frozen sea to Karaga Island, and only just escaped.

During 1744 the scattered members of the Second Kamchatka Expedition were recalled to St Petersburg. Steller sailed for Okhotsk in August, the voyage being uneventful though he did record that a Crested Auklet flew on board.

Steller's Eider

At Irkutsk he was charged with freeing the seventeen natives without authority but he was acquitted at once. Proceeding westwards he passed through the Ural Mountains in April 1746 and spent some time at the home of Gregorij Demidov, an amateur botanist and landowner with whom Steller was at last able to enthuse about his ideas and discoveries after years of scientific isolation. In May he left for St Petersburg but had not gone far when he returned to continue botanizing with Demidov and spent three enjoyable months exploring the forested mountains and valleys around Perm. Steller seems to have been in no hurry to return, perhaps realizing that his commitments in St Petersburg would severely curtail the freedom to which he had become accustomed.

On 15 August he and Demidov returned to Solikamsk, where Steller found himself under arrest by a courier from St Petersburg because news of his acquittal had not yet arrived there. He was given one day to prepare for the 2000 mile journey back to Irkutsk, during which Steller characteristically worried more about the fate of his collections rather than the fact that he was unprepared for winter travel. It was arranged that Demidov would take care of his live plants and Professor J. E. Fischer, who happened to be in Solikamsk at that time, agreed to take his specimens, papers and manuscripts on to St Petersburg. Steller had travelled a third of the way back to Irkutsk when a second courier caught up with them ordering the naturalist's release. Returning westwards again, Steller caught a fever but he insisted on travelling day and night. When he arrived at Tyumen on 14 November he was dying. Two naval surgeons who had been on the *St Paul* and who knew him well happened to be there and attended to him, but Steller died the same day, aged only thirty-seven.

A Lutheran clergyman wrapped the body in his own red mantle and buried him in a shallow grave, the ground being frozen hard, on a high bluff overlooking the River Tura. Several nights later the cloak was stolen and the body left lying in the snow, but friends reinterred him and placed a large stone on the grave. In December 1770 when Pallas was twenty-nine, he visited the site and correctly predicted that the high bluff would eventually be eroded by the river. Steller's widow re-married soon after the official report of his death was made public.

It was an ignominious end for one of the greatest explorer-naturalists of all time. Steller died before Linnaeus introduced the binomial system of classification and his discoveries have consequently been redescribed and renamed, serving to enhance the careers of several other naturalists (including Pallas). Steller was not just a collector of plants and animals: he was a most careful and accurate observer, with a broad concept of the geographical and environmental variation of plants, and there is evidence that he had his own ideas on evolution, in the Lamarckian sense. But for his untimely death, he would have been able to write far more about his ideas and discoveries. His *De Bestiis Marinis* was written in a hut on Bering Island under the most appalling conditions, yet few alterations needed to be made on his safe return to the mainland; his dissection and description of a Steller's Sea Cow remains a zoological classic. Among the birds named after him, he is most fittingly remembered by Steller's Eider, which then, as now, wintered in large numbers just off the shores of the island on which he was shipwrecked.

STURM. *GERMAN BIRD-ARTIST AND COLLECTOR.*

Johann Heinrich Christian Friedrich Sturm (1805-1862)

DWARF BITTERN *Ardeirallus sturmii* (Wagler)

Ardea Sturmii Wagler, 1827. *Systema Avium, Ardea*, No. 37: Senegambia

Sturm was born in Nuremberg on 6 February 1805 and he died in the same city, fifty-seven years later, having rarely left the environs of his home town. And yet Sturm was known throughout the world, honoured by both German and foreign societies for his contribution to ornithology: not for any thorough investigation of the biology, distribution or habits of birds, nor for any extensive revision of classification but chiefly for his remarkable qualities as a bird illustrator.

He belonged to a talented family, exceeding both his father and younger brother in their artistic skills. Trained at art school from the age of fifteen until he was twenty-three, he had a broad interest in natural history which included the study of zoology, keeping pigeons, hunting and adding to the famous museum of natural history which he founded at Nuremberg. To begin with he helped his father, Jakob, to illustrate books on zoology, and even though his father encouraged him towards entomology and botany he became more and more attracted to ornithology, whenever possible drawing only from living specimens. Between 1829 and 1834, together with his brother Johann Willhelm, he produced eighteen copper engravings of birds for *Deutschlands Fauna* [German

Dwarf Bittern

Fauna]; the short but adequate text was partly written by Joann Wagler and Karl Michahelles. Another notable work by Sturm was a series of thirty-eight engravings carried out between 1841 and 1847 for a German edition of John Gould's *Monograph on the Rhamphastides, or Family of Toucans*. Sturm later made some new engravings, and re-did a few original drawings, for a supplement to J. F. Naumann's *Naturgeschichte der Vögel Deutschlands* [Natural History of German Birds] (1860).

Sturm continued working until 1857, his birds becoming more lifelike with each subsequent commission. After his death, on 24 January 1862, his bird collection went to the State of Bavaria and was housed at Munich but was destroyed in the Second World War. Sturm's life was not without personal tragedy as his two children, both daughters, each died at an early age, and his good friend Wagler also died prematurely, under tragic circumstances. While out collecting birds he accidentally shot himself in the arm. It was only a small wound but blood poisoning set in and the arm was not amputated in time to prevent his death. It was Wagler who gave the Dwarf Bittern the complimentary name of *Ardea Sturmii*, from a specimen in the Sturm collection originally from Senegambia. The only record of the species occurring in the Palearctic was on Tenerife in 1889–90,[1] but considering the shy and secretive nature of these birds and the paucity of observers along the northern extent of its range, from Senegal and Nigeria to Chad and Ethiopia, it may well have occurred more often.

William Swainson
(1789-1855)

SWAINSON'S THRUSH *Catharus ustulatus* (Nuttall)

Turdus ustulatus Nuttall, 1840. *Manual of the Ornithology of the United States and Canada*, 2nd edn, Vol. 1, p. vi, 400: Fort Vancouver, Washington

Swainson's Thrush is a rare vagrant to the Western Palearctic from North America, where it is sometimes known as the Olive-backed Thrush, a vague descriptive name which fails to distinguish it from a number of similar close relatives. Called Little Tawny Thrush by William Swainson in 1831, from specimens collected in the boreal forests of Saskatchewan, it was re-named by Thomas Nuttall a few years later. Swainson's Hawk and Swainson's Warbler are two other North American species that perpetuate the name of this naturalist and artist whose main connections with that continent (which he never visited) were his important contributions to the *Fauna Boreali-Americana* (1829–37) and his friendship with John James Audubon.

In his native land of England, Swainson is remembered primarily as an early bird illustrator. He was one of the first to develop the new technique of lithography, a process which involved drawing directly onto the stone which did away with the requirements of an intermediate professional engraver. Swainson's illustrations, which were accurate and skilful representations, preceded the productions of John Gould whose *Birds of Europe* (1832–37) and *The Birds of Britain* (1862–73) contain some of the finest early examples of lithography.

Throughout his life, William Swainson was interested in various aspects of natural history but he managed to concentrate all his major ornithological work into a space of twenty years. As a boy he sketched and studied his father's shell collection and longed to visit tropical regions. His father, who lived at Hoylake in Cheshire, was a high-ranking official in the Liverpool Customs and at fourteen years of age William was employed there as a junior clerk. After four years his father obtained a position for him in the commissariat, with the army stationed in the eastern Mediterranean, and Swainson remained there for the next eight years from 1807 until 1815, most of the time based on Sicily. On his annual leave of six weeks he visited Greece or parts of Italy and at other times was stationed at Genoa and Malta.

Although the Napoleonic Wars were raging through much of Europe, the Sicilian garrison was not on active service and Swainson had ample time to

SWAINSON. *ENGLISH NATURALIST AND ARTIST WHO SPENT SOME OF HIS EARLY YEARS IN THE CENTRAL MEDITERRANEAN REGION, AND MADE A SHORT EXPEDITION TO BRAZIL. WELL KNOWN IN HIS DAY AS A PRODUCTIVE AUTHOR, HIS BOOKS OFTEN GIVE VALUABLE INSIGHTS INTO THE DEVELOPMENT OF NATURAL HISTORY IN THE EARLY NINETEENTH CENTURY. HE WAS ONE OF THE FIRST BIRD ILLUSTRATORS TO USE LITHOGRAPHY.*

pursue his own interests and was able to collect and draw plants, insects, shells and fishes. Whilst on Malta, plague broke out, and he was confined by the authorities to his house for two months; while all around seemed to be dying Swainson put the time to good use by working on his sketches from Sicily and Greece. He went back to Palermo, on Sicily, in 1814, but in the following year when peace came he returned to England with his collections because his health had deteriorated. He retired from the service on half pay and lived with his father at Liverpool for about a year. His mother had died many years before when he was very young.

Swainson found it difficult to fit into English society again and in the autumn of 1816 he planned a voyage to Brazil. He tried without success to secure some financial support from various museums and horticultural bodies, and so he set off under his own modest means. He landed at Recife at the end of December but just as he was preparing for a trip inland, a revolution broke out and he was forced to confine his collecting to nearby areas; it was no hardship as even the immediate vicinity had never been explored by naturalists and was rich in new plants and birds. Eventually, in June, he headed into the interior with a small party towards the Rio San Francisco and then followed the river down to the sea and took a boat to San Salvador, where he arrived in August. He explored the coastal region there very thoroughly and then headed inland again until March, all the while collecting and sketching. In April he sailed to Rio de Janeiro, chiefly to compare it with the areas he had already visited rather than to search for more new specimens, as the south had already been well explored. Indeed, when he arrived at Rio he met a number of European naturalists.

Swainson returned to England in August 1818 with a collection of over 20,000 insects, plants of more than 1200 species, and drawings of 120 species of fish, with the smaller fish preserved in spirit. He had also acquired about 760 bird skins, a good proportion of them humming-birds and toucans.

In 1819 he wrote a very brief account of his Brazilian travels which appeared in the first volume of the *Edinburgh Philosophical Journal*. It was not Swainson's first publication. When he was eighteen, before he left for the Mediterranean, he drew up at the request of the Liverpool Museum, *Instructions for Collecting and Preserving Subjects of Natural History* which was later expanded into his *Naturalist's Guide* (1822).

After returning from South America Swainson based himself in London and, on the suggestion of his friend William Leach, he began to investigate the technique of lithography. For three years he worked so hard learning the process that he claimed to have lived like a hermit. Between 1820 and 1823, although there were a number of technical problems, he produced three volumes of *Zoological Illustrations*, which contained 182 plates all drawn, printed and hand coloured by himself; it was probably his finest illustrative work. In 1822 he also managed to bring out *Exotic Conchology, or Coloured Lithographic Drawings of Shells*.

When Leach was forced to resign his position as Assistant Keeper at the British Museum because of illness, Swainson quickly applied for the vacancy, but despite letters of recommendation from Cuvier, Hooker and a number of other eminent naturalists, his application was rejected. The post was filled by

J. G. Children, a physicist by training and inclination who happened to have the more influential support of Sir Humphrey Davy. Children's appointment was a set-back for ornithology only rectified by his retirement in 1840, when J. E. Gray took over. Swainson himself may not have been the ideal candidate because he lacked scientific training but on the practical side he was extremely well qualified. At the beginning of the nineteenth century, museums displayed nearly all their bird specimens fully mounted in sealed cases, which meant that they could only be examined through glass. Sometimes birds were mounted on perches which could be slotted in and out of large open cases but both these methods took up a vast amount of space. William Swainson was among the first to adopt the now standard alternative. In 1836 he wrote:

> "The last and best method of arranging birds is by leaving them, as it is technically called, 'in their skins'. It is now twenty years since we [Swainson] began this plan, to the great surprise and disapprobation of our scientific friends; but the practice has now become almost general. It is simply arranging the birds in drawers . . . and he may by this means have them compactly, and even beautifully, arranged in his library or drawing room, without any risk of the plumage being injured by the light . . . and ready, with a moments trouble, to be handled and examined. To each specimen a strip of cord is attached, with the name etc., written thereon, and tucked beneath the wing."[1]

Swainson urged that the tags should record the original colour of the soft parts and of the plumage, the sex, and details of where the skin had been collected or where further information could be obtained, such as in field notebooks. Once this had all become the normal procedure, museums quickly changed from being mainly public displays and began their long career as storehouses of scientific records.

In 1825, after five years in London, Swainson married the only daughter of John Parkes and went to live with his father-in-law in Warwick. When his own father died and left him less money than he had expected, Swainson decided to become a full-time artist and author. He moved with his wife to Tittenhanger Green in Hampshire and for the next ten years he worked almost unceasingly on his various publications.

Swainson's Thrush

The most influential of these ornithological works was Richardson and Swainson's second volume of the *Fauna Boreali-Americana; or the Zoology of the Northern Parts of British America* (1831). Dr John Richardson, who had twice accompanied Franklin on his overland travels through Canada to the Arctic coast, wrote the specific descriptions; Swainson wrote the greater part of the letterpress and provided all the illustrations. When combined with the other volumes on the mammals, fish and insects (and as a companion to W. J. Hooker's *Flora Boreali-Americana* (1833–40)), it was part of a monumental investigation of lasting importance, contributing greatly to the study of Arctic biology.

To cope with the increasing amount of work Swainson and his family moved to St Albans to be nearer to the London publishers. Swainson brought out a second series of *Zoological Illustrations* (1832–33) and in 1834 a small pictorial book, without text, on *The Birds of Brazil and Mexico*; all but ten of the seventy-eight plates depicting Brazilian species. This last publication contrasted sharply with the lavish productions of Audubon who was still using an engraver and with whom Swainson had earlier become associated. In 1828 Swainson and his wife had accompanied Audubon on an eight-week visit to Paris and there was a proposal that the two artists work together, but the project came to naught. Ten years later Bonaparte invited Swainson to Italy so that they could collaborate on a catalogue of all the birds then known, and although Swainson at first agreed, this idea also had to be abandoned.

Meanwhile, Swainson busied himself by contributing eleven volumes to Lardner's *Cabinet Cyclopaedia* which were published between the years 1834 and 1840. During this period Swainson's wife suddenly died and he was left with five children to bring up. He felt the loss of his wife deeply but continued to produce more ornithological literature, contributing three volumes to William Jardine's *Naturalist's Library*; two on the *Birds of Western Africa* (1837) and another on *The Natural Arrangement and History of Flycatchers* (1838).

But by now Swainson wanted a complete change. He had made little profit from his books and in 1837 had lost money by speculating in Mexican silver mines. He decided to sell the bulk of his collections to Cambridge and after two years had increased his funds sufficiently to be able to buy three 100-acre plots of land in New Zealand. His last volume of the *Cabinet Cyclopaedia* entitled *Taxidermy: with the Biographies of Zoologists* appeared in 1840 and contained an autobiographical sketch of his life almost up to the time that he set sail for New Zealand with his new wife, Anne Grasby of Yorkshire.

When they arrived at Wellington in June 1841 the Swainson family established themselves on their estate and Swainson planted a number of trees, shrubs and plants which he had acquired when their ship had called at Brazil. Unfortunately it was not the ideal new start in life that he had hoped for. The Maori chief Taringa Kuri objected to the European invasion and started to fell trees and cultivate some of the newly purchased land, virtually making Swainson a prisoner who now lived in constant dread of an attack by Maoris. Swainson joined the local militia but there was little progress made in his favour for a number of years. He never published any more bird work, but between 1841 and 1849 he completed a series of sketches of Wellington and the Hutt River valley region where he lived. He did, however, render assistance and instruction to a young ornithologist, [Sir] Walter Buller, one of New Zealand's greatest early naturalists and author of a *History of the Birds of New Zealand* (1873).

William Swainson died on 6 December 1855, at Lower Hutt, after only fourteen years in the country. He was survived by his wife and his children. Almost fifty years later one of his daughters sold Swainson's collection of correspondence to the Linnean Society of London. Only fifteen of the letters are by Swainson himself; the rest were written by an astonishing variety of naturalists. There are more by Rafinesque Schmaltz (a friend from his days in Palermo) than by any other person; others are from well-known naturalists of the period including Audubon, Bonaparte, Bullock, Richardson, Rüppell, Waterton and Yarrell, and are chiefly about proposed publications, books that were already being compiled or the exchange of specimens; yet others are from lesser known individuals such as the Reverend James Bulwer, a fellow shell-enthusiast.

Robert Swinhoe
(1836-1877)

SWINHOE'S STORM-PETREL *Oceanodroma monorhis*
(Swinhoe)

Thalassidroma monorhis Swinhoe, 1867. *Ibis*, p. 386: near Amoy

SWINHOE'S SNIPE *Gallinago megala* Swinhoe

Gallinago megala Swinhoe, 1861. *Ibis*, p. 343: between Taku and Peking

Robert Swinhoe was born in Calcutta and educated in England, but, like Père Armand David, he will always be remembered as one of China's pioneer naturalists. For twenty years he worked in the British Consular Service and devoted all his spare moments to studying the Chinese flora and fauna. In 1863 he compiled the first checklist of Chinese birds and his revised list of 1871 increased the number of known species from 454 to 675. This was achieved despite frequent ill health and partial paralysis which developed in his mid-thirties.

At the age of eighteen he sailed out to Hong Kong where he was appointed as a supernumerary interpreter, and the following year, in 1855, he was transferred to the Consulate on Amoy, a barren island in the shelter of a huge bay on the coast of Fukien. His first scientific paper, 'Remarks on the Fauna of Amoy', published in *The Zoologist* in 1858, was succeeded by a lifelong flow of reports on the habits and distribution of the birds and mammals of the Chinese littoral, frequently interspersed with descriptions of newly discovered species. That same year he also began his study of the natural history of Formosa (Taiwan), making two visits to the mountainous, tropical island.

Early in 1860 he was granted three months leave and went down the coast to explore the environs of Hong Kong, Macao and Canton, an ornithological account of which appeared in *The Ibis* the next year. Swinhoe was nearing the end of his leave, rambling through the narrow painted and gilded streets of Canton, inspecting its old yamens and pagodas, when he was ordered to immediately join the forces assembling in Hong Kong, as the staff interpreter to General Napier and Sir Hope Grant. The combined English and French fleet sailed northwards in June, and in early August the troops, with all their auxiliary services, landed in heavy rain on the coast nearest to Peking.

SWINHOE. *DEDICATED ENGLISH NATURALIST WHO SERVED IN THE BRITISH CONSULAR SERVICE IN CHINA AND FORMOSA FOR TWENTY YEARS. DESPITE A CRIPPLING ILLNESS, HE PIONEERED THE ORNITHOLOGY OF THESE REGIONS AND ACCUMULATED A LARGE AND IMPORTANT BIRD COLLECTION.*

On the 12th they were attacked by six or seven thousand Tartars, who fought courageously on horseback with bows and arrows, spears and a few matchlocks, but they were easily defeated by the well-armed European army of twice their strength. The forts at Taku were soon taken, and the armies turned inland towards Tiensin. During these warm, September days, Swinhoe noted thousands of Sand Martins, Swallows and Red-rumped Swallows swarming above the camps, where every tent was blackened inside by insects. When they reached the town, he was surprised to find baskets and baskets of Lapland Buntings for sale, all plucked and trussed. He persuaded a hunter to bring him some feathered specimens, and bought two dozen; but he found that travelling with an army afforded few opportunities for collecting. The success of the North China Campaign was assured when Peking surrendered peacefully, the Emperor having fled. By the Treaty of Tiensin, Kowloon was ceded to the British and numerous other privileges were granted which greatly increased the trading opportunities.

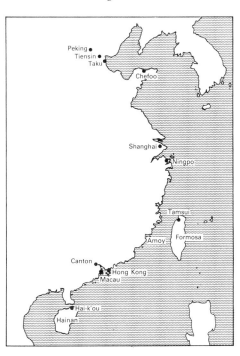

COASTAL CHINA

Soon after his return to Amoy, Swinhoe was appointed Vice-Consul in Formosa and was the first foreign, diplomatic officer to be stationed there. He arrived in January 1861, at the age of twenty-four, and during that year the Consulate moved from town to temple to steamer, finally being established in an old Spanish fort in Tamsui. In November Swinhoe took ill and had to return to Amoy for treatment and rest, but he returned a month later and began to travel extensively over the island, taking an interest in the mammals, fish, molluscs, insects and plants, as well as the birds, regularly sending notes and specimens to the British Museum. In the winter he frequently visited the markets to inspect the many species on sale there; teal, for example, were sold alive, after being caught in nets at dusk as they flew into specially cleared patches of open water among the reedy lagoons.

In May he became ill again and returned to England. He remained in London until the autumn of the following year, being elected an Honorary Fellow of King's College, London, and an Honorary Member of the British Ornithologists' Union.

He sailed back to Formosa via Egypt, Bombay and Ceylon, arriving at Tamsui on 31 January 1864. He built an aviary there and chiefly stocked it with the rare, endemic Swinhoe's Pheasant. This splendid bird was not easily procured, for they only inhabit the mountain forests of the interior, and Swinhoe's best collector was on one occasion robbed of £50 and nearly murdered while in search of it. Another Formosan bird which Swinhoe discovered was the Whistling Green Pigeon. The first specimen, which was brought to him in 1861, was a female, and for the next few years he naturally looked forward to acquiring a male. At last, in 1865, a Chinese sportsman shot one just a few miles from Tamsui and presented it to Swinhoe—neatly plucked! Fortunately, one of Swinhoe's own collectors brought him a perfect male specimen just a month later, so that he was able to examine and describe the lovely grassy-green head and neck, the maroon shoulder patch and the soft greens and greys of the rest of the plumage.

It was then comparatively easy for an ornithologist to make original discoveries in places such as Formosa which had hardly ever been visited by Europeans with any knowledge of natural history. The isolation from western scientific circles was also, of course, a disadvantage, and made correspondence with other naturalists essential. Swinhoe kept in touch with Père David, the missionary and naturalist who made enormous contributions to our knowledge of interior China, as well as Edward Blyth at Calcutta. When Swinhoe found the new species of snipe now named after him, he sent it to Blyth, noting that it was almost identical to the Great Snipe, but that it had a different number of tail feathers. The snipe were so similar that when Blyth wrote back, he expressed the opinion that the birds were of the same species.

Swinhoe's Storm-petrel

Swinhoe also had to contend with disasters which rarely befell his colleagues in Great Britain. In October 1865 he wrote:

"I have been very unfortunate with regard to my scientific books. The two closing numbers of 'The Ibis' for 1864 went down with the mail-steamer in a typhoon; and some other works have since been carried off by pirates on the capture of a schooner bound from Amoy to this port with the mails."[1]

He left Formosa the following May after being appointed H.M. Consul at Amoy, a post which lasted for several years. As usual he went collecting whenever possible, and on 11 November 1866 he was out on the river below Chang-chou, a town on the mainland near Amoy. As it was high tide the marshes were covered and a strong north-east wind was blowing, raising choppy waves which rocked the boat and spoilt his aim as he tried to shoot some of the wild and wary ducks which were feeding in the shallows. A small black bird skimming over the water caught his attention, and he realized immediately that it was a petrel, the first that he had seen in China. As it flew closer he fired twice, but missed each time. Unalarmed, it settled on the surface near him, and "a charge of dust fetched it". The body was a nearly uniform sooty colour, and exuded a strong, musky odour. Later, on dissection, he found it to be a female with well-developed follicles in the ovary. This bird provided the first description of Swinhoe's Storm-petrel which breeds on small, uninhabited islets off the coasts of Japan, Korea and Shantung. (The only one known to have reached the Western Palearctic was found exhausted at Elat, Israel, in January 1958.)

After Swinhoe's red-letter day, the next was something of an anticlimax, although the wind had dropped and birds abounded. As he rowed downstream against the tide, Lapwings flew by in small flocks above the ploughed fields and Pied Kingfishers hovered over the river. He later wrote:

> "Commenced war again against the wildfowl . . . Thousands of Ducks and Geese were floating lazily on the mirror-like expanse, waiting for the outflow, rising in flights with a rushing sound of wings as my small boat came slowly towards them. My head felt dizzy in trying to think out the different species that dotted the water before me. I observed a small group of pied birds floating in a clump. Not Sheldrakes, for two or three genuine Sheldrakes are paddling not far from them! Mergus albellus? [Smew] Too close together! Must be a novelty in the Duck line! My heart throbs with excitement. A few strokes more, and my cartridge can reach them. The Ducks keep on fluttering away on all sides; but the pied group still remain. I fire; one pied fellow remains motionless, the rest, seven or eight in number, stream away with what speed they can, which is not much. As they rise I note the long legs and curved bill, and am annoyed to find that my new Duck is only an Avocet!"[2]

During 1868 his work necessitated frequent travel and in the spring he spent two months at Hainan investigating the commercial opportunities of the island, with a view to establishing a port there for European trade. He was sent on the gunboat *Algerine* and the Captain had orders to hunt out local pirates. As Swinhoe had been given permission to spend his leisure time pursuing the local fauna he found his armed companions to be a great help when they were ashore together. In all he collected 172 different species of birds there, nineteen of which were new to science.

From the capital, now Hai-k'ou, Swinhoe embarked for the interior in a flat-bottomed boat with chairs and bearers and spent the next week, between visits to villages, in pursuit of the forest birds. The accompanying mandarin was

Swinhoe's Snipe

greatly bewildered by this strange occupation, and followed him on all his rambles, from time to time offering tea, cakes, pipe and a stool to sit on.

Swinhoe rejoined the gunboat early in March and soon afterwards they captured and burned a pirate junk, whose crew escaped ashore. A few days later they chased two vessels and took thirty-three prisoners. After handing the pirates over to the authorities they sailed back up the west coast, frequently making trips ashore, visiting, feasting and exploring.

In the summer of 1869 Swinhoe journeyed back to England by way of Japan, California and the North Pacific Railway, but less than two years later he was again in China, further north than before, serving as H.M. Consul at Ningpo. The bird life of the plains was unremarkable but he found the inland hills teeming with new and interesting species.

Sadly, it was during this time that he became partially paralysed, and was relieved of his charge. Chefoo being recognized as the healthiest station, he was directed there early in 1873 but because Chefoo harbour was frozen that winter Swinhoe spent February, March and early April in Shanghai, where he was able to get about in a type of wheelbarrow and visited the market every alternate day. In this manner he was still able to learn about the local ducks and waders; Mallard, Wigeon, Pintail, Teal, Shoveler, Goldeneye, Scaup and Baer's Pochard were for sale in large numbers and Mandarin Ducks could usually be purchased alive. On the 16 April Swinhoe toured the dealers' shops as usual. Searching among the many baskets of Knot, Great Knot and Bar-tailed Godwits he was delighted to find a brace of Terek Sandpipers, several Sharp-tailed Sandpipers, two Lesser Sand Plovers and, to his great joy, two Spoon-billed Sandpipers.[3]

A week later he at last left for Chefoo, arriving before the summer migrants. He immediately realized that a string of small offshore islands would be attractive to birds on passage and he enlisted the help of the lighthouse keeper, who sent him Kestrel, Oystercatcher, Pechora Pipit and many other species. Despite his paralysis, Swinhoe became familiar with the district by travelling in a sedan chair through the nearby woods and lower slopes of the hills, where Yellow-browed Warblers, Magpies and Azure-winged Magpies were common. The government buildings were pleasantly situated on a hill forming one side of the small inner harbour, but, even so, Swinhoe found the summer to be insufferably hot and the winter so bitter that he left in October and returned the next spring. In 1875 he became physically unable to carry out his duties and in October he left China for the last time and returned to London.

He took up residence in Chelsea and during the last two years of his life he enjoyed the frequent contact with his fellow naturalists and continued to work unceasingly on his own collections, as well as those sent to him from Asia. He died on 28 October 1877 at the age of only forty-one. The following year his invaluable collection of 3700 skins which included 650 species and 200 types was declined by the British Museum. Luckily, most of it was belatedly deposited there as part of the Henry Seebohm collection.

Swinhoe's brother, Charles, was also an outstanding naturalist. Several years after Robert's death he sent contributions to *The Ibis* on the birds of southern Afghanistan and central India, and also donated 300 bird skins from each of those countries to the British Museum. His main interests were butterflies and moths, and in the course of his career in the Bombay Staff Corps, Colonel Swinhoe built up one of the largest and most comprehensive collections of Indian lepidoptera then in existence.[4]

TEMMINCK. *DUTCH ORNITHOLOGIST AND LONG-SERVING FIRST DIRECTOR OF THE LEYDEN NATURAL HISTORY MUSEUM. HE WAS THE AUTHOR OF SOME VERY IMPORTANT EARLY BOOKS ON BIRDS, ESPECIALLY THE* MANUEL D'ORNITHOLOGIE.

Coenraad Jacob Temminck (1778-1858)

TEMMINCK'S STINT *Calidris temminckii* (Leisler)

Tringa Temminckii Leisler, 1812. *Nachträge zu Bechstein's Naturgeschichte Deutschlands*, p. 64: near Hanau am Main, Germany

TEMMINCK'S HORNED LARK *Eremophila bilopha* (Temminck)

Alauda bilopha Temminck, 1823. In C. J. Temminck and M. Laugier, *Nouveau Recueil de Planches coloriées d'Oiseaux*, Pt 41, Pl. 244, Fig. 1: Aqaba

When Professor Temminck died he was said to have achieved his life's ambition: under almost forty years of his direction the Natural History Museum at Leyden had developed into one of the finest in the world, equal to those at Paris, London, Berlin and Philadelphia, and in many ways surpassing them in its systems of arrangement and quantity of material.

Coenraad Jacob Temminck was born at Amsterdam on 31 March 1778. He had no early scientific training and at the age of seventeen became an auctioneer with the Dutch East India Company, of which his father was the Treasurer. Several factors then combined to help him towards the career that he was later to adopt. Temminck's father had helped François Levaillant, the French explorer of southern Africa, in his production of *Histoire naturelle des oiseaux d'Afrique* (1796–1808) and he had acquired a number of Levaillant's specimens which the young Temminck was able to examine and study. Through his contact with Levaillant and other collector-friends of his father, many of whom also possessed exotic menageries, Temminck absorbed a great deal of information about birds and mammals, and soon learnt to speak and write in French, then one of the principal languages of science. In addition, through his own activities as an auctioneer he met seafaring men from all over the world who later proved to be useful contacts as his passion for collecting developed.

With the dissolution of the East India Company in 1800 Temminck decided to devote himself entirely to natural history and his home in Amsterdam soon became almost filled with specimens. In April 1804, together with his young wife, he went to stay for six months with Bernhard Meyer of Offenbach from whom he gained both theoretical and practical instruction, becoming a skilled taxidermist of birds and more especially of fish. Temminck also became a good friend of Dr J. P. A. Leisler who was a regular visitor to the Meyer household. This friendship was commemorated in 1812 when Leisler obtained a small, newly identified wader from Hanau am Main and named it *Tringa Temminckii*.

Two years after his return to Holland Temminck published a *Catalogue systématique du cabinet d'ornithologie et de la collection de Quadrumanes* (1807). It contained a detailed list of the thousand or so bird species in his collection, many of which were from his father and Levaillant, plus some others from Leschenault de la Tour.

Through no fault of his own, Temminck's next work had a stormy and controversial beginning. He wrote the text for the first volume of *Histoire naturelle générale des Pigeons* (1808–11) which was illustrated by the accomplished artist Madame Knip and which was to be issued in fifteen parts. Unknown to Temminck, from the ninth part onwards, Madame Knip made a number of alterations, suppressed Temminck's introduction and index, and made herself the principal author. He did not discover that the format had been changed for some time because he had been given eight copies of the work as it should have been printed. Temminck's belated protests were ineffectual and so, between 1813 and 1815 he produced his own version: *Histoire naturelle générale des Pigeons et des Gallinacées*. The first volume contained the same text as the 1808 work while the second two volumes on the Gallinaceous birds were entirely

Temminck's Stint

new; together they established him as the leading Dutch ornithologist and one of the most promising in Europe. He was honoured with the Order of Union by King Louis, the brother of Napoleon, who had been created ruler of Holland after its French occupation. Following the Battle of Waterloo the country once more became a free nation but in the troubled times afterwards Temminck took up arms and for a while served as a captain of a volunteer corps of cavalry, without seemingly neglecting his studies.

After a period as Director of the Academy of Science and Arts at Haarlem, just west of Amsterdam, he moved southwards in 1820 to the newly completed museum at Leyden and became its first director. From the 12 January 1822, by royal decree, the state subsidies formerly paid to Amsterdam were transferred to Leyden and it thus became the Dutch National Museum of Natural History; Temminck's own huge collection being conveyed there in 1823. Under his direction the museum rapidly grew in importance, not only because of the increasing number and quality of its specimens and their systems of arrangement but also because his influential publications served to enhance its reputation.

In 1815 he had issued his famous *Manuel d'Ornithologie, ou Tableau systématique des Oiseaux qui se trouve en Europe*, and this was later expanded into four parts, issued between 1820 and 1840. In part one he also gave a detailed classification of the birds of the world and although not simple it was adopted by naturalists in many countries. More importantly the work gave good descriptions of the birds, detailed remarks on their habits, plumage variations and geographical distribution as far as it was then known. There was also a list of synonyms for each species, an indispensable addition in those early days of ornithology when some species could boast a dozen names or more. As an all-embracing work on European birds it was not superseded until the publication of Dresser's magnificent *The Birds of Europe* (1871–81).

At the same time as Temminck was working on the *Manuel d'Ornithologie* he was also collaborating with Baron Meiffren Laugier de Chartrouse on their *Nouveau Recueil de Planches coloriées d'Oiseaux* (1820–39). Whereas the former work was small and spartan, the latter was a huge-format, luxurious and very expensive production with over 600 coloured plates depicting about 800 bird species. Issued in 102 parts, Temminck is credited with all of the scientific material and all of the nomenclature but although widely acclaimed, later generations of ornithologists found the text to be meagre, and, apart from the physical descriptions of the birds, it was sadly lacking in other information about them. Many new species, from various parts of the world, were first illustrated in the work and one such species was later called Temminck's Horned Lark; it had originally been obtained by Rüppell, near Aqaba, the specimens reaching Temminck via Dr Cretzschmar of the Senckenberg Museum in Frankfurt.

Although much of Temminck's time was taken up with writing and taxidermy, his life was not, as might be supposed, an entirely sedentary one. In 1816 he wrote to J. F. Naumann saying, "I am the one who mounts all the birds, fish, and quadrupeds; in search of one or the other I vary my trips, sometimes by the seashore, or beside our lakes, or near our swamps . . ." Moreover, in 1817, in a special carriage which was adapted for carrying bird skins, he and his wife set out on a tour of Europe. After visiting Offenbach and Stuttgart they made their way to Lausanne to spend the winter with Temminck's ageing father. They then travelled down to Turin to visit Bonelli, went north again to the Italian lakes, eastwards to the Dalmatian coast and then up to the Hungarian marshes. As they returned homewards at the end of 1818, they called upon Johann Natterer, Hinrich Lichtenstein, K. A. Rudolphi, J. F. Naumann and several other leading naturalists.

Temminck's Horned Lark

Between 1844 and 1850, in association with his colleague Hermann Schlegel, Temminck contributed to the mammalian sections of Philipp von Siebold's twelve-part *Fauna Japonica*, excellently illustrated by Joseph Wolf. Siebold, a German aristocrat, sent most of his botanical collections from the Far East to Leyden which then boasted the finest botanical garden in Europe; his most important book was the *Flora Japonica*. Many years earlier Temminck had been involved with the works of another naturalist known primarily as a botanist. On a visit to London in 1819 he studied some parrot and pigeon skins that had been collected by the Scottish botanist Robert Brown during Flinders's exploration of the Australian coast. Temminck later contributed 'An Account of some new Species of Birds of the genera *Psittacus* and *Columba* in the Museum of the Linnean Society', to the *Transactions* of that same society.

Many Dutch and foreign societies bestowed their honours upon him and his success was aided by his robust bodily health and powerful mental capabilities both of which he retained until the last year of his life. In time he became increasingly unable to cope single-handedly with the number of collections sent to him, yet jealously prevented his assistants from handling some of the ornithological and mammalian material, allowing them only to study the fish and amphibians. Much of the material from the Dutch East Indies, often originally collected there under Temminck's instigation, suffered in this way.

The last occasion on which he left his home at Lisse was to make a visit to the museum to which he had devoted almost half his life. He died on 30 January 1858, and was survived by his third wife and three sons. Afterwards Hermann Schlegel was named Director of the Leyden Museum, with Professor van der Hoevan as over-Director, but on the latter's resignation two years later, Schlegel became the sole Director; for the next twenty-four years he ably filled the gap left by Temminck.

Pehr Gustaf Tengmalm (1754-1803)

TENGMALM'S OWL *Aegolius funereus* (Linnaeus)

Strix funerea Linnaeus, 1758. *Systema Naturae*, 10th edn, p. 93: Sweden

Tengmalm was born in Stockholm on 29 June 1754, and although his parents were poor they made every effort to educate him well. At the age of eighteen he was sent to Uppsala to study medicine at the University. He lodged with his uncle and in his spare time he worked as a tutor to some of the wealthiest families there, acquiring polished manners as well as financing his education. Despite the demands of studying and teaching he found time for ornithology and became an accomplished and unusually progressive taxidermist, taking great care to mount his specimens in life-like postures. Whenever he could, he made excursions into the surrounding low-lying countryside, where he studied Tawny Owls and Red-backed Shrikes in particular, and published his observations in the Transactions of the Swedish Academy of Science in 1781 and 1782.

When he received his degree in 1785 he moved to the town of Eskilstuna, about fifty miles west of Stockholm, where he worked for the next seven years as the provincial medical officer. During this time he economized until he had saved sufficient funds to give up his post and travel abroad. He visited Scotland and England where he met various naturalists, including Sir Joseph Banks, and he returned to Stockholm in 1793.

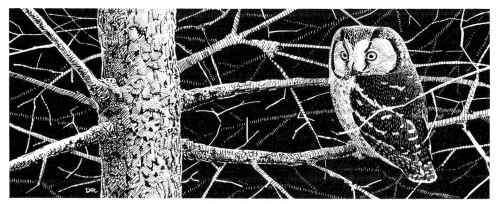

Tengmalm's Owl

*TENGMALM. SWEDISH MEDICAL OFFICER WHO WAS INTER-
ESTED IN ORNITHOLOGY AND TAXIDERMY.*

He then became the medical officer for the district of Västmanland, a lowland area with shallow lakes and reedbeds, where he was able to study many of the water birds, concentrating mainly upon the grebes. He contributed several more papers, of high quality, concerning both medicine and ornithology to the Transactions of the Swedish Academy and was made a member of the Academy in 1797.

Tengmalm became highly regarded as a trustworthy and attentive doctor, but sadly, while attending to his patients as an epidemic of dysentery scoured the countryside, he contracted the disease himself and succumbed on 27 August 1803 at the age of forty-nine. He had never married.

Tengmalm's Owl is a small nocturnal owl of the northern coniferous forests, with a circumboreal distribution. In the Scandinavian languages it is called the 'Pearly Owl' because of the white spangling over the rich chocolate-brown upperparts and wings. This descriptive name is rather more appropriate than the eponym, for although J. F. Gmelin named the owl *Strix Tengmalmi* in 1788 believing that Tengmalm had been the first to distinguish it, this has since been disproved. Some time before 1746, Professor Olof Rudbeck of Uppsala prepared some coloured plates of the owl and sent them to Linnaeus who therefore knew of the owl before Tengmalm was even born; but Gmelin's specific name was used for so many years that the bird is still known as Tengmalm's Owl in English, French and Spanish.

As Tengmalm was particularly interested in all the Swedish owls he well deserves to be remembered for his pioneer studies: he simplified and improved upon Linnaeus's rather complex owl classification in his paper *Utkast til uggelslägtets, i synnerhet de svenska arternas, naturalhistoria* [A natural history of some of the owls, especially the Swedish species], published in two parts in the Transactions of the Academy in 1793.

TICKELL. *BRITISH ARMY OFFICER WHO SERVED IN INDIA AND BURMA. HE WAS AN INDUSTRIOUS FIELD ORNITHOLOGIST, AUTHOR AND ARTIST; BUT THE BULK OF HIS BIRD PAINTINGS WERE NEVER PUBLISHED.*

Samuel Richard Tickell (1811-1875)

TICKELL'S THRUSH *Turdus unicolor* Tickell

T[urdus] Unicolor T[ickell], 1833. *Journal of the Asiatic Society of Bengal* 2, p. 576: Borabhum and Dholbhum [Bengal]

Each spring, all along the foothills of the Himalayas up to about 7000 ft, the ashy-grey Tickell's Thrush pours forth its Blackbird-like song, often from the very summit of the forest trees. They generally nest in open deciduous woodland, groves, gardens and orchards, usually in the fork of a tree from six to twenty feet above the ground. At the end of the breeding season they move lower down the mountains and most winter in Bangladesh, Orissa and Bengal and indeed the species was first discovered and described by Tickell from a specimen wintering in west Bengal. Other birds winter regularly on the other side of the Indian continent in northern Baluchistan but it is only an accidental visitor to the Western Palearctic.

Several species in the Indian avifauna bear the name of Tickell including Tickell's Babbler, Tickell's Flowerpecker, Tickell's Leaf Warbler and Tickell's Redbreasted Blue Flycatcher, and at one time the whole genus of flycatcher-warblers was known as the 'Tickellia'. Although Samuel Tickell is not ranked alongside those three great early ornithologists of India; Jerdon, Blyth and Hodgson who were his contemporaries, Tickell nevertheless made his own significant contribution. He wrote ornithological papers, he discovered many new species and races, he often sent specimens to Edward Blyth at Calcutta[1] and even worked for a short period with Brian Hodgson, the British Resident in Nepal. In Britain, under the pen-names of *Ornithognomon* and *Old Log*, Tickell was known for his regular contributions to *The Field* on various natural history subjects including articles on the game-birds and wildfowl of India.

Tickell was born on 19 August 1811 at Cuttack, some hundred or so miles south-west of Calcutta. He was educated in the British Isles and did not return to India until he was nineteen, having already enlisted in the Bengal Native Infantry. From 1832 to 1833 he served with his regiment in the Kol Campaign, in the hillier and wilder regions of south-west Bengal, but thereafter passed into the civil department of the army and spent two years conducting survey work in the Kol country after which he was promoted to Lieutenant.

He continued to serve in Bengal until May 1840 when he became the Assistant Resident and commander of Hodgson's military escort at Katmandu. Tickell's sister had married Hodgson's brother, William, but unfortunately William and their infant child had recently died and the widow had returned to England. Because of this family connection the two naturalists already knew each other well. Their association could have been a long and profitable one for zoology but political events dictated otherwise: Hodgson resigned after disagreeing with the newly arrived and high-handed Governor-General and returned to England. Tickell went back to Bengal in February 1843, after spending nine months leave at the Cape. In July of the following year he married Maria Templer at Bankura and three years later on his promotion to Captain they were moved to lower Burma.

Throughout his time in India, Tickell had studied birds whenever possible and contributed to Volume 17 of the *Journal of the Asiatic Society of Bengal*, the first published observations on the nests and eggs of the birds of the plains of India. Volume 18 of the same journal shows that he continued his pursuits in Burma for it contained 'An Itinery, with Memoranda, chiefly Topographical and Zoological, through the Southerly portion of the District of Amherst, Province of Tenasserim'. Unfortunately, in January 1852 the second Burmese War irrupted and the British, after some initial setbacks, succeeded in subduing the Burmese by the end of the year. Tickell then became the principal assistant to the commander of the Tenasserim and Martaban Provinces. He was rapidly promoted to Major and then again, in 1863, to Lieutenant-Colonel and Commander of the Pegu Division in British Burma.

During these upheavals he again continued his ornithological interests and made various expeditions including a long winter excursion into the Tenasserim Mountains in 1855. In 1864 he sent a paper to *The Ibis* on the hornbills of India and Burma. Indeed hornbills appear to have been amongst his particular favourites for he kept several at his home:

> "Those I possessed used to roost on the roof, flying in and out at pleasure. One in particular, which we kept for nearly two years, became a great favourite . . . It would fly to me or the children from any distance in the garden or grounds; and especially attached itself to the young folks, allowing them to scratch its neck . . . and never on any occasion hurting them with its formidable bill."[2]

Tickell's Thrush

In January 1865, at the age of fifty-four, Tickell retired from the service as an Honorary Colonel, and afterwards settled in the Channel Islands. In 1870, following a fishing trip off the coast of Brittany, his eyes suffered an inflammatory attack which cost him the sight of one eye and then the other. He died on 20 April 1875 at Cheltenham, after much suffering in his final year.

His deteriorating eyesight had forced him to abandon his manuscript work entitled 'Illustrations of Indian Ornithology' which he had intended to be a complete history of the Indian avifauna. Some of his earlier sketches and the texts for several families had been lost but there were seven folio volumes describing 448 species, accompanied by 261 plates of birds depicting 276 species, and five plates of the eggs of forty-two species, all by Tickell's own skilful hand. The birds were illustrated in their natural surroundings, often with scenes of everyday Indian life in the background which added greatly to the overall pictorial quality of the plates. In addition there were ninety-four small oval vignettes of village scenes, native customs, and shooting and hunting parties. Viscount Walden, commenting on Tickell's illustrations, wrote that "It may be affirmed that nearly all are good, and that many are almost perfection". The paintings of the swallows and the hornbills were described as amongst the best. A year before Colonel Tickell died he donated the unfinished work to the Zoological Society of London, and it remains unpublished.

TRISTRAM. *ENGLISH CLERGYMAN, TRAVELLER, NATURALIST AND ANTIQUARIAN. HE HAD A SPECIAL INTEREST IN THE FLORA AND FAUNA OF THE HOLY LAND WHERE HE MADE SEVERAL LONG JOURNEYS AND WAS THE FIRST TO COMPILE A QUANTITATIVE ORNITHOLOGICAL SURVEY FOR THE REGION. THE RED-BEARDED EXPLORER IS DRESSED HERE (IN A DUR-HAM STUDIO) IN HIS FULL TRAVELLING OUTFIT FOR THE MIDDLE EAST.*

Henry Baker Tristram
(1822-1906)

TRISTRAM'S WARBLER *Sylvia deserticola* Tristram

Sylvia deserticola Tristram, 1859. *Ibis*, p. 58: "southern Algerian Sahara"

TRISTRAM'S GRACKLE *Onychognathus tristramii* (P. Sclater)

Amydrus Tristramii P. Sclater, 1858. *Annals and Magazine of Natural History*, Ser. 3, No. 2, p. 465: Dead Sea Depression, Palestine

TRISTRAM'S SERIN *Serinus syriacus* Bonaparte

Serinus syriacus Bonaparte, 1850. *Conspectus Generum Avium*, Vol 1, p. 523, *ex* Hemprich and Ehrenberg MS: "Bischerre" [Lebanon]

Henry Baker Tristram was born at the vicarage in Eglingham, a small village near Alnwick, between the Cheviot Hills and the Northumberland coast. As a boy he was often taken on field trips by friends of his father who taught him much about birds and insects. His first collection of eggs included those of Raven, Peregrine and Hen Harrier from the nearby moors, and in the local woods he climbed to the nests of Buzzard and Red Kite. His early inclinations were very much in the family tradition, as the Hon. Daines Barrington, one of Gilbert White's correspondents, was his great uncle. Tristram's mother had died when he was a child and at the age of fifteen he suffered the additional loss of his father and was sent away to Durham School. At the Durham Museum the curator encouraged him to try his hand on one of the tough-skinned crows and in the workshop above the museum he produced his first proud trophy which was a Jackdaw.

On leaving school he went up to Lincoln College, Oxford, graduated in Classics in 1844 and spent six months travelling in Switzerland where he studied the habits of Wallcreepers, Nutcrackers, Alpine Accentors and Snow Finches and for a while resumed his lessons in taxidermy at Geneva. He spent a year in Italy and took the opportunity to visit Professor Savi at Pisa University, where the eminent naturalist lectured in zoology and comparative anatomy.

At the age of twenty-three Tristram was ordained to the curacy of Morchard

Bishop in Devon, but after two years he was suffering so seriously from tuberculosis that his doctor advised him to seek a warmer climate. As a result, he sailed out to Bermuda and worked there for three years as naval and military chaplain and secretary to the Governor. During this time he met several other keen ornithologists, including Colonel Drummond-Hay (the first President of the British Ornithologists' Union) and Colonel Wedderburn, both of whom became lifelong friends. They collaborated on a study of the migrant birds and many species were added to the Reverend Tristram's collection, including Roseate Tern, Grey Phalarope, Spotted Sandpiper and Eskimo Curlew.

However, the change of climate failed to cure his condition, so after travelling for six months in the United States and Canada he sailed back to England and became rector of Castle Eden in County Durham, where he held the living for the next ten years. Soon after his return he married Eleanor Bowlby, and during their long and happy marriage she gave birth to seven daughters and a son.

Tristram's Warbler

Tristram's next excursion abroad was to northern Norway where he triumphantly found the nests of Great Snipe, Green Sandpiper and Bar-tailed Godwit, the eggs of which were figured in the second edition of W. C. Hewitson's work on British oology. Tristram's own first natural history publication appeared in *The Zoologist* of 1853, 'On the Occurrence of the Little Auk in Durham'.

By the age of thirty-three the clergyman's health had deteriorated to such an extent that he was forced to go abroad for the next two winters, and each time was scarcely expected to return alive. Fortunately, the dry, invigorating climate of Algeria was so beneficial for him that his lungs completely recovered. He made numerous excursions into the interior, continually watching and studying the bird life, collecting eggs and skins, enjoying the hospitality of French army officers and nomadic Bedouin chiefs and writing about all he experienced. Many of the birds were familiar to him, for Chiffchaffs, Willow Warblers and Whitethroats occurred in all the gardens and Swallows swooped low over the wells in pursuit of the swarming mosquitoes. The Hoopoe was also common and he noted how it "solemnly stalks on every dunghill, a cherished and respected guest".

One of Tristram's favourite places was Lake Hallula with its teeming thousands of ducks and herons and during both his visits to North Africa he stayed well into the breeding season so that he could collect there. Once, he found the nests of over thirty species round the lake in a single day; he took the eggs of Squacco and Night Heron, Glossy Ibis and Crested Coot, all of which have since decreased or ceased to breed in Algeria. Black-necked Grebes also occurred there and he found that Whiskered Terns had laid in some of the grebes' old nests. As he journeyed southwards he discovered a completely new species of warbler, similar to the Dartford Warbler, but smaller and paler with rufous wings, which he named *Sylvia deserticola*, now commonly known as Tristram's Warbler.

For some months, Tristram possessed two Griffons taken from the nest. They were doubtless well fed while travelling with him, as he described how they "remained contentedly about the tents, or perched on the backs of the baggage-camels *en route*. They took a peculiar interest in taxidermy, scrutinising, head on one side, the whole operation of bird-skinning, and perfectly aware of the moment when a morsel would be ready, exhibiting a more than ordinary excitement when they saw the skin drawn back over the head, and knew that the whole carcase would soon be cut off for them. I have seen our pet, 'Musha Pasha', attack the entrails of a camel, and, as his crop became distended, sink upon his breast unable to stand, till at length, even this position being too much for him, he lay on his side still eating, until overpowered and helpless he fell asleep. This enormous capacity for food, combined with the power of long abstinence, is a wonderful provision of Creative Wisdom for carrion-feeders, whose supply is so uncertain, while the necessity for the immediate removal of offensive matter is so urgent. The strength of the Vulture's stomach is equal to its capacity, for on one occasion one of our griffons devoured a half-pound pot of arsenical soap with no further inconvenience than a violent fit of vomiting."[1]

The large numbers of Griffons which sometimes congregated at a carcass led him to wonder whether they located it by smell or by watching other vultures, and he came to the latter conclusion, since proved to be correct. It occurred to him that if vultures spaced themselves aerially so that each soaring bird remained in sight of its neighbour, they could follow each other down to carrion from a great distance away. He went on to mention that the Arabs "believe that the vultures from all North Africa were gathered to feed on Russian horses in the Crimea, and declare that during the war very few 'Nissr' were to be seen in their accustomed haunts."[2]

Tristram gave a full and fascinating account of his Algerian travels in his first book, *The Great Sahara* (1860), though he had, in fact, only penetrated the northern edge of this vast desert.

The following winter he was cruising in the eastern Mediterranean with a friend, calling at many places along the coasts of Greece and Turkey. On one of the Greek islands he had a narrow escape when he spotted a rare lizard and pounced on it—only to realize that it was actually a deadly nose-horned viper which proceeded to coil itself tightly round his wrist. Having no weapon handy, he called to the boatmen for a knife, but they refused to lend him one, fearing that in doing so they would interfere in what was obviously divine judgement! Fortunately Tristram noticed an empty soda water bottle lying on the sand and managed to force the snake's head into the neck, then prised off the rest of its body from his arm. Not one to waste such an opportunity, as soon as he was on board the boat he filled the bottle with whisky and thus preserved the specimen!

In the spring of 1858 he visited Palestine for the first time. One of his most memorable days was spent in the Qidron Valley, between Bethlehem and the Dead Sea. Near the monastery of Mar Saba, whose buildings cling to the steep cliffs of the ravine like a cluster of martins' nests, Tristram noticed some glossy-brown starling-like birds. As they flew amongst the rocks they displayed large, translucent orange wing patches which flashed in the strong sunshine and the cliffs echoed with the music of their clear, piercing, melodic whistles. Tristram sent two specimens to his friend Philip Sclater who named them *Amydrus tristramii*; now usually known as Tristram's Grackle in English, and 'Tristram's Bird' in Hebrew. The discovery of these beautiful birds in the desolate ravines at the northern end of the great Rift Valley was of particular interest, as until then the grackles were considered to be an exclusively African group. This exciting find and the rich variety of all of Palestine's wildlife convinced Tristram that it would be well worth planning a future expedition to the country to make a prolonged investigation of its natural history.

Later that same year, in Tristram's study at Castle Eden, plans of a different nature took shape when the idea of forming an exclusively ornithological society was put forward while John Wolley, Alfred Newton and Osbert Salvin were on a visit. In November they were together again at a meeting of the British Association in Cambridge, and at Magdalen College they and other friends formed the British Ornithologists' Union and agreed to establish a 'Quarterly Magazine of General Ornithology'. At the publisher's suggestion it was called *The Ibis*, Tristram contributing to the first and many subsequent volumes.

During the next five years he remained in Britain, becoming the vicar of Greatham, Durham, in 1860. Even this relatively uneventful period of his life was not without its ornithological highlights, for he later recounted how, "One morning in August 1862, my children came running into my study at Greatham Vicarage, to tell me a black stork was walking about in the Seaton fields. (They were familiar with the bird, as a mounted specimen stood in the hall). I went out and watched the bird for an hour, marching about in a swampy meadow."[3] Although the stork was shot the following day it was not killed by Tristram, who was critical of what he considered to be indiscriminate and purposeless collecting.

Tristram's Grackles at Mar Saba

In the autumn of 1863 the Reverend Tristram returned to Palestine, as he had long hoped to do, accompanied by a botanist, a photographer, a zoological assistant and various friends including the crack shot Henry Morris Upcher. Tristram spent ten months travelling between the Dead Sea depression and the high mountains of Lebanon, his finds in the latter area including the Syrian or Tristram's Serin. On the northern side of Mt Hermon, in June, in some pear orchards above Rasheiya, he was attracted by some clear and musical notes which were quite unknown to him. After searching about he found the songster deep among the trees, and succeeded in shooting it and four others. His companion, Edward Bartlett, trapped a hen as she sat on her nest and collected the clutch. The little finch bred high in the hills, descending to the villages on the edge of the snow-line in winter. Henry Dresser later named it Tristram's Serin *Serinus canonicus*, though it had in fact been discovered earlier by Hemprich and Ehrenberg in 1824.[4]

Tristram's party was continually impressed by the high density of birds of prey everywhere they went and no less than forty-three species were claimed to have rewarded their researches. From one of his camp sites, Tristram watched a pair of Lammergeirs which had an eyrie nearby. As they flew, they repeatedly dropped what appeared to be sticks and stones, then swooped down to pick them up and drop them again. Bewildered by this strange behaviour, he went

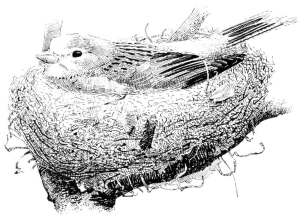

Tristram's Serin

forward to investigate and discovered that the stick-like objects were snakes, and found the surrounding ground littered with tortoise shells. The vultures had been dropping each tortoise up to a dozen times until the carapace shattered, much as gulls in Britain will smash cockles and mussels. Tristram recalled that in 456 BC the Greek poet Aeschylus was said to have met his death on account of a tortoise falling on his head in this way! (See Upcher for further details of Tristram's 1863–64 expedition, with a map of his route.)

Once Tristram was again settled in Durham he wrote extensively about the Holy Land, his publications including *The Land of Israel* (1865), *Natural History of the Bible* (1867) and much later, *The Fauna and Flora of Palestine* (1884) for the Survey of Western Palestine. Tristram was the most productive and important of the early pioneering naturalists of the Holy Land, but, like a prophet who is without honour in his own land, Tristram is now little appreciated in Britain though held in great respect in Israel. His observations regarding the status and distribution of many of their birds and animals during the second half of the last century are frequently referred to in Israeli publications.

He also took great pains to correctly identify many of the birds mentioned in the Bible, a task largely beyond the ability of ordinary translators who lacked ornithological knowledge. For example, he realized that in the book of Micah (Ch. 1, v. 16), the prophet was referring to the baldness of the Griffon Vulture, yet it had long been translated as 'eagle'. In Old Testament times, the Griffon would have been familiar to everyone in Israel, as Tristram considered the bird to be the most striking ornithological feature of the country, and found it impossible, almost anywhere, to look up without seeing some.

The biblical account of the Israelites in the desert being fed by the Lord on manna and Quail (Exodus Ch. 16), prompted Tristram to comment on the migration of Quail in vast flocks northwards from Africa in the spring: "I have myself found the ground in Algeria, in the month of April, covered with quails for an extent of many acres at daybreak, where on the preceding afternoon there had not been one. They were so fatigued that they scarcely moved till almost trodden upon."[5] In all his investigations into the physical and natural history of the Holy Land, he was deeply impressed by the truth of many incidental allusions in Scripture to the facts of nature, climate and geographical position, which, though perhaps of little importance in themselves, confirmed the accuracy of the writers in faithfully recording what they had observed, and which, therefore, increased his confidence in their honesty when recording incidents which cannot be corroborated.

On both of his visits to the Middle East he had longed to explore the blue hills of Moab which lay shimmering in the heat and the haze, beyond the Dead Sea, not far away and yet scarcely traversed by any European explorer since the fall of the Roman Empire. He approached the Palestine Exploration Fund for help but they strongly advised him to avoid the country. Biblical lands, however, held far too great a fascination for Tristram for him to be so easily deterred. On his earlier visits to Palestine he had tried to approach Moab from the north, but had only got as far as Mount Nebo; another time he had tried the southern route, but feuding Arab tribes had forced him to return before his curiosity was satisfied.

In 1872 he made his third attempt by leading a well-organized expedition which sailed from England in January. Less than two weeks later they landed at Jaffa, rode via Jerusalem to Hebron and then descended to the shores of the Dead Sea at Engedi. While searching among the trees and shrubs there on 2 February, Tristram's attention was drawn to an unfamiliar call and among the Sardinian Warblers he noticed a pair of a different species which he pursued for some time and eventually succeeded in shooting. He later described the new Sylviad in *The Ibis* of 1872 as *Sylvia melanothorax*, and though at first called the Palestine Warbler it is now known as the Cyprus Warbler; it winters in Israel but breeds only on the island of Cyprus.

From Engedi the expedition rode southwards past the great rock of Masada to the Brook Zered, accompanied by an armed party of Arabs. As they crossed the brook, the ancient boundary line between Edom and Moab, about a hundred and fifty near-naked Bedouin dashed towards them from a narrow opening in the reeds, all armed with guns, spears, swords and clubs. There was a scuffle, but when the attackers realized that none of the other Arabs were of the Ta'amirah tribe, with whom they had a blood feud, the party was allowed to continue on its way, with only some loss of property.

By the end of February Tristram was noting the first signs of spring. Hoopoes had returned and a Swallow took refuge in one of the tents. By the eastern shores of the Dead Sea he watched Lesser Whitethroats, Chiffchaffs and Blackcaps feeding among the large yellow, pink and white flower spikes of the many shrubs and bushes.

The only major discovery in Moab was the ruins of the great Persian palace at Mashita which was built by Chosroes about AD 614 and which had lain deserted and almost entirely forgotten for many centuries.

On his return to England Tristram was elected Canon of Durham Cathedral and for a number of years he avoided foreign travel, being content to serve within the Church and his local community, but he continued his interest in foreign birds by working on collections sent to him from distant parts of the world. *The Land of Moab* was published in 1873 and six years later Tristram was offered the Bishopric of Jerusalem, but he declined. In 1881 he made an expedition to the ruins of Ur of the Chaldees, which was of interest to Tristram as the city which Terah and Abram had left in order to go to Canaan, and for seven months Tristram travelled in Mesopotamia and Armenia, spending some time also in northern Syria and in Palestine. These journeys were followed at the end of the 1880s by a worthwhile investigation into the ornithology of the seven major islands of the Canaries, which he undertook with his younger friend Edmund Meade-Waldo.

At the age of sixty-nine Tristram sailed to Japan to visit one of his daughters who had been working there as a missionary for several years. *Rambles in Japan* (1895) is a collection of perceptive observations of a society which charmed the Canon by its beauty and contrast to western culture. He described the butchers' shops decorated with vases and flowers, the cleanliness of the women who coaled the ships, the chequered carpets of golden rape and green cotton fields, the mission church with its porch well stocked with fans for the comfort of the worshippers, a winding stream with long rows of images of the Buddha on either side, the glory of the blossoming cherry and peach trees of every hue from pure white to deepest crimson, and the shrines at Shima, sacred to the memory of the Shoguns and decorated with barbaric magnificence. Tristram wrote little about the ornithology of the islands as his priority was to assess the work of the Church Missionary Society, learn about the Japanese religions and lifestyle, and spend time with his daughter whom he feared he might not see again.

In 1894 Canon Tristram was drawn back to the Holy Land and three years later, at the age of seventy-five, made his last trip there. While riding with a party of friends he had his leg broken by the kick of a vicious mule and had to spend some weeks in hospital in Jerusalem, but was soon his old sprightly self again.

In February 1900 Tristram and his wife celebrated their golden wedding anniversary and enjoyed three more years together until her death on 8 March

1903. In the summer of 1905 the Canon's health began to fail and he passed away the next spring on the third anniversary of his wife's death, at his residence in the College, Durham, aged eighty-three.

On the following Monday afternoon the nave and transepts of Durham Cathedral were packed with mourners; family, clergymen, freemasons, friends and many others who felt deeply the loss of one of Durham's greatest men. There must have been a few among the great assembly who marvelled that the man who had almost succumbed through ill health in his thirties, had enjoyed such an active and eventful life for another fifty years.

His influence within the Church and local politics had been considerable, but it was in the field of natural history that he had made the most outstanding contribution. Besides being an exceptional ornithologist he was interested in, and knowledgeable about, almost every aspect of natural history. In his introduction to the 'Ornithology of North Africa', in *The Ibis* of 1859, he stated his conviction that "it is impossible to gain a just view of the ornithology of any country without considering in the first place its physical and geological characters". Thus, when he wrote his *Natural History of the Bible*, he discussed Palestine's physical geography, geology and meteorology as well as describing the mammals, birds, reptiles, fish, invertebrates, trees, shrubs, herbs and flowers to be found there. His knowledge of the country was unrivalled. Because of his ability to combine accuracy with an entertaining narrative, the books of his travels were widely read during his lifetime and he made over seventy contributions to *The Ibis*.

An inveterate collector of bird skins and eggs, he also took more interest in bird behaviour than ornithologists of his time are generally given credit for. His large and valuable collection of eggs is now in the British Museum (Natural History). In 1896 he gave his priceless collection of skins to the Liverpool Museum as he feared the possibility of the collection being dispersed after his death. The catalogue, which he had carefully prepared, listed over 17,000 skins of about 6000 different species, of which about 130 were types. Even though Tristram was then seventy-four years of age, so ingrained was his habit of collecting, and so well established was his network of correspondents, that he immediately began another collection! In his remaining years he succeeded in selectively accumulating 7000 specimens of some 3000 species, which later went to Philadelphia.

Among the Liverpool specimens which Tristram had cherished most were those of several extinct species, including the Norfolk Island Parrot and the very last known Labrador Duck, which he listed as a gift from Colonel Wedderburn, an old friend from his days in Bermuda. Sir Hugh Gladstone wondered how Wedderburn had acquired the duck, and wrote to his widow in 1913. He received the following reply:

"My husband often regretted having shot the last Labrador duck,[6] in the Harbour of Halifax, N.S. in 1851. He did not know at the time how rare a bird it was, and valued the specimen very much. He had no intention of parting with it, but his friend Canon Tristram, who was a *rapacious* collector, happened to call one day when my husband was just starting to catch a train, and he insisted on begging for the bird, persuading my husband that as he, my husband, had *pairs* of most birds, this single specimen was not of so much interest! I suggested that my husband should think it over for a day or two, but Dr. Tristram was so persistent that in the end he walked off with the duck under his arm!"[7]

UPCHER. *NORFOLK SQUIRE AND KEEN SPORTSMAN WITH A LIFELONG INTER-EST IN BIRDS. AN EXCELLENT MARKSMAN, HE COLLECTED IN ICELAND AND ACCOMPANIED THE REVEREND TRISTRAM ON HIS MOST IMPORTANT EXPEDITION TO PALESTINE.*

Henry Morris Upcher (1839-1921)

UPCHER'S WARBLER *Hippolais languida* (Hemprich and Ehrenberg)

Curruca languida Hemprich and Ehrenberg, 1833. *Symbolae Physicae. Avium*, folio cc: Syria

Upcher's Warbler was so named by the Reverend H. B. Tristram after his friend, Henry Morris Upcher, who accompanied him on his travels through Palestine early in 1864. Unlike the nomadic clergyman, Upcher spent almost all of his life at home in England, farming for many years near Ely and later managing the family estate.

Born on 15 December 1839, the eldest of six sons, Upcher was fortunate to grow up at Sheringham Hall, just a few miles east of Cley, on the north Norfolk coast, one of the best places in Britain for the observation of migrating birds. From an early age he learnt to shoot game and to hunt for nests and eggs in the gardens and surrounding countryside. He was educated at Harrow, where he became a keen cricketer and went up to Trinity College in October 1857. After leaving Cambridge he spent three months in Iceland with his friends G. G. Fowler, a Suffolk naturalist, and the Reverend C. W. Shepherd of Maidstone who led the expedition and later wrote a short, entertaining account of their travels.

They sailed on 20 April 1862, called at the Faeroe Islands where they had one day ashore and landed at Reykjavik on 28 April. Their plan was to explore the little-known north-west peninsula and climb at least one of its peaks, then cross the northern part of the island to Lake Myvatin and examine its population of breeding ducks. They also hoped to establish whether or not Greylag Geese, Sanderling and Knot bred in Iceland. On their arrival they discovered that spring was not so far advanced as they had expected. Much of the country was boggy because of the melting snow; roads, such as they were, were still blocked by drifts and there was nothing for the baggage ponies to feed upon. The fishermen who often acted as guides in the summer were still at sea. While making enquiries they spent the first week fishing for trout on the nearby Laxa River and collected the skins of Red-breasted Merganser, Goosander, gulls, ducks and Ptarmigan.

For the next month they had to endure snowstorms and gales, retreating to local farmhouses when their little tent threatened to blow away. By the time they could set off northwards from Reykholt at the end of May, Redwings were rearing their young and some had already fledged. On the morning that they planned to leave they woke early to driving sleet and resigned themselves to another wasted day in their sleeping-bags. However, the appearance of their guide outside the tent, bareheaded and in his shirtsleeves, urging them to rise and pack, made their reluctant departure inevitable. The strong winds continued as they travelled but at least the daylight hours were long and they were able to search some of the high ground for breeding geese and waders, but only found Purple Sandpipers feeding by the ice-fringed pools. They were disappointed not to find the nests of Sanderling or Knot, but it is now known that their nearest breeding grounds are in east Greenland.

For a week they rode over sodden hills and through swampy valleys until they reached the coast where they found a wreck of Razorbills and guillemots, their emaciated bodies lying in great heaps on the shore. Thousands of Eider and large flocks of Purple Sandpipers were sheltering in the bay and the travellers themselves sought shelter in the little church at Fell. They were awoken during the night by some local people coming in and out of the building, but did not realize why until the morning when they found a coffin laid out beside them, and, on examination, discovered that a smaller box by their sleeping-bags also contained a corpse. Thereafter the intrepid explorers preferred their tent, whatever the weather.

On 17 June they climbed to the summit of Drangajokull and then, with one ambition achieved, they sailed next day from Hamar to Isafjordhur, where they waited for a boat to Hofsas. In the meantime their guides travelled eastwards with the ponies, by land, so as to meet the collectors there. A few days later the trio made an excursion to Vigr Island where they found the shores covered in Eider nests and many more ducks sitting all around the single farmhouse, some even incubating on the turf slopes of the roof. Each year the farmer's wife pickled many of their eggs for the winter and supplemented the family income by gathering nearly a hundred pounds of the soft down. After a week Upcher and his friends sailed to Hofsas, where their landlady fed them daily on an unrelieved diet of stewed guillemots, so that when the guides arrived the Englishmen gladly left for the horrors of Myvatin. When they reached the lake mosquitoes rose up around them in clouds. Undeterred by such conditions they borrowed a boat and spent several days exploring the area where Scaup, Long-tailed Ducks, Barrow's Goldeneye, Harlequins, Mergansers and Common Scoters all bred. Red-necked Phalaropes brooded their young within a few feet of the strangers, and with a net they caught some of the adult birds as they flew around them.

They had hoped to cross the mountainous interior on their return, but bad weather made this impossible and so they took the usual route to Reykjavik via Akeyri, and consequently missed any chance of coming across the breeding grounds of the Pink-footed Goose. They reached the capital on 29 July with a good collection of skins and eggs and with new information about the breeding range of Greylag Geese and the wildfowl population of Lake Myvatin.

At the end of the following year Upcher and Shepherd went away together again, this time to Palestine where they took part in a lengthy expedition planned and led by the Reverend Tristram. The two friends stayed for only ten weeks but Upcher gave invaluable assistance and earned the name *Abou-'eyn-t'nin* (Father of two eyes), so impressed were the Arabs by his marksmanship. Towards the end of December 1863 Upcher and Shepherd reached Jerusalem where Tristram, his young assistant Edward Bartlett, the botanist B. T. Lowne, the photographer H. T. Bowman and the artist W. C. P. Medleycott were all camped, just outside the city.

Their plan was to travel down the west shore of the Dead Sea, then cross the Ghor and explore the large flat peninsula of El Lisan and the southernmost part of Moab up to Kerak. Tristram later wrote a vivid and detailed account of the expedition in *The Land of Israel* (1865), in which he described their departure on 30 December in his usual meticulous but entertaining style:

> "After a very short night's rest, we were roused by the fragrance of cups of hot coffee, presented under our noses. Our bedding was quickly rolled up, we united in prayer in the quiet corner, and, soon after daybreak, our boxes lumbered up the access to the cafe, and our throng of animals and attendants crowded the road. It is no easy matter to effect an early start from a city, and hopeless to attempt to hurry Orientals, who, with all their keen appreciation of the value of money, have never yet learned the value of time."

Under the guardianship of Sheik Mohammed whose territory they were traversing, they passed through the Damascus Gate in a long cavalcade of over thirty horses, asses and mules, with two dozen mounted Bedouin carrying long spears and some dozen more on foot. From Bethany they descended a rocky staircase for several hundred feet down to the Jordan valley and reached Jericho later that day. They set up camp north of the town at Ein es Sultan and during the next fortnight they explored the hills and rocky gorges to the west and the oases and plains to the east.

The days were busily spent in writing, photographing, shooting, collecting, skinning or sketching, depending on vocation, and Sunday was always welcomed as a day of rest. On the first Sabbath afternoon at Ein es Sultan the camp was visited by a group of shabby, scantily dressed women from a nearby village. They proceeded to form a circle in front of the tents and performed a graceful dance, but the Englishmen were not favourably impressed: "The women of the Ghor, unlike Moslems of the towns, do not veil, and truly there is no need for them to do so."

Upcher regularly set traps and examined them himself every morning, but on 12 January he was roused at sunrise with the news that a lynx had been caught and he rushed out to find that it was a fine specimen of the Jungle Cat *Felis chaus*. In another trap there was a curious little sandy-coloured rodent, the Sinai Spiny Mouse *Acomys dimidiatus*.

The next day they broke camp and rode southwards down the shore of the Dead Sea. Dunlin and Redshank were running along the sandy beach, Smyrna Kingfishers hunted quietly from their concealed perches and a gull which flew low over the warm waters fell to Upcher's gun and had to be retrieved by one of the swimmers. Dusk fell before they reached their destination, but fortuitously so, for nightjars flicked past them in the gloaming and when Bartlett procured one, they found it to be a small, sand-coloured bird, a race of the Nubian

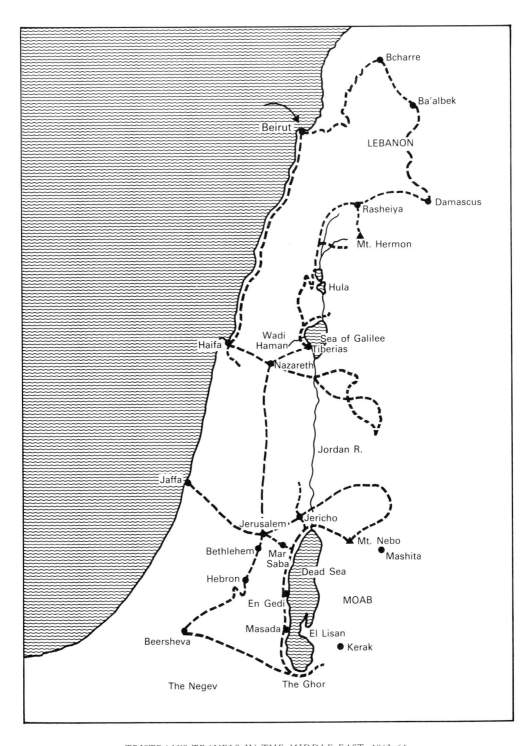

TRISTRAM'S TRAVELS IN THE MIDDLE EAST, 1863–64

Nightjar as yet undescribed. A few days later they had to leave the protection of Sheik Mohammed who insisted that they must first be entertained in his own camp, and so they reluctantly accepted the loss of a day of research. After the feast the seven travellers rode on in a leisurely fashion to the monastery at Mar Saba where they spent Sunday with the monks. Two days later they continued their journey, discovering a completely new species, the Dead Sea Sparrow. The next day Upcher and Shepherd rose early and each shot one of the males before breakfast.

When they reached the great rock of Masada they camped at the base, 1300 ft below the ancient fortress where nearly a thousand Jewish Zealots had taken their own lives in AD 73, rather than submit to the besieging Romans. Tristram's party all laboured up the steep slope to explore the crumbling ruins, except for Bartlett who, on their return, presented them with a Fan-tailed Raven he had shot and the remains of a Pochard which a Lanner had dropped in surprise on suddenly spotting human life in that desolate place.

At the end of the month, escorted by Sheik Abou Dahuk and seventy-six of his armed men, they entered the rich green oasis which stretched for several miles below the red sandstone hills at the very southern end of the Salt Sea. They had not gone far when the advance guard returned with six prisoners, armed tribesmen whom they had found skulking in the dense cover. Because of this, although the wild thickets and fertile glades teamed with birds, the Sheik inflicted torture on the foreigners by insisting that not a shot be fired. The wisdom of his precaution was realized when they reached the village where they had planned to camp. As they passed through the reed-wattled stockade they beheld smouldering hovels and naked bodies strewn around the ruins. While the naturalists watched in horror, the Bedouin, with yells of glee, plundered and looted in all directions, filling every spare sack with the precious indigo which they found stored below the huts. Only with the greatest difficulty did Tristram persuade the Sheik to set up camp away from the village. As darkness fell twenty-five men were detailed for patrols and thirty-five more were stationed around nine large watchfires so that if the raiders returned they would assume that a large force slept inside the encampment. In fact, few slept at all throughout the long and anxious night, during which twelve more prisoners were taken.

As soon as dawn began to break they doused the fires and loaded their beasts who moved slowly, under all the plunder, back in the direction of their last safe quarters on the other side of the Ghor. As they moved off, Black Kites and vultures were gathering in the skies above, but well out of range. However, as ravens flapped overhead towards the unclean feast, Upcher and his friends shot specimens of all three species that occur there: the Common, Fan-tailed and Brown-necked Ravens.

The next day Tristram and Upcher rose before dawn and walked two miles for a wash in some rain pools: "Nature had provided us with beautiful marble baths, and we each selected one. The water was icy cold, for the sun cannot reach the deep fissure, and not having as yet adopted the hydrophobic principles of our hosts, we enjoyed a wash and a thorough soaping, which effaced all remembrance of the feverish anxiety, the heat and the dust, of the last three days."

After leaving the environs of the Dead Sea they rode westwards through almost birdless country into the barren hills of the Negev, from which rose only the occasional sandgrouse or lark. As they neared Beersheva large flocks of sheep, goats, camels and horned cattle were more frequently seen, and Upcher distinguished himself by bringing down a Caspian Plover. The desert bloomed with blue iris and crimson *Ranunculus* as they turned northwards from Abraham's Well towards Hebron. There they lingered to examine the glass-works and tanneries, but by the second week of February they were back at their old campsite outside Jerusalem.

Upcher's last fortnight was devoted to exploring the bird life of the hills and plains north-west of the Sea of Galilee. The whole area was densely populated by raptors and in some of the deep gorges hundreds of Griffon Vultures nested in colonies. One morning Upcher and Shepherd shot five of these huge birds, all of which were skinned and prepared the next day by Bartlett. Collecting their eggs was much more difficult and a whole week was dedicated to the task. One morning Upcher was trying to reach a Griffon's nest in the Wadi Haman when an Eagle Owl swept out of one of the caves. As he shot it, a startled Woodcock rose up from nearby and was swiftly brought down with the other barrel. Bonelli's Eagles, Lanners and Kestrels all inhabited the wadi but the sight which impressed them more than any other was that of the Lammergeiers soaring above the rugged limestone cliffs, rising up and up on motionless outspread wings early each morning.

During the second week of March, as the spring migrants streamed into the country, Tristram lamented the fact that Upcher and Shepherd had to depart for England:

> "In them we lost the most energetic collectors and sportsmen of our party. For the last time their little trim Iceland tent stood by the camp fire, and no longer was Upcher to pay his morning visits to the traps, or Shepherd to cheer us as he dispensed soup and jokes at our dinner table."

Several months later, Tristram was still investigating the flora and fauna of Palestine. He recorded the events of 4 June 1864, in *The Ibis*, as follows:

> "Our first recognition of Upcher's warbler was from finding a nest in an orchard under Mount Hermon, from which a bird stole off, which I took to be an

Upcher's Warbler

[Olivaceous warbler], till I noticed the eggs to be of a rich salmon ground and almost as large as those of the Olive-tree warbler. I waited till the bird returned, and then secured both parents, when I ascertained that I had got hold of an exactly intermediate species. Its note is unlike that of the [Olivaceous warbler]; and it frequents very different localities, the uplands of Hermon and Lebanon, in the vineyards and oak-coppices. The nest was usually placed in a bush of *Vitex agnus-castus*, or Linden tree, never more than a yard or two from the ground, neat and conspicuous. We found this bird very abundant in its restricted localities."[1]

Earlier that same day Tristram had found the little serin which is sometimes named after him, and so, as he sat down under the pear trees to blow the eggs of Upcher's Warbler he had good reason to feel pleased with himself. After his return to England, Tristram was disappointed to discover that Ehrenberg had obtained both species in the Lebanese Mountains in the summer of 1824 while travelling there with Hemprich. Ehrenberg's description of the warbler was rather vague, so Tristram redescribed the bird and named it *Hippolais upcheri*.[2] Since then, only the vernacular name has been retained as Ehrenberg's priority has been upheld for the scientific name.

Although Upcher's travels in the Holy Land lasted only a few months, the memories delighted him for the rest of his life. Forty-four years later, at the Jubilee gathering of the British Ornithologists' Union in 1908, Upcher, as the oldest surviving elected member, was called upon to present some medals and in his speech he took pleasure in referring to "dear old Canon Tristram"—the "Sacred Ibis" as he often called him. Upcher had become a member of the B.O.U. on his return to England in 1864, and he was made a Fellow of the Zoological Society that same year. His ornithological interests were thereafter chiefly confined to the birds of Norfolk, although he made occasional short trips to the Continent, and went to Royal Deeside for the salmon fishing. Shooting gamebirds was a lifelong passion, and it was not unusual for the Sheringham Hall game-book to record an annual bag of over 100 Woodcock, his favourite quarry. Until his father's death Upcher farmed some 2000 acres at East Hall, Feltwell, near Brandon. His wife Maria, whom he married when he was twenty-nine, was the daughter of the Reverend Sparke, the Rector of Feltwell and later the Canon of Ely Cathedral for many years.

In February 1876, a Great Bustard appeared on Upcher's land on the Hockwold Fens. Bustards had not bred in Norfolk since 1830 so the bird's arrival caused great excitement. Alfred Newton, Lord Lilford and other friends came over to view the gigantic bird and Lord Lilford agreed to send across a hen bird from his aviary, near Oundle. She was soon released into the same coleseed field as her potential mate. Upcher wrote to neighbouring landowners and posted up notices, asking that the birds be protected, but the female accidentally drowned in a nearby ditch and after a stay of seven weeks, the male disappeared.[3]

In 1883 Upcher was elected president of the Norfolk and Norwich Naturalists' Society, of which he had long been a member, and in 1889 he contributed his only paper to their transactions, on 'A Day's Bird's-nesting in Norfolk'.[4] 1888 was the year of the great invasion of Britain by Pallas's Sandgrouse, when more than a thousand arrived in Norfolk alone, and Upcher's genuine interest in wild birds was again reflected in the fact that he refrained from shooting them and urged his friends to do likewise. Instead he made every effort to compile an accurate record of their distribution in collaboration with other Norfolk ornithologists.

Upcher inherited Sheringham Hall in 1892. It was an attractive two-storeyed house of grey brick which he decorated with trophies from Iceland and the Middle East. The Hall had been designed for his grandfather, Abbot Upcher, by John Adney Repton around 1815; the beautiful gardens with their fine rhododendrons had been landscaped by Humphrey Repton, and are said to have been his favourite work. For almost thirty years Upcher managed the estate, and contributed greatly to the progress and popularity of the seaside resort of Sheringham, where he was affectionately known as 'The Squire'. He encouraged the establishment of a golf course and a large recreation ground for various other sports, built part of the Promenade at his own expense and erected groynes to protect the village from the encroaching North Sea. He always took an active part in the Church life of the Parish and gifted land for the extension of the graveyard. Among the numerous committees on which he served was that for the Protection of Wild Birds and the Eastern Sea Fisheries Joint Committee. On the occasion of his golden wedding anniversary in June 1919, he was presented by the fishermen with a photograph of the lifeboat, the *Henry Ramey Upcher* and her crew. The first local lifeboat, which had saved a remarkable number of lives, had been provided by his grandmother in 1839, and some fifty years later, Upcher's mother had replaced it with another in memory of her husband. The squire continued the family tradition and bore the expense of its upkeep.

Two years after the golden wedding celebrations, following a major operation and a long illness, Upcher died on 6 April 1921, survived by his widow, two sons and two daughters.

Sheringham Hall and the surrounding parkland was acquired by the National Trust in 1986. Most of the furniture was sold by auction, but Upcher's bird collection still remains there.

Jules Pierre Verreaux (1807-1873)

VERREAUX'S EAGLE *Aquila verreauxii* Lesson

Aquila Verreauxii Lesson, 1830. *Centurie Zoologique*, p. 105, Pl. 38: in the interior of Cape of Good Hope, i.e. Central Cape Province

The Verreaux's or Black Eagle occurs within the Western Palearctic only in the Middle East, where there have been sporadic breeding attempts in Israel and the Sinai Peninsula. The eagle's main breeding areas are from Ethiopia southwards down through eastern Africa to the Cape, and it is at this southern end of its range that one finds the connection with Jules Pierre Verreaux.

Several members of the Verreaux family had a strong interest in natural history. Throughout much of their lives the brothers Jules, Edouard and Alexis Verreaux collected birds or handled skins; their father, Pierre Jacques, bought and sold natural history specimens, while their uncle, the famous explorer-naturalist, Pierre Antoine Delalande, was himself the son of a taxidermist who worked at the Paris Museum. Delalande had been sent on collecting forays to Portugal, Provence and Brazil, and in 1818 he set off for southern Africa. He was so successful that his achievements excelled those of all other naturalists who had preceded him to the Cape, including Levaillant, Sparrman, Barrow and Lichtenstein. Throughout his expedition Delalande was accompanied by one of his small nephews; when they first set foot in the settlement on False Bay in November 1818, Jules Verreaux was just eleven years old.

Three days after their arrival, Delalande and Verreaux set off eastwards with three Hottentots but their journey was curtailed when they received news of an advancing Xhosa army. In July they tried again and reached the Oliphant River. In the course of their travels they came across the remains of a hippopotamus which provided a complete skeleton, the first to reach the Paris Museum. They soon set off on a third trip which lasted eight months and involved a 400-mile sea voyage eastwards from the Cape to Algoa Bay, together with a long trek into the interior as far as the Keiskanna River. On their return they spent a few months at Algoa Bay sorting through their collections. Under the tuition of his uncle, Verreaux had quickly acquired a thorough background in natural history and had become an excellent taxidermist, a skill which remained invaluable throughout his long career. An unlucky riding accident prevented Delalande from undertaking a fourth expedition and so, after almost two years at the Cape, they returned to Paris.

VERREAUX. *MEMBER OF A WELL-KNOWN FRENCH FAMILY WHO DEALT IN NATURAL HISTORY SPECIMENS ON AN ENORMOUS SCALE.*

The collection which was brought home consisted of a staggering 131,405 specimens, most of which were plants. Other items included 288 mammals, 2205 birds, 322 reptiles, 265 fish, 3875 shellfish, human skulls of Hottentots, Namaquas and Bushmen, and nearly two dozen skeletons unearthed from an old Cape Town cemetery and from the Grahamstown battlefield of 1819. The botanical success was reduced by the decay of many of the plants and it was mainly the seeds that proved of lasting value.

After five years studying under Cuvier, and after his uncle's death, Verreaux returned to southern Africa. This time he was nineteen years old. In June 1825, a year and a half before his arrival, the South African Museum had been established at Cape Town with the Scottish surgeon [Sir] Andrew Smith as its first superintendent. The Cape Colony was once more under British rule and Verreaux now found that he had to apply for permission to hunt, but this was quickly granted when Verreaux promised not to abuse his permit and agreed to help provide new material for the museum. In 1828 when Smith went on an expedition to Namaqualand, Verreaux was authorized to take charge of the museum until his return, almost a year later. Verreaux still found time to either purchase or gather specimens for himself; so much so, that he sent for his younger brother, Edouard, to help in the collection's arrangement and to transport it back to Paris.

Among the birds was a large black eagle, which was bought by an amateur ornithologist from Verreaux's father. René Primevère Lesson gained access to the bird and made use of it in his *Centurie Zoologique* (1830), in which he named the eagle after "M. Verreaux, voyageur naturaliste". Lesson's thorough description, and the brief comment that it was from "l'interieur du cap du Bonne-Esperance", was accompanied by a rather stiff looking painting by J. G. Prêtre, which shows a view of the bird's back and its distinguishing white markings on rump and mantle. Many more birds, and some mammals, now also commemorate the name of Verreaux.

In 1832 Edouard returned to the Cape with the youngest brother, Alexis, and in the following year Edouard travelled on a French ship to Sumatra, Java, the Philippines and Indo-China. When he returned to Paris in 1834 he took over the family business which traded in natural history specimens of all kinds, the so-called *Maison Verreaux* at 9 Place Royale: "one of the greatest, if not the greatest emporium of natural history that the world has ever seen".[1] By the 1850s there were said to be more than 3000 mammals and 40,000 birds stored in its warehouses.

Meanwhile Jules Verreaux continued to collect in southern Africa and from 1834 to 1836, while Smith explored beyond the northern boundaries of the Colony, he again took over the directorship of the museum. When Smith arrived back, Jules and Alexis helped to mount the specimens from the expedition (some of which later went to the British Museum), but in 1848 Verreaux decided to return to Paris to help in the family business. Alexis stayed on at Cape Town where he ran a gunpowder shop and continued to supply his two brothers with African birds and other animals.

After four years in Paris, undaunted by the disastrous wreck of the *Lucullus* which had sunk off the French coast with a huge collection of their African specimens, or even perhaps spurred on by the need to make good the loss, Jules Verreaux sailed to Australia and Tasmania to seek more new and exotic material for the *Maison Verreaux*. He spent five years gathering another collection of insects, mammals, reptiles and birds which he eventually conveyed safely to Paris where it was found to consist of 11,500 items. It was his last great expedition and thereafter he was content to live in France helping Edouard, and sometimes going on more local collecting excursions.

In his later years a number of articles began to appear in a variety of journals including *The Proceedings of the Zoological Society*, *The Ibis*, *Revue Zoologique* and *Nouvelles Archives du Muséum*; those in the latter chiefly related to the discoveries of Père David in China. Together with Edouard Verreaux he compiled a book on the geography of Australia, and with Des Murs he wrote about the birds of New Caledonia. On his own account he wrote some biological notes on the island of Réunion. He also worked on a monograph of the *Nectarinidae* or sunbirds, but he died before it could be completed, and his collection of sunbirds, manuscript notes and other books went to the Paris Museum.

Verreaux was said to have "possessed an immense knowledge of birds, probably greater than any man of his generation".[2] Many, though not all of the birds he discovered or purchased were given to other naturalists to describe, and so he has lost much of the credit for his contribution to ornithology. He produced few publications but during the heyday of the *Maison Verreaux* his handwriting was more widely known than that of any other ornithologist. A large label was always attached to each specimen that was sent out, on which he wrote out the synonomy from Bonaparte's *Conspectus Generum Avium*, indeed he had helped considerably with the second part of the book, published in 1857. Verreaux sometimes failed to mention the exact locality from which the skin had originated and the firm more than once sent out material completely mislabelled. Lord Lilford once helped to unpack a consignment of eggs sent to Paris from southern Russia. He watched in amazement as the Verreaux brothers suddenly attributed the eggs to a variety of species apparently at random: crane eggs were said to be those of eagles, marsh tern eggs now served as pratincole eggs, Redshank eggs became those of rare plovers, and eggs of Eagle Owls were transformed into Black Stork eggs![3] Henry Dresser occasionally dealt with the business and also complained of their unreliability. But the natural history world

Verreaux's Eagle

at that time was rife with ignorance, incompetence and even deliberate deception. The reputation of the *Maison Verreaux* was in fact better than most.

In 1864 Jules Verreaux took an opportunity to become an assistant naturalist at the Paris Museum where he worked under Henri Milne-Edwards. In 1870, when France was at war, Verreaux managed to escape from the city and its subsequent siege by German troops and he found refuge in England. For ten years he had been one of the original Honorary Members of the British Ornithologists' Union, amongst whose members he had several personal friends. He received a warm welcome in London, where he stayed with Bowdler Sharpe. When it was safe to do so, Verreaux returned to Paris and he died there on 7 September 1873, at the age of sixty-six. His two younger brothers had both died in 1868.

WHITE. *ENGLISH CLERGYMAN. AUTHOR OF THE MUCH-LOVED* NATURAL HISTORY OF SELBORNE. *THIS SKETCH WAS FOUND IN A COPY OF POPE'S TRANSLATION OF* THE ILIAD, *GIVEN BY THE AUTHOR TO WHITE.*

Gilbert White (1720-1793)

WHITE'S THRUSH *Zoothera dauma* (Latham)

Turdus Dauma Latham, 1790. *Index Ornithologicus*, Vol. 1, p. 362: India [= Kashmir]

White's Thrush breeds throughout the forest zones of Siberia and winters in China and other parts of south-east Asia. It is more frequently seen in the eastern regions of the Western Palearctic than in Britain where it is only a rare vagrant. The first White's Thrush recorded in Britain was shot by the Earl of Malmesbury on his estate at Heron Court, near Christchurch, in January 1828. "It attracted his attention, on disturbing it, in passing through a plantation, where it appeared to have established a haunt in a high furze brake, as it returned to it repeatedly before he could succeed in shooting it."[1] The Earl sent the bird to Thomas Eyton who later included details of it in his *History of the Rarer British Birds* (1836). Because it had been found in Hampshire, and not knowing that it had previously been described in Europe (and originally from India), Eyton named it White's Thrush:

> ". . . in memory of one with whom everybody is familiar by name, the late Gilbert White, author of "The Natural History of Selborne", a work which has and will afford many hours amusement and instruction to hundreds, and is deservedly classed among our standard books on British natural history."[2]

Since that time there have been well over 150 editions of the book which has delighted people throughout the world, even in countries with a completely different flora and fauna.

Though little is known about White's early life there is considerable documentation concerning the numerous parishes to which he was the curate and of his travels to relatives and friends. Born at Selborne on 18 July 1720 Gilbert was educated by private tutor at Basingstoke, afterwards going on to Oriel College, Oxford. He obtained his Master of Arts degree in 1746 and his deacon's orders in the following year.

For many years White was vicar of Moreton Pinkney in Northamptonshire, where he installed a curate. White in turn took the place of an absent rector, becoming curate of Farringdon in Hampshire, a position he held for twenty-four years. Because Farringdon was in the neighbouring parish to Selborne it enabled him to live at the *Wakes*, the house that had been his grandfather's and uncle's property and which White inherited in 1763. Only when aged sixty-four (and until his death) did he become the curate of Selborne. Thus the Reverend Gilbert White was not the *vicar* of Selborne as might be supposed; at most he was only the curate of the parish. It was not the vicarage that he made famous but his own house which can be visited today as the Gilbert White Museum.

White led a simple but active life. In his early years he travelled more widely and more frequently than is generally believed, usually on horseback, and so much so that his lifelong college friend, John Mulso, called him the "hussar-parson". He mainly visited friends and relatives, in particular his aunt Rebecca at Ringmer in Sussex, where he went at least once a year while she was alive. White also travelled to Norfolk, Rutland, Essex, Wiltshire, Gloucestershire, Devon and even the Derbyshire Peak District, and must therefore have been familiar with much of southern England. He made many trips to London and it was on one of these visits, in 1767, that he met Thomas Pennant with whom he later began the long correspondence that forms the basis of his famous book.

The first edition of *The Natural History and Antiquities of Selborne* was published in 1789 by his brother Benjamin White. The first letters in the book are dated 1767, at a time when Gilbert White had ceased travelling to any great extent, and for this reason most of the letters refer to his home area. The latter part of the book on the 'Antiquities' was very important to White who spent a great deal of time researching original documents relating to Selborne, in particular its ancient priory. However, it is for the more popular first part on general natural history that he is most often remembered. It recorded his many patient observations as he communicated them to Pennant and Daines Barrington.

Concentrating here only upon some of his notes concerning birds, it is hard for us to understand some of the problems that White struggled with. The question of whether Swallows migrated or remained buried in mud or hidden in chimneys throughout the winter was never resolved by White. This was despite the fact that his brother John, who was resident in Gibraltar, wrote to Gilbert telling him about the Swallows that flew through southern Spain at the end of each year. Swallows seen in England very late in the autumn, and letters from Barrington who did not believe that the birds migrated, did not make it easier for White. At a time when migration was very poorly understood White was probably as well informed as anybody. He was the first to note the passage of Ring Ouzels through southern England, rightly believing them to be of Scandinavian origin. Many of White's other ornithological observations have become of great interest because they reflect upon the changing status of birds

White's Thrush

in the southern counties. He was able to write that the Chough "abounds, and breed on Beechy Head and on all the cliffs of the Sussex coast"; he recorded Ravens nesting near his home year after year, until the tree was felled; and on one occasion in Sussex he saw sixteen 'fork-tailed kites' in the air at one time. Stone Curlews seem to have been very numerous for White wrote about a friend in Sussex "near whose house these birds congregate in vast flocks in autumn" and, at Selborne, "on any evening [in summer] you may hear them round the village, for they make a clamour which may be heard a mile". And on the South Downs the Great Bustard still bred.

In 1751 White started a *Garden Kalendar* in which he noted his activities in his beloved garden; it later developed into his *Naturalist's Journal*. He continued to make entries until a few days before he died on 26 June 1793. Although not affluent White had been better off than many clergymen of the time, especially as he never married and kept only one servant in the house. He seems not to have led a lonely life for with several brothers and sisters he had many family ties. Two years before his death he proudly recorded that he had fifty-eight nephews and nieces, one of whom remembered him as "only five feet three inches in stature, of a spare form and remarkably upright carriage". This brief description, confirmed by a villager who recalled that he was "a little, thin, prim, upright man", White's own admission that he had stumpy legs, and two pen and ink sketches, are all that we know for certain about his physical appearance. Two other alleged portraits of Gilbert White are of doubtful validity.[3]

MR. JOHN WHITEHEAD, AGE 32.

WHITEHEAD. *INDEPENDENT, HIGHLY-MOTIVATED, PROFESSIONAL BIRD COLLECTOR. TWO EXPEDITIONS TO CORSICA WERE FOLLOWED BY MORE AMBITIOUS PROJECTS, OFTEN OF AN EXTREMELY PERILOUS NATURE. HE DISCOVERED LARGE NUMBERS OF NEW BIRDS, MAMMALS AND INSECTS.*

John Whitehead (1860-1899)

CORSICAN NUTHATCH *Sitta whiteheadi* Sharpe

Sitta whiteheadi Sharpe, 1884. *Proceedings of the Zoological Society of London*, p. 233, Pl. 36: mountains of Corsica

John Whitehead was born at Muswell Hill, in London, on 30 June 1860. He was educated at Elstree and later at the Edinburgh Institution, where his interest in natural history was encouraged to such an extent that within a few years he became, according to Ogilvie-Grant, "one of the best, perhaps the best, of the field naturalists of his time". This happened despite, or even perhaps, because of his lung trouble, which he is said to have developed after pursuing the outdoor life too vigorously whilst in Scotland. Having been advised to go abroad he spent the winter of 1881–82 in the Engadine region of the Swiss Alps and the following winter in Corsica.

In November 1882 Whitehead arrived at Ajaccio on the west coast of the island and stayed in that area until January, shooting and collecting birds. He crossed over the mountains to Aleria and worked his way down the east coast to the southernmost point before returning to Ajaccio. He then headed north to the large lagoon near Bastia but the shooting was poor so he went back to Ajaccio. For much of April, May and June Whitehead was on the east coast but he kept out of the unhealthy marshes in the hottest weather and consequently missed some of the best days of the spring passage. Instead he spent much of the time in the mountains and this fortunately led to his new discovery:

> "On the 12th June 1883, I left a small village to visit the nest of an eagle which the shepherds had told me of. Starting at 4 a.m. with a mule and a guide (taking provisions for two days), it was not until 2 p.m. that we reached the summit of the mountain. As it was close upon 6 o'clock before the nest had been visited, I decided to pass the night in a small stone hut . . . The next morning wishing to get a shot at some Alpine Swifts, which were nesting on a high crag near, I got up early, and when returning heard a curious whistle, which I thought was that of the Crested Titmouse. After I had waited a few minutes a Nuthatch crept out of the end of a pine-bough and was promptly shot. The bird being badly hit in the head, I skinned it at once, and thought no more about it . . ."[1]

In October, after about a year on the island, Whitehead returned home to London. The young collector, only just twenty-three years old, must have found it very hard to contain his impatience as he waited for the next breeding season because Bowdler Sharpe at the British Museum had told him that the nuthatch he had shot was new to science! When he arrived in Corsica, on 9 May, he made directly for the pine forest where he had discovered the nuthatch but found nothing. The following morning was equally unproductive but in the early afternoon he shot a male and a few minutes later a female. To his surprise he found that, unlike many other nuthatches, the sexes were different. The male had a black cap and white stripe above the eye and the female a grey cap and a less-pronounced stripe. Later in the same day Whitehead shot three more of the birds. Then, to his dismay he found that most of the nuthatch nests were between 70 and 100 ft above the ground, in enormous rotten pines. Unlike the Nuthatch *Sitta europaea* (which does not occur on Corsica), these nuthatches had disregarded the old woodpecker holes and had excavated their own, thereby eliminating the need to plaster them with mud in order to reduce the entrance diameters. It took Whitehead three hours hard work to reach the first nest to secure the clutch of five eggs. The second nest was only 40 ft up and he managed to climb an adjacent tree and swing across with the aid of ropes. In all he found nine occupied holes and preserved one of the nests by pulling a great pine tree down with ropes—after he had removed the eggs.

Despite these depredations Whitehead was deeply concerned about the survival of the nuthatches. He believed them to be extremely rare and so never divulged the exact locality where he found them. Later discoveries have shown that they are more widespread than he had realized, but they are confined to the remnant pine forests of Corsica between about 2500 and 6000 ft. Outside the breeding season they can sometimes be seen foraging amongst the trees at lower altitudes, in the company of Firecrests, Goldcrests and Coal Tits.

Whitehead's article on the birds of Corsica appeared in *The Ibis* of 1885, together with a magnificent colour plate of "Whitehead's Nuthatch" by J. G. Keulemans. The young naturalist described all the species that he encountered there and gave some comments on their status. Since then the populations of some of the birds have become much reduced. Only a handful of Lammergeirs remain and the White-headed Duck no longer breeds there. Fortunately the lovely songs of the Citril Finch and the Serin can still be heard; the former in the montane coniferous forests, the latter often among the olive and cork groves, and in and around the villages.

For the rest of his relatively short life Whitehead had little to do with Western Palearctic birds. Only a few months after his return to England, making no

Corsican Nuthatch

concessions for his lung trouble, he prepared himself for a four-year expedition to the jungles of North Borneo.

He left England in October 1884 and later recounted his many adventures in his book *The Exploration of Mount Kina-Balu* (1893). It was a lavish, large-format, single-volume work illustrated by himself with village scenes, views of the mountain and colour plates of some of the birds, mammals, butterflies and other insects which he had brought back. In his introduction he wrote: "Essentially and by choice a 'field naturalist', I find it far easier to explore an unknown tract of country than to write an account of my researches." Nevertheless it was a well-written and interesting account of his travels in Borneo and adjacent Palawan and Java, in which he made light of the many difficulties and dangers. For example, he mentioned casually that "several tribes about the foot of Kina-Balu had been misbehaving themselves after their manner, by collecting a few heads to celebrate their harvest thanksgiving"!

The reality of the situation was far more serious. On his first attempt to penetrate the area he came across a police patrol which had been attacked and watched helplessly as one of their number slowly died from a number of wounds. On his second attempt Whitehead also failed to get far up the side of the mountain, but by then he was learning to overcome some of the enormous problems.

There was little hope of living off the land and so food and shelter had to be transported into the jungle by native porters who often proved to be a source of considerable frustration. They were superstitious, sometimes refusing to work for no sensible reason and sometimes becoming quite hostile towards him. Even when things were going well they did not share the naturalist's concept of the value of time. The ever present leeches, brown or green and yellow, caused his clothes to become saturated

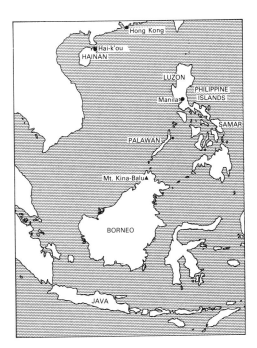

BORNEO

with blood, and the tiny wounds could irritate for weeks afterwards and often developed into running sores. He also had to cope with attacks of dysentery and malaria. As if this was not enough, he had to endure torrential rain every day for six or seven of the twelve hours of daylight! Indeed the top of Kina-Balu, at over 13,000 ft, was rarely out of the clouds. The nights were usually clear but they became increasingly cold the higher he ascended.

The area had been visited a few years earlier by Sir Hugh Low and Thomas Lobb and each had startled the botanical world with the new species of giant insectivorous pitcher plants which they had sent back to Europe along with splendid collections of orchids. The main attraction for Whitehead was that most of North Borneo was still virgin territory for the zoologist and he was able to obtain a large number of birds, mammals and insects which were new to science. On 25 February 1887, after several months of collecting and notwithstanding his earlier discovery of the Corsican Nuthatch, he wrote:

> "Today has been the grandest day for me since I took an interest in ornithology, and has brought to light the first specimens of the large green Cock-of-the-Rock (Calyptomena Whiteheadi)—the plumage of this superb bird being bright emerald-green, which shines like glass, picked out with jet-black markings."[2]

It is now known as Whitehead's Broadbill.

Further up the mountain the vegetation became less dense and the variety of birds diminished; once above 7000 ft he found only ten new species but four of these he was able to place in new genera. Eventually, after three separate attempts, he reached the bare rocky summit of the mountain. He wrote a message with the date (11 February 1888), his name and the names of the natives with him, put it in a sauce bottle and placed a cairn of stones over it; a small gesture interpreted by his companions as a religious ceremony of the "Orang-puteh'. Whitehead was not the first to conquer the mountain but it provided a satisfactory turning point to the expedition and after a few more months of travelling he arrived back in England.

He spent much of the next few years distributing his collections and labouring over his book, his only major publication. There were separate appendices on the reptiles, mammals, beetles and butterflies compiled by leading specialists of the day, and the ornithological section, co-written with Bowdler Sharpe, contained the descriptions of about forty-five new species. The book was completed by May 1893 and Whitehead then prepared to return to the Far East, this time to the Philippines. In December of the same year he was already exploring the island of Luzon.

He hired native bearers to assist him but again had trouble finding suitable hunters and taxidermists. "Worse than useless" he called one of his men who repeatedly brought him specimens that were wingless or so badly blasted that he could not keep them. In all Whitehead made nine expeditions to various parts of the Philippines, each time returning to Manila to send specimens home, renew his supplies and sometimes change his assistants. As usual he struggled in appalling conditions: "To cut a long story short, it rained all November, all December, and all January: one deluge began on the 11th December, and was perhaps second only to that which floated Noah and his great zoological collection, for it continued until the 6th of January 1896! . . . In such weather it was hardly to be expected that we should do very much . . ." Over and over again he was racked by fever, but now and then he was spurred on by new finds, such as the discovery of five new genera of rodents on the heights of Mt Data. It was a mixed blessing when one series of his collections, made on the island of Samar, was destroyed by fire on its return passage, because when he went back to the island to replace the losses, he acquired a new species of eagle that had eluded him on his previous visit. At that time the forests of the island were still vast, but even so, much of the timber, especially on the west coast, had been felled for several miles inland, leaving ranges of undulating hills that were badly eroded. On the Pacific coast most of the forest was in pristine condition and some of the trees were more than 200 ft tall.

> "In these lofty forests the Great Philippine Eagle has made his home, with no enemies to trouble him. He is well known to the natives as a robber of their poultry and small pigs, but chiefly as a destroyer of monkeys, which are the only animals sufficiently abundant in these forests to support such a large bird . . . One morning . . . my servant Juan returned with this huge bird, which he shot with an old muzzle loader, luckily putting one buckshot into its neck. The Eagle fastened its talons round the branch in its death-grip and hung firmly at the top of the tree . . . [Juan] climbed the tree and secured the prize. When he handed it over to me it was so heavy that I could hardly hold it out at arm's length in my then enfeebled state of health . . ."[3]

This eagle, long known as the Philippine Monkey-eating Eagle, was given the scientific name *Pithecophaga jefferyi* because Whitehead especially asked Ogilvie-Grant to name the bird after his father Jeffrey Whitehead, a London stockbroker, "by whose generous aid this and my Bornean expedition have been carried out". The bird is now one of the rarest raptors in the world. In the hundred years since Whitehead was on Samar much more of the forest has been destroyed and it has not been seen there since 1934. However, it still occurs in small numbers on some of the other islands.

On 22 October of the same year, satisfied that he had covered most of the different habitats on most of the islands, and having more than made good his losses due to the fire, he set sail for England. Less than three years later he returned, hoping to complete his researches, but the Spanish–American War forced him to alter his plans and many species in the Philippines were left to other collectors to discover; Edgar Mearns, the famous American ornithologist, being among the more notable.

After several frustrating weeks in Manila, Whitehead sailed to Hong Kong and thence to the island of Hainan. To Whitehead it must have seemed a poor substitute, as he knew that Robert Swinhoe had already collected in many parts of the island. In mid-March he set off into the interior hoping to cover some new ground but he and his twenty-eight porters were quickly overtaken by fever in the Five-Finger Mountains. His diary entries became increasingly difficult to maintain.

> "April 2nd. V. seedy with dysentery. Juan shot a silver pheasant which may be new, and a fine paradise flycatcher. Heat and sand-flies awful.
> 3rd–19th. All ill with fever and dysentery.
> 19th–30th. The bird collecting is going along slowly—my men being all ill one day or another; one or two have been ill every day with fever. I am perhaps in better health than I have been for some time. Lū women catching caterpillars for food. It rains heavily and thunders every afternoon, and our life here, owing to fever, is most miserable.
> 21st–23rd (May). Nearly dead with fever—no food—no depression of temperature."
> [This was the final entry.][4]

Whitehead died on 2 June, less than a month before his thirty-ninth birthday. His Chinese servants carried his body, all his equipment and collections, on a nineteen-day journey back to the northern port of Hai-k'ou where he was buried in the cemetery by the sea.[5] The British Consul forwarded his 250 perfectly preserved bird skins to the British (Natural History) Museum.

In many ways it was a wonder that he had lasted so long. There seems to be little similarity between the cautious young man who had deliberately kept out of the marshes of Corsica and the John Whitehead who had endured so many privations in the humid jungles of the East. It would have been hard for him to have found an unhealthier location in which to pursue his passion for collecting and exploring. Yet unlike many others, Whitehead did not collect primarily for himself; most of his discoveries were given to other naturalists to describe. Nevertheless he enjoyed the thrill of finding new species and may not have been entirely honest with himself when he wrote in his introduction to *Kina-Balu*:

> "I did not visit these lands for the purpose of collecting hides and horns for my trophies, but rather the more lasting beauties of the East, and especially, if possible, to add some little everlasting stone to that ever increasing cairn of human knowledge . . ."

Alexander Wilson (1766-1813)

WILSON'S STORM-PETREL *Oceanites oceanicus* (Kuhl)

Pro.[cellaria] oceanica Kuhl, 1820. *Beiträge zur Zoologie*, Pt 1, p. 136, Pl. 10, Fig. 1: No locality. South Georgia designated by Murphy

WILSON'S PHALAROPE *Phalaropus tricolor* (Vieillot)

Steganopus tricolor Vieillot, 1819. *Nouveau Dictionnaire d'Histoire Naturelle, Nouvelle édition*, Vol. 32, p. 136: Paraguay.

HOODED WARBLER *Wilsonia citrina* (Boddaert)

Wilsonia Bonaparte, 1838. *Geographical and Comparative List of the Birds of Europe and North America*, p. 23. Type, by subsequent designation, *Motacilla mitrata* Gmelin = *Muscicapa citrina* Boddaert (Ridgway, 1881)
Mucicapa Citrina, Boddaert, 1783. *Tables des Planches Enluminées*, p. 41: Louisiana

Alexander Wilson was born in Paisley on 6 July 1766 and was baptized soon afterwards by the Reverend John Witherspoon. The minister later emigrated to North America and in 1776 was the only clergyman to sign the Declaration of Independence. Twenty years later, disillusioned with life in Scotland, Wilson also sailed to the New World and became, like Witherspoon, one of the most famous early citizens of the United States, as the author of the *American Ornithology* (1808–14).

Generally considered only to have become interested in birds after his arrival in America, Wilson had in fact already written about the waterfowl of Lochwinnoch, hunted gamebirds on the moors and enjoyed watching the Gannets and the other seabirds of the Firth of Forth. During his years of travel around central Scotland, he had become used to walking great distances, travelling rough and living off the land, long before he began his great "pedestrian achievements" abroad.

Known in his early years as Sandy, he made such rapid progress at school that his mother began to cherish great hopes for him; she had greatly admired Witherspoon and decided that Sandy should follow him into the ministry. Soon the boy was being tutored by a divinity student, though he much preferred to

WILSON. *SCOTTISH WEAVER AND POET WHOSE ACCUSATORY VERSES LED TO IMPRISONMENT; ON HIS RELEASE HE EMIGRATED TO THE UNITED STATES OF AMERICA TO BEGIN A NEW LIFE. AMAZED BY THE BEAUTY OF THE NEW WORLD BIRDS HE BEGAN TO OBSERVE AND PAINT THEM, EVENTUALLY PRODUCING THE AMBITIOUS AND INNOVATIVE* AMERICAN ORNITHOLOGY.

spend his time by the river, fishing, swimming, gathering mussels, or rabbiting along the banks. However, when he was ten his mother died and his schooling came to an abrupt end.

Wilson's father had given up smuggling at the time of his marriage and had become a prosperous weaver in Paisley, then the fastest growing town in Scotland and famous for its thread-making and weaving industries; he owned a number of looms and hired other weavers to work for him. After the death of his wife he immediately remarried, to a widow with children and Sandy was sent from the crowded house to a farm near Beith where he stayed until the age of thirteen, working as a cowherd. Then, when his sister Mary married a Paisley weaver Sandy became his apprentice. Meanwhile, Sandy's father and the rest of his family had moved into Auchinbathie Tower, a grim old fort in the hills three miles south-east of Lochwinnoch, where he had taken up weaving in smuggled silk. When Sandy's three-year apprenticeship was completed he too moved into the tower and spent the next two years working in Lochwinnoch as a journeyman weaver.

Each morning he set off early from the tower and followed the road which ran between Barr Meadows and Castle Semple Loch. In winter he often stopped to watch as gaggles of grey geese flew over, or listened as the Whooper Swans flighted in. Throughout the day, while he drove the shuttle, Pope or Milton's works would be propped up on his loom, then walking back home in the evening, he played with words, trying to express his own responses to the people and the countryside around him. In *Lochwinnoch, a Descriptive Poem* he wrote about the waterfowl he had seen on Castle Semple Loch:

> "Adjoining this, 'midst bordering reeds and fens,
> The lengthened lake its glossy flood extends,
> Slow stealing on with lazy silent pace,
> The Peel lone rising from its wat'ry face.
> Here stalks the heron gazing in the lake,
> The snowy swan and party-coloured drake;
> The bittern lone that shakes the solid ground,
> While thro' still midnight groans the hollow sound;
> The noisy goose, the teal in black'ning trains,
> And long-billed snipe that knows approaching rains;
> Wild fowl unnumbered here continual rove,
> Explore the deep or sail the winds above."

Sometimes, in winter, the loch froze over, and with his friends, Sandy skated around the old Peel. (Today, the ruins of this tower lie on the boundary of the R.S.P.B. Lochwinnoch Reserve which includes part of Castle Semple Loch and Barr Meadows.) In the worst weather he lodged in the village. But whenever he could, Wilson escaped from the hated loom to go out walking and rhyming, or poaching Red Grouse on the surrounding moorland.

When his sister's husband opened a business at Queen's Ferry, near Edinburgh, Sandy Wilson went to work for him once more. He spent most of the next four years peddling their lengths of muslins and silk, handkerchiefs and ribbons around the countryside. When the weather was very bad he slept in inns, but usually he sought shelter in a barn or some old ruin to save money. He was continually writing verses in imitation of the great English poets, but when Robert Burns published his first book of poems and songs in 1786, all in his native Lallans, Sandy was set free by his influence and began to write in his own dialect.

Whereas Burns was an Ayrshire farmer who "rov'd by bonie Doon", Wilson was more familiar with the Black Cart River and the weaving sheds of Paisley. He wrote on the conventional topics of love and nature but he was also the first poet to write successfully from his own experience about machine industry and life in the factories. Although his poems met with some interest, the acknowledgement he had hoped for failed to materialize at a time when all Scotland was thrilled by Burns's powerful verses.

Wilson eventually returned to the loom again in Paisley but tension between the weavers and the mill owners grew rapidly. There had been revolution in France and America—increasingly punitive action was being taken against Scottish reformers. By the summer Wilson had been arrested, and, between periods of bail, he languished for the next one and a half years in Paisley jail. He was known to

Wilson's Storm-petrel

have published several anonymous satires against the mill owners and when a libellous poem was received by Mr Sharp, owner of the Long Mills in Paisley, Wilson was immediately suspected. The poem, *The Shark, or Lang Mills Detected*, accused the recipient of cheating the weavers, and an accompanying letter threatened that the poem would be published unless five guineas were paid to suppress it. Wilson's part in the whole affair is still mysterious: the satirical verse was much in character but extortion was not. Yet when he was arrested, he admitted writing the letter but would not acknowledge authorship of the poem. As a result, instead of being charged with libel, which would have led to an examination of the well-founded allegations and perhaps his vindication, Wilson was convicted of blackmail; a slur on his character which haunted him even in America.

Whatever the truth about the whole puzzling affair, it was Wilson who suffered. He had lost any hope he had of patronage or marriage into a good family and he was penniless. During his imprisonment his roistering poem *Watty and Meg* had swept the country, selling more than 100,000 copies, but the public credited it to Burns and Wilson's profits only cleared his debts to his printer. When he was finally released he only worked long enough to raise his passage to the United States. Then early one morning in May 1794, he set off with his nephew, William Duncan, who had pleaded to go with him. They walked to Portpatrick in Wigtownshire and sailed to Belfast where they found deck space on board the *Swift*, bound for Delaware Bay. They arrived there a week after Wilson's twenty-eighth birthday, owning nothing except a flute and a 'fowling piece', and with only a few shillings lent to them by a kindly fellow passenger. As they walked the thirty miles to Philadelphia, Wilson shot a Red-headed Woodpecker, so delighted by its beauty that he immediately regretted his action.

At first, Alexander Wilson and William Duncan accepted any employment that they were offered, then Wilson settled down as a schoolteacher, living beside the Delaware River at Milestown for five years. In Scotland he had always been aware of birds but he paid no special attention to them because most of the birds he saw were familiar to him. Now he was living on one of America's greatest flyways and he was thrilled by the vast numbers of migrating ducks, geese and swans. He had never before seen birds in such numbers or such brilliantly varied colours. He kept some as pets but it was not until after he moved to Gray's Ferry, just outside Philadelphia, that he began to seriously draw and paint them. He soon realized that he worked best from live specimens, and wrote, rather poignantly:

"I have had live crows, hawks, owls, opossums, squirrels, snakes and lizards so that my own room sometimes reminded me of Noah's ark; but Noah had a wife in one corner of it and in this particular our parallel does not altogether tally."

He began to dream about painting and describing all the American birds, but he had no scientific training and his early artwork left much to be desired. Fortunately, one of his closest neighbours was William Bartram, then in his sixties but still a keen naturalist with a fine library which he made available to Wilson. There he studied the works of Linnaeus, Pennant, Catesby and Buffon, realizing how little was known about the rich and varied bird life around him. He began to spend all his spare time either out in the field birdwatching or indoors, painting.

In June 1804 he was proud to become a United States citizen, and, in the autumn, set off with his nephew and a friend to walk to Niagara Falls. During the two-month trip they covered about 1300 miles and Wilson collected several new bird species. His hopes for his book on American birds began to become a reality in 1806 when the publisher, Samuel Bradford, offered him the job of assistant editor of Abraham Ree's *Cyclopaedia*. Wilson told him about his proposed book and showed him some engravings which he had already completed. Bradford agreed to publish the work in ten volumes, with ten colour plates in each. Wilson was now able to resign from his teaching post and put all his energies into the two projects.

One of the greatest problems which he faced was that of finding suitable colourists for his engravings, as many of the early plates were spoilt through streaking or too heavy a wash. When he discovered that Bradford's seventeen year old apprentice, Charles Robert Leslie, was a gifted artist, his problem was partly solved. Thereafter Leslie coloured many of the plates with great care and accuracy and grew to admire Wilson enormously. It says much for Wilson's generosity that although he was dependent on Leslie's skills, he and some friends bought up his apprenticeship after three years and sent him to England to study art. He later became one of the greatest Victorian artists, a court painter to the Queen and one of her favourites. In his old age, Leslie wrote an autobiography and in it recalled Wilson's physical appearance and his enormous patience:

> "He looked like a bird: his eyes were piercing, dark and luminous, and his nose shaped like a beak. He was of a spare, bony form, very erect in his carriage, inclining to be tall; and with a light, elastic step, he seemed [perfectly] qualified by nature for his extraordinary pedestrian achievements . . . I assisted him to color some of his first plates. He worked from birds which he had shot and stuffed and I remember the extreme accuracy of his drawings, and how carefully he had counted the number of scales on the tiny legs and feet of his subject."

The first volume of the *American Ornithology* illustrated common passerines such as the Blue Jay, Baltimore Oriole, Wood Thrush and Golden-crowned Kinglet. Wilson was greatly encouraged when Meriwether Lewis gave him specimens which he had collected on his Pacific coast expedition with Clark, as well as his ornithological notes. In their honour Wilson named two of the new discoveries Lewis's Woodpecker and Clark's Crow (now Clark's Nutcracker).

The autumn of 1808 awakened old memories of his peddling days in Scotland when he set off northwards with a copy of the first volume to solicit subscribers. His early travelling days must have set him in good stead, for he thought nothing of lengthy journeys in all types of weather, and was long accustomed to only his own company for days on end.

In the early winter he went southwards to Washington, where Thomas Jefferson, the President, welcomed him warmly and took out a subscription. Wilson then rode south to North Carolina. Outside Wilmington he shot three Ivory-billed Woodpeckers one of which was only slightly wounded, so he carried it back to the inn, delighted that he had a live bird to draw. He locked it in his room, attended to his horse and, on returning, discovered that his bed was covered in plaster. The woodpecker had already drilled a hole the size of a man's fist but had not quite reached the outer wall. Had Wilson not tied a string round its leg and the bedroom table it would soon have made its escape. Wilson's embarrassment was by this time mixed with considerable respect for his captive and he went in search of food for it, while the bird proceeded to destroy the fine mahogany table. Wilson then wisely decided to paint the bird without any further delay, receiving several gashes from its powerful bill before he was finished.

From Savannah he sailed to New York, pleased at having obtained 250 new subcribers and to have discovered more new species. During the next year he worked on the *Ornithology* until the first copies of volume two were ready, then he set off alone to New Orleans, with the usual dual aim of obtaining subscriptions and collecting birds. It was his longest expedition. He travelled first to Pittsburgh where he bought a rowboat and called it *The Ornithologist* (a name assumed by its next owner to be that of an Indian chief). As soon as the ice broke up on the Ohio Wilson started downriver with his baggage and his gun. Among the most memorable birds that he encountered were the flocks of Carolina Parakeets, now extinct. They were then so common that when flocks settled on the ground, whole fields turned scarlet, yellow and green. He

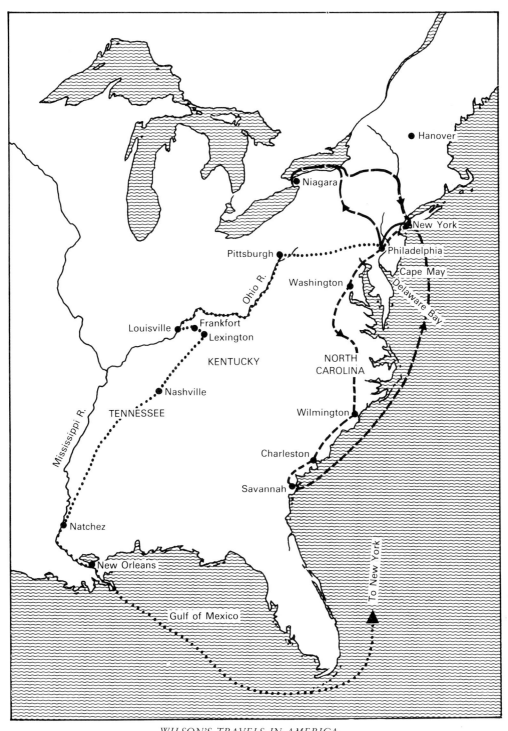

WILSON'S TRAVELS IN AMERICA:

━━━━━━━ AUTUMN 1804

━ ━ ━ ━ ━ WINTER 1808-9

· · · · · · · · · JANUARY TO AUGUST 1810

Hanover

Niagara

New York

Pittsburgh
Philadelphia
Cape May

Washington

Ohio R.

Louisville
Frankfort
Lexington

Delaware Bay

KENTUCKY

NORTH
CAROLINA

Nashville

TENNESSEE

Wilmington

Charleston

Savannah

Mississippi R.

Natchez

To New York

New Orleans

Gulf of Mexico

shot one, wounding it slightly on the wing and thereafter *Poll* travelled with him, either in the stern of the boat, or, when he walked, wrapped in a silk handkerchief in his pocket. Wilson was interested in the factors determining their range and decided that their preferred food, the cockle burr, was more influential than climate.

When he reached Louisville he sold his boat and visited a local storekeeper who gave drawing lessons, hoping that he would become a subscriber. The man behind the counter was John James Audubon, who was sufficiently impressed by the two volumes to be about to sign the contract when his partner suggested that Audubon's own paintings were superior and so he changed his mind. Much has been written of this first chance meeting between the two great ornithologists. There is no doubt that later, Audubon far exceeded Wilson in artistic ability; the lively beauty of his creatures and his strength of composition contrast greatly with the stiffness of Wilson's birds. But just as over twenty years before, Wilson had broken free from writing laboured English verses through the powerful influence of Robert Burns's broad Scots, so Wilson now inspired Audubon. Until their meeting Audubon had painted on any and every subject; now he realized that natural history was a subject worthy of his skills, although it was some years before he channelled all his talents in that direction.

After watching Whooping Cranes in the surrounding marshes, Wilson walked on to Lexington, Kentucky, making a detour to examine a wood where Passenger Pigeons had bred. He found a great forest of dead beech trees, covering about 120 square miles, with up to ninety nests in one tree and many branches broken off through the sheer weight of the birds. The next day, pigeons began to fly overhead in vast numbers as far as the eye could see. Wilson had seen huge flocks which darkened the sky before, but he was so impressed by this movement that, "Curious to determine how long this appearance would continue, I took out my watch to note the time, and sat down to observe them. It was then half past one. I sat for more than an hour, but instead of a diminution of this prodigious procession, it seemed rather to increase both in numbers and rapidity; and anxious to reach Frankfurt before night, I rose and went on."[1] When he reached the town at 4 o'clock they were still passing overhead and continued to do so till six in the evening. The number of birds in this flock has been estimated to be in excess of two thousand million!

In Lexington he bought an excellent horse and rode through Kentucky and Tennessee as warblers arrived from the south, finding two new species which he named after these two states. In Nashville he spent eight days painting all his new specimens and wrote to his friend Sarah Miller, whom he had known since his Milestown days, informing her that *Poll* was now learning to talk and came when called, and that he was about to set off on an 800-mile journey through Indian country. Though warned against it, Wilson followed the Natchez Trace, an ancient Indian trade route along a crest of ridges. Before leaving Philadelphia he had been saddened by news of the mysterious death of the explorer Captain Lewis, and he wanted to investigate the story for himself. At Grinder's Stand, where Lewis was buried, he paid for the care of the grave and after questioning a witness, concluded that Lewis had been murdered, though the official verdict was suicide.

Near Charleston Wilson suddenly became seriously ill with fever but he managed to reach Natchez and was invited by a fellow Scot to stay at his elegant plantation house deep in the oak woods. There he regained his strength and formed close friendships, doubly welcome after his solitary travels. It was here that he discovered and shot the Mississippi Kite, though he had to paint it with a bandaged hand because the wounded bird had struck him with its claws. His host introduced him to so many acquaintances that he gained the surprising total of twenty-three subscriptions in and around the small town.

In June, after travelling 3000 miles in less than six months, he sailed from New Orleans well pleased to have discovered a dozen new birds. For some time the ship lay becalmed in the Gulf of Mexico, thus making it possible for Wilson to row to some of the islands off the Florida coast. Poor *Poll*, his companion for so long, flew overboard and drowned. Later the weather became rough and stormy petrels followed the ship. In his *Ornithology* Wilson condemned the sailors' superstition that because of the birds' association with storms they were connected with Satan, and despite their protestations he shot fourteen and succeeded in retrieving them with the aid of a small boat. He examined the petrels' stomach contents—as he always did, to learn about feeding habits—and also noted that one bird, easily identified by the loss of some flight feathers, had followed the ship for nearly a week, for over 400 miles.

Believing these birds to be identical to the Storm Petrel, Wilson referred to them as *Procellaria pelagica* (Linnaeus's name for them). Later, Charles Bonaparte realized that, though very similar, they were a distinct species which he named *Procellaria Wilsonii*,[2] unaware that they had been described and named by Heinrich Kuhl four years earlier, in 1820. Despite this, the vernacular name of Wilson's Storm-petrel continues to be used in North America and some European countries for this small seabird, perhaps the most numerous bird in the world.[3] Bonaparte also created the genus *Wilsonia* which includes the Hooded, Wilson's and Canada Warblers.

Wilson returned to Philadelphia in August and resumed work on the *Ornithology*, resigning his editorship of the *Cyclopaedia* early in the next year so that he could concentrate his energies. In a letter to a friend in Paisley he wrote:

Wilson's Phalarope

"I was a wanderer when I was in Scotland, and I have been much more so since my arrival here. Few Americans have seen more of their country than I have done, and none love her more."

He made only one more long journey, this time to Hanover, near the Canadian border, but he made many short trips to the New Jersey coastal marshes, sometimes in the company of George Ord, a wealthy young sportsman who discovered the Cape May Warbler for him. In March 1813 Wilson completed the seventh volume and went to the coast for a month in the summer, then returned to the boarding house in Philadelphia, his home since he first moved to Gray's Ferry. On the 19 August he was sufficiently weak from dysentery to require a doctor; afterwards Wilson made his will leaving everything to his friend Sarah Miller, except for a set of the *Ornithology* to his nephew William Duncan and two sets to his father. Four days later, he died.

Alexander Wilson was among the very first to study American birds in their natural habitat and was their first true *field* ornithologist. For the last ten years of his life he had worked on the *American Ornithology* complementing the notes of

Hooded Warbler

many correspondents with his own original observations. This he did in such a way that Joseph Sabine declared that Wilson had "produced a work which, for correctness of description, accuracy of observation, and acuteness of distinction, will compete with every publication of natural history yet extant . . . the beauty of the style, and perspicuity of the narrative, add unrivalled charms to its scientific merits."[4] The work is most valuable today for its detailed text, in particular its information on species which are now endangered or extinct, among them the Ivory-billed Woodpecker, Eskimo Curlew, Labrador Duck and Carolina Parakeet; his vivid descriptions of the Passenger Pigeons which then occurred in vast numbers have often been quoted. Wilson's extensive journeys through the American wilderness added forty-eight new species of birds to those already known, and by the time of his death he had completed the text and illustrations for the first eight volumes of the *Ornithology*. He had also left sufficient illustrations for a ninth volume for which George Ord provided the text.

Wilson's Phalarope was not described in the *American Ornithology*, despite the fact that Wilson acquired a specimen and made a painting from it which was in his portfolio when he died. The omission was due to an oversight by Ord, and Wilson's discovery lay neglected until Bonaparte searched through the artist's material in preparation for his sequel to the work; but by then Vieillot had already described the wader from a wintering individual procured in South America. By a happy coincidence, the bird owes its popular name to Joseph Sabine who, ignorant of the fact that Wilson and others had already discovered the phalarope, described it in his zoological appendix to the narrative of Franklin's first overland Canadian expedition. Sabine called it *Phalaropus Wilsoni*, simply because of his enormous respect for him as the Father of American Ornithology.

Bibliography and Notes

General Bibliography

Mullens, W.H. and Swann, H.K. 1917. *A Bibliography of British Ornithology*. MacMillan & Co., London.

Prestwich, A.A. 1963. "I name this parrot . . ." Prestwich, Edenbridge.

Vaurie, C. 1959–1965. *The Birds of the Palaearctic Fauna*, 2 vols. H.F. & G. Witherby, London.

Wynne, O.E. 1969. *Biographical Key—Names of Birds of the World—to Authors and those Commemorated*. Wynne, Fordingbridge.

Introduction

See e.g. Thomson, A.L. 1985. Nomenclature, *in* Campbell, B. and Lack, E. (Eds) *A Dictionary of Birds*. Calton (Poyser).

1. *Quoted in* Cutright, P.R. and Brodhead, M.J. 1981. *Elliott Coues, Naturalist and Frontier Historian*, p. 321. University of Illinois Press, Chicago.

Adams

Adams, E. 1878. Notes on the Birds of Michalaski, Norton Sound. *Ibis*, pp. 420–442.

Bury and Norwich Post 17.12.1856. Obituary.

Collinson, R. 1889. *Journal of H.M.S. Enterprise on the expedition in search of Sir John Franklin's ships by Behring Strait 1850–55*. Samson Low & Co., London.

1. These drawings by Adams were said to have been deposited at the British Museum but their present whereabouts are unknown. They may be in private hands (*see* Günther, A. (Ed.) 1904–12. *The History of the Collections Contained in the Natural History Departments of the British Museum*, Vol. II, p. 251. BM publication, London).

2. At least two publications erroneously connect the White-billed Diver with Royal Navy Surgeon Arthur Adams who also visited the Arctic and who also made a number of zoological sketches: Warren, R.L.M. 1966. *Type Specimens of Birds in the British Museum (Natural History)*, Vol. I; and Coomans de Ruiter, L., *et al.* 1947. *Beteekens en Etymologie van de Wetenschappelijke namen der Nederlandsche Vogels*. Club van Nederlandsche Vogelkundigen.

3. Seebohm, H. 1885. On the occurrence of the White-billed Diver, Colymbus adamsi, on the British coasts. *Zoologist*, pp. 144–145.

Alexander

Alexander, B. 1896. Ornithological Notes from Romney Marsh and its neighbourhood; Notes on Birds in Kent; Ornithological Notes from Rye. *Zoologist*, pp. 246–253; 344–349; 408–416.

Alexander, B. 1898. An Ornithological Expedition to the Cape Verde Islands. *Ibis*, pp. 74–118.
Alexander, B. 1903. On the Birds of Fernando Po. *Ibis*, pp. 330–403.
Alexander, B. 1907. *From the Niger to the Nile*, 2 vols. E. Arnold, London.
Alexander, B. 1912. *Boyd Alexander's Last Journey* [with memoir by H. Alexander]. E. Arnold, London.
Grant, W.R.O. 1910. Boyd Alexander and his Ornithological Works. *Ibis*, pp. 716–729.
1. Alexander, B. 1898. *op. cit.*, p. 97.

Allen

Allen, W. 1855. *The Dead Sea, a New Route to India, with other Fragments and Gleanings in the East*, 2 vols. Longman & Co., London.
Allen, W. and Thomson, T.R.H. 1848. *A Narrative of the Expedition sent by H.M. Government to the River Niger in 1841*, 2 vols. R. Bentley, London.
Dictionary of National Biography 1885–1900. Vol. I, p. 322. London.
Gentleman's Magazine 1864. New series, Vol. XVI, pp. 659–660. Obituary.
O'Byrn, W.R. 1849. *A Naval Biographical Dictionary*, pp. 11–12. J. Murray, London.
Southern Times 6.2.1864. Obituary.
1. Allen, W. and Thomson, T.R.H. 1848. *op. cit.*, Vol. I, pp. 332–333; Vol. II, p. 507.

Amherst

Beebe, W. 1921. *A Monograph of the Pheasants*, Vol. IV, pp. 26–35. H.F. & G. Witherby, London.
Coats, A.M. 1969. *The Quest for Plants*, pp. 94, 151–153. Studio Vista, London.
Complete Peerage 1945. Vols I and X. St. Catherine Press, London.
Heber, R. 1828. *Narrative of a Journey through the Upper Provinces of India, from Calcutta to Bombay 1824–5*. J. Murray, London.
Ritchie, A.T. and Evans, R. 1894. *Rulers of India. Lord Amherst and the British advance eastwards to Burma*. Clarendon Press, Oxford.

Aristotle

Encyclopaedia Britannica 1875. 9th edn, Vol. II, pp. 510–523. Edinburgh.
Stresemann, E. 1975. *Ornithology, from Aristotle to the Present*, pp. 1–23. Harvard University Press.
1. *Quoted in* Stresemann, E. 1975. *op. cit.*, pp. 5–6.

Audouin

Audouin, J.V. 1826. *Explication sommaire des planches d'Oiseaux de l'Égypte et de la Syrie*. Paris.
Dictionaire de Biographie Française 1933–. Vol. IV, columns 431–433. Paris.

Baillon

Gladstone, H.S. Unpublished MS, from: Prarond, E. 1852–57. *Mémoires de la Société Impériale d'Emulation d'Abbeville*. Abbeville; and from information supplied by the Bibliothèque Nationale, Paris.
1. Stephens, J.F. 1824. *In* Shaw, G. *General Zoology*, Vol. XII, p. 228. London.

Baird

Cutright, P.R. and Brodhead, M.J. 1981. *Elliott Coues, Naturalist and Frontier Historian*. University of Illinois Press, Chicago.
Dall, W.H. 1915. *Spencer Fullerton Baird 1823–1887, a Biography*. J.B. Lippincott Co., Philadelphia and London.
1,2. *Quoted in* Cutright, P.R. and Brodhead, M.J. *op. cit.*, pp. 256; 37.

Barrow

Barrow, J. 1801. *An Account of Travels into the Interior of Southern Africa in the years 1797 and 1798*, Vol. I. T. Cadell & W. Davies, London.
Barrow, J. 1847. *An Autobiographical Memoir of Sir John Barrow, Bart., Late of the Admiralty*. J. Murray, London.
Dictionary of National Biography 1885–1900. Vol. III, pp. 305–307. London.
Lloyd, C. 1970. *Mr. Barrow of the Admiralty; A Life of Sir John Barrow 1764–1848*. Collins, London.
1. Ross, J.C. 1847. *A Voyage of Discovery and Research in the Southern and Antarctic Regions, during the years 1839–43*, Vol. I, p. 187. J. Murray, London.
2. Richardson, J. and Swainson, W. 1831. *Fauna Boreali-Americana*, Vol. II, pp. 456–457. J. Murray, London.
3. Lloyd, C. *op. cit.*, p. 90.

Bartram

Cantwell, R. 1961. *Alexander Wilson*. J.B. Lippincott Co., Philadelphia and New York.
Dictionary of American Biography 1928–36. Vol. II, pp. 28–29. New York.
Kastner, J. 1978. *A World of Naturalists*, pp. 79–112. J. Murray, London.
1. Wilson, A. 1808–14. *American Ornithology*, Vol. VII, p. 63. Bradford & Inskeep, Philadelphia.

Bergius

Dictionary of South African Biography 1968–1981. Vol. III, pp. 61–62. Cape Town.
Ffolliott, P. and Liversidge, R. 1964. Carl Heinrich Bergius, Cape Apothecary and Collector, 1816–1818. *Quarterly Bulletin of the South African Library*, March, pp. 134–142; June, pp. 183–192.

Berthelot

Dictionaire de Biographie Française 1933–. Vol. VI, columns 201–202. Paris.
Dictionary of National Biography 1885–1900. Vol. LX, pp. 105–107. [P.B. Webb], London.
1,2. *Quoted in* Dresser, H.E. 1871–81. *A History of the Birds of Europe*, Vol. III, pp. 293; 292.

Bewick

Bain, I. (Ed.) 1981. *Thomas Bewick. My Life*. Folio Society, London.
Dictionary of National Biography 1885–1900. Vol. IV, pp. 452–460. London.
Goddard, T.R. [1929] *A History of the Natural History Society of Northumberland, Durham and Newcastle upon Tyne 1829–1929*, pp. 35–37. A. Reid & Co. Ltd, Newcastle upon Tyne.
1. Latham, J. 1824. *General History of British Birds*, Vol. X, p. 219. Winchester.
2. *Transactions of the Natural History Society of Northumberland, Durham and Newcastle upon Tyne* 1830, **1**: 1–2; 17–25.
3. Yarrell, W. 1830. *Transactions of the Linnean Society of London* **16**: 453.
4. Audubon, J. J. 1832–39. *Ornithological Biography*, letterpress to pl. 118. Edinburgh.

Blyth

Dictionary of National Biography 1885–1900. Vol. V, pp. 276–277. London.
Gladstone, H.S. Unpublished MS, from: *Ibis* 1908, Jubilee Supplement, pp. 175–176; *Journal of the Asiatic Society of Bengal* 1875, part 2, extra number; Mullens, W.H. and Swann, H.K. 1917. *Bibliography of British Ornithology*, p. 73. MacMillan & Co., London.
1,2. *Quoted in Dictionary of National Biography op. cit.*, p. 277.

Bolle

Bannerman, D.A. and Bannerman, W.M. 1968. *Birds of the Atlantic Islands*, Vol. IV, pp. 18–19. Oliver & Boyd, Edinburgh and London.
Gebhardt, L. 1964. *Die Ornithologen Mitteleuropas*, p. 44. Giessen.
1. *Quoted in* Mercer, J. 1980. *The Canary Islanders, their prehistory, conquest and survival*, pp. 170–171. R. Collings, London.

Bonaparte

Brodhead, M.J. 1978. The Work of Charles Lucien Bonaparte in America. *Proceedings of the American Philosophical Society* **122**: 198–203.
Lias, A. 1975. Napoleon's brother was a 'prisoner' at Ludlow. *Shropshire Magazine*, July, p. 13.

Jones, R. 1954. Lucien, brother of the Great Napoleon. *Shropshire Magazine*, December, pp. 19–20.

Proceedings of the Linnean Society of London 1859, **3**: 41–44. Obituary.

Stresemann, E. 1975. *Ornithology, from Aristotle to the Present*, Ch. 9: 'Charles Lucien Bonaparte', pp. 153–169. Harvard University Press.

1. *Quoted in* Stresemann, E. 1975. *op. cit.*, p. 155.
2. Richardson, J. and Swainson, W. 1831. *Fauna Boreali-Americana*, Vol. II, pp. 425–426. J. Murray, London.
3. *Quoted in* Dresser, H.E. 1871–81. *A History of the Birds of Europe*, Vol. IX, p. 390. London.
4. *Quoted in* Stresemann, E. 1975. *op. cit.*, pp. 160–161.

Bonelli

Dizionario Biografico degli Italiani 1960–. Vol. XI, pp. 754–756. Rome.

Passerin d'Entrèves, P. and Sella Gentile, G. 1985. Franco Andrea Bonelli, Zoologo trasformista. *Studi Piemontesi* **14**: 34–48.

Rolando, A. 1985. L'ornitologia di Franco Andrea Bonelli nel bicentenario della nascita. *Rivista Italiana di Ornitologia, Milano* **55**: 41–60.

1. The *Dizionario Biografico degli Italiani* gives Bonelli's dates as 11.11.1784–11.6.1830.
2. Temminck, C.J. and Laugier, M. 1823. *Planches coloriées*, Vol. I, letterpress to pl. 288. Paris.

Brehm

Baege, L. Personal communication.

Gebhardt, L. 1964. *Die Ornithologen Mitteleuropas*, pp. 50–53 [A.E., C.L. & R. Brehm]. Giessen.

Hildebrandt, H. 1932. Christian Ludwig Brehm: a German Ornithologist. *Ibis*, pp. 308–316.

1. In *Naumannia* 1858, p. 210 Thekla Brehm's father gives her date of death as "6. Julius 1858". According to the church records at Renthendorf, the correct year is 1857 (Baege, L. Personal communication).

Bruce

Bruce, H.J. 1872. Some of the Familiar Birds of India. *American Naturalist* **6**: 460–471.

Bruce, H.J. 1875. Missionary Touring in India. *Missionary Herald* **71**: 65–67.

Bruce, H.J. 1877. A New Region Visited—The People Eager to Hear. *Missionary Herald* **73**: 155–157.

Missionary Herald 1909, **105**: 282–283. Obituary.

[Additional information supplied by the Bangor Theological Seminary, Maine.]

Brünnich

Brünnich, M.T. 1764. *Ornithologia Borealis*. Hafniae.
Gladstone, H.S. Unpublished MS, from: Collin, J. 1934. *Dansk biografisk Leksikon*, Vol. IV, pp. 276–277. København.
1. Sabine, E. 1818. A Memoir of the Birds of Greenland. *Transactions of the Linnean Society of London* **12**: 538.
2. Pennant, W. 1766. *British Zoology*, Vol. II, p. 434. B. White, London.

Buchanan

Buchanan, F. 1926. *Journal of Francis Buchanan kept during the survey of the district of Shahabad in 1812–13*. Bihar and Orissa, Patna.
Dictionary of National Biography 1885–1900. Vol. VII, p. 186. London.
Prain, D. 1905. *A Sketch of the Life of Francis Hamilton (once Buchanan)*. Bengal Secretariat Press, Calcutta.

Bulwer

Gladstone, H.S. 1946. British Birds named after Persons: Bulwer's Petrel. *Transactions and Journal of Proceedings of the Dumfriesshire and Galloway Natural History and Antiquarian Society 1940–44*. Ser. 3, **23**: 178–184, 188–189.
[Lyall, A.] 1827. *Rambles in Madeira and Portugal*. Dublin.
1. *Ibis* 1886, pp. 531–532. [Sale of the Jardine Ornithological Collection.]

Butler

Army Lists, October 1883.
Butler, E.A. 1877. Astola, a Summer Cruise in the Gulf of Oman. *Stray Feathers*, pp. 283–304.
Butler, E.A. 1878. My Last Notes on the Avifauna of Sind. *Stray Feathers*, pp. 173–191.
Ibis 1916, p. 644. Obituary.
Ibis 1940, pp. 348–350. Obituary [A.L. Butler].
Yarmouth Mercury 22.4.1916. Obituary.
1. *Stray Feathers* 1878, p. 316; *Stray Feathers* 1877, p. 300. (For details of an even earlier specimen, in the Tristram collection, *see Stray Feathers* 1878, pp. 416–417.)
2. Günther, A. (Ed.) 1904–12. *The History of the Collections Contained in the Natural History Departments of the British Museum*, Vol. II, pp. 325–326. BM publication, London.
3. Butler, E.A. 1877. *op. cit.*, pp. 283–304.

Canute

Encyclopaedia Britannica 1882. 9th edn, Vol. V, pp. 39–40; Vol. XIV, p. 129. Edinburgh.
1. Camden's statement is: *Knotts, i Canuti aves, vt opinor e Dania enim aduolare credunter.*

Cetti

Gladstone, H.S. 1946. British Birds named after Persons: Cetti's Warbler. *Transactions and Journal of Proceedings of the Dumfriesshire and Galloway Natural History and Antiquarian Society 1940–44*, Ser. 3, **23**: 177–178, 188.
Tyndale, J.W.W. 1849. *The Island of Sardinia*, 3 vols. London.
1. For full details on the history of the naming of this species *see* Marmora, A. della 1820. Mémoire sur deux oiseaux du Compté de Nice observés en . . . 1819. *Memorie della Reale Accademia delle scienze di Torino* **25**: 253–261.

Clot

Dictionaire de Biographie Française 1933–. Vol. IX, columns 29–30. Paris.
Foriegn Quarterly Review July 1841, pp. 362–393. [Review of Clot-Bey's *Aperçu Général sur l'Egypte.*]

Cory

Osgood, W.H. 1922. Charles Barney Cory. *Auk* **34**: 151–166.
1, 2. *Quoted in* Austin, E. (Ed.) 1967. *Frank M. Chapman in Florida. His Journals and Letters*, pp. 51, 91. University of Florida Press.
3. *Bulletin of the Nuttall Ornithological Club* 1881, **6**: 84.

Cretzschmar

Neue Deutsche Biographie 1952– . Vol. III, pp. 411–412. Berlin.

Denham

Bovill, E.W. (Ed.) 1964–66. *Missions to the Niger. Vol. II: The Bornu Mission 1822–25.* Cambridge University Press (for Hakluyt Society).
Denham, D. 1831. *Narrative of Travels and Discoveries in Northern and Central Africa*, 4 vols. J. Murray, London.
Dictionary of National Biography 1885–1900. Vol. XIV, pp. 341–342. London.
1, 2. Denham, D. 1831. *op. cit.*, Vol. II, pp. 205; 162.
3. *Quoted in* Bovill, E.W. (Ed.) 1964–66. *op. cit.*, Vol. II, p. 115.

Dunn

Army Lists 1900–04, 1919.

Bath and Wiltshire Chronicle 22.10.1952. Obituary.

Günther, A. (Ed.) 1904–12. *The History of the Collections Contained in the Natural History Departments of the British Museum*, Vol. II, pp. 30, 343. BM publication, London.

National Army Museum archives, London.

Who was Who 1951–60. Vol. V, p. 328, London.

1. In the original description of Dunn's Lark, Shelley notes that the bird had been collected by "Major W. H. Dunn". However there is no such person mentioned in the *Army Lists* for that period. We have examined the labels attached to the type specimen (housed at Tring) which show that whereas "Capt W. H. Dunn" appears on the *museum* label, "Capt H. N. Dunn" is written on the *original* label.

2. Grogan, E.S. and Sharp, A.H. 1900. *From the Cape to Cairo*, pp. 300–303. Hurst & Blackett, London.

Dupont

Biographie Universelle 1855. Vol. XII, pp. 22–23. Paris.

Lyon, G.F. 1821. *A Narrative of Travels in Northern Africa in the years 1818, 19, and 20*, pp. 1–20. J. Murray, London.

1. Mulsant, E. and Verreaux, E. 1877. *Histoire Naturelle des Oiseaux-Mouches ou Colibris*, Vol. 4, p. 14. Lyon.

Eleonora

Tyndale, J.W.W. 1849. *The Island of Sardinia*, Vol. II. London.

Waite, V. 1977. *Sardinia*. B.T. Batsford Ltd.

Walter, H. 1979. *Eleonora's Falcon: Adaptations to Prey and Habitat in a Social Raptor*, pp. 310–314. University of Chicago Press.

1. Gené, G. 1840. Descrizione di un nuovo falcone di Sardegna (Falco eleonorae). *Memorie della Reale Accademia delle scienze di Torino*, Ser. 2, **2**: 41–48.

Eversmann

Gebhardt, L. 1964. *Die Ornithologen Mitteleuropas*, pp. 87–88. Giessen.

Gladstone, H.S. Unpublished MS, from: Eversmann, E. 1823. *Reise Orenburg nach Buchara*. Berlin; *Bulletin of the Imperial Society of Natural Science, Anthropology and Ethnology: Proceedings of the Zoology Department of the Society, 1891*, Vol. LXX. Moscow [title translated from the Russian]; and other sources.

Finsch

Finsch, O. 1877. Ornithological Letters from the Bremen Expedition to Western Siberia. *Ibis*, pp. 48–66.

Finsch, O. 1885. Letter from Mioko, Duke of York Is. *Ibis*, p. 339 [and various other letters from the Pacific *Ibis* 1880–82].

Gebhardt, L. 1964. *Die Ornithologen Mitteleuropas*, pp. 92–93. Giessen.

Ibis 1918, pp. 304–306. Obituary.

Stresemann, E. 1975. *Ornithology, from Aristotle to the Present*, Ch. 12: 'Otto Finsch', pp. 220–233. Harvard University Press.

Fischer

Gebhardt, L. 1964. *Die Ornithologen Mitteleuropas*, p. 95. Giessen.

Neue Deutsche Biographie 1952– . Vol. V, pp. 212–213. Berlin.

Forster

Dictionary of National Biography 1885–1900. Vol. XX, pp. 15–16. London.

Hoare, M.E. 1976. *The Tactless Philosopher. Johann Reinhold Forster (1729–98)*. Hawthorn Press, Melbourne.

1. *Philosophical Transactions of the Royal Society of London, 1772*, Vol. LXII, Article XXIX, pp. 421–422.

Franklin

Dictionary of National Biography 1885–1900. Vol. XX, pp. 191–196. London.

Franklin, J. 1823. *Narrative of a Journey to the Polar Sea, in the years 1819–22*. J. Murray, London.

Johnson, R.E. 1976. *Sir John Richardson*. Taylor & Francis, London.

1. Richardson, J. and Swainson, W. 1831. *Fauna Boreali-Americana*, Vol. II, pp. 424–425. J. Murray, London.

Gené

Sismonda, E. 1851. Notizie Biographiche del Professore Cavaliere Giuseppe Gené. *Memorie della Reale Accademia delle scienze di Torino*, Ser. 2, **11**: 1–19.

Godlewski

Gebhardt, L. 1964. *Die Ornithologen Mitteleuropas*, pp. 79–80, 116. Giessen.

Ibis 1931, pp. 101–102. Obituary [B. Dybowski].

1. Some Polish sources give 1833 as his date of birth.
2. For explanation and further references *see* Ludlow, F. 1944. The Birds of South-eastern Tibet (with notes by N.B. Kinnear). *Ibis*, p. 364.

J. E. and G. R. Gray

Dictionary of National Biography 1885–1900. Vol. XXIII, pp. 7–11. London.
Gunther, A.E. 1975. *A Century of Zoology at the British Museum. Through the Lives of Two Keepers. 1815–1914*. Dawsons, London.
Gunther, A.E. 1980. *The Founders of Science at the British Museum, 1753–1900*. Halesworth Press, Suffolk.
Ibis 1872, pp. 340–342. Obituary [G.R. Gray].
Lancaster, E.R. 1904. *A Short History of the Collections*. BM publication, London.

Güldenstädt

Gebhardt, L. 1964. *Die Ornithologen Mitteleuropas*, p. 126. Giessen.
Neue Deutsche Biographie 1952– . Vol. VII, pp. 254–255. Berlin.
[Pallas, P.S.] 1784–81. *Histoires des découvertes faites par divers savans voyageurs … 1784–81*, Vol. I, pp. 1–31. Lausanne.
1. Walters, M. 1981. The Problem of Güldenstädt's Redstart. *Sandgrouse* **2**: 86–90.

Hemprich

Hanstein, J. 1877. *Christian Gottfried Ehrenberg. Ein Tagwerk auf dem Felde der Naturforschung*, pp. 17–31. A. Marcus, Bonn.
Neue Deutsche Biographie 1952– . Vol. IV, pp. 349–350 [Ehrenberg]; Vol. VIII, pp. 514–515 [Hemprich]. Berlin.
Stresemann, E. 1962. Hemprich und Ehrenberg zum Gedenken. Ihr Reise zum Libanon im Sommer 1824. *Journal für Ornithologie* **103**: 380–388.

Hey

Landsborough-Thomson, A. 1965. Orthography of the name Ammoperdix heyi (Temm.). *Bulletin of the British Ornithologists' Club* **85**: 117–119.
Mertons, R. 1949. *Eduard Rüppell: Leben und Werk eines Forschungsreisenden*. Frankfurt am Main.
1. *Quote translated from* Mertons, R. 1949. *op. cit.*, p. 338.

Hodgson

Hunter, W.W. 1896. *Life of Brian Houghton Hodgson*. J. Murray, London.
1. *Quoted in* Hunter, W.W. 1896. *op. cit.*, pp. 306–307.

Hornemann

Gladstone, H.S. Unpublished MS, from: Christensen, C. 1936. *Jens Wilken Hornemann. Dansk biografisk Leksikon*, Vol. X, pp. 599–603; Ostermann, H. 1936. *Carl Peter Holbøll. Dansk biografisk Leksikon*, Vol. X, pp. 368–369, and other sources.
1. *Quoted in* Dresser, H.E. 1871–81. *A History of the Birds of Europe*, Vol. IV, p. 56. London.
2. *British Birds* 1946, **34**: 151 [footnote].

Hume

Dictionary of National Biography 1912–21. pp. 277–278. London.
Günther, A. (Ed.) 1904–12. *The History of the Collections Contained in the Natural History Departments of the British Museum*, Vol. II, pp. 390–393. BM publication, London.
Sharpe, R.B. 1885. The Hume Collection of Indian Birds. *Ibis*, pp. 456–462.
Wedderburn, W. 1913. *Allan Octavian Hume, C.B. Father of the Indian National Congress*. T.F. Unwin, London.
1. Blanford, W.T. 1873. Notes on 'Stray Feathers'. *Ibis*, pp. 211–225.
2. *Stray Feathers* 1881, p. 461.

Jouanin

Barloy, J.J. 1976. *Le Bon, La Bête et Le Chasseur, La Grande Aventure de la protection de la faune*, pp. 251–260. Stock, Paris.
Jouanin, C. Personal communication.
1. Greenway, J.C. 1967. *Extinct and Vanishing Birds of the World*, 2nd edn, p. 12. Dover Publications Inc., New York.
2. *See e.g.* Roux, F. and Jouanin, C. 1968. Studies of less familiar birds. 147. Cory's shearwater. *British Birds* **61**: 163–168.

Kittlitz

Gebhardt, L. 1964. *Die Ornithologen Mitteleuropas*, pp. 182–183. Giessen.
Greenway, J.C. 1967. *Extinct and Vanishing Birds of the World*, 2nd edn, pp. 74–77. Dover Publications Inc., New York.
Kittlitz, F.H. von 1861. *Twenty-four views of the vegetation of the coasts and islands of the Pacific*. Longman, Green, Longman and Roberts, London.
Mertons, R. 1949. *Eduard Rüppell: Leben und Werk eines Forschungsreisenden*. Frankfurt am Main.
Neue Deutsche Biographie 1952– . Vol. XI, pp. 694–695. Berlin.

Kramer

Höfer, F. 1886. Guielmus de Kramer. *Verhandlungen der kaiserlich-königlichen zoologische-botanischen Gesellschaft in Wien* **36**: Sitz-Ber. 40–41.
1. White, G. 1789. The Natural History and Antiquities of Selborne. Letter XXXII to Pennant.
2. Lockwood, W.B. 1984. *The Oxford Book of British Bird Names*, p. 121. Oxford University Press.

Krüper

Auk 1922, pp. 148–149. Obituary.
Gebhardt, L. 1964. *Die Ornithologen Mitteleuropas*, pp.200–201. Giessen.
1. *Quoted in* Dresser, H.E. 1871–81. *A History of the Birds of Europe*, Vol. III, p. 190. London.
2. Sclater, P.L. 1865. Notes on Krüper's Nuthatch and on the other known species of the genus Sitta. *Ibis*, pp. 306–311.

Leach

Dictionary of National Biography 1885–1900. Vol. XXXII, pp. 311–312. London.
Gladstone, H.S. Unpublished MS, from: Mullens, W.H. 1917–18. *Museums Journal* **17**: 51–56, 132–137, 180–187; Mullens, W.H. and Swann, H.K. 1917. *Bibliography of British Ornithology*, pp. 343–344. MacMillan & Co., London; and other sources.
Smith, E. 1980. Some early Nineteenth Century Devonshire Naturalists. *Transactions of the Devonshire Association* **112**: 8–13.
Swainson, W. 1840. *Lardner's Cabinet Cyclopaedia of Natural History, Vol. XI; Taxidermy: with the Biography of Zoologists, and notices of their works*, pp. 237–240. London.
1. Günther, A. (Ed.) 1904–12. *The History of the Collections Contained in the Natural History Departments of the British Museum*, Vol. II, pp. 208–245. BM publication, London.
2. Temminck, C.J. 1820. *Manuel d'Ornithologie*, 2nd edn, Vol. II, pp. 812–813. Paris.
3. *Quoted in* MacGillivray, W. 1837–52. *A History of British Birds*, Vol. V, p. 454. W.S. Orr & Co., London.
4. Swainson, W. 1840. *op. cit.*, p. 239.

Ledant

Burnier, E. 1976. Une nouvelle espèce de l'avifaune paléarctique: la sittelle kabyle *Sitta ledanti*. *Nos Oiseaux* **33**: 337–340.
Ledant, J.-P. 1977. La sittelle kabyle (*Sitta ledanti* Vielliard) espèce endémique montagnarde récemment découverte. *Aves* **14**: 83–85.
Ledant, J.-P., Jacobs, P., Ochando, B. and Renault, J. 1985. Dynamique de la Forêt

du Mont Babor et Préférences Écologiques de la Sittelle Kabyle *Sitta ledanti. Biological Conservation* **32**: 231–254.

Ledant, J.-P. Personal communication.

van den Berg, A.B. 1985. PhotoSpot 11. Algerian Nuthatch. *British Birds* **78**: 265–268.

Leschenault

Nouvelle Biographie Générale 1855–66. Vol. XXX, columns 923–927. Paris.

Stresemann, E. 1975. *Ornithology, from Aristotle to the Present*, pp. 116–117. Harvard University Press.

Levaillant

Dictionary of South African Biography 1968–81. Vol. II, pp. 396–399. Cape Town.

Stresemann, E. 1975. *Ornithology, from Aristotle to the Present*, Ch. 5: 'François Levaillant', pp. 85–98. Harvard University Press.

The details concerning J.-J.-R. Levaillant are from:

Laplatte, G. [undated] *Biographie du Général Jean Le Vaillant*, pp. 1–7 [in the collection of the Bibliothèque municipale de Sézanne].

Loche, V. 1867. *Exploration Scientifique de l'Algérie*, pp. 83–85. Paris.

Seurat, L.G. 1930. *Exploration zoologique de l'Algérie de 1830 à 1930*, pp. 37–38, 646–647, 649. Paris.

Stresemann, E. 1975. *op. cit.*, p. 92.

Lichtenstein

Dictionary of South African Biography 1968–81. Vol. III, pp. 520–523. Cape Town.

Gebhardt, L. 1964. *Die Ornithologen Mitteleuropas*, pp. 215–216. Giessen.

Lichtenstein, H.M.C. 1812. *Travels in Southern Africa in the years 1803, 1804, 1805 and 1806*. H. Colburn, London.

Proceedings of the Linnean Society of London 1859, **3**: 44–45. Obituary.

Whittel, H.M. 1954. *The Literature of Australian Birds*, pp. 444–446. Paterson Brokenska Pty., Perth.

1. Temminck appears to have named the sandgrouse after Lichtenstein because Lichtenstein recognized this bird as being the same as the Ganga bibande of Temminck's *Histoire naturelle des Gallinacés*, Vol. III, p. 247. *See* Temminck, C.J. 1823. *Planches coloriées*, letterpress to pls 355, 361.

2. Swainson, W. 1840. *Lardner's Cabinet Cyclopaedia of Natural History, Vol. XI; Taxidermy: with the Biography of Zoologists, and notices of their works*, p. 249. London.

McDougall

Anon. 1814. *A Catalogue of a Choice Collection of British and Foreign Birds, comprehending many curious and rare specimens in high preservation. The entire collection of the late Dr. Peter M'Dougall.* J. Smith, Glasgow [in the collection of Glasgow University Library].

Duncan, A. 1896. *Memorials of the Faculty of Physicians and Surgeons of Glasgow*, p. 144. Glasgow.

Glasgow Directory 1804–13. W. M'Feat & Co., Glasgow.

Glasgow Chronicle 5.5.1814.

Glasgow Courier 30.4.1814–11.6.1814.

Laskey, J. 1813. *A General Account of the Hunterian Museum Glasgow*, p. vi. Glasgow.

Montagu, G. 1813. *Supplement to the Ornithological Dictionary*. S. Woolmer, Exeter.

Parish Records: Kilsyth; Ramshorn and Blackfriars (Glasgow).

1. In the eighteenth and nineteenth centuries *Mc* and *Mac* were often interchangeable. There was no significance between the difference and both were frequently abbreviated to *M'*. The baptismal record refers to Peter's father as Alexander McDougall and this version has been adopted throughout.

   Two Glasgow University publications refer to the younger McDougall as Patrick or Patricius. All other documents, including his baptismal entry, death notices and burial record give his name as Peter.

2,3. Montagu, G. 1813, *op. cit.* Letterpress for Roseate Tern.

4. Graves, G. 1821. *British Ornithology*, Vol. III, letterpress to pl. 39. London.

Marmora

Inciclopedia Italiana 1929–37. Vol. XX, pp. 401–403. Treves.

Mauri

Journal für Ornithologie 1856, pp. 419–21.

Palmer, T.S. 1931. The scientific name of the western sandpiper—who was Mauri? *Condor* **33**: 243–244.

Ménétries

Anon. 1863. Notice Biographique sur Mr. Edouard Ménétriès. *Horae, Societatis entomologicae rossicae* **2**: 1–7.

Essig, E.O. 1931. *History of Entomology*, pp. 706–707. MacMillan, New York.

Hagen, H.A. 1862. *Bibliotheca Entomologica*, pp. 531–532. Leipzig.

Ménétries, E. 1832. *Catalogue raisonée des objets de Zoology*, pp. 1–15. St Petersburg.

Papavero, N. 1971. *Essays on the History of Neotropical Dipterology*, Vol. I, pp. 52–54. Museo de Zoologia, University of São Paulo.

Seebohm, H. 1883. Notes on the Birds of the Caucasus. *Ibis*, pp. 1–37.

Młokosiewicz

Coats, A.M. 1969. *The Quest for Plants*, pp. 60–61. Studio Vista, London.
Gebhardt, L. 1964. *Die Ornithologen Mitteleuropas*, p. 244. Giessen.
1. *Quoted in* Dresser, H.E. 1871–81. *A History of the Birds of Europe*, Vol. VII, p. 221. London.

Montagu

Cleevely, R.J. 1978. Some background to the life and publications of Colonel George Montagu 1753–1815. *Journal of the Society for the Bibliography of Natural History* **8**: 445–480.
Cunnington, G. 1857. Memoir of George Montagu. *Wiltshire Magazine* **3**: 89–94.
Dictionary of National Biography 1885–1900. Vol. XXXVIII, pp. 246–247. London.
Gladstone, H.S. Unpublished MS, from: Cummings, B.F. 1913. A Biographical Sketch of Col. George Montagu. *Zoologisches Annalen Würzburg* **5**: 306–325; *Gentleman's Magazine* 1815, Parts I and II; Fairweather, J. [*c*.1912] *Salcombe, Kingsbridge and Neighbourhood*, 3rd edn. Fairweather, J., Salcombe and Kingsbridge; Montagu, G. 1792. *The Sportsman's Directory: or, Tractate on Gunpowder*. London; Mullens, W.H. 1909. *British Birds* **2**: *361*; Mullens, W.H. and Swann, H.K. 1917. *Bibliography of British Ornithology*, pp. 409–411. MacMillan & Co., London; information supplied by the Society for Army Historical Research, Linnean Society of London, Public Record Office, Probate Office and other sources.
Montagu, G. 1802. *Ornithological Dictionary: or, Alphabetical Synopsis of British Birds*, 2 vols. London.
Montagu, G. 1813. *Supplement to the Ornithological Dictionary*. S. Woolmer, Exeter.
1. Various dates have been given for Montagu's year of birth: the *Dictionary of National Biography, op. cit.*, gives 1751; Cummings, B.F. 1913. *op. cit.*, Cunnington, G. 1857. *op. cit.*, and Montagu's coffin plate give 1754 or 1755; Cleevely, R.J. 1978. *op. cit.* gives 8.4.1753 but no source is given.
2. Gladstone, H.S. Unpublished MS.
3. Vassall, E. Baroness Holland 1908. *The Journal of Elizabeth, Lady Holland (1791–1811)*, Vol. II, p. 20. Longman & Co., London.
4. The valuable library, chiefly collected by their ancestor Sir Charles Hedges, had already been sold off by Leigh & Sotheby on 27.4.1798 and the three following days. *Cf. Dictionary of National Biography, op. cit.*
5. Montagu was accused of: 1. Joining a Subaltern's Club under the title Ensign Montagu, formed on principles destructive of the harmony of the corps. 2. Proposing the formation of a separate mess to exclude Captains Awdry and Houlton. 3. Inducing other officers not to associate with the two Captains. 4. Denouncing the two Captains as incendiaries. 5. Trying to extort details of private conversations. 6. Dressing the servant of a soldier in uniform so that he could receive army pay even though he was not enlisted or sworn in. Montagu was found guilty on all charges except number 4, on which he was acquitted on grounds of insufficient evidence.
6. In fact, Montagu was given command of the South Devon Corps of Guides following invasion threats in 1803. *See* Cleevely, R.J. 1978. *op. cit.*, p. 449.
7. Albin, E. 1734. *A Natural History of Birds*, Vol. II, p. 5, pl. 5. London.
8. Coues, E. 1880. Fourth Instalment of Ornithological Bibliography. *Proceedings of the United States National Museum* **2**: 372.
9. Cleevely, R.J. 1978, *op. cit.*, p. 463.
10. *Field* 90. 24.7.1897.

Moquin-Tandon

Nouvelle Biographie Générale 1855–66 Vol. XXXVI, columns 434–435. Paris.
1. *See* Bonaparte, C.L. 1856. *Comptes Rendus de l'Académie des sciences, Paris* **43**: 1020;
   Dresser, H.E. 1871–81. *A History of the Birds of Europe*, Vol. IX, letterpress to pl. 711.
   London.
2. Bannermann, D.A. 1963. *Birds of the Atlantic Islands*, Vol. I, pp. 90–93. Oliver &
   Boyd, Edinburgh and London.

Moussier

Extracts from French army records. [Supplied by General Delmas, head of the army
   historical service, Ministère de la Défense, Paris; *per* C. Jouanin.]
Seurat, L.G. 1930. *Exploration zoologique de l'Algérie de 1830 à 1890*, pp. 154, 656.
   Paris.
1,2. *Quoted in* Dresser, H.E. 1871–81. *A History of the Birds of Europe*, Vol. II,
   pp. 302–303; 302. London.

J.A. and J.F. Naumann

Baege, L. Personal communication.
Gebhardt, L. 1964. *Die Ornithologen Mitteleuropas*, pp. 256–258. Giessen.
Gladstone, H.S. Unpublished MS, from: *Journal für Ornithologie* 1857, pp. 360–362.
1. *See e.g.* Dresser, H.E. 1871–81. *A History of the Birds of Europe*, Vol. II, p.60.
   London.
2. Thomsen, P. and Stresemann, E. 1957. *Johann Friedrich Naumann, der Altmeister
   der deutschen Vögelkunde*. J.A. Barth, Leipzig.

Neumayer

Barnhart, J.H. 1965. *Biographical Notes upon Botanists*, Vol. 2, p. 547. G.K. Hall &
   Co., Boston, Massachusetts.
Bulletin de la Société Impériale des Naturalistes de Moscou 1885, **61**: 49.
Gebhardt, L. 1964. *Die Ornithologen Mitteleuropas*, p. 242. [K. Michahelles] Giessen.

Nordmann

Gladstone, H.S. Unpublished MS, from: Eichwald, E. von. 1870. *Nils von Nordenskiold
   und Alexander von Nordmann nach ihren leben und wirken*, pp. 25–109; and other
   sources.
1. Demidoff, A. 1853. *Travels in Southern Russia and the Crimea; through Hungary,
   Wallachia and Moldavia during the year 1837*, Vol. 1, pp. 317–318. J. Mitchell,
   London.

Pallas

Coats, A.M. 1969. *The Quest for Plants*, pp. 52–56. Studio Vista, London.

Pallas, P.S. 1802. *Travels through the Southern Provinces of the Russian Empire, 1793–4*, 2 vols. London.

Smith, C.H. 1843. Memoir of Pallas, *in* Jardine, W. (Ed.) *The Naturalist's Library. Vol. IV, Mammalia; iii, Dogs*, part 1, pp. 17–76. Edinburgh.

Urness, C. (Ed.) 1967. *A Naturalist in Russia. Letters from Peter Simon Pallas to Thomas Pennant*. University of Minnesota Press, Minneapolis.

1. *Quoted in* Smith, C.H. 1843. *op. cit.*, p. 41.

Radde

Freshfield, D.W. 1869. *Travels in the Central Caucasus and Bashan*. Longmans Green & Co., London.

Gebhardt, L. 1964. *Die Ornithologen Mitteleuropas*, pp. 284–285. Giessen.

Ibis 1903, pp. 439–440. Obituary.

Radde, G. 1858. Notes on the River Amur and the adjacent Districts. *Royal Geographical Society Journal* **28**: 418–425.

Ravenstein, E.G. 1861. *The Russians on the Amur; its Discovery, Conquest and Colonisation*. Trübner & Co., London.

1,2. Freshfield, D.W. 1869. *op. cit.*, pp. 295; 103.

3. Radde, G. 1858. *op. cit.*, p. 419.

4. *Ibis* 1866, pp. 118–119. [Recent Ornithological Publications: 4. Russian.]

Richard

Gladstone, H.S. Unpublished MS and correspondence.

1. Oliver, W.R.B. 1955. *New Zealand Birds*, pp. 460–461. A.H. & A.W. Reed, Wellington, N.Z.

2. Holandre, J.J.J. 1851. Catalogue des animaux vertébrés, observés et recuillis dans le département de la Moselle. *Bulletin de la Société d'Histoire naturelle de la Moselle* **6**: 101.

3. Yarrell, W. 1871. *History of British Birds*, 4th edn, Vol. I, p. 600. London.

4. Vieillot, L.P. 1818. *Nouveau Dictionnaire d'Histoire Naturelle, Nouvelle édition*, Vol. XXVI, p. 492. Paris.

5. Stresemann, E. 1975. *Ornithology, from Aristotle to the Present*, p. 86. Harvard University Press.

Ross

Dictionary of National Biography 1885–1900. Vol. XLIX, pp. 265–269. London.

Dodge, E.S. 1973. *The Polar Rosses. John and James Clark Ross and their Explorations*. Faber & Faber, London.

Parry, W.E. 1824–25. *Journal of a Second Voyage for the Discovery of a North-West*

Passage from the Atlantic to the Pacific. Performed in the years 1821–3, 2 vols. J. Murray, London.

Ross, J.C. 1847. *A Voyage of Discovery and Research in the Southern and Antarctic Regions, during the years 1839–43*, 2 vols. J. Murray, London.

Ross, M.J. 1982. *Ross in the Antarctic*. Caedmon of Whitby.

1. Buturlin, S.A. 1906. The Breeding-grounds of the Rosy Gull. *Ibis*, pp. 131–139, 333–337, 661–666.
2. Parry, W.E. 1824. *op. cit.*, p. 449.
3. MacGillivray, W. 1842. *Manual of British Ornithology*, Vol. II, part ii, pp. 252–254. London.
4. Richardson, J. and Swainson, W. 1831. *Fauna Boreali-Americana*, Vol. II, p. 427. J. Murray, London.
5. Ross, J.C. 1847. *op. cit.*, Vol. I, p. 315.

Rüppell

[Cretzschmar, P.J., *et al.*] 1826–28. *Atlas zu der Reise im nördlichen Afrika von E. Rüppell*. Senkenbergische Naturforschende Gesellschaft, Frankfurt.

Foreign Quarterly Review 1841, 28 (55): IV: pp. 64–90. [Review of Rüppell's *Reise in Abyssinien*.]

Ibis 1885, pp. 336–368. Obituary.

Mertons, R. 1949. *Eduard Rüppell: Leben und Werk eines Forschungsreisenden*. Frankfurt am Main.

Rüppell, E. 1835–40. *Neue Wirbelthiere zu der Fauna von Abyssinien gehörig*. Frankfurt.

Sabine

Dictionary of National Biography 1885–1900. Vol. L, pp. 74–79. London.

Parry, W.E. 1821–24. *Journal of a Voyage for the Discovery of a North-West Passage from the Atlantic to the Pacific; performed in the years 1819–20* [with appendices on mammals, birds, fish by E. Sabine]. J. Murray, London.

Ross, J. 1819. *A Voyage of Discovery . . . for the purpose of exploring Baffin's Bay*. J. Murray, London.

Sabine, E. 1819. A Memoir of the Birds of Greenland. *Transactions of the Linnean Society of London* **12**: 527–559.

1. Sabine, E. 1819. *op. cit.*, p. 543.
2. Ross, J.C. 1847. *A Voyage of Discovery and Research in the southern and Antarctic Regions during the years 1839–43*, Vol. I, p. 183. J. Murray, London.
3. Günther, A. (Ed.) 1904–12. *The History of the Collections Contained in the Natural History Departments of the British Museum*, Vol. II, p. 460. BM publication, London.
4. Richardson, J. and Swainson, W. 1831. *Fauna Boreali-Americana*, Vol. II, pp. 428–429. J. Murray, London.

Savi

Gladstone, H.S. Unpublished MS, from: *Atti della Reale Accademia delle scienze, Torino* 1871–72, **7**: 140–183; and other sources.

Ibis 1874, pp. 451–452. [Review of *Ornitologia Toscana*.]

Schlegel

Cordier, H. 1903. Nécrologie. Le Dr. Gustave Schlegel. *T'oung Pao*, Ser. 2, **4**: 407–415.
Ibis 1884, p. 364. Obituary [H. Schlegel].
[Additional information supplied by the Rijksmuseum van Natuurlijke Historie, Leiden.]
1,2. Seebohm, H. 1901. *Birds of Siberia*, pp. 126–127. J. Murray, London.

Schrenck

Coats, A. 1969. *The Quest for Plants*, pp. 58–59. Studio Vista, London.
Gebhardt, L. 1964. *Die Ornithologen Mitteleuropas*, p. 325. Giessen.
Ibis 1861, pp. 203–208. [Review of Schrenck's *Reisen und Forschungen im Amur-lande ... 1854–56.*]
Ibis 1894, p. 459. Obituary.
Ravenstein, E.G. 1861. *The Russians on the Amur; its Discovery, Conquest and Colonisation*, Trübner & Co., London.

Schwarz

Gladstone, H.S. Unpublished MS, from: Poggendorff, J.C. 1898. *Biographisch-Literarisches Handwörterbuch*, Vol. III, p. 1223. Leipzig.

Steller

Stejneger, L. 1936. *Georg Wilhelm Steller, the Pioneer of Alaskan Natural History.* Harvard University Press.

Sturm

Gebhardt, L. 1964. *Die Ornithologen Mitteleuropas*, p. 352. Giessen.
Hauck, H. 1862. J.H.C.F. Sturm. Nekrolog. *Journal für Ornithologie* **56**: 157–160.
1. Meade-Waldo, E.G.B. 1890. Further Notes on the Birds of the Canary Islands. *Ibis*, pp. 429–438.

Swainson

Dictionary of National Biography 1885–1900. Vol. LV, pp. 192–193. London.
Dictionary of New Zealand Biography 1940. Vol. II, pp. 350–352. Wellington.
Proceedings of the Linnean Society of London 1900, pp. 14–61. [The President's Anniversary Address; Catalogue of the Swainson Correspondence in the possession of the Linnean Society.]

Swainson, W. 1819. Sketch of a Journey through Brazil in 1817 and 1818. *Edinburgh Philosophical Journal* 1: 369–373.
Swainson, W. 1840. *Lardner's Cabinet Cyclopaedia of Natural History, Vol. XI; Taxidermy: with the Biography of Zoologists, and notices of their works*, pp. 338–352. London.
1. Swainson, W. 1836. *On the Natural History and Classification of Birds*, Vol. I, pp. 276–277. London.

Swinhoe

Beebe, W. 1921. *A Monograph of the Pheasants*, Vol. II, pp. 78–83. H.F. & G. Witherby, London.
Ibis 1861–77. [Various articles and correspondence by Swinhoe.]
Ibis 1878, pp. 126–128. Obituary.
Swinhoe, R. 1861. *Narrative of the North China Campaign of 1860*. Smith, Elder & Co., London.
Takahashi, Y. 1965. Biography of Robert Swinhoe 1836–1877. *Quarterly Journal of the Taiwan Museum* 18: 335–338.
1. Swinhoe, R. 1866. A Voice on Ornithology from Formosa. *Ibis*, p. 130.
2. Swinhoe, R. 1867. Jottings on Birds from my Amoy Journal. *Ibis*, p. 400.
3. Swinhoe, R. 1873. Letter from Chefoo. *Ibis*, pp. 423–427.
4. *Ibis* 1924, pp. 362–363. Obituary [C. Swinhoe].

Temminck

Gladstone, H.S. 1946. British Birds named after Persons: Temminck's Stint. *Transactions and Journal of Proceedings of the Dumfriesshire and Galloway Natural History and Antiquarian Society 1940–44*, Ser. 3, 23: 184–189.
Proceedings of the Linnean Society of London 1859, pp. 47–50. Obituary.
Stresemann, E. 1975. *Ornithology, from Aristotle to the Present*, pp. 110–125, 147–152. Harvard University Press.
Whittel, H.M. 1954. *The Literature of Australian Birds*, pp. 709–712. Paterson Brokenska Pty., Perth.

Tengmalm

Gladstone, H.S. Unpublished MS, from: Hedin, S. 1814. *Åminnelsetal öfver . . . Pehr Gustaf Tengmalm*. Stockholm; Löwegren, J. 1936. *Svensk uppslagsbok*, Vol. 27. Malmo; and other sources.
Lindroth, S. 1967. *Kungliga Svenska Vetenskapsakademiens Historia 1739–1818*, pp. 446–447. Kungliga Vetenskapsakademien, Stockholm.

Tickell

Field 5.6.1875. Obituary.
Hay, A. [Viscount Walden]. 1876. Notes on the late Colonel Tickell's manuscript Work entitled 'Illustrations of Indian Ornithology'. *Ibis*, pp. 336–357.

Hodson, V.C.P. (Ed.) 1947. *List of the Officers of the Bengal Army, 1758–1834*, Vol. IV, pp. 276–277. London.

Ibis 1908. Jubilee Supplement, pp. 211–212. Memoir of Tickell.

1. Tickell, S.R. 1863. [Letter complaining that Blyth had named and described some of Tickell's birds against his wishes.] *Ibis*, pp. 111–113.

2. Tickell, S.R. 1864. On the Hornbills of India and Burmah. *Ibis*, pp. 173–182.

Tristram

Dictionary of National Biography, Second Supplement 1901–1911. pp. 535–536. London.

Durham County Advertiser 16.3.1906. Obituary.

Günther, A. (Ed.) 1904–12. *The History of the Collections Contained in the Natural History Departments of the British Museum*, Vol. II, pp. 499–501. BM publication, London.

Ibis 1906, p. 602. Obituary.

Ibis 1908. Jubilee Supplement, pp. 153–156. Memoir of Tristram.

Tristram, H.B. 1860. *The Great Sahara*. J. Murray, London.

Tristram, H.B. 1865. *The Land of Israel*. Christian Knowledge Soc., London.

1,2. Tristram, H.B. 1859. On the Ornithology of Northern Africa. Part II. *Ibis*, pp. 281, 280.

3. Tristram, H.B. 1905. The Birds of County Durham, *in* Page, W. (Ed.) *The Victoria History of the Counties of England. Durham*, Vol. I, p. 184. A. Constable & Co., London.

4. Dresser, H.E. 1871–81. *A History of the Birds of Europe*, Vol. III, p. 555. London.

5. Tristram, H.B. 1867. *The Natural History of the Bible*, p. 232. S.P.C.K., London.

6. The last recorded specimen is not Wedderburn's, but another, shot in the autumn of 1875 on Long Island, New York. *See* Greenway, J.C. 1967. *Extinct and Vanishing Birds of the World*, 2nd edn, p. 173. Dover Publications Inc., New York.

7. Unpublished letter, H. S. Gladstone collection.

Upcher

British Birds 1921, **15**: 16–17. Obituary.

Eastern Daily Press 6.4.1921. Obituary.

Ibis 1921, pp. 540–543. Obituary.

Shepherd, C.W. 1867. *The North-West Peninsula of Iceland*. Longmans, Green & Co., London.

Tristram, H.B. 1865. *The Land of Israel*. Christian Knowledge Soc., London.

1. Tristram, H.B. 1867. On the Ornithology of Palestine, Part V. *Ibis*, p. 82.

2. Tristram, H.B. 1864. Report on the Birds of Palestine. *Proceedings of the Zoological Society*, p. 438.

3. Wollaston, A.F.R. 1921. *A Life of Alfred Newton*, pp. 55–56. J. Murray, London.

4. Upcher, H.M. 1889. A day's bird's-nesting in Norfolk, with a few birdy notes added. *Transactions of the Norfolk and Norwich Naturalists' Society* **4**: 679–682.

Verreaux

Dictionary of South African Biography 1968–81. Vol. II, pp. 811–812 [Verreaux]; Vol. III, p.204 [Delalande]. Cape Town.

Günther, A. (Ed.) 1904–12. *The History of the Collections Contained in the Natural History Departments of the British Museum*, Vol. II, pp. 208–245. BM publication, London.

Ibis 1874, pp. 467–468. Obituary.

Stresemann, E. 1975. *Ornithology, from Aristotle to the Present*, pp. 162–163 [footnote]. Harvard University Press.

Whittel, H.M. 1954. *The Literature of Australian Birds*, pp. 729–730. Paterson Brokenska Pty., Perth.

1,2. Günther, A. (Ed.) 1904–12. *op. cit.*, p. 503.

3. Trevor-Battye, A. (Ed.) 1903. *Lord Lilford on Birds*, pp. 263–264. Hutchinson & Co., London.

White

Dictionary of National Biography 1885–1900. Vol. LXI, pp. 36–48. London.

White, G. 1981. *The Illustrated Natural History of Selborne*. Compiled by R. Davidson-Houston. Introduction by J.E. Chatfield, pp. 6–12. Webb & Bower, London; in collaboration with Gilbert White Museum.

White, R.H. 1901. *The Life and Letters of Gilbert White of Selborne*. J. Murray, London.

1,2. Eyton, T.C. 1836. *A History of the Rarer British Birds*, pp. 92, 93. Longman, London.

3. Chatfield, J.E. Personal communication.

Whitehead

Country Life 20.1.1900. pp. 72–73.

Dictionary of National Biography 1885–1900. Vol. LXI, p. 104. London.

Grant, W.R.O. 1900. On the Birds of Hainan. *Proceedings of the Zoological Society*, pp. 457–461.

Whitehead, J. 1885. Ornithological Notes from Corsica. *Ibis*, pp. 24–48.

Whitehead, J. 1893. *The Exploration of Kina Balu, North Borneo*. Gurney & Jackson, London.

Whitehead, J. 1899. Field Notes on Birds collected in the Philippine Islands in 1893–6. *Ibis*, pp. 81–111, 210–246, 381–399, 485–502.

1. Whitehead, J. 1885. *op. cit.*, pp. 28–29.

2. Whitehead, J. 1893. *op. cit.*, p. 117.

3. Whitehead, J. 1899. *op. cit.*, p. 91.

4. *Quoted in* Beebe, W. 1918–22. *A Monograph of the Pheasants*, Vol. II, pp. 72–75. H.F. & G. Witherby, London.

5. The *Dictionary of National Biography, op. cit.*, maintains that Whitehead managed to struggle back to the coast and died at Hai-k'ou.

Wilson

Cantwell, R. 1961. *Alexander Wilson*. J.B. Lippincott, Philadelphia and New York.

Dictionary of National Biography 1885–1900. Vol. LXII, pp. 75–76. London.

Henderson, J. 1857. *The Poetical Works of Alexander Wilson*. Belfast.
Leslie, C.R. 1860. *Autobiographical Recollections*, Ch. XII. London.
Wilson, A. 1808–14. *American Ornithology*, 11 vols. Bradford & Inskeep, Philadelphia. Philadelphia.

1. Wilson, A. 1808–14. *op. cit.*, Vol. V, p. 106.
2. Bonaparte, C.L. 1824. An Account of Four Species of Stormy Petrels. *Journal of the Academy of Natural Sciences of Philadelphia* **3**: 2.
3. Fisher, J. and Lockley, R.M. 1954. *Sea-Birds*, p. 61. Collins, London.
4. Sabine, J. 1823. Appendix V, pp. 669, 691, *in* Franklin, J. *Narrative of a Journey to the Shores of the Polar Sea*. London.

Appendices

$\mathcal{A}$*ppendix* 1

A miscellaneous selection of naturalists commemorated by species of uncertain status within the Western Palearctic, together with some naturalists who have had well-known races of birds named after them.

AUDUBON, John James (1785–1851). American ornithologist. Famous as the illustrator of *Birds of America* (1827–38) and *Viviparous Quadrupeds of North America* (1842–54). Text for the former work published separately as the *Ornithological Biography* (1831–39).

Audubon's Shearwater *Puffinus lherminieri* Lesson, 1839. One Palearctic record, England 1936, now deleted from the official list. It was called Audubon's Shearwater in the A.O.U. checklist of 1886, following Baird, Brewer and Ridgway's 1884 suggestion of Audubon's Dusky Shearwater.

The scientific name commemorates Félix-Louis L'HERMINIER (1779–1883). Pharmacist and botanist; born and died Paris. Collected natural history specimens in Guadeloupe, Antilles, Antigua and the United States east coast while attached to the French military services.

BAROLO, Carlo Tencredi Fallet (1782–1838). Born at Turin. His father's political influence gained the Marchese di Borolo a position in Napoleon's *Corps des Pages* in Paris. He and his wife thereafter divided their time between the two cities, or travelled. In Italy they devoted themselves to the care of the poor, the improvement of hospitals, and education of the young. He possessed a fine library and a vast number of pictures, engravings, tapestries and a small collection of birds.

Little Shearwater *Puffinus assimilis baroli* (Bonaparte, 1857). Bonelli appears to have acquired the original specimen from Baillon in 1820. Bonaparte adopted the name *baroli* which may have been a creation of Temminck's or Bonelli's, probably the latter.

COUES, Elliott (1842–1899). American army surgeon, historian and author. One of the greatest of all ornithologists. Born Portsmouth, New Hampshire. He came under the influence of Baird at an early age and gained a place on an expedition to Labrador where he studied and collected seabirds. After medical school and the horrific experience of treating Civil War wounded, he was posted to Arizona. "The Apaches are so hostile and daring" he wrote to Baird, "that considerable *caution* will have to tinge my collecting enthusiasm, if I want to save my scalp." In fact his spell in the West was remarkable for the size and quality of his collection, the discovery of species of birds and mammals new to science and the large volume of published material that ensued. (Despite the hostile Indians he still managed to contribute to *The Ibis*!) Afterwards he served on the east coast and wrote his *Key to North American Birds* (1872), possibly his most important work, it certainly influenced a whole generation of American ornithologists. His *Check List of North American Birds* (1873) appeared when Coues was back in Indian country at Fort Randall in South Dakota. Four years later Custer was killed at the nearby valley of Little Big Horn, but Coues was then working with the British and Americans on the Northern Boundary Commission. In 1876 he was transferred to the U.S. Geological Survey of the Territories to Colorado, and remained connected with it until 1880. Most of this last period was spent at Washington editing survey publications but he also produced *Birds of the North West* (1874) and *Birds of the Colorado Valley* (1878). He retired from the army and spent much of the rest of his life writing, one of his self-appointed tasks being the documentation of the lives and travels of the early frontier explorers—to which he added zoological notations. Coues was one of the most prolific ornithological writers that America has produced: in one year he had over fifty publications. He was one of the three principal founders of the A.O.U. and was a friend and advisor to the bird artist Fuertes. His outspoken views on ornithology and other subjects often made him a controversial character but even those he had antagonized were willing to acknowledge the value of his work, much of which was considered to be brilliant. He died in Baltimore and was buried at Arlington National Cemetery.

Coues's Redpoll *Acanthus hornemanni exilipes* (Coues 1862). The English name for this redpoll arose after the publication of *A Monograph of the Genus Aegiothus* [now *Acanthus*], *with Descriptions of New Species*. Coues wrote it on his return from Labrador at the age of nineteen. It appeared in the *Proceedings of the Academy of Natural Sciences of Philadelphia* and reviewed previous studies of redpolls including the Hoary or Coues's Redpoll which breeds across Arctic Canada, Russia and the northern tip of Norway.

FEA, Leonardo (1852–1903). Italian collector, born in Turin. An assistant at the Civic Museum, Genoa, he was inspired by collections received from the Far East and he set out for Burma in 1885. He spent almost four years there amassing a truly extraordinary collection of insects and birds (including Fea's Thrush from the mountains of Tenasserim). After his return to Italy he planned a second expedition, to Malaysia, but his declining health forced him to choose a drier climate and instead he spent 1898 in the Cape Verde Islands. He found eleven new species for the islands, collecting, in all, 308 specimens of forty-seven species.

Soft-plumaged Petrel *Pterodroma mollis feae* (Salvadori, 1899). This very scarce race of petrel is restricted to the Desertas and Cape Verde Islands, and is known locally as the Gon-Gon. It perhaps deserves specific status. The type was collected by Fea on São Nicolau on 10 December 1898.

FELDEGG, Baron Christoph (1780–1845). Austrian army officer and naturalist. Born at Kruman in Bohemia. He took part in the Battle of Asperne in 1809 and distinguished himself at the siege of Dresden in 1813. For his many gallant deeds he received, at the end of the campaign in 1815, the *Ritterkreuz* (Knightly Cross) of Maria Theresa and was created a Baron in 1817. He served many years in Spalato and elsewhere in Dalmatia, but died, as Colonel and Commanding Officer of the 6th Battalion of Chaseurs, while on leave in Leipzig. His natural history collection contained 4549 birds, twenty-four stuffed mammals and 3037 marine crustacea, corals, sea-urchins and shells. He was a correspondent of C.L. Brehm, John Gould and Hermann Schlegel and was also a friend of Dr Michahelles, the ornithologist who was based with him on the Yugoslav coast from 1829 to 1832. A collection of 328 bird pictures formed by Baron Feldegg is in the Vienna Natural History Museum.

Falco biarmicus feldeggii, the Lanner of southern Europe, from Italy to Turkey, was named in 1843 by Schlegel from examples taken by the Baron in Dalmatia in 1829.

Motacilla flava feldegg, the Black-headed Wagtail of the Balkans and the Black Sea, was named by Michahelles in 1830 from specimens collected in southern Dalmatia by Feldegg.

GRAELLS, Mariano de la Paz (1809–1898). Brehm called him "the father of Spanish Natural History". Born at Tricio in the province of Lograno. He studied at Barcelona where he became the founder and curator of the museum of natural history of the Academy of Science and Arts. He studied zoology, geology and palaeontology, and published a flora of Catalonia in 1831. Six years later he became Professor of Zoology at Madrid where he enjoyed the friendship of the Spanish Royal Family. Latterly he became Professor of Comparative Anatomy in the University of Madrid, and Director of the National Museum of Natural Sciences and of the Botanical Gardens—appointments he held until his death. He was a thorough investigator, an all-round naturalist and Spain's most illustrious entomologist. He is perhaps best known for his discovery of the handsome Spanish Moon Moth *Graellsia isabellae*, found locally only in the mountains of central Spain and in parts of the French Alps.

Larus fuscus graellsii Brehm, 1857. This is the Lesser Black-backed Gull of Iceland, Britain, France and north-west Spain. When it was first described it was only a winter visitor to Spain, but it now breeds there in small numbers.

HARCOURT, Edward William Vernon (1825–1891). Descended from the distinguished Vernon family; the additional name Harcourt was assumed only in the 1830s. His father William was Canon of York, founder, first Secretary and afterwards President of the British Association. Edward Harcourt was M.P. for Oxford, 1878–85, but he mainly led the life of a country gentleman. He made at least two trips abroad, publishing *Sketch of Madeira* (1851) and *Sporting in Algeria* (1859). The former contains his description of a new species of petrel; the latter has several appendices on birds and mammals but they are summaries of the work of Malherbe and Loche. Five of his papers on the birds of Madeira are listed in Bannerman's *Birds of the Atlantic Islands*, Vol. 2, pp. xiii–xiv.

Madeiran Storm-petrel *Oceanodroma castro* (Harcourt, 1851). This species has two distinct breeding ranges in the tropical regions. Those occurring in the Pacific are now more often referred to as Harcourt's Storm-petrel than those in the Atlantic, even though the species was first described from a specimen from the Desertas, off Madeira.

HEUGLIN, Theodor von (1824–1876). German explorer and ornithologist, who originally trained as a mining engineer. At the age of twenty-five he helped Baron Muller in the examination of his African collection and thereafter decided to follow his own lifelong interest in birds. Continuing the work begun by Hemprich, Ehrenberg and Rüppell he made arduous expeditions to north-east Africa in 1852–53, 1857–58, 1861–62, 1862–64 and in 1875. His classic two-volume *Ornithologie Nord-Ost Afrikas* (1869–74) dealt with the birds of Ethiopia, the coastal areas of the Red Sea and northern Somali Land, and was complemented by fifty-one of his own illustrations. By way of contrast, he made trips to the Arctic in 1870 and 1871, afterwards producing ornithological reports upon Finnmark and Spitzbergen. He also wrote popular, but modest, accounts of his travels. His collections chiefly went to museums in Vienna and Stuttgart.

Larus fuscus heuglini Bree, 1876. This race of the Lesser Black-backed Gull breeds in parts of Arctic Russia but was named from a specimen from the Red Sea where some birds over-winter.

KUMLIEN, Thure Ludwig Theodor (1819–1888). Swedish-born naturalist. Graduated at Uppsala in 1843, and in the following year emigrated to Wisconsin. He collected natural history specimens for the Smithsonian Institute, the museums of Stockholm, Leyden and London and enjoyed frequent correspondence with J. E. Gray, Alfred Newton and Henry Dresser. After a period as a teacher he was employed by the Wisconsin Natural History Society, 1881–83, and for the last five years of his life he was Conservator of the Milwaukee Public Museum. One of his publications was entitled

Contributions to the History of Arctic America in connection with the Howgate Polar Expedition 1877–78 (1879).

Kumlien's Gull *Larus glaucoides kumlieni* Brewster, 1883. This is a race of the Iceland Gull, first described from specimens taken in the Canadian Arctic.

McCORMICK, Robert (1800–1890). Royal Navy surgeon, geologist and naturalist. Born at Great Yarmouth. He had a liking for polar climates and an extreme dislike for the tropics. He served in the West Indies and began a long battle with the naval authorities who persisted in sending him to such regions. In 1827 he volunteered for Arctic service with Parry (and James Ross) and sailed to Spitzbergen in an unsuccessful attempt to gain the North Pole. On return posted to the West Indies, Brazil, the Dutch coast and the West Indies again. One such post was surgeon and naturalist on the *Beagle*, but he invalided himself off and left all the natural history honours to Darwin! McCormick then spent four years travelling throughout England and Wales in pursuit of interesting species and minerals. In 1839 he accompanied Ross to the Antarctic for four years, as surgeon of the *Erebus*. He was completely overshadowed as a naturalist on this expedition by the much younger Joseph Hooker, though McCormick afterwards wrote up the geological findings. He returned to the Arctic in 1852 but failed to achieve the promotion he sought and in 1865 was put on the retirement list. His autobiography *Voyages of Discovery in the Arctic and Antarctic Seas and around the World* (1884) lists many of the birds he was so fond of shooting.

Stercorarius maccormicki (Saunders, 1893). The South Polar Skua has not yet been added to the list of Western Palearctic birds, although sight records have been claimed for British coastal waters. McCormick shot the type specimen on 12 January 1841, on Possession Island, Victoria Land, Antarctica.

MACQUEEN, — . The identity of Macqueen remains a mystery. In the 1940s, Sir Hugh Gladstone made extensive enquiries concerning Macqueen at the British Museum, the Royal Scottish Museum, the India Office and the Bombay Natural History Society. He also placed advertisements in national newspapers and though he received several suggestions there was no Macqueen with any ornithological connection. Whoever he was, Macqueen must have had more than a passing interest to acquire, preserve and transport a large bustard skin from India to Britain.

Chlamydotis undulata macqueenii J. E. Gray, 1832. The name Macqueen's Bustard, for this eastern race of the Houbara, was first used by Gray in his *Illustrations of Indian Zoology, chiefly selected from the collection of Major-General Hardwicke F.R.S.* The original specimen at the British Museum (Natural History) has no contemporary label. It is indexed in the catalogue, without a date, as – *Otis Macqueenii. Himalayas : purchased : Mr. Macqueen.* Later entries mention a General Macqueen but this assertion is of doubtful validity.

MEADE-WALDO, Edmund Gustavus Bloomfield (1855–1934). Field ornithologist and conservationist. Educated Eton and Cambridge, he managed a country estate in Kent. He travelled in the Atlas Mountains of Morocco, and in Spain. The eggs that he collected in the Canaries (sometimes in company with Tristram) can now be found at the British Museum (Natural History). He was a keen falconer and a fine shot and took an active part in the preservation of the Red Kite in Wales. He was Vice-President of the B.O.U. in 1923.

Haematopus moquini meadewaldoi (Bannerman, 1913). The Canarian Black Oyster-catcher was given specific status by Hayman, Marchant and Prater in *Shorebirds* (1986) but was treated as a race of the African Black Oystercatcher *H. moquini* in BWP, Vol. 3 (see Moquin-Tandon).

PLESCHANKA, — . The Pied Wheatear *Oenanthe pleschanka* (Lepechin, 1770) is sometimes referred to as Pleschanka's Chat or Pleschanka's Wheatear (see e.g. Ali, S. and Ripley, S.D. *Handbook of the Birds of India and Pakistan* (1968–75) Vol. 9, p. 55 and Walters, M. *The Complete Birds of the World* (1980) p. 202).

There are no grounds for calling this bird Pleschanka's Wheatear. Pleschanka is derived from the Russian word 'plesch' meaning 'bald spot on a head' and does not refer to a person but to the pattern of the bird's plumage.

REEVES, John (1774–1856). English naturalist, mainly known for the material he collected in China. The youngest son of the Rev. Jonathan Reeves of West Ham, he became orphaned when very young. After being educated at Christ's Hospital he started work with a firm of tea-brokers and a few years later joined the East India Company in England. When he was thirty he was sent to their Chinese depot at Canton where he soon became Chief Inspector of Teas. He could only stay in Canton when the merchant fleet was present and, like all other foreigners, he had to live nearby at Macao. During his seventeen years on the coast of China he had no real collection of his own and liberally dispersed all the items he acquired to contacts in Britain. On his first leave, in 1816, he exhibited to the Horticultural Society a hundred living plants which he had carefully established in pots months before leaving the Far East. Among the many plants which he was responsible for introducing to Britain is the popular climbing plant *Wisteria sinensis*. John Richardson wrote a valuable report on the icthyology of the seas of China and Japan based on specimens and drawings (by Chinese artists) which Reeves had sent to him. Reeves himself produced only one paper, which entered the *Transactions of the Medical Botanical Society* in 1828. He returned to England in 1831 and settled in Clapham where he seems to have lived quietly until his death. His son, John Russell Reeves, spent many years at Macao and gave valuable assistance to the well-known plant hunter Robert Fortune.

Reeves's Pheasant *Syrmaticus reevesii* (J. E. Gray, 1829). Native to the hill and mountain woodlands of central and northern China, this pheasant has been evident in Chinese art for centuries. Marco Polo even made a reference to it in the thirteenth century: "There be plenty of Feysants and very greate, for 1 of them is as big as 2 of ours, with tales of eight, 9 and tenne spannes long, from the Kingdom of Erguyl or Arguill, the W. side of Tartary". In Europe it was considered for a long time to be a mythological bird on account of its extraordinary tail, often over 6 ft in length. Thomas Beale managed to keep a bird in captivity at Macao from 1808 until it died in 1821. It was presumably this individual that Reeves sent to England, to be made known to the scientific world in 1829 under the name *Phasianus reevesii*, since Beale was unable to obtain any more of the pheasants until 1831. This time he received four birds and Reeves brought one of them with him when he returned to England later that same year; it was the first Reeves's Pheasant to be seen alive in Europe. More birds were sent from China and the first breeding in captivity eventually took place at London Zoo in 1867. Several attempts have since been made to introduce this strong and fast-flying pheasant as a sporting bird. Feral groups have existed in Scotland, Austria, West Germany and France but it has not yet been added to any of their national lists.

SAUNDERS, Howard (1835–1907). English ornithologist, born and died in London. He became a merchant banker and travelled widely. In 1855 he went to Brazil and Chile. He returned to England in 1862 but devoted much of his time to the ornithology of Spain, publishing several articles in *The Ibis*. He visited the Pyrenees, 1883 and 1884; Switzerland, 1891; and France, 1893. He became an authority on the gulls and terns of the world, producing a number of articles for the *Proceedings of the Zoological Society* and the *Journal of the Linnean Society*. He was therefore selected to write the twenty-fifth volume of the British Museum's *Catalogue of Birds* (1896) which dealt with those groups. He also compiled *An Illustrated Manual of British Birds* (1889) which proved very popular. Secretary of the B.O.U. 1901–07. Co-editor of the fifth and seventh series of *The Ibis*.

Sterna saundersi Hume, 1877. Saunders's Little Tern is extremely similar to the Little Tern. There are some unconfirmed records of *S. saundersi* in the Iranian Gulf just within the borders of the Western Palearctic.

SCHINZ, Heinrich Rudolph (1777–1862). Swiss naturalist and medical doctor. He practised at his home town of Zurich, devoting his spare time chiefly to zoology. In 1815 he assisted Meisner in his book *Die Vögel der Schweiz*: a descriptive catalogue of the birds of Switzerland. In 1830 he published a picture-book which dealt with the nests and eggs of central European birds but especially those of his own country. He had numerous other publications, including *Europäsche Fauna* (1840).

Calidris alpina schinzii C. L. Brehm, 1822. This is the race of Dunlin that breeds in Britain, Iceland and south-west Greenland.

SCHLEGEL, Hermann (1804–1884). German ornithologist who lived most of his life in The Netherlands. Born in Altenburg, Saxony, he studied in Vienna, joined the staff of the Leyden Museum in 1825 and was Director from 1860 until his death. He made a great contribution to ornithology, his most important works dealing with the Dutch overseas possessions. He also co-authored faunal studies of Japan and Madagascar. He greatly encouraged Joseph Wolf, Joseph Smit and J. G. Keulemans in their artistic careers.

Atlantic or Schlegel's Petrel *Pterodroma incerta* (Schlegel, 1863). There is a sight record of this petrel from near Elat, Israel, in May 1982. (The Kermadec Petrel has also been known as Schlegel's Petrel.)

SEEBOHM, Henry (1832–1895). Yorkshire-born steel manufacturer and traveller whose hard business-like character often antagonized other ornithologists. The Seebohms had lived for several generations in Germany but were originally from Sweden. He made trips to the Pechora in 1875 (with Harvie-Brown) and the Yenisey in 1877; popular accounts of each were later combined together as *The Birds of Siberia* (1901). His other published works include papers in *The Ibis*, a monograph on wader distribution and *A History of British Birds, with Coloured Illustrations of Their Eggs* (1883–85). His *Coloured Figures of Eggs of British Birds* (1896) was edited by R. B. Sharpe, with a memoir and portrait. Seebohm's *Monograph on the Turdidae* (1902) was also issued after his death and was again edited by Sharpe. His huge collection of Palearctic birds and eggs passed to the British Museum (Natural History); the thrushes, waders and *Phylloscopus* warblers being particularly well represented.

Seebohm's Wheatear *Oenanthe seebohmi* Dixon 1882. This wheatear is sometimes given specific status. It was discovered in the Province of Constantine, Algeria, by Charles Dixon who named the bird after his patron and employer; Seebohm had sent him there for collecting purposes. It is more often classed as a race of the Wheatear *Oenanthe oenanthe*.

SMITH, Sir Andrew (1797–1872). Scottish army surgeon, explorer, government emissary and zoologist. First director of the Cape Town Museum. He led three politically motivated expeditions in southern Africa under the guise of scientific exploration. Returning to Britain in 1837, after sixteen years at the Cape, the expedition collections were exhibited in London and then dispersed by auction. His private collection was donated to Edinburgh University. Author of the five-volume *Illustrations of the Zoology of South Africa* (1838–47), he was also the first describer of a vast number of African bird species. He later suffered unjust criticism for his medical role in the Crimean War, and following the death of his wife in 1864 he became increasingly reclusive.

Cape Shoveler *Anas smithii* (Hartert, 1891). First described from a specimen from the Cape Province. A pair seen off the coast of Morocco in April 1978 were probably escapees.

STRICKLAND, Hugh Edwin (1811–1853). English geologist, ornithologist and systematist. Educated Oriel College, Oxford. In 1835 he travelled with W. J. Hamilton to Greece and the coast of western Turkey (where he discovered the Olive-tree Warbler and Cinereous Bunting). In 1837 he made a geological tour of northern Scotland. His *Rules of Zoological Nomenclature* was published in 1841 and four years later his translation of Bonaparte's *Observations on the State of Zoology in Europe* appeared. In 1845 he also married the second daughter of Jardine and toured many of the museums of Europe. He later co-authored *The Dodo and its Kindred* (1848). He was killed by a train in a cutting near Clareburgh, whilst pursuing his geological interests; on a double track, he stepped out of the way of a goods train and was killed by an express coming the other way. His *Ornithological Synonyms*, edited by his wife and father-in-law, was published in 1855. Strickland's collection of 6000 birds went to Cambridge in 1867.

Eastern Pied Wheatear *Oenanthe picata opistholeuca* (Strickland, 1849). Sometimes referred to a Strickland's Wheatear. Its first description appeared in Jardine's *Contributions to Ornithology*. (Strickland's Bunting is now an obsolete name for the Cinereous Bunting.)

SYKES, Colonel William Henry (1790–1872). Indian army officer, politician and ornithologist. Entered Bombay Army in 1804 and commanded a native regiment at the battles of Kirkee and Poona, 1817–18. He retired from the East India Company service in 1837 and returned to Britain shortly afterwards. Became long-standing M.P. for Aberdeen in 1857. Elected President of the Royal Asiatic Society, 1858. While in India he made extensive zoological collections. His catalogues of the birds and mammals of the Deccan, which appeared in the *Proceedings of the Zoological Society* 1831–32, was the first for that area; fifty-six of the birds were described as new species. He also studied the fishes of the Deccan and wrote papers on the quails and hemipodes of India.

Motacilla flava beema—the Blue-headed Wagtail of south-east Russia which winters in India. It was named *Budytes Beema* by Sykes in 1832 (Beema is a river in the Deccan where Sykes may have first met with the bird). The term Sykes's Wagtail for this race was first used by Ticehurst in *British Birds*, 1907.

THUNBERG, Carl Peter (1743–1828). Swedish doctor, botanist and traveller. A pupil of Linnaeus at Uppsala, he was engaged by the Dutch East India Company to go to Japan in a medical capacity. He stopped off at the Cape and made two lengthy expeditions with the Scottish botanist Francis Masson. He then continued on to Japan, Java and Ceylon before returning firstly to England and subsequently to Germany. His travels occupied nine years and he accumulated a rich harvest of plants and insects. Latterly he was director of the botanic gardens at Uppsala.

Motacilla flava thunbergi—the Grey-headed Wagtail of north Scandinavia and Russia. It was named by G. J. Billberg in 1828.

VIDAL, Ignacio (died 29 December 1859). Spanish naturalist. Doctor of medicine and science. Professor of Mineralogy and Zoology at the University of Valencia and Director of the Zoological Museum of the same city. He took part in public work and served on the provincial council being especially interested in matters of public health.

His chief ornithological work was *Catalogo de las aves de la Albufera (de Valencia)* (1850–56).

Athene noctua vidalii—the Little Owl of Spain northwards to The Netherlands (and the race introduced to Britain). Named by A. E. Brehm in 1858.

YARRELL, William (1784–1856). English naturalist. Born in central London, his father was a newsagent and he succeeded to the business. His leisure was spent shooting and fishing but he later turned his attention to ornithology and abandoned all field sports in order to study zoology systematically. In 1823 he began to send birds to Bewick, and became a friend and correspondent of Gould, Jardine and many other naturalists. One of the original members of the Zoological Society and its Secretary from 1836–38. In 1836 he completed a *History of British Fishes*. His *History of British Birds* (1837–43) went into several editions and became the standard text for a generation of British ornithologists. He died while on a trip to Great Yarmouth and a memorial was afterwards erected in St James Church, Piccadilly. His collection of books, birds and fishes was sold by public auction.

Motacilla alba yarrellii—the British Pied Wagtail. It was originally treated as a separate species from the White Wagtail. Yarrell's name was attached to the bird by his friend John Gould in 1837.

References

AUDUBON—*see e.g.* Kastner, J. 1978. *A World of Naturalists*, pp. 207–239, 330. J. Murray, London. [L'HERMINIER—Gibourt, G. 1834. Notice sur Félix-Louis l'Herminier. *Journal de Chimie Médicale* 10: 221–224.]

BAROLO—Gladstone, H.S. Unpublished MS, from: Masse, D. 1941. *Un precursore nel campo pedagogico il Marchese Barola*. Alba; Pellico, S. 1866. *The Life of the Marchesa Giulia Falletti di Barolo*. London.

COUES—Cutright, P. R. and Brodhead, M. J. 1981. *Elliott Coues, Naturalist and Frontier Historian*. University of Illinois Press, Chicago.

FEA—Bannerman, D. A. and Bannerman, W. M. 1968. *The Birds of the Atlantic Islands*, Vol. IV, pp. 25–28. Oliver & Boyd, Edinburgh and London; Gestro, R. 1904. Leonardo Fea ed i suoi Viaggi. *Annali Museo Civico di Storia naturali Giacoma Doria* 41: 95–152.

FELDEGG—Gladstone, H. S. Unpublished MS, from: Hirtenfield, J. 1857. *Der Militar-Maria Theresien Orden und seine Mitglieder*, Vienna; *Ornithologisches Jahrbuch* 1896, 7: 238–241.

GRAELLS—Gladstone, H. S. Unpublished MS, from: *Actas de la Sociedad Espanola de Historia Natural Madrid* 1898, pp. 65–67; Agenjo, R. 1943. *Graellsia* 1: 7–12.

HARCOURT—*Burke's Peerage* 1959, p. 2284.

HEUGLIN—Gebhardt, L. 1964. *Die Ornithologen Mitteleuropas*, pp. 153–154. Giessen.

KUMLIEN—*Auk* 1889, pp. 204–205. Obituary.

McCORMICK—*Dictionary of National Biography* 1885–1900. Vol. XII, p. 455. London.

MACQUEEN—Gladstone, H.S. Unpublished MS; *Ibis* 1948, pp. 337–338.

MEADE-WALDO—*Ibis* 1934, pp. 399–402. Obituary.

PLESCHANKA—Professor V. Filov, Leningrad, personal communication.

REEVES—Beebe, W. 1922. *A Monograph of the Pheasants*, Vol. III, pp. 145–157. H.F. & G. Witherby, London; *Dictionary of National Biography* 1885–1900. Vol. XLVII, p. 416. London; *Proceedings of the Linnean Society of London* 1857, pp. 43–45. Obituary.

SAUNDERS—*Ibis* 1908, pp. 169–172. Obituary.

SCHINZ—Gladstone, H.S. Unpublished MS, from: Locher, A. 1863. *Naturforschende gesellschaft. An die Zürcherische Jugend auf des Jahr 1863*, **65**: 18.

SCHLEGEL—*Ibis* 1884, p. 364. Obituary.

SEEBOHM—*Ibis* 1896, pp. 159–162. Obituary.

SMITH—*Dictionary of South African Biography* 1968–81. Vol. I, pp. 731–734. Cape Town.

STRICKLAND—*Dictionary of National Biography* 1885–1900. Vol. XIX, pp. 50–52. London; Jardine, W. 1858. *A Memoir of Hugh Strickland*. London.

SYKES—*Dictionary of National Biography* 1885–1900. Vol. XIX, p. 258. London; *Ibis* 1872, pp. 343–344. Obituary.

THUNBERG—Coats, A. M. 1969. *The Quest for Plants*, pp. 64–66, 204–205, 251–256. Studio Vista, London.

VIDAL—Gladstone, H.S. Unpublished MS, from: *Memorias de la Real Academia de ciencias de Madrid* 1850, **1**: 167–199 and 1856, **4**: 401–429.

YARRELL—Yarrell, W. 1859. *A History of British Fishes*, 3rd edn, Vol. I, pp. 5–23. London.

Appendix 2

A selection of naturalists mentioned in the main text.

ALBIN, Eleazor (fl. 1713–1759). Few biographical details exist for this professional water-colourist. He published an early series of British birdbooks: *A Natural History of Birds* (1731–38) and *A Natural History of English Song-Birds* (1737).

ALEXANDER, Wilfrid Backhouse (1885–1965). English ornithologist. Numerous expeditions in Australia where he worked from 1912 to 1926. Keeper at Western Australia Museum and Librarian of Western Australasian Ornithologists' Union. Director of Edward Grey Institute, Oxford, 1938–45, and librarian of its Alexander Library until 1955. Various papers in the *Emu, Ibis* and *British Birds* but best known for his *Birds of the Ocean* (1928).

AUDUBON—see Appendix 1.

BAER, Karl Ernst von (1792–1876). Born Estonia, educated Reval, Dorpat and Würzburg. Natural History Professor for seventeen years at Königsberg, where he was mainly interested in embryology. In 1834 appointed librarian of the Russian Academy of St Petersburg and undertook several expeditions in Russia. Other interests included geography and anthropology. Baer's Pochard *Athya baeri* of the Eastern Palearctic was named by his friend Radde in 1863.

BANKS, Sir Joseph (1743–1820). Wealthy English naturalist and patron. Returned from Cook's first great expedition (1768–71) with huge collection of plants. Afterwards made voyage to Iceland. Influential President of the Royal Society, 1778–1820.

BANNERMAN, David Armitage (1886–1979). Widely travelled long-serving staff member of British Museum (Natural History). Best known for his *Birds of Tropical West Africa* (1930–51), *The Birds of the British Isles* (1953–63) and *The Birds of the Atlantic Isles* (1963–68).

BARTLETT, Edward (c.1836–1908). English ornithologist. Accompanied Tristram to Palestine, 1863–64. Collected Amazon basin and eastern Peru, 1865–69. Curator at Maidstone Museum, 1875–90. In 1891 he began working at the Brooks Museum in Sarawak but returned to England in 1897. He compiled a *Monograph of the Weaver Birds* (1888–89) and was co-author of *Notes on the Birds of Kent* (1907).

BRANDT, Johann Friedrich (1802–1879). German physician and naturalist. Director of the Zoological Museum at St Petersburg. Published many papers concerning collections made by others, particularly from the Russian North Pacific possessions.

BREHM, Christian Ludwig (1787–1864). German pastor and ornithologist. Born near Gotha, studied at the University of Jena. Soon afterwards became the minister at

Renthendorf where he remained for the rest of his life. A prolific author, his more important works include *Beiträge zur Vögelkunde* (1820–22) in which 104 species of German birds are minutely described. He tried unsuccessfully to sell his lifelong collection of birds to the Berlin Museum. After his death it lay undisturbed in his attic for nearly forty years. Eventually Otto Kleinschmidt persuaded Lord Rothschild to buy the skins for his museum at Tring. (They were later sold to North America to raise funds for a blackmailer.) Brehm's son Alfred Edmund (1829–1884) collected birds Egypt and Sudan 1847–52; Spain, 1856; Norway, 1860; the Altai and Russian Arctic, 1876. Another son, Reinhold (1830–1891), a doctor in Madrid, collected birds on a smaller scale. Their step-brother Oskar Brehm (1823–1850) who died in Dongola was also interested in birds.

BREWER, Dr Thomas Mayo (1814–1880). American naturalist and oologist. Author of *North American Oology* (1857) and co-wrote (with Baird and Ridgway) *A History of North American Birds* (1874).

BUFFON, Georges-Louis-Leclerc, Compte de Buffon (1707–1788). Wealthy French naturalist appointed keeper of the Jardin du Roi and its museum. Published thirty-six of the proposed fifty-volume *Histoire Naturelle, générale et particulière* (nine volumes on birds, 1770–83). Brought together many previously isolated facts of natural history in intelligible form. Buffon's Skua (an obsolete name for the Long-tailed Skua) once commemorated his name.

CABANIS, Jean Louis (1816–1906). Influential German ornithologist of international renown. Most of his working life was spent at the Berlin Museum. He founded the *Journal für Ornithologie*, edited it for forty-one years, and thereby laid down the direction for German ornithology. He also revitalized the D.O-G.

CASSIN, John (1813–1869). American businessman and ornithologist, based on the east coast. Curator of ornithology and Vice-President of the Philadelphia Academy of Natural Sciences. Wrote *Birds* (1858). One of the best systematic ornithologists.

CATESBY, Mark (1683–1749). Born and died in England. Collected plants Virginia, 1710–19. Returned to America 1722–26. Produced *Natural History of Carolina* (1731) which contained 200 of his hand-coloured etchings, many of which were birds.

COOPER, James Graham (1830–1902). American ornithologist, born New York city. Surgeon and naturalist on the Pacific Railroad Survey expedition and on the Geological Survey of California. Remained on the west coast and produced a *Report on the Birds of California* (1870). His father, William, was a friend of Bonaparte, Nuttall and Audubon.

COUES—see Appendix 1.

CUVIER, Baron Georges (1769–1832). French zoologist and palaeontologist. Professor of Comparative Anatomy at the Museum d'Histoire Naturelle de Paris. Famous for *Règne Animal* (1817) on structure of living and fossil animals; second expanded edition issued 1829–30. He was the most eminent French naturalist of his day.

DALL, William Healey (1845–1927). American naturalist, born Boston. When Kennicott died he took over as leader of the Western Union International Telegraph Expedition in Alaska, 1855–68. He worked on the United States Coast Survey, mainly in the Aleutians, 1871–84, and became the leading authority on the natural history of the region publishing *Alaska and its Resources* in 1870. Curator of Molluscs at U.S. National Museum 1880. Compiled a biography of Baird.

DAVID, (Père) Armand (1826–1900). Lazarist missionary and naturalist. Born and died in France, he taught in Italy 1851–61. Ordained at thirty-six and sent to China (Tche-li and Peking). Explored Mongolia, 1866; Tibet, 1868–70; central China, 1872–74. Greatly enriched zoological and botanical collections of Paris Natural History Museum. Author of several publications, relating to his travels and discoveries. *Plantae Davidianae* (1884–86) catalogues his plant collection.

DRESSER, Henry Eeles (1838–1915). Wealthy English businessman and ornithologist. Travelled widely in Europe (and eastern Canada). Collected eggs and skins for most of his life. *The Birds of Europe* (1871–81) and its supplement (1896) are his best known works. They were followed by *The Eggs of the Birds of Europe* (1910). Huge collection to Manchester University Museum. Also wrote monographs on bee-eaters (1884–86) and rollers (1893).

EHRENBERG, Christian Gottfried (1795–1876). German naturalist, friend and companion of Hemprich in Egypt, Sinai and Lebanon, 1820–26. On return, Professor of Faculty of Medicine, Berlin. Published 'Scientific Travels through Northern Africa and Western Asia' (1828) and *Symbolae Physicae Avium, Insectorum etc.* (1828–34) which detailed his Middle Eastern discoveries. With Humboldt to the Urals and Altai, 1829. Latterly concentrated on microscopic organisms.

FRASER, Louis (fl. 1866). Natural history dealer who owned shops in Knightsbridge and Regent Street, London. Niger River expedition, 1841–42. Also collected in North Africa and Ecuador. Author of *Zoologia typica* (1849), which concentrated on new type specimens. Business unsuccessful, emigrated to California and Vancouver. Son Oscar worked at the Calcutta Museum.

GLADSTONE, Sir Hugh Steuart (1877–1949). Scottish ornithologist and bibliophile who managed country estate Dumfriesshire. Educated Eton and Cambridge. Lieutenant in South Africa, 1900–02; Captain in Great War. Chairman of Wild Birds Advisory Committee (Scotland), 1920. Publications include *The Birds of Dumfriesshire* (1910), *Birds and the War* (1919), *Shooting with Surtees* (1927) and *Thomas Watling, Limner of Dumfries* (1938).

GMELIN, Johann Friedrich (1748–1804). German naturalist. Professor of Medical Sciences, University of Göttingen, for about thirty years until his death. Known mainly for editing thirteenth edition of Linnaeus's *Systema Naturae* (1788–93).

GMELIN, Johann Georg (1709–1755). German botanist and naturalist. Professor of Chemistry and Natural History at St Petersburg, sent on ten-year expedition to Siberia by the Russian Empress. Returned 1743. Issued *Flora Sibirica* (1747). Uncle of J. F. Gmelin.

GMELIN, Samuel Gottlieb (1744–1774). Botanist and traveller. Professor of Botany at St Petersburg. Explored Don and Volga, western and eastern coasts of Caspian Sea. Seized in the Caucasus as hostage and died there 1774. Nephew of J. G. Gmelin.

GODMAN, Frederick du Cane (1834–1919). English ornithologist. Founder member of B.O.U. Large house in London a meeting place for noted ornithologists and a depository for collections. Co-author, with Osbert Salvin, of *Biologia Centrali-Americana* (1879). Author of *Natural History of the Azores* (1870) and a *Monograph of the Petrels* (1907–10).

HARTERT, Ernst (1859–1933). Born Hamburg, died Berlin. German ornithologist who travelled in Africa, South America and India. Curator of birds at the Rothschild Museum at Tring, 1892–1929. With Rothschild published the journal *Novitates Zoologicae*; and with Jourdain, Ticehurst and Witherby compiled *Hand List of British Birds* (1912). Author of *Die Vögel der paläarktischen Fauna* (1903–22). Hartert's and Rothschild's general contribution to ornithology usually underrated.

HOOKER, Sir Joseph Dalton (1817–1911). Botanist and traveller. With James Ross to Antarctica, 1839–43. To Himalayas, 1848–52. With Asa Gray through western United States, 1877. Assistant Director at Kew, 1855, succeeding his father as Director, 1865. Responsible for introducing many fine rhododendrons and other plants from the Himalayas to Britain. Second wife was the widow of Jardine.

HOOKER, William Jackson (1785–1865). Professor of Botany, Glasgow University. Produced *Flora Scotica* (1821), *Flora Boreali-Americana* (1833–40), and *British Flora* (1830). From 1840, Director at Kew. Father of J. D. Hooker.

HUMBOLDT, Alexander von (1769–1859). Celebrated German explorer, scientist and geographer. Expeditions to Central and South America, 1799–1804; Russia and central Asia, 1829. *Kosmos* (1845–62) gives his physical description of the Earth.

IRBY, Lieutenant-Colonel Leonard Howard Lloyd (1836–1905). British army officer and ornithologist. Served in Crimea, China and India. 1868 stationed at Gibraltar. Few publications despite immense knowledge on birds. Persuaded to write *The Ornithology of the Straits of Gibraltar* (1875).

JARDINE, Sir William (1800–1874). Studied medicine Edinburgh and Paris. At twenty-one inherited estate of Jardine Hall, Dumfries, and devoted spare time to ornithology. With Selby produced *Illustrations of Ornithology* (1825–43). Compiled a *Naturalist's Library* (1838–43) and *Contributions to Ornithology* (1848–52). Much respected in his day. Second daughter married Hugh Strickland.

JERDON, Thomas Claverhill (1811–1872). Of Scottish descent, he was an excellent field ornithologist who travelled extensively in India, Assam and Burma. Entered East India Company as an assistant surgeon at Madras, 1835. *Illustrations of Indian Ornithology* (1844) and *The Birds of India* (1862–64) were his greatest works, especially the latter. Viscount Walden declared that "No man, with so long a career, made fewer bad 'species' than Dr. Jerdon, proof by itself of his knowledge on his subject". First discoverer of Jerdon's Warbler (now Paddyfield Warbler) and many other birds. Jerdon's Courser, long thought to be extinct but rediscovered in 1986, also commemorates his name.

KENNICOTT, Robert (1835–1866). North American naturalist and explorer. Born New Orleans, he came under the influence of Baird and collected for the Smithsonian Institute in Arctic America 1859–62. Died of heart failure at Nulato, on the Yukon River, while leading a surveying expedition in Alaska.

KEULEMANS, John Gerrard (1842–1912). Dutch bird artist who worked in England from 1869. His consistently high standard on a huge range of species made him much in demand. He was a regular illustrator for *The Ibis, The Proceedings of the Zoological Society* and many important bird books of the period. Buller's *A History of the Birds of New Zealand* (1873) contains some of his best work.

KUHL, Heinrich (1796–1821). Talented young German zoologist. Collected for Leyden Museum in Java but died there with his companion. Published several ornithological papers before leaving Germany, including a monograph of the petrels, the first to be attempted.

LATHAM, John (1740–1837). English naturalist. Doctor at Dartford in Kent (where he collected the Dartford Warbler). Retired 1796 and settled in Hampshire. His *General History of Birds* (1821–28) and *A General Synopsis of Birds* (1781–1801) established him as a leading British ornithologist.

LEADBEATER, Benjamin (fl. 1760–1837). Established a natural history business in London about 1800. His son John, and grandson Benjamin, continued the family business.

LESSON, René Primevère (1794–1849). French naturalist, born Rocheforte. Numerous ornithological publications relating to the discoveries made on the 1822–25 round-the-world voyage of the *Coquille*, on which he served as surgeon. Afterwards became Professor of the school of naval medicine at Rocheforte. His other works include *Manuel d'Ornithologie* (1828) and *Traité d'Ornithologie* (1831).

McCORMICK—see Appendix 1.

MACGILLIVRAY, William (1796–1852). Scottish naturalist whose boyhood was spent in Harris. At Aberdeen University, 1808–20, then moved to Edinburgh. From 1831 until 1841 he was Conservator of the Museum of the Edinburgh College of Surgeons but returned to Aberdeen and was Professor of Civil and Natural History until his death. He wrote a large part of the text for Audubon's *Ornithological Biography* (1831–39). His best work, *A History of British Birds* (1837–52), was original, accurate and of lasting value but was over-shadowed by the more popular works of Bewick and Yarrell. His nomenclature and classification were often controversial.

MAXIMOWICZ, Carl (1827–1891). Russian botanist of German extraction, educated at Dorpat. Conservator of the Herbarium of St Petersburg Botanic Garden, 1852. He collected in the Amur, 1854–56, and later revisited the area and extended his travels to Korea and Japan, 1859–64. Director of the St Petersburg Botanic Gardens, 1869.

MEADE-WALDO—see Appendix 1.

MEARNS, Edgar Alexander (1856–1916). American army surgeon and ornithologist. Founder member of A.O.U. Collected Arizona and Texas, 1884–88; Philippines, 1903–07; British East Africa, with President Roosevelt, 1909; Abyssinia, 1911, 1912. At the time of his death, more than one tenth of the bird specimens in the U.S. National Museum were either collected or contributed by him.

MILNE-EDWARDS, Henri (1800–1885). French zoologist. The son of an Englishman, he spent most of his life in France. Early work on crustaceans with Audouin followed by *Histoire naturelle de Crustacés* (1837–41), a standard work for many years. Professor of Natural History 1841, and twenty-one years later Professor of Zoology at the Paris Museum. His son Alphonse (1835–1900) was a well-known ornithologist.

NEWTON, Alfred (1829–1907). English zoologist. Founder member of B.O.U. Won Cambridge Travelling Fellowship in pursuit of ornithology: to Lapland, 1855; North America, 1857; Iceland (to search for the Great Auk), 1858; Spitzbergen, 1864. First Professor of Zoology at Cambridge, from 1866 until his death. Best known for completing *Ootheca Wolleyana* (1907) and for *A Dictionary of Birds* (1893–96). Brother of Edward Newton (1832–1897) who worked (and collected) in Mauritius.

NUTTALL, Thomas (1786–1859). Yorkshire printer, arrived in U.S. at twenty-two. Travels to Arkansas, Rocky Mountains, California and Hawaii. An excellent field botanist, he wrote the *Genera of North American Plants and a Catalogue of Species* (1817). He later turned to zoology and produced *A Manual of the Ornithology of the United States and Canada* (1832–34). Self-exiled to England to fulfil the legal requirements of the estate he inherited.

OGILVIE-GRANT, William Robert (1863–1924). Educated at Edinburgh, he joined the British Museum (Natural History) in 1882. In charge of the ornithological section in 1885 while Sharpe in India retrieving Hume's collection. He remained in the department after Sharpe's return and helped to raise its status to the best in the world. He collected in Sokotra, Madeira, the Canary Islands and the Azores, and organized and encouraged the expeditions of other naturalists. Edited the *Bulletin of the B.O.C.*, 1904–14; contributed to the museum's *Catalogue of Birds*, Vols 17 (part), 22, 26; author of *British Game Birds and Wildfowl* (1912) and numerous ornithological papers.

OLPH-GALLIARD, Victor Aimé Léon (1825–1893). French zoologist. Wrote *Contributions à la Faune Ornithologique de l'Europe Occidentale* (1884–92) and compiled a *Catalogue des Oiseaux des Environs de Lyon* (1891).

ORD, George (1781–1866). American naturalist who inherited a prosperous ship-chandlery, but retired in 1829 to live as a gentleman of leisure. After Wilson's death he completed the *American Ornithology*, and thereafter needlessly defended his friend's reputation by trying to discredit Audubon. He went with Titian Peale and Thomas Say to Florida and Georgia, 1818. He died a recluse amongst his books.

PENNANT, Thomas (1726–1798). British naturalist. Author of *The British Zoology* (1761–66), *Arctic Zoology* (1784–87) and *Indian Zoology* (1790). Produced a number of other publications which related to his various tours around the U.K. Corresponded with most of the eminent naturalists of his day, notably Pallas and White.

PONTOPIDDAN, Erik (1698–1764). Danish prelate, historian and antiquary. Professor of Theology, Copenhagen, 1738. Bishop of Bergen, 1748. A treatise on the *Natural History of Norway* (1755) followed by his seven-volume *Danske Atlas* (1763–81).

RAFFLES, Sir Thomas Stamford (1781–1826). British colonial governor and patron. Joined East India Company. Went to Malaya in 1805 and was made Lieutenant-Governor of Java in 1811. He also served Sumatra and Singapore, privately supervising zoological and botanical collecting throughout his time in the East. Returned to England, 1824. Founded the Zoological Society and became its first President.

RAFINESQUE-SCHMALTZ, Constantine Samuel (1784–1842). Born Constantinople of French father and Greek–German mother. At nineteen spent three years in North America as a shipping clerk but returned to live in Sicily, where he became a friend of Swainson (and first discovered the Fan-tailed Warbler). He made his fortune and sailed to America again but was shipwrecked and arrived penniless. Became Professor of Natural History in Kentucky, later died in poverty. Discovered many new American plants, fish and mammals and became a friend of Audubon. A scatterbrained genius.

RICHARDSON, Sir John (1786–1865). Scottish naval surgeon, Arctic explorer and zoologist. Born Dumfries, where father an intimate friend of the poet Burns. Franklin's companion on two overland Arctic expeditions. Unsuccessful search for Franklin, with Dr Rae, 1848–49. Retired to the Lake District, buried in 'Wordsworth's Cemetery', Grasmere. Contributed the volumes on quadrupeds and fishes to his own *Fauna Boreali-Americana* (1829–37) and assisted Swainson with the volume on birds. He wrote the zoological appendices to accounts of several naval expeditions, including some of those of Parry, Franklin and James Ross.

RIDGWAY, Robert (1850–1929). At the height of his career he was the leading American ornithologist. Born Illinois, he corresponded as a boy with Baird who later placed him on a survey of Utah, Nevada and Wyoming as the zoologist. Joined staff of Smithsonian Institute 1869. Curator of birds in U.S. National Museum from 1880 until his death.

SABINE, Joseph (1770–1837). Lawyer and inspector-general of taxes. An original Fellow of the Linnean Society. Hon. Secretary of the Horticultural Society, 1810–30. Afterwards Treasurer and Vice-President of the Zoological Society. Most of his publications are of a botanical nature. Brother of Edward Sabine.

SALVIN, Osbert (1835–1898). English ornithologist. Tunisia and eastern Algeria (with W.H. Simpson and H. B. Tristram, the latter a cousin by marriage), 1857. Guatamala 1857, 1858 and 1861 (with F. Godman). Appointed to the Strickland Curatorship of Cambridge University. Editor of *The Ibis*, Secretary of B.O.U. Nearly 100 papers on Central and South American birds to *The Ibis* and *The Proceedings of the Zoological Society*. Contributed the volumes on petrels and humming-birds to the *Catalogue of Birds*.

SAY, Thomas (1787–1834). American naturalist. Author of *American Entomology* (1824–28)—a pioneer study. He made expeditions to the Rocky Mountains, Minnesota, Florida and Mexico. He later eloped with the girl who made the illustrations for his *American Conchology* (1830–34) and lived at the Utopian village of New Harmony until his death. Grandnephew of William Bartram.

SCHLEGEL, H.—see Appendix 1.

SCLATER, Philip Lutley (1829–1913). English lawyer and zoologist. First editor of *The Ibis*, 1859, and Secretary of the Zoological Society for forty-three years. A prolific author, most of his publications refer to non-British birds. His collection of American bird skins went to the British Museum (Natural History). His son, William Lutley Sclater (1863–1944) absorbed his ornithological interest.

SCOPOLI, Giovanni Antonio (1723–1788). Born in the Tyrol, he graduated from Innsbruck University in 1743. After studying botany at Venice he practised medicine in Vienna. About 1754 became physician at the quicksilver mines of Idria in Carniola, and remained there about ten years. Afterwards Professor of Mineralogy at Schemitz, Hungary. In 1776 he transferred to Pavia as Professor of Chemistry and Botany and died there twelve years later. In his day, known throughout the world as a botanist and entomologist. British ornithologists are best acquainted with his *Annus I Historico-Naturalis* (1769) which is several times mentioned by Gilbert White. This work gave rise to the oft-quoted saying "every kingdom, every province, should have its monograph". Scopoli was the first describer of a number of birds including the Bridled Tern (once known as Scopoli's Sooty Tern).

SEEBOHM—see Appendix 1.

SELBY, Prideaux John (1788–1867). English ornithologist, botanist and artist, born Alnwick. Produced *Illustrations of British Ornithology* (1821–34) and (with Jardine) *Illustrations of Ornithology* (1825–43). Often worked on same scale as Audubon—many of his birds are painted life-size. Also wrote and illustrated *A History of British Forest-trees* (1842).

SHARPE, Richard Bowdler (1847–1909). English ornithologist. Librarian of Zoological Society at twenty. Published monograph on the kingfishers (1868–71) and would have assisted in Dresser's *Birds of Europe* but G. R. Gray died in 1872 and Sharpe took charge of the bird collection of the British Museum (Natural History). He wrote thirteen and a half of the twenty-seven-volume *Catalogue of Birds* and innumerable other publications. He conceived the idea of the British Ornithologists' Club and edited its bulletin for a number of years.

SHELLEY, George Ernest (1840–1910). English geologist diverted to ornithology. He retired early from the Grenadier Guards to pursue his interest. An excellent shot, he travelled in South Africa and Ethiopia. Wrote *Handbook of the Birds of Egypt* (1872) and *Birds of Africa* but only completed four volumes of the latter due to partial paralysis in 1906. Authority on sun-birds. Youngest son of the famous poet's younger brother.

SLOANE, Sir Hans (1660–1753). Physician and naturalist of Scottish extraction. Settled London, where studied medicine. Collected Jamaica and West Indies. Secretary to Royal Society 1693, later President. On his death, his library of 50,000 volumes and natural history collection originated the British Museum.

SMITH, Sir A.—see Appendix 1.

SMITH, Sir James Edward (1759–1828). Wealthy English botanist, born Norwich. Responsible for purchase of the Linnean collection from Sweden, and thus the founder (and first President) of the Linnean Society. Wrote *Flora Britannica* (1804) and, with Sowerby, *English Botany* (1807).

SPARRMAN, Anders (1748–1820). Swedish naturalist. Student of Linnaeus. Collected plants in China and at the Cape. Joined the Forsters on Cook's second Pacific voyage, returning to Sweden in 1776. In Senegal, 1787. Became Professor of Natural History at Stockholm.

STEJNEGER, Leonhard Hess (1851–1943). Norwegian-born naturalist, studied birds Norway and the Tyrol. Arrived U.S. 1881, next year to Commander Islands for

Smithsonian Institute. Returned to Bering Sea 1895–97. Curator of Biology at U.S. National Museum, 1911. Besides birds, he wrote extensively on amphibians and snakes. Compiled exhaustive biography of Steller.

STRESEMANN, Erwin (1889–1972). One of the most outstanding ornithologists of the twentieth century. He explored the East Indies in his early twenties. In 1921 he began revitalizing the bird department of the Berlin Museum, and encouraged a host of young Germans in their scientific careers. Longstanding editor of the *Journal für Ornithologie* (from 1922 on). A prolific author, his greatest work was his 900-page *Aves* (1927–34) which dealt with all aspects of avian biology. His *Entwicklung der Ornithologie*, a masterly review of the development of ornithology from Aristotle to the present, was translated into English in 1975.

STRICKLAND—see Appendix 1.

SYKES—see Appendix 1.

TACZANOWSKI, Ladislas (1819–1890). Polish ornithologist, trained at Paris Museum. Conservator of the Zoological Museum of Warsaw from 1855 until his death. Visited Algeria winter 1866–67. 'Birds of Poland' (1882), 'Ornithology of Peru' (1884–86) and a memoir on the birds of Siberia are among his chief works.

THUNBERG— see Appendix 1.

VIEILLOT, Louis Jean Pierre (1748–1831). French ornithologist. Born Yvetot, France. In business on the island of St Domingo, he took refuge in the U.S. during the French Revolution. Returned to France, but despite authorship of some important works he is believed to have died in poverty in Rouen. Issued *Histoire naturelle et Générale* (1802) and *Ornithologie Française* (1823–30). Contributed to *Nouveau Dictionaire d'Histoire Naturelle* (1803–19). Described a great many new European, Australian and American bird species.

VIGORS, Nicholas Aylward (1785–1840). Zoologist, born Ireland. Served Peninsula War, 1809–11, M.A. Oxford 1818. Secretary to Zoological Society of London, 1826. Later returned to Ireland and became M.P. for Carlow. Author of about forty papers, mainly ornithological. Assisted Jardine and Selby with *Illustrations of Ornithology*. Described the birds in the *Zoology of Captain Beechey's Voyage* (1839), and is sometimes credited with helping Children with the natural history of Denham's travels.

WAGLER, Johann Georg (1800-1832). Professor and Director of the Zoological Museum of the University of Munich. His *Systema Avium* (1827) and a monograph on the parrots (1832) both showed early promise but he died, aged thirty-two, from an accidental gunshot wound.

WALDEN, Viscount (Arthur Hay), 9th Marquis of Tweeddale (1824–1878). Served Grenadier Guards India and Crimea. Expeditions to Himalayas and eastern Europe. Wrote many papers for *The Ibis* and *The Proceedings of the Zoological Society*, specializing in the birds of India, Celebes and Philippines. He described the birds collected by his nephew, R. Wardlaw-Ramsay, from the Andaman Islands, Burma and India.

YARRELL—see Appendix 1.

Index of English and Scientific Names of Birds

Index of People